Enlightenment Key Bindings

Task	Key Binding
Move a window on the desktop	Alt+left-click
Resize a window	Alt+middle-click
Display menu of current desktop	Alt+middle-click
Align windows on the desktop neatly	Ctrl+Alt+Home
Exit Enlightenment and log out of GNOME	Ctrl+Alt+Delete
Restart Enlightenment	Ctrl+Alt+End
Raise window to the top	Ctrl+Alt+Up-arrow
Lower window to the bottom	Ctrl+Alt+Down-arrow
Go to the previous desktop	Ctrl+Alt+Left-arrow
Go to the next desktop	Ctrl+Alt+Right-arrow
Close window	Ctrl+Alt+X
Iconify window	Ctrl+Alt+I
Kill window	Ctrl+Alt+K
Shade/Unshade window	Ctrl+Alt+R
Stick/Unstick window	Ctrl+Alt+S
Switch focus to next window	Alt+Tab
Move to the virtual desktop on the left	Shift+Alt+Left-arrow
Move to the virtual desktop on the right	Shift+Alt+Right-arrow
Move to the virtual desktop above	Shift+Alt+Up-arrow
Move to the virtual desktop below	Shift+Alt+Down-arrow

GNOME File Manager Key Bindings

Task	Key Binding
Open a file	F3
Select All in a directory	Ctrl+A
Search	Ctrl+S
Open Run Command dialog box	F2
Close File Manager Window	Ctrl+W

XFree86 Key Bindings

Task	Key Binding
Increase screen resolution mode setting	Ctrl+Alt+plus key
Decrease screen resolution mode setting	Ctrl+Alt+minus key
Emergency exit from X (kills X server)	Ctrl+Alt+Backspace
Go to virtual console number 0 to 11 from within an X session	Ctrl+Alt+(F1 to F12)
Return to X session from a virtual console	F7

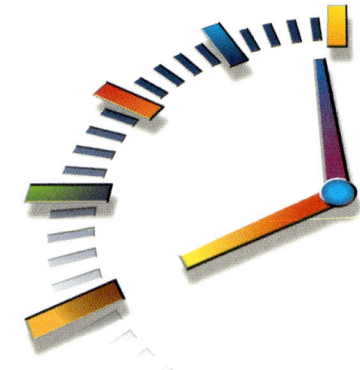

Installation Order for GNOME Packages (with Enlightenment)

To satisfy dependencies, install `rpm` packages and tarballs in the following order:

    libjpeg
    libpng
    libungif
    libtiff
    libgr
    ImageMagick
    zlib
    guile
    Berkeley DB
    audiofile
    esound
    glib
    libxml
    ORBit
    GTK+
    imlib
    fnlib
    gnome-audio
    gnome-libs
    lib-gtop
    libghttp
    enlightenment
    xloadimage
    xscreensaver
    gnome-core
    mc
    control-center
    libglade
    gnome-print
    ee
    gtop
    extace
    gnome-media
    gnome-pim
    gnome-utils
    gnome-games
    gnome-users-guide
    gnumeric

Judith Samson

SAMS
Teach Yourself
GNOME
in 24 Hours

SAMS

A Division of Macmillan USA
201 West 103rd St., Indianapolis, Indiana, 46290 USA

Sams Teach Yourself GNOME in 24 Hours

Copyright © 2000 by Sams Publishing

All rights reserved. No part of this book shall be reproduced, stored in a retrieval system, or transmitted by any means, electronic, mechanical, photocopying, recording, or otherwise, without written permission from the publisher. No patent liability is assumed with respect to the use of the information contained herein. Although every precaution has been taken in the preparation of this book, the publisher and author assume no responsibility for errors or omissions. Nor is any liability assumed for damages resulting from the use of the information contained herein.

International Standard Book Number: 0-672-31714-1

Library of Congress Catalog Card Number: 99-6361

Printed in the United States of America

First Printing: May 2000

02 01 00   4 3 2 1

Trademarks

All terms mentioned in this book that are known to be trademarks or service marks have been appropriately capitalized. Sams Publishing cannot attest to the accuracy of this information. Use of a term in this book should not be regarded as affecting the validity of any trademark or service mark.

Warning and Disclaimer

Every effort has been made to make this book as complete and as accurate as possible, but no warranty or fitness is implied. The information provided is on an "as is" basis. The author and the publisher shall have neither liability nor responsibility to any person or entity with respect to any loss or damages arising from the information contained in this book or from the use of the CD-ROM or programs accompanying it.

ACQUISITIONS EDITOR
Neil Rowe

DEVELOPMENT EDITOR
Laura N. Williams

MANAGING EDITOR
Lisa Wilson

PROJECT EDITOR
Carol Bowers

COPY EDITORS
Mary Ellen Stephenson
Rhonda Tinch-Mize

INDEXER
Kevin Kent

PROOFREADER
Katherin Bidwell

TECHNICAL EDITORS
David Gay
Jim Westveer

MEDIA DEVELOPER
Jason Haines

INTERIOR DESIGNER
Gary Adair

COVER DESIGNER
Aren Howell

COPY WRITER
Eric Bogert

PRODUCTION
Darin Crone
Steve Geiselman

Contents at a Glance

		Introduction	1
PART 1		**Installing and Running GNOME**	**5**
Hour	1	Introducing GNOME	7
	2	Installing GNOME	15
	3	Starting and Logging Out of GNOME	27
	4	Working with Window Managers	37
PART II		**Using and Customizing GNOME**	**53**
Hour	5	Exploring the Desktop	55
	6	GNOME Under the Hood	69
	7	Using the Panel and the Main Menu	79
	8	Managing Files in GNOME	89
	9	Common File Manager Tasks	103
	10	Exploring Enlightenment	123
	11	Customizing Your GNOME Environment	141
	12	Understanding and Using Themes	155
PART III		**System Administration with GNOME**	**165**
Hour	13	GNOME Processes	167
	14	Setting Up a Remote Connection in GNOME	185
	15	The Internet and GNOME	199
	16	Managing Printing with GNOME	215
PART IV		**GNOME Applications**	**227**
Hour	17	Installing and Running GNOME Applications	229
	18	Using GNOME for Your Business	243
	19	Working With Graphics in GNOME	257
	20	Fun with GNOME	271

Part V Advanced GNOME Topics — 287

Hour 21	Uninstalling GNOME and Getting Help	289
22	Upgrading GNOME and Joining the GNOME Project	301
23	GNOME Technologies	315
24	Anatomy of a GNOME Application	321
Appendix A	Troubleshooting	333
B	Answers	339
	Index	367

Contents

Introduction	1

PART I Installing and Running GNOME   5

Hour 1 Introducing GNOME   7

The GNU Network Model Environment = GNOME! 8
    Goals of the GNOME Project 9
A Brief History of the GNOME Project 9
Free Software and the Free Software Foundation 10
    Copylefting 11
GNOME and KDE 11
The Future of GNOME 12
Summary 12
Q&A 13
Workshop 13
    Quiz 13
    Exercises 13

Hour 2 Installing GNOME   15

Preparing to Install GNOME 15
    Necessary Hardware 16
    Necessary Software 16
    Finding Installed Components 16
Choosing an Installation Method 19
    Installing GNOME from a CD-ROM 19
    Installing GNOME from Downloaded rpms 21
Solving Dependency Errors 24
Solving Version-Dependency Errors 25
Summary 25
Q&A 26
Workshop 26
    Quiz 26
    Exercises 26

Hour 3 Starting and Logging Out of GNOME   27

Preparing to Start GNOME 28
Starting GNOME from the Command Line (xinit) 29
    Possible Problems 30
Starting GNOME When X Starts at Boot (xdm) 31
    Possible Problems 31

Using Switchdesk to Switch Between GNOME and KDE 32
Summary 34
Q&A 34
Workshop 35
    Quiz 35
    Exercises 35

Hour 4 Working with Window Managers 37

How GNOME Works with Window Managers 38
    The Desktop Environment 38
    The Graphical Interface 38
    The Window Manager 38
    How It All Comes Together 40
GNOME-Compliant Window Managers 41
    Enlightenment 41
    IceWM 44
    sawmill 47
    Installing sawmill 48
    Other Window Managers 49
Switching Window Managers 49
Summary 50
Q&A 50
Workshop 51
    Quiz 51
    Exercises 51

Part II Using and Customizing GNOME 53

Hour 5 Exploring the Desktop 55

A Word on Three-Button Mouse Emulation 56
The GNOME Desktop 57
    Desktop Icons 57
    The Main Menu 60
    The GNOME Panel 61
Working with GNOME Windows 63
Some Useful GNOME Utilities 64
    gEdit 64
    gnotepad+ 64
    GNOME Virtual Terminals 65
Session Management 65
Summary 66
Q&A 66

Workshop	67
Quiz	67
Exercises	67

Hour 6 GNOME Under the Hood   69

GNOME and Linux	70
Understanding the Multiuser System	70
GNOME Libraries	72
GNOME Executable Files	72
The $PATH/share Directory	73
The /usr/share/pixmaps Directory	73
The .gnome Directory and GNOME Configuration Files	74
The Session Files	75
The .desktop Files	76
User Directory .desktop Files	77
Summary	78
Q&A	78
Workshop	78
Quiz	78

Hour 7 Using the Panel and the Main Menu   79

Configuring and Using the GNOME Panel	80
Adding an Application Launcher	80
Using Drawers to Organize Your Launchers	81
Adding Useful Applets to the Panel	82
Configuring Panel Properties	83
Using the Main Menu	84
Parts of the Main Menu	85
Editing the Main Menu	86
Summary	87
Q&A	87
Workshop	88
Quiz	88
Exercises	88

Hour 8 Managing Files in GNOME   89

The Basics of GNOME File Manager	90
Opening File Manager	90
Closing a File Manager Window	90
File Manager Window	91
File Manager Menus	92
The File Menu	92
The Edit Menu	93
The Settings Menu and the Layout Menu	94
The Commands Menu and the Help Menu	94

The Toolbar 95
    Right-Click Menus 95
Setting Preferences in File Manager 97
    The File Display Tab 98
    The Confirmation Tab 98
    The Desktop Tab 99
Summary 101
Q&A 101
Workshop 101
    Quiz 101
    Exercises 102

HOUR 9 Common File Manager Tasks   103

Customizing Your View 104
Selecting Files 106
Copying, Deleting, Moving, and Renaming Files 107
    Copy 107
    Move 108
    Delete 108
    Renaming Files 109
    Using Drag-and-Drop 109
    Viewing Directory and File Sizes 111
Finding Files 111
    Search 112
    Find File 112
    Sorting Files 113
    Symbolic Links Versus Hard Links 114
    Viewing File Properties 115
    Using Filters 118
The Virtual File System 119
    Viewing Compressed and Archived Files 119
Summary 119
Q&A 120
Workshop 120
    Quiz 120
    Exercises 121

HOUR 10 Exploring Enlightenment   123

Enlightenment Tools 124
    Iconbox 124
    The Enlightenment Pager 124

Contents

Enlightenment Menus	125
Main Enlightenment Menu	125
Window Border Menu	129
Customizing the Menus	131
Desktops	132
Virtual Desktops	132
Multiple Desktops	133
Keybindings	134
Using the Enlightenment External Shell (eesh)	135
Opening eesh	136
Getting Help in eesh	136
Exiting eesh	136
Some Common Enlightenment Problems and Solutions	137
Edit or Delete ~/.enlightenment Directory to Fix a Broken Session	137
Enlightenment Is Slow	137
Sound Does Not Work	138
Segmentation Fault	138
Getting Help	138
Summary	139
Q&A	139
Workshop	139
Quiz	139
Exercises	140

Hour 11 Customizing Your GNOME Environment   141

Using the GNOME Control Center	142
Default Editor	143
Background	143
Screensaver	144
Changing the Font	145
Keyboard Bell	145
Sound Events	146
Keyboard	146
Mouse	147
Applications	148
Session Management	149
Options	149
Non-Session-Managed Startup Programs	150
Browse Currently Running Programs	150
Resetting the GNOME Session	151
Control Center Behavior	152
Summary	152

Q&A	152
Workshop	153
Quiz	153
Exercises	153

Hour 12 Understanding and Using Themes 155

The Magic of Themes	156
How Themes Work	156
Kinds of GTK Themes	158
Components of a gtk Theme	159
Libraries Needed for gtk Themes	160
Obtaining and Installing gtk Themes	160
Installing a gtk Theme	160
Using a New Theme	161
Uninstalling a Theme	161
Installing Enlightenment Themes	162
Downloading an Enlightenment Theme	162
Uninstalling an Enlightenment Theme	163
Summary	163
Q&A	163
Workshop	164
Quiz	164
Exercises	164

Part III System Administration with GNOME 165

Hour 13 GNOME Processes 167

Installing Packages with gnoRPM	168
Exploring gnoRPM	168
Installing and Upgrading rpms	169
Finding rpm Packages	171
Using Rpmfind	171
Querying rpm Packages	172
GnoRPM Preferences	174
GnoRPM and File Manager	177
Other GNOME System Administration Utilities	177
Gnome-linuxconf	177
Gnome-admin	177
System Information	179
GNOME DiskFree	179
Working with MIME Types	180
Viewing MIME Types	181
Editing MIME Types	181
Adding MIME Types	181

Summary	182
Q&A	182
Workshop	182
Quiz	182
Exercises	183

Hour 14 Setting Up a Remote Connection in GNOME 185

Gathering Information About Your ISP	187
Gathering Information About Your Modem	187
Is Your Modem Compatible with Linux?	188
Which Serial Port Is the Modem Connected To?	188
Special Initialization String	189
Setting Up a New Account in GNOME PPP Dialer	190
Dial Tab	190
Authentication Tab	191
IP Address Tab	191
DNS Server Tab	191
Script Tab	192
PPP Tab	192
Modem Tab	192
Making a Connection	193
Monitoring Your Connection	194
PPP Applet	195
Modem Lights	195
Summary	196
Q&A	196
Workshop	196
Quiz	196
Exercises	197

Hour 15 The Internet and GNOME 199

A Word About Netscape Communicator	200
Getting and Sending Email with Balsa	200
Setting Preferences in Balsa	202
Uploading and Downloading Files with gFTP	204
Exploring the gFTP Window	204
Using gFTP	207
Connecting to an FTP Site	208
Navigating the File Systems	208
Downloading and Uploading Files	208
Comparing Windows	209
Configuring gFTP Options	209
General Options	210
Using GNOME File Manager for FTP	212

Summary		212
Q&A		212
Workshop		213
Quiz		213
Exercises		213

Hour 16 Managing Printing with GNOME   215

Setting Up Your System for Printing	216
The Printing Process	217
Printing Tools	218
`lpr`	218
`lpd`	218
`lpq`	218
`lprm`	219
GNOME Printing Tools	219
`ggv`	219
`cpanel`	219
Gnome-print	220
Printing Graphics Files from GIMP	222
Summary	224
Q&A	224
Workshop	225
Quiz	225
Exercises	225

Part IV GNOME Applications   227

Hour 17 Installing and Running GNOME Applications   229

Running Applications	230
Running Applications from the Command Line	231
GNOME Applications—Behind the Scenes	232
Finding New GNOME Applications	233
The GNOME Software Map	233
Downloading and Installing GNOME Applications	239
Tarballs Versus Binary Packages Revisited	239
Summary	241
Q&A	241
Workshop	241
Quiz	241
Exercises	242

Hour 18 Using GNOME for Your Business — 243

- GNOME in an Enterprise ... 244
  - The GNOME Solution to Complexity ... 244
  - The Business Advantage of GNOME ... 245
  - Disadvantages of GNOME ... 245
- GNOME Office ... 246
  - AbiWord ... 246
  - Gnumeric ... 247
  - GNOME-PIM ... 249
  - Dia ... 251
- Other Productivity Applications ... 252
  - Gaby ... 253
  - TimeTracker ... 254
- Summary ... 254
- Q&A ... 254
- Workshop ... 255
  - Quiz ... 255
  - Exercises ... 255

Hour 19 Working with Graphics in GNOME — 257

- Eye of GNOME ... 258
  - Using Eye of GNOME ... 259
- Electric Eyes ... 260
  - Viewing Files in Electric Eyes ... 261
  - Editing Images in Electric Eyes ... 263
- Changing the Default Image Viewer ... 264
- Introducing the Graphics Image Manipulation Program (GIMP) ... 265
  - Getting the Latest Version of GIMP ... 266
  - GIMP Basics ... 266
  - Further Reading on the GIMP ... 267
- Summary ... 267
- Q&A ... 267
- Workshop ... 268
  - Quiz ... 268
  - Exercises ... 268

Hour 20 Fun with GNOME — 271

- Setting Up GNOME for Sound ... 272
  - Configuring Your Desktop for GNOME/Enlightenment Sound ... 272
- Using the GNOME CD Player ... 273
  - Using Track Editor ... 275
  - Customizing the CD Player ... 276
  - Quit ... 277

GNOME Games 277
   AisleRiot 278
   Gnome Mines 278
   Gnome Tetravex (Gnotravex) 279
   Gnome Tali (GTali) 279
   Iagno 279
   Mah-jongg 281
   Same Gnome 281
   Gnibbles 282
   GNOME Robots II 282
   Gnome-Stones 282
Panel Amusements 283
   Other GNOME Entertainment 284
Summary 285
Q&A 285
Workshop 286
   Quiz 286
   Exercises 286

PART V Advanced GNOME Topics   287

Hour 21 Uninstalling GNOME and Getting Help   289

Uninstalling GNOME from Binary Packages 290
   Uninstalling GNOME Using GnoRPM 291
   Uninstalling Binary Packages from the Command Line 292
   Uninstalling GNOME Tarballs 293
   Uninstalling Enlightenment 293
The GNOME Help Browser 294
   The GNOME User's Guide 296
   The GNOME FAQ 296
   Other GNOME Help Documents 296
   The GNOME Documentation Project 296
   The Mailing Lists 297
Summary 299
Q&A 299
Workshop 299
   Quiz 300
   Exercises 300

Hour 22 Upgrading GNOME and Joining the GNOME Project   301

Installing GNOME from Source Code 302
The Source Code Advantage 303
How to Install GNOME Software from Source Code 304
   Obtain the Compilation Tools 304

Tarball Installation Process	306
Delete Old Versions of the Software	306
Untar the Tarballs	306
Configure the Makefile	307
Compile and Install	308
Clean Up	308
Uninstalling a Tarball	308
Using CVS to Get Development Versions	309
Becoming a GNOMEr	311
Reporting Bugs	311
Writing Documentation for GNOME	311
Programming for GNOME	312
Other Ways to Contribute	312
Summary	312
Q&A	312
Workshop	312
Quiz	313

HOUR 23 GNOME Technologies 315

GNOME Technologies	315
CORBA	316
ORB	317
Bonobo	318
Language Bindings	318
Summary	319
Q&A	319
Workshop	320
Quiz	320

HOUR 24 Anatomy of a GNOME Application 321

What Is a GNOME Application?	322
How Do Graphical Interface Programs Work?	322
Some Programming Terms Defined	323
Parts of a GNOME Application	323
GNOME Libraries	324
Libgnome	325
Libgnomeui	325
GTK	326
GDK, Glib, and Xlib	327
Glade	327
Learning More	328
Summary	328
Q&A	329

Workshop 329
    Quiz 329
    Exercises 329

APPENDIX A Troubleshooting   **333**

APPENDIX B Answers   **339**

Index   **367**

About the Author

Judith Samson is a technical writer and Linux for business evangelist. She regularly contributes to *TechRepublic*, as well as the GNOME Documentation Project. Judith is also pursuing graduate studies in mathematics and computer science at Eastern Michigan University. Send email to judith@samsonsource.com, or visit www.samsonsource.com.

Dedication

To Alain

Acknowledgments

First, I would like to give a very special thanks to Miguel de Icaza, and everyone on the GNOME Project. Now that the book is finished, I will be able to work on all the documentation I've been promising. Thanks to Neil Rowe, acquisitions editor, for giving me this opportunity and cheering me along; Laura Williams, for being the best development editor in the world; Carol Bowers, for running the show; Mary Ellen Stephenson and Rhonda Tinch-Mize, for making sure that my English is gud enuff. Thanks to Jim Westveer and David Gay, for making sure that I won't get a flood of emails from GNOMErs pointing out errors in the book. Thanks to George Cager and David Drake, for starting the whole thing. And most of all, thanks to the staff of the Washtenaw County Jewish Community Center, for taking such excellent care of Adrian so I could get some work done; to Adrian, for being a good boy; and to Alain, for all your support and encouragement, and for doing the dishes when it wasn't your turn.

Tell Us What You Think!

As the reader of this book, *you* are our most important critic and commentator. We value your opinion and want to know what we're doing right, what we could do better, what areas you'd like to see us publish in, and any other words of wisdom you're willing to pass our way.

You can fax, email, or write me directly to let me know what you did or didn't like about this book—as well as what we can do to make our books stronger.

Please note that I cannot help you with technical problems related to the topic of this book, and that due to the high volume of mail I receive, I might not be able to reply to every message.

When you write, please be sure to include this book's title and author as well as your name and phone or fax number. I will carefully review your comments and share them with the author and editors who worked on the book.

- Fax: 317-581-4770

- Email: linux_sams@macmillanusa.com

- Mail: Mark Taber
  Associate Publisher
  Sams Publishing
  201 West 103rd Street
  Indianapolis, IN 46290 USA

Introduction

Few people who read the newspaper or watch cable television news have not heard of Linux. Linux and open-source software are the latest technology buzzwords in the mainstream media. If you have been reading about this latest technology phenomenon, you might have found yourself asking these questions:

- Just what is it about Linux that is so revolutionary?
- How can it be any good if it doesn't cost anything?
- If it doesn't cost anything, how do people make money with Linux?
- Why should I replace my Windows system with Linux?
- Now that I have Linux, how do I use it?

The answers to all these questions can be found by learning about GNOME, Linux's answer to the Windows and MacOS desktops.

What Is GNOME?

GNOME, officially pronounced "guh-nohm," is several things, depending on the level at which you ask the question. GNOME is a windowed, graphical desktop environment for UNIX and UNIX-like computer systems. It is a collection of integrated applications, specifically created for Linux. GNOME is also a set of standards and tools for developing integrated applications that maintain a standard look and feel and can be seamlessly used, embedded within each other, and controlled together.

The word "GNOME" is an acronym, which stands for GNU Networked Object Model Environment. Consisting entirely of free software, the GNOME Project is supported by hundreds of volunteers all over the globe, including application developers, code developers, writers, user interface specialists, and free software advocates.

Some people would say that GNOME is the hole in the dike of the monopolistic hold that companies such as Microsoft have had on the desktop computing industry. Others might say that GNOME is the "killer app" that will eventually fuel and maintain the meteor-like growth of Linux. You could also say that GNOME is a desktop windowing environment that combines the MacOS's or Windows's intuitive ease of use with the custom features and power of UNIX. But most importantly, GNOME is simply fun to use.

Why Teach Yourself GNOME and Who Is This Book For?

Sams Teach Yourself GNOME in 24 Hours is written with the beginning Linux user in mind, but the book is rich enough in content and in-depth enough for the experienced Linux or UNIX user to also benefit from reading it. This book will arm you with practical knowledge of how to accomplish tasks in GNOME *and* an understanding of how the system works.

Sams Teach Yourself GNOME in 24 Hours assumes no prior knowledge of GNOME on the reader's part, and you only need the most basic knowledge of Linux to understand the book. If you are learning Linux for the first time, this book is an ideal companion to an introductory Linux book. Although advanced topics are discussed, topics that are addressed to advanced Linux users are clearly delineated, and there are references in almost every chapter to resources from which you can learn more about the Linux subject discussed.

If you are an experienced Linux user, this book also has plenty for you. Although Linux topics are explained in detail to help the beginning user, this book does not skimp on content, nor does it dumb-down the coverage of advanced topics.

If you would like to learn how to develop GNOME applications, or if you are simply interested in how GNOME programs work, there are chapters that discuss the technologies behind GNOME and how GNOME applications are constructed. These chapters are written from a user's standpoint, and provide a gentle introduction to application development.

After reading *Sams Teach Yourself GNOME in 24 Hours*, you will be able to use the full power of the GNOME desktop, understand how to unleash GNOME's potential as the front end to Linux, be able to fully customize GNOME, and develop a simple GNOME application—even without any programming experience.

Linux is rapidly growing in importance as a commercial operating system, and more Windows users are embracing it. As Linux ceases to exist solely within the hacker's arena and enters the mainstream-computing world, an understanding of GNOME will become essential to anyone who uses Linux.

What's Included on the CD-ROM

The CD-ROM that accompanies *Sams Teach Yourself GNOME in 24 Hours* provides you with everything you need to use GNOME and to follow the chapters and do the exercises in this book, including

Introduction

- A full Mandrake 7.0 distribution of Linux, which includes the full base GNOME installation
- Enlightenment, IceWM, sawmill, and WindowMaker window managers
- The full GNOME Office suite of applications
- Extra GNOME games and amusements
- The popular blueHeart theme for GTK and Enlightenment
- The GNOME C program discussed in Hour 24, "Anatomy of a GNOME Application"
- A list of URLs for the Web resources mentioned in the book

The CD-ROM is organized into folders that coincide with the chapters, for easy reference.

How To Use This Book

Sams Teach Yourself GNOME in 24 Hours is designed to teach you the basics of the GNOME desktop in 24 one-hour lessons. Each lesson begins with an overview of the topics that will be covered in that hour.

The main body of each hour presents the lesson, with the major topics broken down into simpler, easily digestible parts.

Throughout each lesson, you will find additional information provided in the form of Notes, Tips, and Cautions.

A Tip gives you special hints, shortcuts, or advice on how to perform a task that is often missed by new GNOME users.

A Note presents interesting information that is pertinent to the lesson, but not necessarily integral to your understanding.

A Caution alerts you to a possible problem or common pitfall, and gives you advice on how to avoid the problem.

At the conclusion of each hour is a Summary to help you review the lesson, a Question-and-Answer section that answers common questions about the topic, or helps you solve problems that are frequently encountered by new GNOME users. The hour ends with a quiz to help you test yourself on what you have learned. The exercises following the quiz are designed as a starting point for you to begin using the practical knowledge you have acquired.

I hope that you enjoy this book and that it helps you acquire a full understanding and appreciation of GNOME!

PART I
Installing and Running GNOME

Hour

1 Introducing GNOME

2 Installing GNOME

3 Starting and Logging Out of GNOME

4 Working with Window Managers

HOUR 1

Introducing GNOME

Once upon a time, there lived a young programmer named Miguel, who lived in the computer dungeons of a university in the middle of a vast, dusty city. Miguel loved the new operating system called Linux that he had been working with, and decided that it would be wonderful if ordinary people all over the world could enjoy it too, without having to undergo the strenuous and fearsome initiation rites into the ancient and secret brotherhood of UNIX hackers. He decided to create a special key to unlock the secrets of UNIX. The key was called the GNOME desktop environment. The world would never be the same again....

Welcome to the wonderful world of the GNU Network Model Environment, or GNOME.

In this hour, you will

- Explore the basics of the GNOME desktop environment.
- Review a brief history of the GNOME Project.
- Learn about the GNU Project and the free software movement.
- Look into the future of GNOME.

GNOME is a simple, easy-to-use graphical interface to UNIX-like operating systems, particularly Linux. It uses point-and-click and drag-and-drop to do the tasks that previously required an encyclopedia of text-based commands. GNOME has many faces and appearances. It can make your desktop applications change color, shape, and form as often as you change your clothes. Eventually it will have a cadre of applications more powerful and more customizable than—and as easy to use as—the most expensive office productivity suite in existence. And every piece of software, every line of code, is completely free.

The GNU Network Model Environment = GNOME!

UNIX can be arguably called the world's most powerful operating system. Its true multi-tasking capability, infinite configurability, network transparency, power, and stability have made it the world's most widely-used operating system. For the ordinary desktop computer user, however, it can be unwieldy and impossibly difficult to use. There is so much syntax to learn, so many arcane commands to remember, so many different ways of doing the same function, that simply learning the basics of UNIX is a task that most people in the everyday work world, not to mention many computer professionals, cannot imagine undertaking.

Not only is the operating system itself difficult to learn, the thousands of applications that run on UNIX, also tend to be difficult to learn and use.

With the advent of Linux and the GNU Project—whose aim was to bring the power of UNIX to the masses in the form of free software—millions of non-technical people all over the globe are being introduced to UNIX.

Until very recently, the problem of Linux's usability remained. Another problem slowing the spread of Linux has been the scarcity of everyday, user-level desktop applications. The GNOME Project was conceived to make UNIX an easy and logical choice for desktop computing. Figure 1.1 shows the GNOME footprint, which is the symbol for the GNOME Project.

FIGURE 1.1
The GNOME footprint, designed by Tigert, symbolizes the GNOME Project.

Goals of the GNOME Project

The goals of the GNOME Project are to

- Create an intuitive, full-featured, easy-to-use desktop environment to provide a graphical interface for the Linux operating system.
- Provide point-and-click and drag-and-drop alternatives to the traditional text-based UNIX interface.
- Develop a suite of applications that have a consistent, recognizable look and feel and are inter-operable.
- Develop a powerful, logical, and conceptually simple framework to encourage and simplify further application development.
- Create a suite of applications for the desktop computer, including ones for word processing, graphic art, spreadsheets, database processing, and Internet and Web use.
- Design a desktop that can be configured on-the-fly by the user, with no programming. This means that a user can change the entire look and feel of her desktop at any time, while programs are running, by using a few simple tools.
- Achieve all these goals with free software.

A Brief History of the GNOME Project

In 1984, Richard Stallman created the GNU Project, which stands for GNU's Not UNIX. Stallman's goal was to create an entire computer system based on free software. The system would include everything that is commonly associated with commercial computer systems, including an operating system, hardware support, networking capability, interfaces, and applications. The operating system that emerged was GNU/Linux, commonly referred to as simply Linux. GNOME was conceived out of the need for a desktop environment for GNU/Linux. Figure 1.2 shows the gnu, the symbol for the GNU Project.

FIGURE 1.2
The goal of the GNU Project is to create an entire computer system of free software.

For Richard Stallman's history of the GNU Project, including his reason for starting the project, see http://www.gnu.org/gnu/thegnuproject.html.

At the time, considerably advanced projects were already underway to develop desktop environments for Linux, including CDE and KDE. Unfortunately, these desktops used widget sets that came with licensing restrictions. Since the GNU project was designed to contain only free and unrestricted software, the restrictions made the desktops unusable.

The members of the GNU Project decided to create a new desktop environment from scratch. With support from Red Hat Software, Miguel de Icaza and a group of volunteers began to create a desktop system that would take GNU permanently out of the realm of geeks and into the reach of ordinary desktop users. Thus, the GNOME Project was founded in 1998.

The goal of the GNOME Project was to create a desktop environment for the GNU Project based entirely on free software. In March 1999, the GNOME Project released version 1.0 of GNOME. In October 1999, the second official release of GNOME was announced. Officially version 1.5.3, it is commonly called October GNOME. October GNOME fixed many major bugs and provided improved documentation and tighter code. GNOME 2.0 should be released in the first quarter of 2000.

Free Software and the Free Software Foundation

GNOME came into existence because of a desire for free software, so it is worth looking at exactly what the term *free software* means. The GNU Project's definition of free software is as follows:

- The freedom to use the program for any purpose that you want
- The freedom to examine and study the inner workings of the program, and change it to suit your needs
- The freedom to distribute as many copies of the program you want to whomever you want
- The freedom to make improvements to the program, and to make those improvements public

Free software does not necessarily mean software that doesn't cost anything, although most GNU software costs nothing to download and use. The fundamental argument of the GNU Project and the Free Software Foundation is that software should be freely available to anybody who wants it, and that users of the software should be completely free to use, study, modify, and give away the software without restriction.

Free software differs in a fundamental way from *open source* software, although the terms are often used interchangeably. *Open source* is a slippery term that can mean the exact same thing as free software, or it can have an insidiously different meaning. Open source means nothing more than the user can look at the source code. Open source software does not always let you modify the software for your personal use without notifying an authority mentioned in the software license. It is not always freely distributable. As the term open source becomes a media buzzword, it is important not to confuse the concept with free software.

Copylefting

GNOME software is "copylefted" with the GNU General Public License (GPL) and the GNU Lesser General Public License (LGPL). These licenses are a way of copyrighting which guarantees that the GNOME software will always be freely distributable. Not only is GNOME copylefted, but any software that is made using GNOME tools or that is derived from GNOME is also freely redistributable.

GNOME and KDE

KDE is the other major desktop environment that was created specifically for Linux, and it shares many of the same features as GNOME. There are some basic differences in design and concept.

GNOME was originally created in response to some controversy around the widget library Qt, which is used in KDE. Owned by Troll Tech, the proprietary software Qt comes with a license that is, for the most part, unrestrictive. Troll Tech does require users to forward to the company any modifications of the software. The members of the GNU Project felt that this policy violated the tenets of free software, and so the GNOME Project was born.

On the programming level, there are some basic design differences between KDE and GNOME. KDE is written in C++, and application developers are restricted to C++. GNOME uses CORBA technology, which enables GNOME applications to be written in any language for which there is a language binding.

The GNOME Frequently Asked Questions page on the GNOME Web Site has an excellent user-level explanation of CORBA, and how it relates to the GNOME architecture. See http://www.gnome.org/gnomefaq/html/x703.html.

GNOME uses the GIMP ToolKit, or GTK, as a widget library. One of the great advantages of GTK is the use of themes to change the appearance of desktop displays. KDE is more restricted in the look and feel of the desktop and applications.

Members of the GNOME and KDE projects work in friendly competition; there's even a mailing list where developers can hash out compatibility issues. You can have both GNOME and KDE installed on your computer and switch between the two, depending on your mood.

The Future of GNOME

The major goals for GNOME in the immediate future are greater configuration and customization, improved user interfaces, and more user-level documentation. Specifically, developers are currently working towards the following goals:

- The ability to configure and customize every aspect of the desktop, including applications, via simple utilities that require no programming or recompiling.
- Themes that affect the entire desktop, not just applications that run on the desktop.
- Integration of GNOME productivity applications with Palm Pilot software.
- A new file manager based on an asynchronous, network-transparent virtual file system.
- Greater customization of the GNOME Panel. You will be able to place the panel anywhere on the desktop, not just around the edges. You will also be able to completely control the size of the desktop panel.
- The capability to support every language in the world, including Klingon!
- The portability of GNOME applications to Windows and BeOS.
- An improved user interface with the creation of the GNOME User Interface Team.
- Creation of an entire office productivity suite of free software, fully comparable to (and probably superior to) currently available proprietary office software suites.

Summary

In this hour, you were introduced to the GNU Project and GNOME Project. You learned about free software, and its importance in the creation of GNOME. You learned about the difference between GNOME and KDE, as well as the goals of GNOME, and you took a peek into the near future of GNOME.

Q&A

Q I just want to learn how to use GNOME to do my everyday tasks at work. I'll never modify source code; I don't even know what source code is. Why should I care about free software?

A If the concept of free software spreads to the mainstream and becomes the norm, the proliferation of custom software will grow exponentially, changing the entire concept of intellectual property and technology as we know it. This is a matter that concerns everybody.

Q Can I run programs that are not GNOME within the GNOME desktop?

A You can run any program that you want within GNOME. Programs do not need to be GNOME-compliant, or even have anything to do with GNOME, in order to run within the GNOME desktop.

Workshop

The quiz questions and exercises are designed to increase your understanding and to encourage you to continue experimenting. Answers appear in Appendix B, "Answers."

Quiz

1. What is the difference between free software and open source software?
2. What larger project is the GNOME Project a part of?
3. What is the basic goal of GNOME?

Exercises

1. Explore the GNOME Web Site at http://www.gnome.org.
2. Read the December 14, 1999 article "GNOME: Its Current State and Future" online at *Linux Today*, http://linuxtoday.com/stories/13678.html, for a detailed look at the future of GNOME.

Hour 2

Installing GNOME

Installing GNOME can be time consuming, but it is not difficult. Some Linux distributions such as Red Hat automatically install GNOME as part of the Linux installation. As we will discuss, however, new releases of GNOME occur so often that the components on the CD are often already out of date by the time the CD is released. In addition, if you ever have to uninstall and reinstall GNOME from scratch, you should understand the components of GNOME and the correct installation order.

In this hour, you will

- Learn what hardware and software you must have to run GNOME.
- Install GNOME from rpm.
- Troubleshoot your installation.

Preparing to Install GNOME

Before you install GNOME, you must be sure that you have sufficient resources on your computer and that you have the necessary software that GNOME needs in order to run.

Necessary Hardware

Your computer must have at least 16MB of memory to run GNOME, and at least 32MB for optimal performance. You must also have a minimum 50MB of disk space if you are installing from binary files (such as `rpms`) or 200MB of disk space if you are installing from source code (tarballs). The memory on your video card is also important—the more you have, the faster GNOME will run. If your video card is low on memory, GNOME will run, but it might be slow, particularly if you have a complex window manager. If your video card has less than 4MB of memory, install a simple window manager like sawmill, and use a simple, clean theme. We will learn more about window managers in Hour 4, "Working with Window Managers," and more about themes in Hour 12, "Understanding and Using Themes."

Necessary Software

To run GNOME you must have a fully functioning X server such as XFree86 installed and configured on your computer. Before installing GNOME try to get the most recent version of your X server. If you are running a common Linux distribution, your X server is most likely XFree86. Install the latest upgrades from `http://www.xfree86.org` before proceeding. At the time of writing, the latest version of XFree86 is 3.3.6.*x*.

> XFree86 version 3.3.6 was released in January 2000. Many bugs are fixed and most video cards are now fully supported. If you have not upgraded, I strongly recommend that you do. You can find tarballs at `http://www.xfree86.org` and `rpms` at `http://www.redhat.com/downloads`.

In addition to an X server, you must have the following software installed before you install GNOME. Make sure that you have the most up-to-date releases. Tarballs are available at `http://freshmeat.net` and `rpms` can be downloaded from `http://www.redhat.com/downloads`. Figure 2.1 shows the freshmeat.net home page.

Finding Installed Components

To learn whether you have a component installed on your computer, use the `locate` command. First, at a command prompt enter

`updatedb`

`Updatedb` updates a database that lists the pathnames for every file on your system.

Next, enter the following command to find a particular file, substituting the actual file name for the placeholder *[file_name]*.

`locate [file_name]`

FIGURE 2.1

Freshmeat.net has downloads for virtually every kind of software made for Linux. The home page has a daily announcement of new software. To find a particular package, use the Find utility.

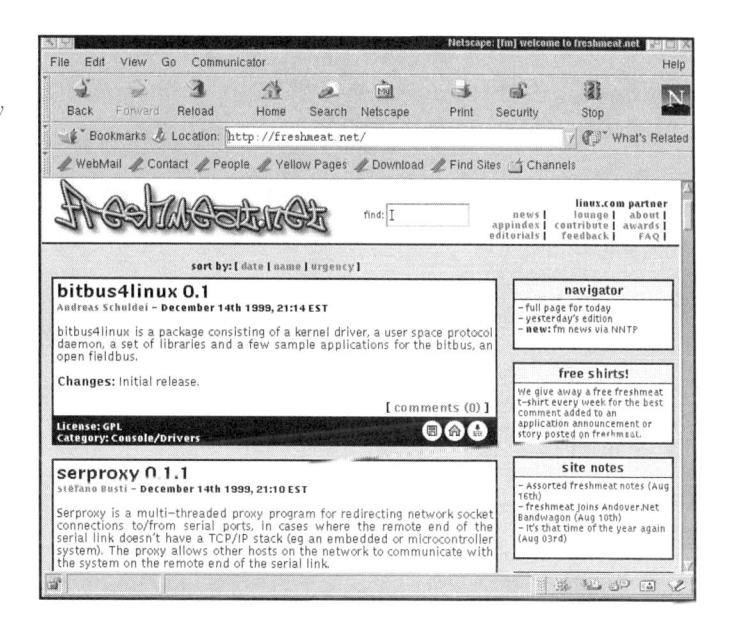

Look at the output of updatedb carefully. You might have the documentation for the component, but not the files themselves, as Listing 2.1 demonstrates.

LISTING 2.1 The *locate* Command and Its Output

```
#Example of locate esound, where the documentation is loaded on the computer,
➥but the actual files are not. Note that you can see the version of the file by
➥looking at the documentation.
[root@localhost i386]# locate esound
/usr/doc/esound-0.2.12
/usr/doc/esound-0.2.12/AUTHORS
/usr/doc/esound-0.2.12/COPYING
/usr/doc/esound-0.2.12/ChangeLog
/usr/doc/esound-0.2.12/INSTALL
/usr/doc/esound-0.2.12/NEWS
/usr/doc/esound-0.2.12/README
/usr/doc/esound-0.2.12/TIPS
/usr/doc/esound-0.2.12/TODO
```

The following list gives the first set of non-GNOME components that you will install on your computer (or verify that you already have), in the order that you should install them:

   libjpeg

   libpng

libungif

libtiff

libgr

ImageMagick

zlib

guile

Berkeley DB

You must also install a window manager that is at least partially GNOME compliant before running GNOME. The window managers that are fully GNOME compliant are

Enlightenment

sawmill

IceWM

WindowMaker

Don't worry about GNOME compliance yet; we will learn all about window managers in Hour 4. For now, we will install Enlightenment as part of our base GNOME installation. If you find that you prefer another window manager, you can easily change window managers later. Figure 2.2 shows the `fvwm` window manager, which some flavors of Linux/UNIX use as the default X Window environment.

FIGURE 2.2
Red Hat and Mandrake Linux display `fvwm` *as the desktop environment when KDE and GNOME are not installed.*

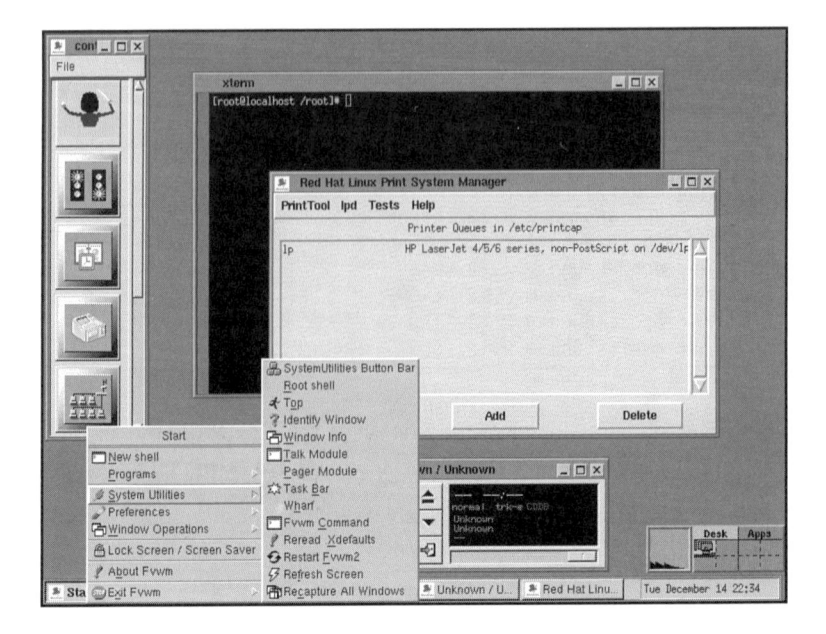

> All the GNOME components listed in this chapter are available on the CD-ROM that comes with this book. After you have a working version of GNOME running, you can follow the instructions in this hour to make upgrades.

Choosing an Installation Method

There are three ways to install GNOME: from a CD-ROM as part of a Linux distribution, from pre-compiled binary packages such as rpms, and from source code. In this section we discuss the advantages and disadvantages of the first two methods. The more complex process of installing GNOME from source code is covered in Hour 22, "Upgrading GNOME and Joining the GNOME Project."

Installing GNOME from a CD-ROM

The easiest way to install GNOME is from a CD-ROM as part of a pre-packaged Linux distribution. If you are new to Linux or just want to get GNOME up quickly and painlessly, this method is for you. All the packages have been scripted to install in the correct order, so you do not have to worry about the errors discussed at the end of this chapter. If you install Linux and GNOME from the same CD, it is unlikely that you will encounter problems.

The major disadvantage to installing from a CD-ROM is that the GNOME components are often out of date. Even if you do your initial installation from CD, you should follow the instructions in this chapter to upgrade your GNOME components after the initial CD installation.

If you have GNOME on your Linux CD-ROM, but didn't install it when you installed Linux, you can either run the installation again as an upgrade (consult your Linux documentation), or you can rpm the files directly from the CD-ROM onto your hard drive.

Insert the CD-ROM into the drive. Mount the CD-ROM using the mount point created in /etc/fstab. (In the following example, the mount point is /mnt/cdrom.)

```
# mount /mnt/cdrom
```

Next, update your file database by entering the command

```
# updatedb
```

Locate each component on the list using the `locate` command. In Listing 2.2, `locate esound` shows that version 0.2.10 of esound is already installed.

LISTING 2.2 Using locate esound

```
# locate esound
/mnt/cdrom/Mandrake/RPMS/esound-0.2.12-6mdk.i586.rpm
/mnt/cdrom/Mandrake/RPMS/esound-devel-0.2.12-6mdk.i586.rpm
/usr/doc/esound-0.2.10
/usr/doc/esound-0.2.10/AUTHORS
/usr/doc/esound-0.2.10/COPYING
/usr/doc/esound-0.2.10/ChangeLog
/usr/doc/esound-0.2.10/INSTALL
/usr/doc/esound-0.2.10/NEWS
/usr/doc/esound-0.2.10/README
/usr/doc/esound-0.2.10/TIPS
/usr/doc/esound-0.2.10/TODO
/usr/doc/esound-0.2.10/esound.sgml
/usr/src/RPM/RPMS/i386/esound-0.2.10-1.i386.rpm
```

As you can see, the version on CD-ROM is a later version, so we will update using the rpm -Uvh command:

```
# cd /mnt/cdrom/Mandrake/RPMS/esound-0.2.12-6mdk.i586.rpm
# rpm -Uvh esound-0.2.12-6mdk.i586.rpm
```

You do not need to update again until you unmount your CD. Locate each component on the CD and install it in the same manner. It is not necessary to repeat the updatedb command unless you unmount and then remount the CD, or change CDs.

Install components in the following order:

- audiofile
- esound
- glib
- libxml
- ORBit
- GTK+
- imlib
- fnlib
- gnome-audio
- gnome-libs
- lib-gtop
- libghttp
- enlightenment

xloadimage

xscreensaver

gnome-core

mc

control-center

libglade

gnome-print

ee

gtop

extace

gnome-media

gnome-pim

gnome-utils

gnome-games

gnome-users-guide

gnumeric

Installing GNOME from Downloaded rpms

An rpm is a package that has been compiled into binary form for you. At present, binary packages are available for Red Hat/Mandrake Linux, Caldera Linux, LinuxPPC, SuSE Linux, Debian, and Solaris. If you are installing GNOME to another system, see "Installing GNOME from Source Code" (tarballs) in Hour 15, "The Internet and GNOME." You can learn more about the various binary packages at http://www.gnome.org/start. Figure 2.3 shows the GNOME installation Web page.

To install GNOME from binary packages, first download the packages to a central location, for example, /usr/src/RPM.

Most of the packages can be found at the GNOME Web site. The Enlightenment packages with supporting libraries are downloaded from the Enlightenment Web site. If you cannot find packages at either the GNOME or the Enlightenment Web site, try the Red Hat site or the Web site of your Linux distribution. The URLs are

    http://www.gnome.org/start

    http://www.enlightenment.org

    http://www.redhat.com/download (or your Linux distribution's Web site)

FIGURE 2.3
Although GNOME only officially supports installation from tarballs, there are many binary packages available from the Project ftp server.

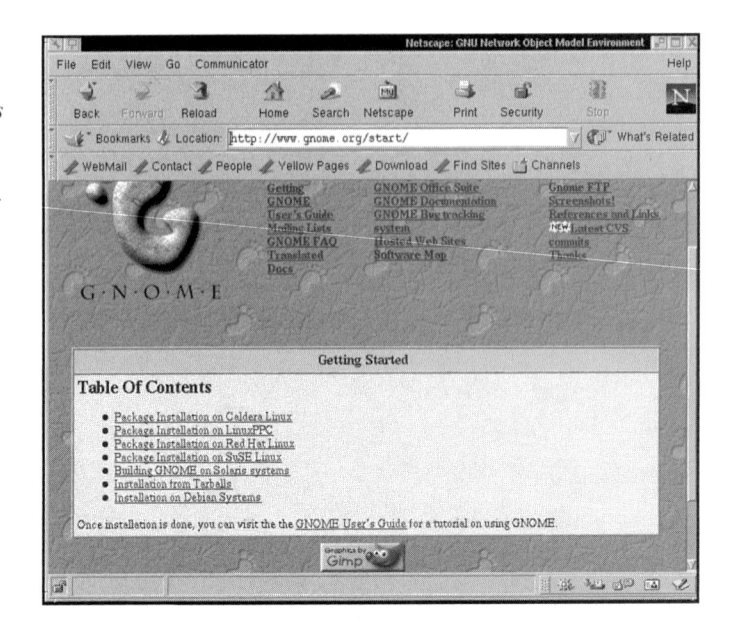

Download all the packages in this list:

audiofile	gnome-core
esound	mc
glib	control-center
libxml	libglade
ORBit	gnome-print
GTK+	ee
imlib	gtop
fnlib	extace
gnome-audio	gnome-media
gnome-libs	gnome-pim
lib-gtop	gnome-utils
libghttp	gnome-games
enlightenment	gnome-users-guide
xloadimage	gnumeric
xscreensaver	

Installing GNOME

You can download GNOME by opening X and using Netscape, or via command line interface using the Lynx browser or the utility wget (most Linux distributions include both). You can find the binary packages of GNOME and the tarballs at http://www.gnome.org.start/.

wget is a useful utility for downloading large files if you have an unstable dial-up connection. If your connection is lost during a download, wget will read the portion of the file that was already downloaded when the connection was lost. When you reconnect, wget will continue where it left off.

To use wget, you must know the complete URL pathname of the file you want to download. You can get the URL via Netscape, and then use wget to perform the actual download. From a command prompt, simply type **wget *[URL pathname]***, for example

wget ftp://ftp.gnome.org/pub/GNOME/stable/latest/sources

Figure 2.4 shows wget in action.

FIGURE 2.4

wget can work in the background or in an xterm to download files.

After you have downloaded all the packages, cd to the directory where the packages are located.

Install each package in the order given for download in the previous paragraph, using the command

rpm -Uvh [package].rpm

You can install all the packages at once by giving the following command:

rpm -Uvh *.rpm

If this is your first time installing GNOME, however, you will probably find it easier to install the packages one at a time, because dependency errors can be confusing to follow.

When you install a package, the output will look something like this:

```
# rpm -Uvh Image*
ImageMagick       ##################################################
#
```

Install each package in the same manner. That's all there is to it! If everything went well, you are ready to start GNOME.

Solving Dependency Errors

The most common installation error when installing from binary package is the dependency error. A dependency error occurs when the package you are trying to install needs some files from another package in order to work. For example, in the dependency error message shown here, we are trying to install guile. We get an error message that we must install umb-scheme before installing guile.

```
[root@localhost i386]# rpm -Uvh guile*
error: failed dependencies:
        umb-scheme is needed by guile-1.3-7
[root@localhost i386]#
```

To clear up the error, download the umb-scheme package and install it using the command

```
rpm -Uvh umb-scheme.rpm.
```

Attempt to install guile again, and the installation works.

Dependency errors can be frustrating if you don't pay attention to what you are doing. As you get a dependency error, write the error down on a piece of paper, noting the file that you are trying to install and the files that you must install to correct the error. As you install the files, check them off. This way, you will not get confused if you end up with dependency errors that go several levels deep. Listing 2.3 shows a dependency error that is a bit more complex than the first example. As you can see, the component gnome-core requires three other components—enlightenment, xscreensaver, and redhat-logos—to be installed first. When we tried to install xscreensaver, we discovered yet another component, xloadimage, had to be installed before xscreensaver.

LISTING 2.3 An Example of a Dependency Error

```
[root@localhost i386]# rpm -Uvh gnome-core*
error: failed dependencies:
        enlightenment >= 0.15.0 is needed by gnome-core-1.0.53-2
        xscreensaver >= 3.17-4 is needed by gnome-core-1.0.53-2
        redhat-logos is needed by gnome-core-1.0.53-2
```

```
[root@localhost i386]#
[root@localhost i386]# rpm -Uvh xscreensaver*
error: failed dependencies:
        xloadimage is needed by xscreensaver-3.17-4
[root@localhost i386]#
```

Solving Version-Dependency Errors

Another common dependency error occurs when you have a component installed on your computer, but a package you are trying to install requires a later version of the package. As you can see in Listing 2.4, we already have `imlib-1.9.7-1` installed. When we try to install `enlightenment-0.16.3-1`, we get a dependency error because `enlightenment-0.16.3-1` requires `imlib-1.9.8`—a later version than the one we already have.

LISTING 2.4 A Dependency Error Requiring a Later Version of a Package

```
[root@localhost i386]# ls
ImageMagick-4.2.9-1.i386.rpm       gtk+-1.2.6-1.i386.rpm
core                               guile-1.3-7.i386.rpm
enlightenment-0.16.3-1.i386.rpm    imlib-1.9.7-1.i386.rpm
esound-0.2.14-1.i386.rpm           libghttp-1.0.4-1.i386.rpm
fnlib-0.5-1.i386.rpm               libgr-2.0.13-20.i386.rpm
glib-1.2.5-1.i386.rpm              libgtop-1.0.5-1.i386.rpm
gnome-audio-1.0.0-7.noarch.rpm     umb-scheme-3.2-9.i386.rpm
gnome-core-1.0.53-2.i386.rpm       wvdial-1.20-1.i386.rpm
gnome-libs-1.0.53-1.i386.rpm
[root@localhost i386]# rpm -Uvh enlightenment*
error: failed dependencies:
        imlib >= 1.9.8 is needed by enlightenment-0.16.3-1
[root@localhost i386]#
```

To solve this error, simply download the later version of the package that must be upgraded, and upgrade it using the same command you use for installing:

`rpm -Uvh [package_name].rpm`

Summary

In this hour, you learned how to install GNOME from CD-ROM distribution and by downloading and installing individual packages. You also learned how to solve some common installation errors.

Q&A

Q **I want to install GNOME, but my computer has Windows, not Linux, on it. Can I run GNOME in Windows?**

A At the time of writing, you must have a Linux/UNIX operating system (including FreeBSD) to run GNOME. There is a project to port GNOME to Windows, but the project is in its infancy. Red Hat Linux, one of the easiest flavors of Linux to install, is included on the CD that comes with this book. Have fun!

Q **I have KDE installed on my computer. Can I still use KDE after I install GNOME?**

A Yes, in fact, KDE and GNOME applications are interchangeable. You can run KDE applications in GNOME, and vice versa. You can set up your system to start one desktop as the default and the other desktop as an alternative, or you can use some utilities that enable you to switch desktops. We will learn more about switching between GNOME and KDE in Hour 3, "Starting and Logging Out of GNOME."

Workshop

The quiz and exercises are provided to help you test your knowledge and improve your understanding. The answers can be found in Appendix B, "Answers."

Quiz

1. Which GNOME installation method is monitored and officially sanctioned by the GNOME Project?
2. What does "dependency error" mean?
3. What should you do if you get a dependency error when installing GNOME?

Exercises

1. Enter the command `man rpm` at a prompt and study the output. What does the -Uvh in `rpm -Uvh [package_name].rpm` mean?
2. Install GNOME as instructed in this chapter, and then create a file called .Xclients using your favorite text editor. (If .Xclients already exists, save it under another name, then return it to its original state after you have finished this exercise.) Enter a single line in the file

    `exec gnome-session`

    Log out of X, and then restart X. Does GNOME appear? If not, don't worry. We'll go over starting problems in the next hour. If it starts, congratulations!

Hour 3

Starting and Logging Out of GNOME

Often, the most frustrating and harrowing part of dealing with new software is getting it to start after you have installed it. Fortunately, GNOME does not require many special configuration steps. After you have installed the required components, there are only a few things to do before you actually start a GNOME session.

In this hour, you will

- Start a GNOME session on your computer.
- Make GNOME the default desktop for one user account.
- Use GNOME as the default desktop for all accounts on your system.
- Switch between GNOME and other desktops, such as KDE, using Switchdesk.

> Packaged Linux distributions that include GNOME, such as Red Hat and Mandrake, include ready-made scripts for starting GNOME and KDE. If your xinitrc, Xsession, or Xclients script already contains references to GNOME or KDE, you can merely comment out references to KDE or use Switchdesk.

Preparing to Start GNOME

GNOME is started as part of the script that starts X on your computer. The command to start a GNOME session is the following:

```
exec gnome-session
```

You can put that command in several places, however, and in order to know the right place, there are three things you must think about:

1. How X is started on your computer
2. Whether you want to use GNOME just for one account on your system or for all accounts
3. If you want to use KDE or another desktop environment as well as GNOME

If you log in using a text-based script and then start X using a command such as startx, xstart, or X11, then your system most likely uses xinit, the X initialization script, to start X. If X starts automatically when you boot, and you log in using some kind of graphical interface such as a dialog box, then you probably use xdm, the X Display Manager, or kdm, the KDE Display Manager, to start X. The method your system uses to start X determines where you must place the command to start a GNOME session.

If you want to use GNOME for just one account on your system, you will place the script to start GNOME in the $HOME directory of that account. If you want to use GNOME for all the accounts in the system, you will place the script in /etc/X11/xinit/xinitrc or /etc/X11/xinit/Xclients.

Finally, if you have another desktop environment such as KDE installed, and you would like to switch back and forth, the utility Switchdesk will take care of the startup scripts for you, and you will not have to manually alter any files to start GNOME.

> If you are new to Linux and feel uncomfortable manually altering files, consider using Switchdesk even if you only have one desktop. Switchdesk will automatically create a GNOME startup script for you.

> See the following man pages to learn more about how X works:
>
> > man X
> >
> > man Xserver
> >
> > man startx
> >
> > man xdm
> >
> > man xinit
> >
> > man xterm
>
> The language is quite technical, but you do not need a programming background to understand it, and the entries provide a fascinating introduction to the intricacies of X.
>
> To open a man page, open an xterm and enter man followed by the term that you want to study, for example: # man startx.

Starting GNOME from the Command Line (`xinit`)

If you start X manually using a command such as `startx`, `xstart`, or `X11`, then your system most likely uses the `xinit` script to start the X server. `xinit` gives the X server instructions on how X should look when it starts, what programs should start automatically with X, and how X should exit.

To get the correct instructions on what to do when it starts the X server, `xinit` looks for a script that will tell it exactly what to do. That script is called `xinitrc`. Some systems have a separate &HOME/.xinitrc file for every account, so that different users can have different ways to run X. For example, you can have one account running GNOME as the desktop environment and another running KDE.

If you want to start GNOME as the desktop environment for just one user, open the user's $HOME/.xinitrc file in a text editor, such as vi. Add the following line to the end of the file:

```
exec gnome-session
```

> The last command in an X initialization script such as &HOME/.xinitrc is called the `magic` command. When you close the process that the `magic` command started, X will also close. You must make GNOME the last command in the &HOME/.xinitrc file so that X will automatically close when you log out of GNOME.

> $HOME is the pathname for the directory where all the user accounts (except root) are kept. In most UNIX systems, this path is /home/[account_name]. For example, if Judy and Bob have accounts on a UNIX system, Judy's .xinitrc file is /home/judy/.xinitrc. Bob's .xinitrc file is located at /home/bob/.xinitrc.

Some systems use one /etc/X11/xinit/xinitrc file for all users, instead of having a separate $HOME/.xinitrc file in each user's home directory. The file is usually located in /etc/X11/xinit. Modify this file the same way as you did the $HOME/.xinitrc file by adding the following line at the end of the file:

exec gnome-session

Make sure that this command is the last command in /etc/X11/xinit/xinitrc.

Possible Problems

xinit looks for a $HOME/.xinitrc file before the /etc/X11/xinit/xinitrc file. If you have an .xinitrc file in your home directory, but you add the line exec gnome-session to the /etc/X11/xinit/xinitrc file, GNOME might not start. You can fix this problem by also adding exec gnome-session to your /$HOME/.xinitrc file.

In some systems, the xinitrc file points to an Xclients file for programs that will start when X starts. If you have an $HOME/.Xclients or /etc/X11/xinit/Xclients file, place the command exec gnome-session at the end of that file instead of the xinitrc file. Otherwise, GNOME will probably start, but X might not close when you log out of GNOME.

Listing 3.1 shows a section of xinitrc that points to .Xclients or Xclients, which will list the X clients the user wants to start with X. If you have an entry similar to Listing 3.1 in xinitrc, then you should add exec gnome-session to Xclients or .Xclients.

LISTING 3.1   .xinitrc Pointing to Xclients or .Xclients

```
# The user may have their own clients they want to run.  If they don't,
# fall back to system defaults.

if [ -f $HOME/.Xclients ]; then
    exec $HOME/.Xclients
elif [ -f /etc/X11/xinit/Xclients ]; then
    exec /etc/X11/xinit/Xclients
```

Starting GNOME When X Starts at Boot (xdm)

If X starts automatically when you boot into Linux, you are probably using xdm, the X Display Manager, to start the X server. For our purposes, xdm runs in a manner similar to xinit, except that the startup script xdm uses is called Xsession, rather than xinitrc.

Edit the Xsession file in exactly the same way as the xinitrc file. If you would like to run GNOME for only one user, edit the $HOME/.xsession file to include the following line as the last entry:

exec gnome-session

Like xinit, xdm uses the system default commands in /etc/X11/xdm/Xsession if there is no $HOME/.xsession file in the user's home directory. The full pathname for the system default Xsession is /etc/X11/xdm/Xsession. Again, enter the line exec gnome-session as the last entry in Xsession.

Also like xinit, xdm sometimes uses an Xclients file to point to certain programs that will run automatically when X starts. If you already have an Xclients file, enter exec gnome-session at the end of the /etc/X11/xdm/Xclients file or $HOME/.Xclients file instead of the /etc/X11/xdm/XSession or $/HOME.xsession file, respectively.

> If you currently use xinit to start X but would like to start X at boottime using xdm, see the X and xdm man pages. xdm is included as part of /etc/init or /etc/inittab, which is your system initialization script. See *The Linux System Administrator's Guide* in the Linux Documentation Project archives at http://metalab.unc.edu/linux/docs.html#guide for more information.

Possible Problems

The possible problems described in the previous section also apply to xdm.

In addition, sometimes xdm specifies a specific desktop environment in the line including xdm in /etc/init. If this is the case, the default desktop will start even if you specify for GNOME to start in /$HOME/.xsession or /etc/X11/xdm/Xsession. If this is the case, you might have to edit your /etc/init or /etc/inittab file to remove the reference to that desktop, or install Switchdesk. See *The Linux System Administrator's Guide* for instructions on editing your system initialization script. Listing 3.2 shows a section from /etc/X11/xdm/Xsession that looks for instructions from xdm regarding which desktop environment to run on. The script takes as input a reference to a desktop in the xdm initialization line in /etc/inittab, and then opens the correct environment. We will not explain the script in detail here, but include it so that you will recognize it if you have a similar script in your Xsession file.

LISTING 3.2 `Xsession` Gives the Path for Opening Each Desktop Environment in `/etc/init`, and Then Opens the Correct Environment

```
# now, we see if xdm/gdm/kdm has asked for a specific environment
case $# in
1)
    case $1 in
    kde)
    exec startkde
    ;;
    gnome)
    exec gnome-session
    ;;
    anotherlevel)
    # we assume that switchdesk is installed.
    exec /usr/share/apps/switchdesk/Xclients.anotherlevel
    ;;
    WindowMaker)
    [ -f $HOME/GNUstep/Defaults/WindowMaker ] || {
        /usr/X11R6/bin/wmaker.inst --batch
    }
    exec /usr/X11R6/bin/wmaker
    ;;
    AfterStep)
    exec /usr/X11R6/bin/afterstep
    ;;
```

Using Switchdesk to Switch Between GNOME and KDE

If you're willing to fall in love with GNOME but don't want to give up KDE just yet, or if you like to change just for change's sake, try a utility called **Switchdesk** that changes desktops for you.

Switchdesk is extraordinarily simple to use. You can download the latest rpms from `http://www.redhat.com/download`. Download and install the following two packages:

`switchdesk-gnome-1.7.x-x.i386.rpm`

`switchdesk-kde-1.7.x-x.i386.rpm`

The GNOME version has a dialog box that lets you select a the desktop. Figure 3.1 shows the Switchdesk Desktop Switcher dialog box.

Starting and Logging Out of GNOME

FIGURE 3.1
Switchdesk enables you to switch desktops without having to manually alter your X scripts.

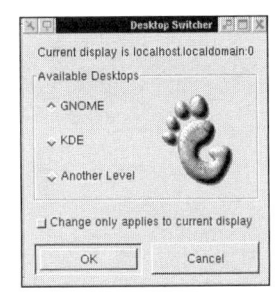

After you select a new desktop environment, the box in Figure 3.2 informs you that you must restart X. Restart X either by logging out of KDE using Logout on the main menu, or by pressing Ctrl+Alt+Backspace.

FIGURE 3.2
You must restart X because Switchdesk automatically generates a new .Xclients script for you.

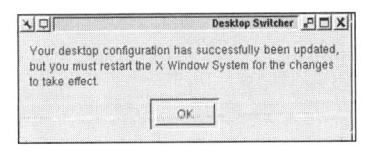

If you are running KDE or another desktop environment, open an xterm and type the following command:

switchdesk

The Switchdesk dialog box will appear. Select your choice, and then log out of X. When you log in again, your new desktop environment will appear.

Switchdesk is also useful if you are unsure about editing your X startup script by hand. When you install Switchdesk, it automatically creates a $HOME/.Xclients script for you. The &HOME/.Xclients script points to a $HOME/.Xclients-default script that contains the command to start the desktop environment you have chosen. Listing 3.3 shows the contents of $HOME/.Xclients and $HOME/.Xclients-default after the user chose GNOME using Switchdesk.

LISTING 3.3 $HOME/.Xclients and $HOME/.Xclients-default Generated by Switchdesk

```
#.Xclients

#!/bin/bash
```

continues

LISTING 3.3 continued

```
# Created by Red Hat Desktop Switcher

if [ -e "$HOME/.Xclients-$HOSTNAME$DISPLAY" ]; then
    exec $HOME/.Xclients-$HOSTNAME$DISPLAY
else
    exec $HOME/.Xclients-default
fi

#.Xclients-default

# Created by Red Hat Desktop Switcher
exec gnome-session
```

> If you use Switchdesk, do not edit $HOME/.Xclients or $HOME/.Xclients-default unless you know what you are doing. If you edit the file incorrectly, Switchdesk will no longer work.

When you are ready to log out of GNOME, open the Main Menu and select Logout. Your X session will end with your GNOME session.

Summary

In this hour, you learned about xinit and xdm, and how they start the X server and GNOME. You learned how to start GNOME as the default desktop environment for one user, and how to make GNOME the default for all the users on your system. You also learned how Switchdesk works to enable you to switch between GNOME and KDE.

Q&A

Q I installed GNOME in a system that already has KDE installed. I entered the correct command into my X initialization script, but when I start X, KDE starts. What to do?

A Check that you entered the command into the correct file, that there is no command preceding the exec gnome-session command to start KDE. Check each script on your system that is mentioned in this chapter for references to KDE. Comment out any references to KDE, then restart X.

Q All this script editing seems really complicated, and I don't want to install Switchdesk. Isn't there an easier way?

A Currently, no. The developers of GNOME are working to make the entire process a bit easier, but at present you still must do a little manual tweaking of your files if you want to use GNOME. Hold on—it will get easier as you become more comfortable with your system.

Workshop

The quiz questions and exercises are designed to increase your understanding and to encourage you to continue experimenting. Answers appear in Appendix B, "Answers."

Quiz

1. What is the difference between xdm and xinit?
2. What is the difference between .xinitrc and xinitrc? Between .xsession and Xsession?
3. Which files does Switchdesk create when it is installed?
4. What is the magic command when dealing with the X server?

Exercises

1. Before installing Switchdesk, determine how the X server is started on your system.
2. Before installing Switchdesk, create a .xsession, .xinitrc, or .Xclients file and input the correct line to start GNOME. Start X and verify that GNOME starts.
3. After installing Switchdesk, open the .Xclients-defaults file in your favorite editor. What does it look like? Switch from GNOME to KDE using Switchdesk, then open .Xclients-defaults again within KDE. What has changed?

HOUR 4

Working with Window Managers

For many people who are new to UNIX-like platforms, the concept of window managers is unfamiliar. In Microsoft Windows, the software that controls the placement and movement of windows is indistinguishable from that which controls the graphical picture that you see on the screen, or the software that makes an application start when you double-click it.

In GNOME all three functions—namely window operation, graphical interface, and desktop shell—are controlled by different pieces of software that work together to create the GNOME environment. GNOME is unique among desktop environments because it works with more than one window manager. For example, the KDE desktop environment works with KWM, which is integrated into the KDE environment. With GNOME, you have a choice of window managers to work with.

In this hour, you will

- Learn about window managers and how they work with the GNOME desktop environment.
- Install and run three window managers that are GNOME compliant.

- Install and run Enlightenment, the default GNOME window manager.
- Discover what it means to be GNOME compliant, and how a GNOME-compliant window manager works with GNOME.

How GNOME Works with Window Managers

GNOME works with window managers a bit differently than other desktop environments do because of its unique features.

To understand how a window manager works and how GNOME works with window managers, it is important to understand exactly what a window manager is and what it is not.

> Like GNOME, the window managers discussed this hour don't work only with Linux, but will work with any UNIX system that has an X server, such as XFree86.

The Desktop Environment

The entire area on your display where you work with windows is the *desktop environment*, or *desktop shell*. A desktop shell enables you to run applications and manipulate files in a graphical setting, rather than using a keyboard to type input. The computer (or more accurately, the kernel) receives the same input as if you had typed in commands—there is just another layer between you and the kernel. The desktop provides an interactive picture that you can use to communicate with the computer.

The Graphical Interface

The foundation of any desktop system that involves pointing and clicking with a mouse is the graphical interface. In UNIX systems, including Linux, the graphical interface is called X. X displays information on your monitor as pictures, or *graphics*. You can interact with the graphics on the screen using a mouse. When you click a button or in a box on the screen, X takes the input from your mouse and translates it into commands that your computer understands. In order for X to work, however, there must be something that tells X what to display and how the display will look. That function is accomplished by GNOME and the window manager.

The Window Manager

Within a graphical interface environment, there is an area called the *desktop* that usually has icons and menus on it. You can click the name of a menu or the icon of an application to run it. The application opens in a window that you can drag anywhere on the desktop.

Working with Window Managers

You can maximize the window to take up the size of the entire desktop, or minimize it so that it disappears from the desktop. Usually there is a border around the window that has the name of the application or file, and possibly some icons that enable you to close and change the size of the window. As shown in Figure 4.1, the window manager controls all these aspects of the window:

- The size of the window
- The window borders
- The window design and appearance
- The window functionality
- Window movement around the desktop
- The general look of the desktop

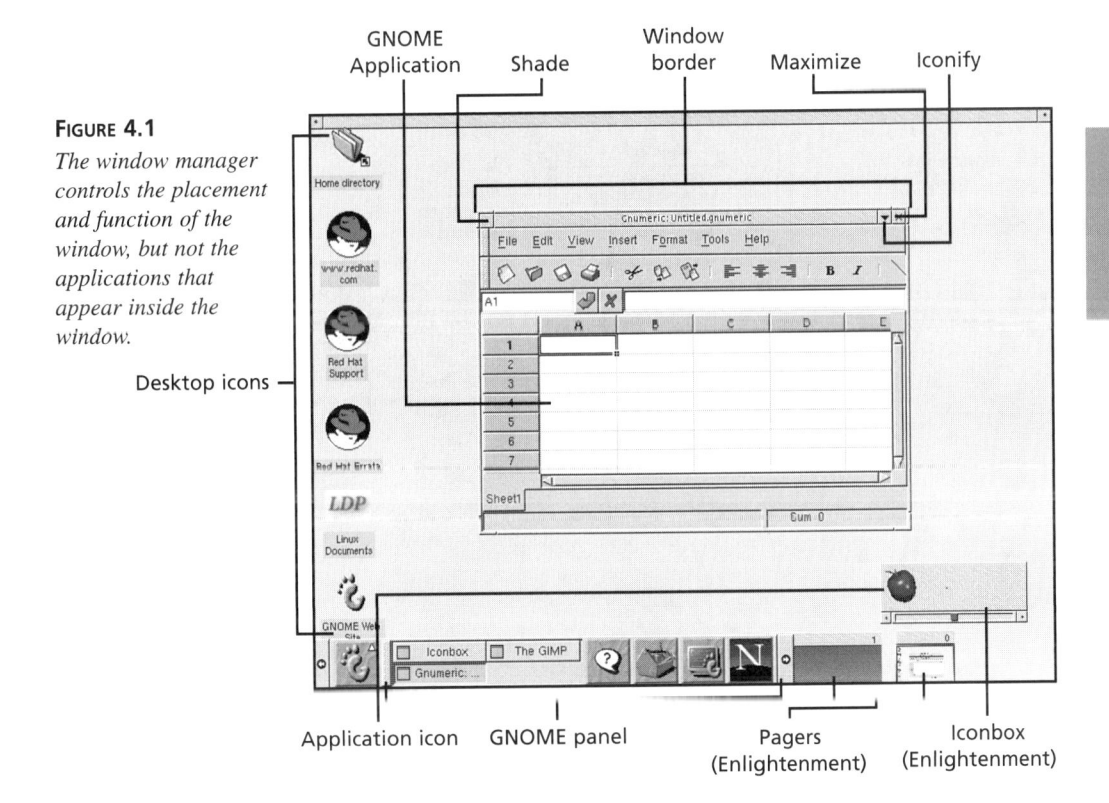

FIGURE 4.1

The window manager controls the placement and function of the window, but not the applications that appear inside the window.

How It All Comes Together

The window manager tells GNOME where windows are located and how they are placed. GNOME also gets information from the window manager about which programs are open and how they are configured. GNOME then uses this information to make the GNOME Tasklist and, when you log out, to save the session. The window manager and GNOME both send information to X, which causes the correct information to appear on the screen.

In his white paper, *GNOME Technologies: A Brief Description of the Technology Behind GNOME*, David Mason described the information exchange between GNOME and the window manager as "hints." If the window manager cannot read the hints from GNOME, the window manager is not GNOME compliant, and the full functionality of GNOME will not be available within that window manager.

Figure 4.2 shows the relationship between X, the window manager, and GNOME.

FIGURE 4.2
GNOME and the window manager work with X to display your interactive desktop on the screen.

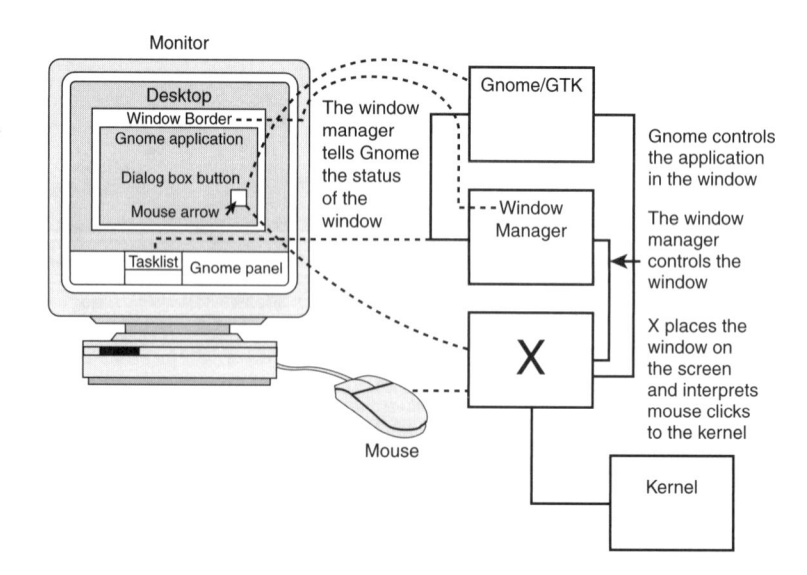

The window manager sends information to GNOME about the file that is open, such as the application name, the path, and the size and placement of the window. GNOME uses the information from the window manager to add the application to the GNOME Tasklist on the Panel.

If you use drag-and-drop within the application, say to move a file from one directory to another in the File Manager, other functions in the GNOME libraries will send that information to the X server. The X server then tells the kernel to move the file.

The window manager also sends information to the X server so that the application appears in the correct place, and so that you can interact with the window using the mouse and keyboard.

GNOME-Compliant Window Managers

If a window manager is "GNOME compliant," it means that you can take full advantage of the functionality of GNOME within the window manager. It can accept directives from GNOME and give information to GNOME in order to keep track of the items that enable features such as the GNOME Tasklist, session management, and drag-and-drop to work.

Although GNOME works to a certain extent with virtually all X window managers, the level of GNOME compliance varies. To date, the only fully GNOME-compliant window managers are Enlightenment, FVWM, sawmill, IceWM, and WindowMaker.

> Red Hat, which supports GNOME as the primary desktop environment, packages several window managers into its distribution, including FVWM, NextStep, AfterStep, and Enlightenment. Check your file system to see what window managers you might have installed already.

Enlightenment

Enlightenment is the default window manager for GNOME. Like the rest of GNOME, Enlightenment is free software. It is continually being developed and expanded by the Enlightenment Project, and anyone with energy and know-how can contribute. The Web page for the Enlightenment Project is http://www.enlightenment.org.

Enlightenment works on the following platforms, in addition to all flavors of Linux:

- Solaris
- FreeBSD
- Linux 2.X [libc5 and glibc2]
- AIX *
- Irix *
- HP/*

> Some extra steps must be taken when installing Enlightenment for AIX, Irix, and HP platforms. See the Enlightenment Web site at http://www.enlightenment.org.

Designed to be highly configurable, Enlightenment has more customization options than any other X window manager. You can design your own window borders, buttons, and menus using a graphic design application like Gimp. You can choose from many options using the Enlightenment Configuration Manager, or download an entire theme.

Enlightenment is also a desktop shell, which means that you can use it by itself to launch applications. According to the Enlightenment Project, eventually Enlightenment will have its own file manager, drag-and-drop, and applet management capability. Currently, however, this functionality is still in the planning stages.

Enlightenment is discussed in greater detail in Hour 10, "Exploring Enlightenment."

Advantages of Enlightenment

- Enlightenment is fully compliant with GNOME.
- The default window manager for GNOME, Enlightenment is relatively simple to install and run.
- Enlightenment was designed to be highly configurable in appearance and functionality.
- Hundreds of themes are available for use with Enlightenment. Many are beautiful and creatively designed (see Figure 4.3).

Disadvantages of Enlightenment

- Because of Enlightenment's many configuration options, some people find it complicated to use at first.
- Enlightenment is complex, compared to other window managers. It takes up lots of system resources, so it can slow down operations, such as loading GNOME and opening windows. If you have a fast processor and a lot of RAM (more than 64MB), this might not be a problem.

Installing Enlightenment: Necessary Software

For these directions, it is assumed that you are running libc6 (or glibc2), that you have an X Window system of Release 6 or higher, and that your system has an Intel-based processor. If you don't have X Window Release 6, check http://www.x11.org to download the latest release. (If you're not sure if you have libc6 or X Window Release 6, see Appendix A, "Troubleshooting"). If you don't have an Intel-based processor, you will

Working with Window Managers

have to compile Enlightenment from source code. See `http://www.enlightenment.org` for more information.

FIGURE 4.3
You can create a stunning desktop look with Enlightenment.

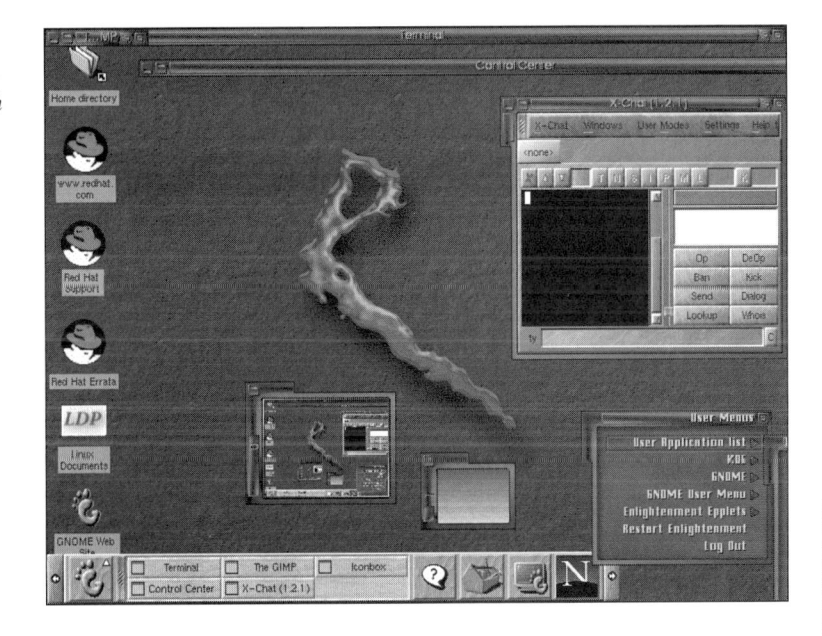

You will also need

- A GCC compiler
- An Imlib package or tarball (the graphics server)
- A Fnlib package or tarball (for pixmap fonts)
- An Enlightenment package or tarball

Optionally, you can install

- ESD (a sound server for sound mixing)
- Eterm (for terminals with pixmaps)
- Eplus (includes a clock and CD player, among other things)
- Emusic (an MP3/MOD/WAV/CD/AU player)
- Gtk-Perl (to edit ConfigEdit)
- Perl (use with Gtk-Perl)

All the modules are available for download at `http://www.enlightenment.org` as tarballs and as `rpm` and `deb` packages. Even if you have Enlightenment included in your Linux distribution, it is a good idea to check the Web site on occasion for the latest version.

Before you install or upgrade Enlightenment, make sure that you have fairly recent versions of Enlightenment's support libraries, Imlib and Fnlib. To make things a little more complicated, you must also have recent versions of the libraries that support Imlib and Fnlib!

Verify that you have the latest stable versions of the following libraries, which are available for download at the Enlightenment Web site in tarball, `rpm`, and `deb` formats:

- Libgif or Libungif
- Libz
- Libpng (for `.png` and `.pnm` files)
- Libtiff (for `.tif` files)
- Libjpeg (for `.jpg` files)
- Gtk (the Gimp Toolkit)
- Glib (Gtk base)
- ImageMagick (image conversion fallback)
- Enlightenment (Window Manager)
- Imlib
- Fnlib

Installing the Components

If you are upgrading from an earlier version of Enlightenment (version 0.13 or older), you must first delete or rename the existing Enlightenment directory, including all old themes and other data.

Next, install the packages (or install and compile the tarballs) in the following order:

1. Libgr, Libz, Libgif or Libungif, Libpng, Libjpeg, Libtiff, ESD, Glib
2. ImageMagick, Gtk
3. Gtk-Perl, Imlib, Fnlib
4. Enlightenment and add-ons, other Enlightenment applications

If you need help installing packages or tarballs, see Appendix A.

IceWM

Marko Macek designed IceWM to be a faster and more-streamlined window manager. The Web page for IceWM reports that IceWM runs under these platforms:

- Digital UNIX
- FreeBSD

Working with Window Managers

- Linux on DEC Alpha (64-bit architecture)
- Linux on Intel compatibles (32-bit architecture)
- NetBSD
- OpenBSD
- OS/2
- Sun Solaris
- Windows

IceWM can be downloaded from the Web site as a tarball or an `rpm`. The Web site also has a few attractive, clean themes available for download (see Figure 4.4).

FIGURE 4.4
GNOME works with IceWM to create a fast, efficient desktop that looks great.

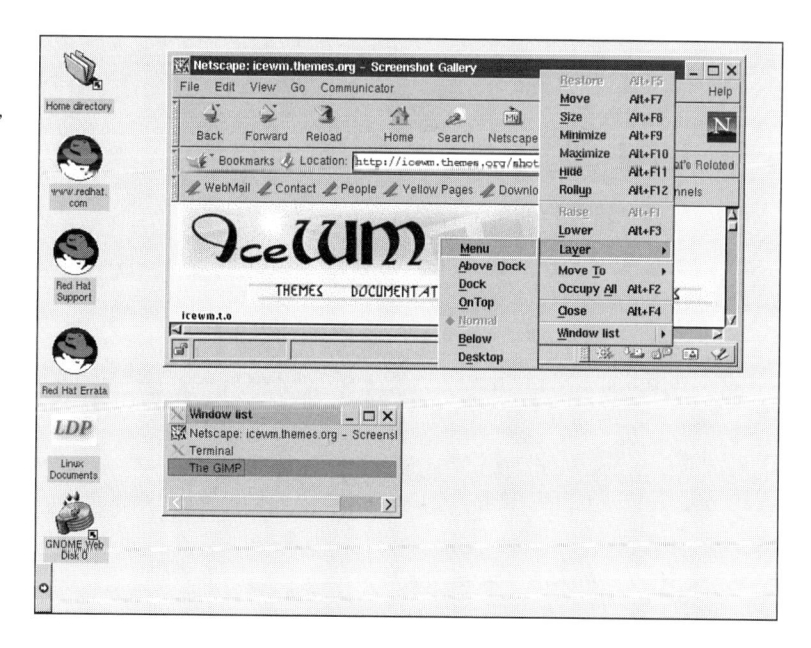

IceWM is unique in that all its functions are available by both keyboard and mouse.

IceWM can be installed either from tarballs or `rpms`.

Installing IceWM from rpm Packages

You will need the following packages to install IceWM:

IceWM
IcePref
PyGtk/PyGNOME

You can obtain them from http://gnome.linuxpower.org. Download the rpms to a temporary directory (usually /var/tmp).

From a GNOME session, open GNOME File Manager and navigate to the directory where you saved the rpms. Right-click each rpm name and select Install. Install the rpms in the following order:

1. PyGtk/PyGNOME
2. IcePref
3. IceWM

Installing IceWM from Tarballs

Download the tarballs for the following software and place them in a temporary directory (such as /var/tmp):

IceWM

IcePref

PyGtk/PyGNOME

Unzip and untar each tarball by entering the following commands:

```
gunzip icewm-0.9.49.src.tar.gz
tar xvf icewm-0.9.49.src.tar
```

Untarring the file will make a new directory called icewm-0.9.49.src, with all the elements from the tar file in it.

Next, compile the files. You can enter ./**configure** --**help** to see all the installation options available. Table 4.1 lists some of the most important.

TABLE 4.1 ./configure Options

Option	Description
--pref	Directory where IceWM binaries should be installed (for example, /usr/bin)
--with-xpm	Use xpm (the standard X pixmap library) for graphics
--with-imlib	Use Imlib for images (recommended)
--with-gnome-menus	Add the GNOME menus to the IceWM start menu (only necessary if you are using IceWM without GNOME)
--infodir	The directory where IceWM info files should be placed
--mandir	The directory where IceWM man files should be placed

Working with Window Managers

You can find the correct pathnames for the options you need by using the `locate` command (see Appendix A).

After the files have compiled, enter the following commands:

```
make
make install
```

Then, remove the extra files and links created during installation and compilation by entering

```
make clean
```

sawmill

sawmill, developed by John Harper, was designed to be even simpler and faster than IceWM. Written in Lisp, sawmill requires some additional libraries from those in basic Linux distributions. Well on its way to full GNOME compliance, sawmill is available at http://www.dcs.warwick.ac.uk/~john/sw/sawmill/ as an rpm or deb package, or as a tarball.

Because of its emphasis on simplicity, sawmill has no desktop backgrounds (see Figure 4.5). It has a few themes that can be downloaded at its Web page. (You will learn more about themes in Hour 12, "Understanding and Using Themes.")

FIGURE 4.5
Although simple in design, sawmill is one of the fastest window managers.

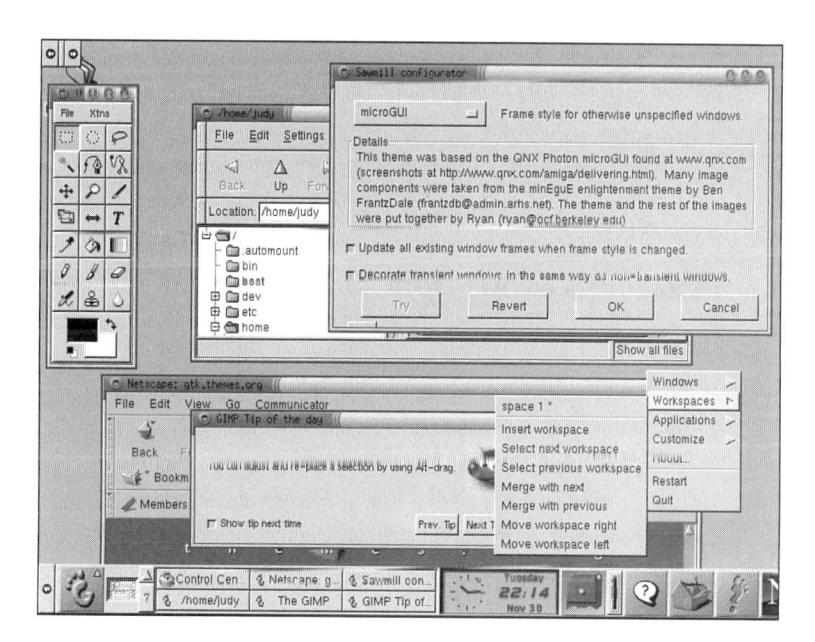

The greatest advantages of using sawmill are its speed and simplicity. It also supports full session management, either within GNOME or alone.

It does not, however, support virtual or multiple desktops.

sawmill has no user documentation, although it comes with a rather comprehensive FAQ and a programmer's manual.

Installing sawmill

sawmill requires three components in addition to the sawmill binaries themselves:

> `librep 0.5` (Lisp interpreter)
>
> `rep-gtk 0.5` (a binding for gtk)
>
> Imlib (this library comes with most distributions of Linux)

You can obtain this software from the sawmill home page at `http://www.dcs.warwick.ac.uk/~john/sw/sawmill/`. All software is available as tarballs or as `rpm` or `deb` packages.

Installing sawmill with `rpms` or `debs`

Download the packages to a temporary directory (usually `/var/tmp`).

From a GNOME session, open GNOME File Manager and navigate to the directory where you saved the packages. Right-click each filename and select Install. Install the packages in the following order:

> Imlib
>
> Rep-gtk
>
> Librep

Installing sawmill from Tarballs

Download the tarballs and place them in a temporary directory (such as `/var/tmp`):

Unzip and untar each tarball, by entering the following commands:

```
gunzip sawmill-0.14.2.tar.gz
tar xvf sawmill-0.14.2.tar
```

Untarring the file will make a new directory called `sawmill-0.14.2`, with all the elements from the tar file in it.

Enter the following commands to install sawmill:

```
./configure
make
make install
make clean
```

After installation, create a file called ~/.sawmillrc and enter the following line:

```
require 'gnome
```

Other Window Managers

In addition to Enlightenment, IceWM, and sawmill, there are other window managers, some of which are listed in Table 4.2. FVWM is fully GNOME compliant. Window Maker is a popular window manager renowned for its stability. AfterStep, designed for use on UNIX platforms, can be used with Linux.

You can learn more about window managers at the X11 Web site, http://www.x11.org.

TABLE 4.2 Other Window Managers

Window Manager	Web Site
AfterStep	http://www.afterstep.org
BlackBox	http://blackbox.alug.org
FVWM	http://www.fvwm.org
Window Maker	http://www.windowmaker.org

Check the GNOME Software Map at www.gnome.org for new window managers.

Switching Window Managers

You can change the window manager you are using within a GNOME session using the Window Manager capplet in the GNOME Control Center. From the Main Menu, select Settings, GNOME Control Center, Window Manager. The Window Manager capplet might take a few seconds to load. Figure 4.6 shows the Window Manager capplet of the GNOME Control Center.

FIGURE 4.6
Use the GNOME Control Center to change window managers as often as you like.

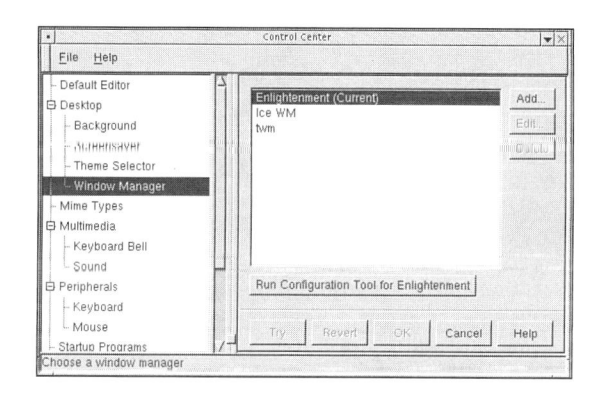

After installing a new window manager from a package, go to the Control Center to verify that the window manager is listed. If you installed the window manager from tarballs, you must add a new entry manually by clicking Add. The Add New Window Manager dialog box is shown in Figure 4.7.

FIGURE 4.7
Adding a new window manager is simple.

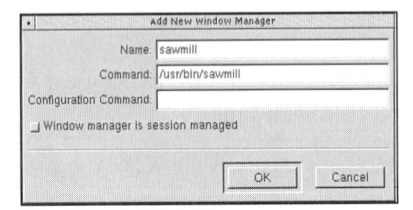

Enter the full pathname of the window manager and the configuration utility executable files. These are usually called something like

```
/usr/[window_manager_name]
/usr//[window_manager_name].conf or .config
```

To switch window managers, simply double-click the window manager entry in the Control Center. The new window manager will load after a short delay.

You can also change the WINDOW_MANAGER environment variable to a new window manager; just log out of GNOME and X, and then start X. GNOME will reappear with the new window manager.

Summary

In this hour, you have learned what a window manager is and how window managers work with GNOME. You have learned how to install and run two simple window managers: IceWM and sawmill, and you have been introduced to Enlightenment, the most powerful and configurable window manager that works with GNOME. Finally, you have learned how to switch window managers within a GNOME session and how to change the default window manager for your system.

Q&A

Q Do I have to use a window manager with GNOME? Can't I just use GNOME?

A GNOME was designed to work with a window manager within the X environment, so it is necessary to have one. Enlightenment is packaged with the GNOME binaries. If you don't want to mess with your window manager, you can use the version of

Working with Window Managers

Enlightenment that came with your GNOME distribution. Eventually, however, you will want to upgrade your window manager, even if you only use Enlightenment.

Even though you can't use GNOME without a window manager, you can use window managers (with minimum functionality) without GNOME.

Q Can I customize sawmill?

A You can customize sawmill, but there is no graphical interface as there is for Enlightenment. The configuration file is called ~/.sawmill.rc, and it is written in Lisp. If you don't know Lisp, you can play with the file and see what effects different changes have. If you mess things up totally, you can uninstall sawmill and then reinstall. See the sawmill FAQ http://tizer.dcs.warwick.ac.uk:8080/sawmill/FAQ for more information.

Q After I changed window managers, I lost my panel and all my icons! Help!

A Some window managers aren't compliant enough with GNOME to support the GNOME Tasklist, session management, or drag-and-drop. But, if everything on your desktop disappears, there is probably something wrong. Check the GNOME mailing list archives and the window manager archives for questions about your particular window manager, to see if someone else had a similar problem. You can also troubleshoot the problem using the techniques and tools in Appendix A. Simply go to the GNOME Control Center and change window managers, and your desktop will go back to normal.

Workshop

The quiz questions and exercises are designed to increase your understanding and to encourage you to continue experimenting. Answers appear in Appendix B, "Answers."

Quiz

1. Which window managers are fully GNOME compliant?
2. Name three aspects of the desktop environment that the window manager controls.
3. How do you change the default window manager?
4. What is the purpose of a desktop shell?

Exercises

1. Go to the X11 Web site at http://www.x11.org, and find the comparison chart on window managers. Which window managers are GNOME compliant? Which GNOME-compliant window manager has the most features?

2. Run a GNOME session with Enlightenment as the window manager. From the GNOME Control Center, switch window managers to sawmill. What looks different on your desktop? What looks the same?
3. From a terminal, change the WINDOW_MANAGER environment variable from the current window manager to IceWM. Restart X. What happens?

PART II
Using and Customizing GNOME

Hour

5 Exploring the Desktop
6 GNOME Under the Hood
7 Using the Panel and the Main Menu
8 Managing Files in GNOME
9 Common File Manager Tasks
10 Exploring Enlightenment
11 Customizing Your GNOME Environment
12 Understanding and Using Themes

HOUR 5

Exploring the Desktop

If you have experience with another graphical interface environment, such as Microsoft Windows or a UNIX desktop shell like KDE, GNOME will probably look familiar when you first log in. You'll see a row of icons on a colored screen, and another row of icons and buttons at the bottom of the screen. When you click the big foot button, a menu appears that looks similar to the menu in Windows. The big difference between GNOME and other desktop environments is that everything you see can be configured, customized, and personalized until your desktop workspace looks and performs in exactly the way that suits you best.

In this hour, you will

- Explore the basic parts of GNOME that you must understand to get up and running with GNOMEit.
- Learn the basics of the GNOME desktop icons, the Main Menu, and GNOME Panel.
- Learn how to add some applets to the GNOME Panel that are of immediate use.

- Learn how to work with windows in GNOME.
- Get a quick introduction to GNOME utilities and the concept of session management.

> Because GNOME is so configurable, no two desktops are alike, and different distributions package the GNOME applications differently. Don't worry if an icon or applet is mentioned that you don't have on your desktop. The material presented in this hour is meant to be a jumping-off point for you to explore your own desktop environment.

A Word on Three-Button Mouse Emulation

Most UNIX graphical interface programs are designed to be used with a three-button mouse, and GNOME is no exception. If you have a two-button mouse, you can configure it so that pressing the left and right buttons simultaneously will substitute for the third mouse button. Also, if you are using a rollerball, you can configure it so that the ball will act as the third button.

To emulate a three-button mouse, you must edit your X configuration file (if you are using XFree86, it is called XF86Config). The full pathname in Linux is usually /etc/X11/XF86Config or /usr/X11R6/lib/X11/XF86Config. Open the XF86Config file in your favorite editor and go to the Pointer Section.

> XF86Config is a simple text file that you can open and edit using any text editor such as vi, emacs, gEdit, or gnotepad+.

You will find a section that deals with three-button emulation. Uncomment the line that reads "Emulate3Buttons." If you do not have such a section, you can manually add the following line at the end of the section:

```
Emulate3Timeout     50
```

Alternatively, if you are nervous about directly editing your XF86Config file, you can use one of the XF86Config-generation scripts, such as xf86config (note the lowercase lettering) or XF86Setup, or if you have Red Hat, Xconfigurator. Listing 5.1 shows an example of the mouse section of an XF86Config script.

LISTING 5.1 XF86Config Script Example

```
# **********************************************************************
# Pointer section
# **********************************************************************

Section "Pointer"
    Protocol    "ps/2"
    Device      "/dev/mouse"

# Emulate3Buttons is an option for 2-button Microsoft mice
# Emulate3Timeout is the timeout in milliseconds (default is 50ms)

    Emulate3Buttons
    Emulate3Timeout    50

EndSection
```

The GNOME Desktop

The GNOME desktop is organized into three sections: the Icon list, the GNOME Panel, and the Main Menu. All these tools can be used to launch applications, access files on a local or shared file system, or even open a URL on the Internet.

Figure 5.1 illustrates a simple GNOME desktop, as it appears in the Mandrake/Red Hat distribution. Red Hat has preconfigured the row of icons on the left. The GNOME Panel along the bottom has a few buttons already added. The small windows on the bottom right are the Enlightenment Pager and Iconbox. They are not strictly part of GNOME, although they work with GNOME. You will learn more about Enlightenment tools in Hour 10, "Exploring Enlightenment."

In the following section, we will explore the purpose and function of each desktop tool. We will look at items that might be set up on your desktop already. Finally, we will begin looking at some of the most common items to add to your desktop.

Desktop Icons

If you installed GNOME from a packaged distribution of Linux, you will probably see a row of icons already on your desktop. There might be an icon with a link to the Linux distribution's Web site, or an icon that will bring up a directory of pre-installed Help documents. If your computer is partitioned, you might see an icon for mounting another partition. At the very least, there will probably be an icon for the GNOME Project Web site and a Home directory folder.

FIGURE 5.1
The GNOME desktop looks simple when you log in for the first time. Your distribution might look slightly different from the desktop pictured here.

You are not limited to the pre-installed icons, however, but can make an icon out of just about anything, including

- Applications
- Other executable files
- Directories
- Web links
- Data files
- Device mount points (such as a floppy disk, CD-ROM, DVD, or zip drive)

Figure 5.2 shows a row of icons that come by default with the Red Hat Linux distribution and some items opened by double-clicking the icons.

Icon Properties

If you cannot determine what the icon does by its name, right-click the icon and select Properties. Figure 5.3 shows the Properties for the Linux Documents icon.

The Properties dialog box will show the full pathname of the icon and the file type: symbolic link, URL, or directory. The Permissions tab shows what permissions are in effect for that icon. You can even change the icon's picture using the Options tab.

Exploring the Desktop

FIGURE 5.2
Desktop icons can open applications, Web URLs, or directories. You can add or delete as many icons as you want.

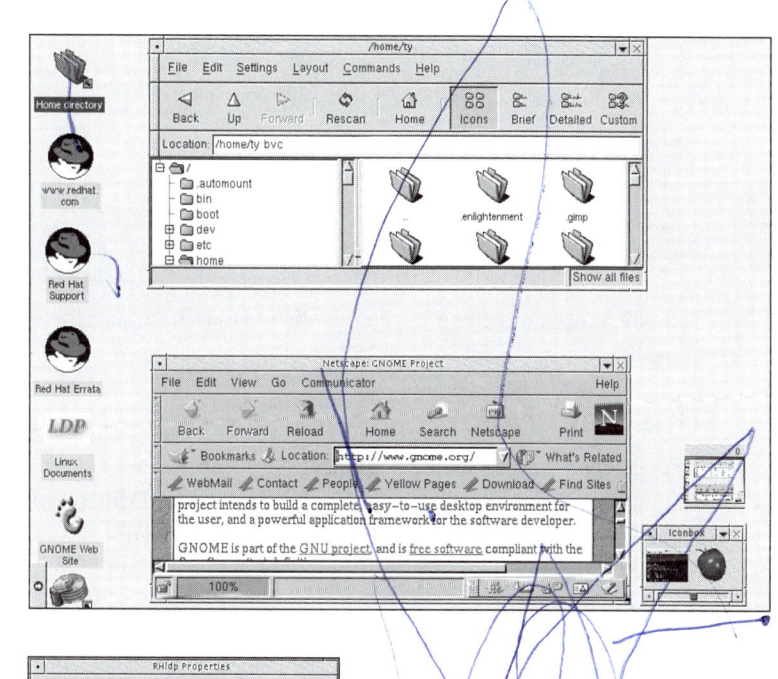

FIGURE 5.3
The URL http://www.redhat.com/mirrors/LDP mirrors the home page for the Linux Documentation Project.

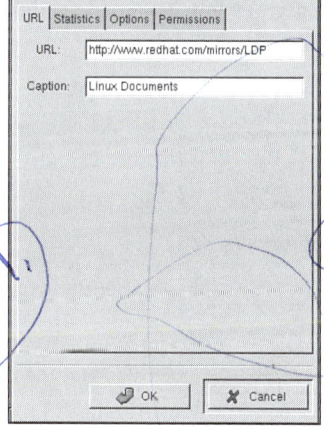

Creating and Removing Icons

You can create desktop icons either by dragging and dropping an item from GNOME File Manager, or by making an entry in $/home/[user]/.gnome-desktop/. To remove an icon from the desktop, right-click the icon and select Delete. To change any aspect of the icon, including the file it opens, right-click the icon and select Properties.

You can create icons to represent

- Applications
- Directories
- URLs
- Data files/databases
- Drive mount points

You will learn more about desktop icons in Hour 7, "Using the Panel and the Main Menu."

The Main Menu

You can open all the GNOME applications, utilities, and configuration tools using the Main Menu. If you have a Linux distribution such as Debian or Red Hat, the Main Menu also can contain the distribution menu. If you have KDE installed on your system, you can access the entire KDE menu from the GNOME Main Menu.

To open the Main Menu, click the foot button, usually located on the bottom left of the GNOME Panel (see Figure 5.4.) Open a submenu by moving the mouse over the submenus until you reach the application you want. The menu will stay open until you click the mouse again.

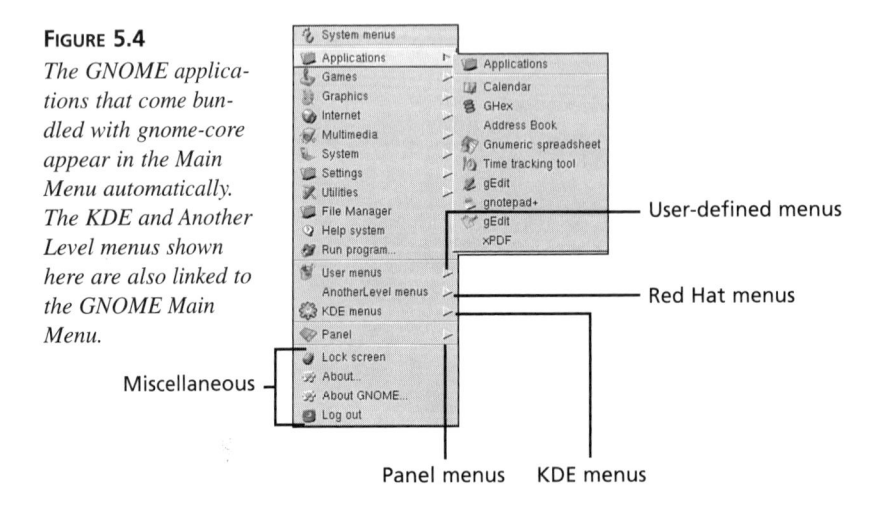

FIGURE 5.4

The GNOME applications that come bundled with gnome-core appear in the Main Menu automatically. The KDE and Another Level menus shown here are also linked to the GNOME Main Menu.

The Main Menu is divided into five sections:

- System menu (settings, file manager, and utilities)
- User menu (a placeholder for user-defined applications)

- Linux distribution and KDE menus
- Panel menu (the menu for the GNOME Panel)
- Miscellaneous items

The items in the Main Menu come bundled with gnome-core. As you add applications to your GNOME desktop, you can make an entry to launch the applications from the Main Menu. We will explore the Main Menu in greater detail in Hour 7, but for now, remember that any gnome-core application can be opened from the Main Menu.

The GNOME Panel

The GNOME Panel is the central point of the GNOME desktop environment. You can configure it to hold launchers for the applications you use most often, which can be organized into *drawers*. You can also add *applets*, which are programs that perform small tasks, ranging from CD players and clocks to utilities that track memory, CPU, and disk usage. The GNOME Panel can be located along any edge of the desktop and can be oriented to any side. You can add as many panels to your desktop as your screen will hold.

Default GNOME Panel Buttons

When you first log in to GNOME, the panel is located along the bottom edge of the desktop, and it already has some default buttons, including one for the Main Menu. Figure 5.5 shows a typical GNOME Panel configuration.

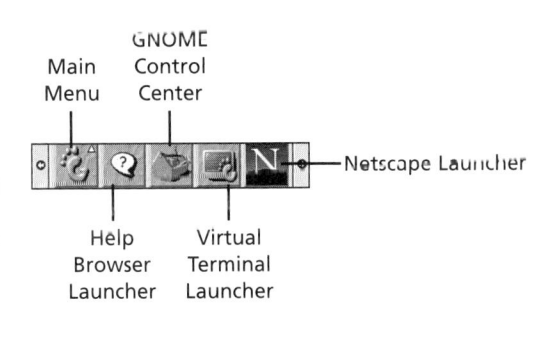

FIGURE 5.5
Use the GNOME Panel to launch the applications that you use most frequently. The panel has many useful applets, and new ones are released almost weekly.

We explored the Main Menu button in the last section. Table 5.1 describes other buttons that appear by default.

TABLE 5.1 Default GNOME Panel Buttons

Button Name	Description
GNOME virtual terminal launcher	This button launches a virtual terminal to give you access to the command line within the desktop shell. You will learn more about virtual terminals later this hour.
GNOME Control Center	The GNOME Control Center is a very powerful tool that enables you to configure virtually every aspect of GNOME, including the choice of window manager, screensaver, your default editor, applications that automatically start when you start GNOME, and many other items. You will learn more about the GNOME Control Center in Hour 11, "Customizing Your GNOME Environment."
Help button	The Help button launches the GNOME Help Browser, which lets you open any documentation or help file, on your computer, the Internet, or an internal network file system or intranet. The default documents loaded into the Help browser include *The GNOME User's Guide*, the info pages, and the man pages.
Netscape Communicator launcher	This button launches Netscape Communicator.

Adding Panel Applets

GNOME comes with many applets you can add to the panel to perform a variety of tasks. You will learn about the panel in greater detail in Hour 7, so this section will introduce just two important applets that you need to get started: a clock and the GNOME Tasklist.

Adding a Clock

To add a clock to the GNOME Panel, right-click an empty section of the panel, and select Add Applet, Clocks. Select the clock you prefer (experiment with the choices!), and it will appear on the panel.

Adding the GNOME Tasklist and Desk Guide

One of the most useful applets in GNOME is the GNOME Tasklist. The GNOME Tasklist keeps track of open and minimized applications, helping you avoid a cluttered desktop.

The Desk Guide works with the Tasklist; it is particularly useful when you are working with multiple desktops. The Guide displays a miniature version of each desktop, so you can see what's available. Switch desktops by clicking on the Desk Guide arrow; a list of open windows for your current desktop will appear.

Working with GNOME Windows

In this section, we will explore the basics of using windows in GNOME, using Enlightenment as an example. As you learned in Hour 4, "Working with Window Managers," GNOME gives you a choice of window managers, and the appearance of open windows varies according to the window manager and theme. The window buttons on your system might look somewhat different from those described here, but you will still be able to understand the basic idea. Figure 5.6 shows an open window with a typical configuration. Table 5.2 describes each GNOME window button. Even if you are familiar with MS Windows, skim this section, because GNOME has some window buttons that do not appear in MS Windows.

FIGURE 5.6

An Enlightenment window manager with some simple window buttons. This window looks different from those in the other figures in this hour because it has a different theme.

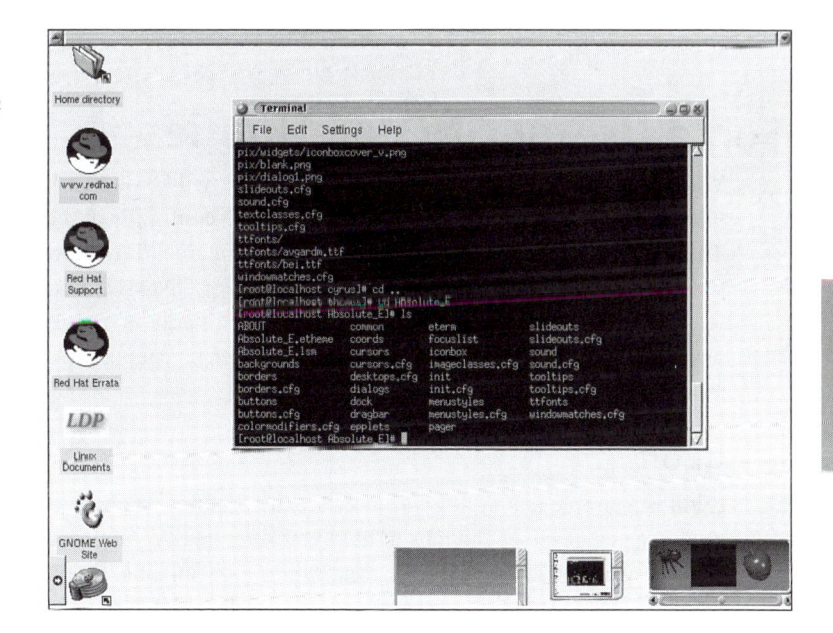

You will learn more about themes in Hour 12, "Understanding and Using Themes."

TABLE 5.2 GNOME Window Buttons

Button Name	Description
Shade/Unshade	Shading a window will cause it to "roll up" like a window shade so that only the top window panel appears. Unshading the window makes the entire window reappear.
Iconify	Pressing Iconify (or Minimize) will cause the window to disappear, although the application is still running. To get the window back, you must be running GNOME Pager, the Enlightenment Iconbox, or a similar Tasklist program.
Maximize/Minimize	Maximize causes the window to expand to the full desktop size. This might be larger than your actual screen size! Click a second time and the window minimizes to a smaller size of your choosing.
Close/Kill	In some window managers and themes, the X button will close the application gracefully, but in others, it will kill it immediately. Be careful with this button!

Some Useful GNOME Utilities

When working in a graphical environment, there will be times when you must look at the inner workings of a system file, such as the Xconfig file at the beginning of this hour. There will also be times when you will need to interact directly with the shell. In this section, you will learn about two basic text editors for GNOME. You can still use vi or emacs within the GNOME environment, but the GNOME editors have some functionality particularly useful within a graphical environment, such as cut and paste. We will also look briefly at the GNOME terminal emulator.

gEdit

gEdit is a simple text editor with useful extra features, such as shortcut keybindings, plug-ins, text reverse, and tabs to help you keep track of multiple open documents. Use gEdit to view files, keep logs, or create simple documents. Open gEdit from Main Menu, Applications. Figure 5.7 shows gEdit's menu of available plug-ins, which can extend gEdit's functionality whenever you are working with a special kind of file. See the gEdit Web site, `http://gedit.pn.org`, for more information.

gnotepad+

gnotepad+ can create simple HTML files. It has a toolbar for adding HTML tags, plus word-wrap and cut-and-paste functionality. gnotepad+ can be opened from Main Menu, Applications.

FIGURE 5.7
You can have multiple files open simultaneously in gEdit. It comes with many useful plugins.

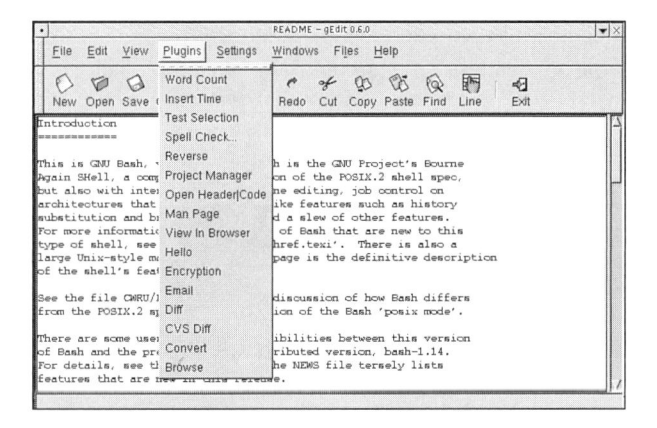

GNOME Virtual Terminals

GNOME comes with two terminal emulators, xterm and the GNOME Terminal. When you start an X environment, you are actually opening a new tty (or terminal) within the system. If you don't have a terminal emulator, you will have to open a new session with the kernel every time you want to use the command line. Terminal emulators enable you to gain access from the command line within GNOME. You can open as many instances of the terminal emulator as you want without actually starting a new session.

The GNOME Terminal is a complete emulation of xterm with a few additional options, including

- Cut-and-paste
- Drag-and-drop of filenames to and from the terminal
- The capability to launch a URL from within the terminal
- Extended color and font configuration options

You can open xterm and the GNOME Terminal from Main Menu, Utilities. If you want to learn more about the GNOME Terminal, see the GNOME Terminal user's guide.

Figure 5.8 shows the GNOME Terminal in action.

Session Management

One of the more unique features of GNOME is session management. With session management, GNOME will remember all the programs you currently have running, their position on the desktop, *and* your current place in the file. To use session management, leave your applications running when you are ready to log out of GNOME. Select Log Out on the Main Menu. A window will appear to confirm the log out. Check the Save

Current Setup box. When you next log in to GNOME, GNOME will automatically restart all the applications so that your desktop appears as it was at the end of the last session.

FIGURE 5.8
The GNOME Terminal uses xterm as a base, but has many more useful features.

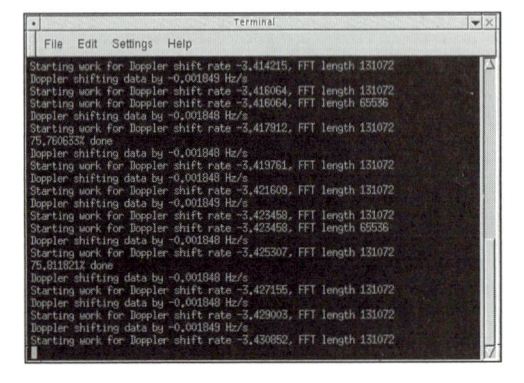

> If you press Ctrl+Alt+Backspace to log out of GNOME, your session will not be saved. This method of exiting is not recommended, because it does not give your X server a chance to disconnect gracefully, and it abruptly kills all the programs you had running in GNOME.

Summary

In this hour, you took a quick tour of the GNOME desktop environment. You learned how to configure a two-button mouse to emulate a three-button mouse. You looked at the three basic parts of the GNOME desktop environment: the desktop icons, the Main Menu, and the GNOME Panel. You saw the basics of how to work with a window in GNOME, and learned about some useful GNOME utilities. Finally, you saw how to save our GNOME session using Session Management, so that we can return to the same desktop when we log back in to GNOME.

Q&A

Q Does GNOME support keyboard hotkeys or shortcuts?

A The current version of GNOME does not provide hotkey alternatives to the mouse functions. Enlightenment, on the other hand, has an extensive collection of hotkey alternatives, and you can also make your own hotkey combinations. You will learn about hotkeys in Hour 10.

Q Do I have to emulate a three-button mouse to use GNOME?

A It is not necessary to have a three-button mouse to use GNOME, because you can choose Cut/Copy and Paste from the Edit menus of most applications. It does, however, make life easier.

Q I deleted my panel by mistake. How do I get it back?

A The Panel menu is duplicated in the Main Menu. If you delete your panel by mistake, you can create a new panel from the Main Menu.

Q I pressed the Iconify button on a window, but it disappeared from my screen. How do I get it back?

A You must have GNOME Pager or Tasklist or a window manager iconbox (more about this in Hour 10) running if you want to minimize, or iconify, windows. If you iconify a window before adding the Tasklist to the panel, don't worry. As soon as you add the tasklist, all applications currently running in GNOME will appear on the Tasklist.

Workshop

The quiz questions and exercises are designed to increase your understanding and to encourage you to continue experimenting. Answers appear in Appendix B, "Answers."

Quiz

1. What is "session management?"
2. Name four items that can be iconified on the GNOME desktop.
3. On the Main Menu, how does the System Menu differ from the User Menu?
4. What does "shade" mean when dealing with windows?

Exercises

1. Examine the properties of each icon on your desktop. Can you tell what the icon does? Double-click the icon to check your guess.
2. Open the properties of an icon on your desktop. Select Options, then click the icon. What happens? Select a new icon graphic for your icon.
3. Open the Main Menu on your desktop, and compare it to the Main Menu in Figure 5.4. If you are running a Linux distribution, does a separate distribution menu appear? Does a KDE menu appear? Select an application from one of these menus. How does the application appear when opened in GNOME?
4. From the Main Menu, open the GNOME Control Center and select Background. Click the Browse button, and navigate to a background filename that interests you. Click it, and then click Try. If you like this background, click OK. Otherwise, click Revert.

HOUR 6

GNOME Under the Hood

Have you ever wondered, "What is really happening when I point and click the desktop? How does the system know what to do when I click a button? How do windows really work?" In addition to teaching you about how to use GNOME, this book tries to answer these questions in a way that the average user, with no programming background, and possibly no Linux background, can understand. The aim of this hour is certainly not to give you all the answers in a few pages, but to lead you into an exploration of the desktop on both the outside and the inside, to encourage you to explore and experiment. We begin this hour with a quick tour through the files and directories that are important to GNOME, in the hopes that this will foster your interest in exploring the mechanisms behind the rest of GNOME.

In this hour, you will

- Explore the multiuser aspect of Linux and how it relates to GNOME.
- Learn about GNOME libraries and executable files.
- Look inside the shared GNOME directories and files.
- Understand configuration files and the session file.

GNOME and Linux

When you type in commands at the command line, you are not really communicating with the Linux kernel directly, but through an interface called the *shell*. Different shells in Linux accept different commands and do things slightly differently.

As you learned in Hours 4, "Working with Window Managers," and 5, "Exploring the Desktop," GNOME works as an interface with the X server, through which you interact with the Linux kernel. You can think of GNOME and X working together as a graphical shell. Like the Bourne-again, C and Korn shells, X is an interface through which you communicate with the kernel to accomplish tasks.

Understanding the Multiuser System

To understand this hour, you must understand that Linux is a multiuser system. When you have GNOME running on your Linux system, every user account can set up GNOME in a different way. Before we discuss how GNOME is configured differently for different users, let's discuss the difference between a single-user system, like MacOS or Windows, and a multiuser system, like Linux.

All UNIX and UNIX-like operating systems are designed to be multiuser, that is, they are designed with the idea that there will be many people using the same computer at the same time to do different tasks.

When you use a Windows or MacOS computer, you turn on the computer and start to use it. Although there may be several user profiles saved on the computer, only one person can use the computer at a time. There is only one user for one operating system. Linux has one operating system and one kernel, but many users. Each user has an account on the system. Before using the Linux computer, the user must log in with a valid username and password.

A rough analogy would be the difference between a single-family house and an apartment building. One family or person lives in the house. One family has the key to the house, and nobody else can enter the house without that family's permission. One family is in charge of the electricity, plumbing, heating, and repairs on the house. Everything in the house belongs to one family, and that family is responsible for everything in the house. That's how Windows operates. (We're not counting NT in this analogy, although if it's not networked, NT acts in much the same way.)

Now imagine an apartment building. There are many people living in the apartment building, and tenants (individuals or families) enter their respective apartments in the building through different doors with different keys. Although they share the same physical building, no one can enter anyone else's apartment without that person's permission.

To each tenant, the only part of the building that concerns him and to which he has access is his own apartment.

Now, there are things in the apartment building that everybody shares. They all get water from the same water heater or steam plant. All the plumbing is on the same system, as well as the heating. They might even share the same laundry room. This apartment building has a landlord who has access to every apartment in the building. The landlord is also responsible for the grounds, the maintenance, and all the services in the building. The apartment building is like a Linux system. Each tenant is like a user; each apartment is like a home directory. The landlord is like the system administrator of a Linux system. Although each apartment contains furniture and personal belongings that the landlord doesn't own or control (the users' files and applications in their home directories), the landlord has a key to every apartment in the building (the root account). The landlord is responsible for the services in the building. The services are similar to the shared directories on the system, such as /usr/bin, /usr/share, and basically everything that isn't in a user's /home directory.

Let's say that the landlord lives in the apartment building. He doesn't use his landlord keys to get into his own apartment; he also is a tenant. In the same way, the system administrator of a Linux system doesn't use the root account for his personal use. He will also have an ordinary user account for doing his daily work. When he needs to do something that requires root access, he will log in to the root account, or become the superuser. When he is performing ordinary user tasks such as writing a letter or using the Internet, he will use his ordinary user account.

> If you are the only user on your Linux system, it might be tempting to always log on as root (this author pleads guilty to the habit). Just be aware that using your root account when you are online can lead to security problems, as well as the potential to inadvertently cause harm to your system.

If you are the only user on your system and you regularly back up your files, don't be afraid to explore and use your system and to make mistakes. It's the only way to learn. A good rule of thumb is to maintain your system in a way that you could format the hard drive and start over again at any time if you had to. That means backing up important files, such as email, home directories, preferences, system files that you have modified, and others.

When experimenting with system administrator tasks, it is helpful to make a backup copy of configuration files. For example, if you want to edit /etc/wvdial.conf, first copy it to /etc/wvdial.conf-backup. Then make changes in the original, and, if it breaks the application, you can always restore the backup copy.

> If you really want to learn by doing, consider maintaining two separate computers or partitions, both running Linux and GNOME. One can be your production system, where all your important files are kept, and the other is the test system, where you see how many ways you can mess things up. Since GNOME is a work in progress, you can actually help a lot by seeing how many ways you can crash an application and then submit bug reports to the GNOME project.

We will now explore some of the shared and user-specific parts of GNOME.

GNOME Libraries

GNOME applications are fast because they make use of shared libraries. The libraries are collections of mini-programs called *functions*, that are used over again by different GNOME programs. The libraries are stored in a central location, so that every GNOME program knows where to look for a particular function or an entire library that it needs. When the GNOME program needs a function, it is entered into memory. Then, if another GNOME program needs the same function and it is already activated, the other program just goes and gets it from memory to use it. GNOME libraries are usually kept in /usr/lib or /usr/local/lib. Different users running GNOME at the same time might make use of the same library, or two different applications can use the same library. You will learn more about GNOME libraries and functions in Hour 24, "Anatomy of a GNOME Application."

GNOME Executable Files

In Linux, applications are run by programs called *executable files*. When you install an rpm, the libraries that the application needs are copied to /usr/lib or /usr/local/lib, and the executable file or files are copied to /usr/bin or /usr/local/bin. If you want to see the entire collection of executable files on your system, poke around in your executable file directory. If you wanted to, you could start any GNOME application by typing the executable file at a shell prompt in an xterm. Figure 6.1 shows a list of GNOME commands in the /usr/bin directory.

> Commands and executable files that are central to a UNIX system are kept separately in the /bin directory. Such commands include ls, cd, cp, and so on.

GNOME Under the Hood

FIGURE 6.1
GNOME and other applications on your system are kept in the /usr/bin directory in Red Hat and Mandrake Linux.

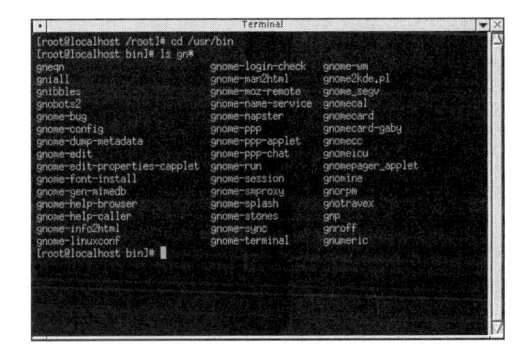

The $PATH/share Directory

The $PATH/share/gnome directory contains all the data and configuration information for applications that is the same for every GNOME user on the system. If you meander through this directory, you will find a file for every GNOME application and desktop component in your desktop environment.

> Depending on how permissions are set up in your system, if you install software as an ordinary user, the executables reside in your home directory, not in /usr/bin or /usr/local/bin.

The /usr/share/pixmaps Directory

Graphic image files that are used in various aspects of the GNOME desktop are contained in /usr/share/pixmaps/gnome directory. If you want to add new backgrounds to the GNOME desktop, copy them to the /usr/share/pixmaps/Backgrounds directory. If you want to add new icons for use in the GNOME desktop environment, add them to the /usr/share/pixmaps directory. You will also find graphic images that are used in certain GNOME applications, such as games or applets. You can use the images in the pixmaps directory in any way you want, not just for their original intended uses. Figure 6.2 shows an image file from the GNibbles game. The image appears when you start the GNibbles game, but you can copy the file and then use it for other nefarious purposes. If you have write permission on the file, you can even edit the image in the GIMP.

FIGURE 6.2
You can add your own image files to the pixmaps directory.

The .gnome Directory and GNOME Configuration Files

As we discussed in the last section, each user has a separate home directory, where he keeps his individual files. The home directory also contains hidden files that store the user's preferences. The first time you run GNOME, GNOME will create a directory called .gnome in your home directory. .gnome maintains the configuration files for your desktop. Configuration files contain all the information about how to set up your individual GNOME desktop environment. Whenever you make a configuration change to your desktop, it is stored in the .gnome directory in the pertinent configuration file.

To view the hidden files in your home directory, cd to your home directory and view the contents by entering the following command:

```
cd /home/user_name
ls -a
```

Figure 6.3 shows a typical listing of hidden files on a home directory.

> A simpler method of getting to your home directory is to type **cd** without specifying a directory.

As you can see, there are hidden files for programs other than GNOME. Some of the hidden files or directories you might see are

- X configuration files
- Netscape files
- Application configuration files

GNOME Under the Hood 75

- Enlightenment configuration files
- Shell configuration files (such as bash)

> You can create your own hidden files and directories by beginning the filename with a dot ".".

FIGURE 6.3
Hidden files are usually created by an application or other process, but you can create your own hidden files by beginning the filename with a dot (.).

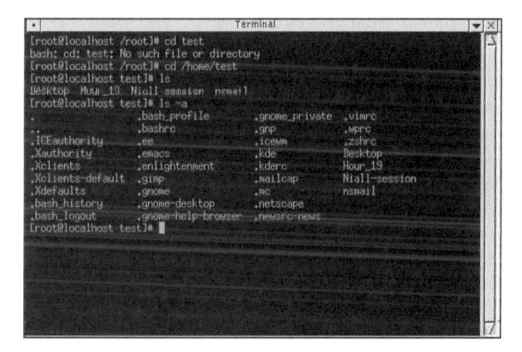

For our purposes, we are most interested in the .gnome directory. To view the contents of the .gnome directory, enter the following command:

`ls -la ~/.gnome`

To see just a list of files without all the detail, enter

`ls -a ~/.gnome`

Figure 6.4 shows the contents of a typical .gnome directory.

FIGURE 6.4
The .gnome directory contains configuration data that is specific to the desktop for your user account.

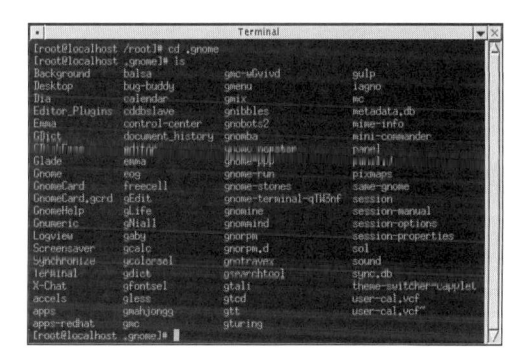

Whenever you run an application in GNOME, a configuration file is created in $HOME/.gnome that saves your setup and configuration information. For example, when you enter values in a Preferences dialog box, the values you set are saved in the configuration file. The next time you open the file, the application will look in the configuration file and maintain the configurations you set the last time. Of all the files in the .gnome directory, the only ones that you will have to deal with directly are the session files.

The Session Files

It is important to be familiar with the session files, because if your GNOME desktop ever behaves strangely or freezes when you log in, you might have to delete one or more of them and restart GNOME. You will need to know what some of the files do, so that you know which ones to back up before deleting the session. This becomes important as you customize your desktop more; it would be a lot of work starting all over again with the customizations.

If your desktop freezes when you first log in to GNOME, delete and log back in. A typical session file is shown in Figure 6.5.

FIGURE 6.5
Whenever you save your session upon logout, a new session file is created in /home/user/.gnome. To look at your session file, open it in your favorite text editor.

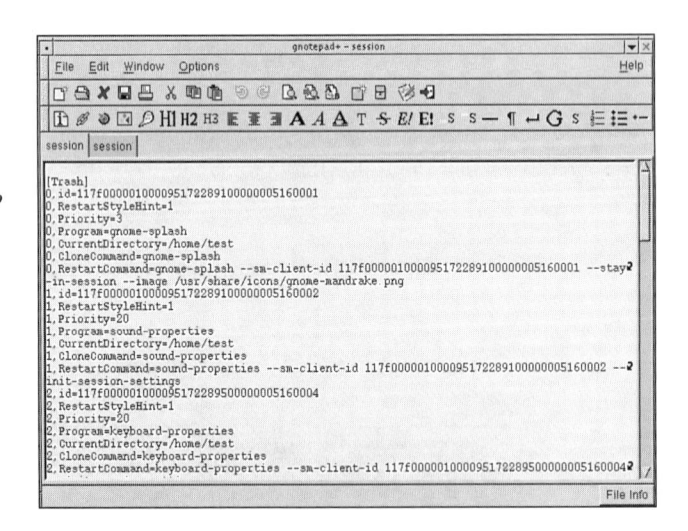

The .desktop Files

The .desktop files contain configuration information about the GNOME programs that you have installed. Located in /usr/share/gnome/apps, /usr/local/share/gnome/apps, or /opt/gnome/share in SuSE, they are in a special format that is read by the program gnome-config. When a new application is added to the desktop by root, a .desktop file is created. Gnome-config uses the information in the file to add the program to the GNOME Main Menu.

GNOME Under the Hood

Unless you really know what you are doing, it is important that you do not manually edit these files. The files are created automatically by the applications, and the information is written in a strict format so gnome-config can read it. If a config file in the share directory is broken, then no user will be able to run the application.

Compare the sample `.desktop` file syntax that follows to the Properties for an application in Figure 6.6. Notice that the Name, Comment, Exec, Econ, and Type entries in the `.desktop` file all coincide directly with the Properties dialog box fields.

```
[Desktop entry]
Name=Emma
Comment=Money management program
Exec=emma
Icon=gnome-money.png
Terminal=0
Type=Application
```

> Remember, to see the Properties for an application, right-click on the application entry in the Main Menu.

FIGURE 6.6
The .desktop *configuration file is used to configure the application on the desktop. This* .desktop *file is for the financial management application, Emma.*

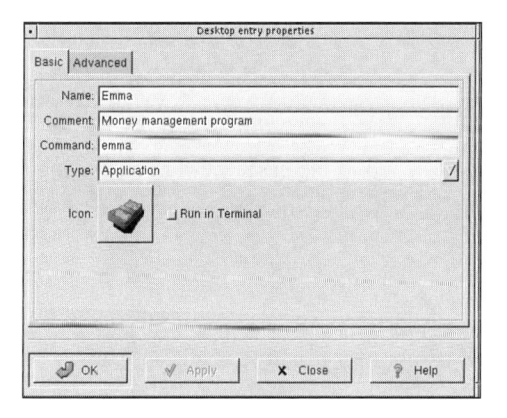

User Directory `.desktop` Files

If you have entries in your User submenu on the GNOME Main Menu, then you have `.desktop` files in your home `.gnome` directory as well. These `.desktop` files perform the same function as those in the `/usr/share` (or `/opt/gnome/share` for SuSE) directory, but they are only for your personal User menu in the GNOME Main Menu. Although you can probably view the contents of a `/usr/share/.desktop` file, usually you must be root to change the file.

You can change any `.desktop` file that is in your own User menu and your home directory.

Summary

In this hour, you were introduced to the shared files and libraries, as well as the configuration files that store information for the GNOME desktop. This isn't, of course, anywhere near the whole story. The point of this hour was to get you thinking of the GNOME desktop as a set of files that do things, just like anything else in Linux. This gives you a simple idea of what is going on behind the scenes. You will learn a lot more about the GNOME environment, how it is created, and how it works throughout the book.

Q&A

Q Can I edit configuration files directly, instead of editing Properties?

A Yes, as long as you maintain the file structure exactly as it was before. It is always better to make your edits within the desktop to be sure that you have done it correctly.

Workshop

The quiz questions are designed to increase your understanding and to encourage you to continue experimenting. Answers appear in Appendix B, "Answers."

Quiz

1. What is the difference between a single-user and a multiuser system?
2. Where are GNOME libraries usually stored?
3. What happens when you type the filename of a GNOME executable file at a shell prompt in an xterm?
4. What is the purpose of the `/usr/share/gnome` directory?

HOUR 7

Using the Panel and the Main Menu

In Hour 5, "Exploring the Desktop," we began to explore the various ways to work within the GNOME environment, using Desktop icons, the Main Menu, and the GNOME Panel. During this hour we will build upon what we've learned to study in greater detail the different ways we can use the GNOME environment.

In this hour, you will

- Use the GNOME Panel to launch applications that you use often. You will organize the application launchers on the panel into drawers according to functionality.
- Use the Main Menu as a central reference and launcher for all the applications on the system.

While reading through this hour, begin thinking of how you want to organize your desktop to make it a useful and efficient workspace. We will devise a generic plan, which will consist of creating icons on the desktop for important files including documents, databases, spreadsheets, programs, and URLs.

Configuring and Using the GNOME Panel

One of the most powerful and useful tools in the GNOME environment is the GNOME Panel. You can make the panel the focus of everything you do in GNOME, or leave it with only its few default items. You can even delete all the items on the panel, or the panel itself.

In our sample setup, we will use the panel to organize the applications and files you use every day. Panel drawers, application launchers, and applets can help you arrange your panel efficiently. We will explore each of these items in detail.

Adding an Application Launcher

An application launcher starts an application with one click on the Panel icon. To create an application launcher, right-click an empty part of the panel, and select Add New Launcher. Enter the name of the application and the full command needed to it. In the Comment field, enter the name that will appear when you place the mouse over the launcher. Finally, specify whether the launcher is for an application or a directory.

If the application you want is listed in the Main Menu, simply drag the Main Menu entry onto the panel; a launcher will be automatically created.

Figure 7.1 shows the dialog box for creating a launcher.

FIGURE 7.1
Application launchers make it easy for you to open applications that you use often.

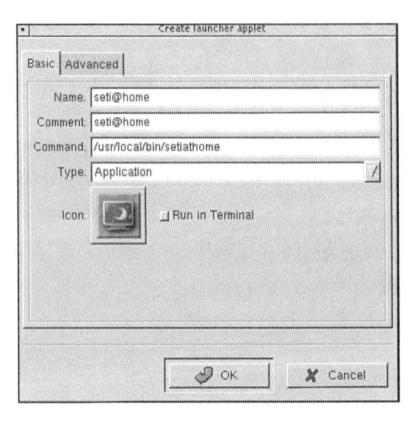

In the Advanced tab, you can add a comment for the user and the pathname of documentation that is associated with the application. After creating the launcher, you can modify it at any time by right-clicking it and selecting Properties.

Using Drawers to Organize Your Launchers

After you have created several application launchers, the drawer where you're storing them can get a little crowded. Drawers help you organize your application launchers and save space on the GNOME Panel. After you have created all your launchers, think about which applications should be grouped together, and then make drawers for those groups.

To create a drawer, right-click on an empty part of the panel and select Add Drawer. An empty drawer appears on the panel. Right-click the new drawer and select Drawer Properties to name the drawer and, if you like, change the drawer icon. Enter the name of the drawer in the ToolTip/Name field. To change the drawer icon, double-click the icon in Properties. From the list that appears, select an icon that best fits the contents of the drawer. In Figure 7.2, we are creating a drawer for graphics, so we will choose an icon that corresponds to graphics, the Electric Eyes.

FIGURE 7.2
Change the drawer name and icon to distinguish it from the other drawers on your panel.

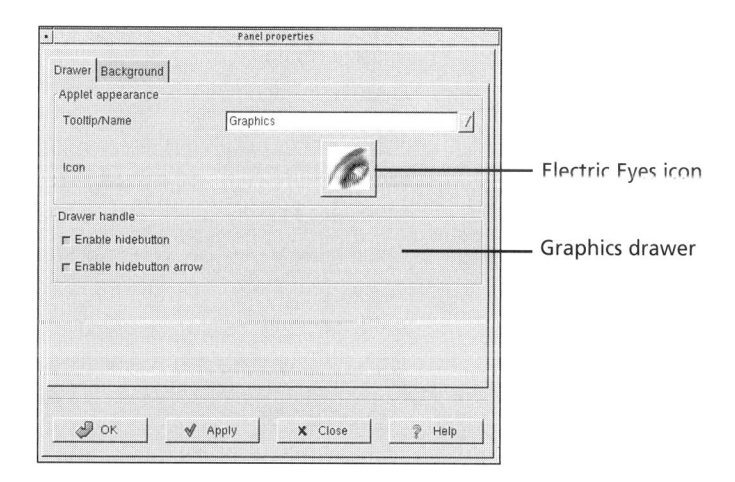

After you have created your drawer, populate it with launchers. To move a launcher into a drawer, right-click the launcher, select Move Applet, and drag it into the drawer.

To add an entire section of the Main Menu as a drawer, right-click the section title, and select Add This As Drawer to Panel. For example, if you right-click User Menus, all the entries in the User menus will appear as launchers in a drawer on the panel.

Adding Useful Applets to the Panel

An applet is a mini-application that performs a small task. GNOME comes with many useful applets that you can add to the panel. Your GNOME release comes with a set of applets, but you can also get new applets from the GNOME Web site. Look for the newest package or tarball of applets under the filename `applet-[version].[tgz/rpm/deb/...]`.

To add an applet to the panel, right-click the panel and select Add Applet. When the applets menu appears, select an applet. It will appear in an empty space in the panel. To remove an applet, simply right-click the applet and select Remove from Panel.

New applets appear constantly. To help you explore the applets in your version of GNOME, Table 7.1 summarizes applets currently available in gnome-core 1.05.3:

TABLE 7.1 GNOME Panel Applets

Category	Applet
Amusements	Fifteen
	Wanda the Fish
	Game of Life
Clocks	After Step clock
	Another clock
	Clock
	Clock and Mailcheck
	JBC Binary clock
Monitors	Battery charge monitor
	CPU/MEM usage
	CPULoad
	Disk usage
	MemLoad
	SwapLoad
Multimedia	CD player
	Mixer
	XMMS player
Network	Clock and Mailcheck
	Mailcheck
	Modem lights
	WebControl

Category	Applet
Utility	Character picker
	Desk Guide
	Drive Mount
	GKB International keyboard
	GNOME Pager
	Mini-Commander
	Printer applet
	QuickLaunch
	TaskList

Configuring Panel Properties

After you have created your application launchers, put them into drawers, and added some applets to the panel, you are ready to configure the look and feel of the panel itself. There are two panel configuration choices:

- This Panel Properties
- Global Panel Properties

If you have multiple panels, you can change the properties of just one panel with This Panel Properties. Changes that you make to Global Panel Properties will affect all your panels.

Figure 7.3 shows a typical GNOME Panel.

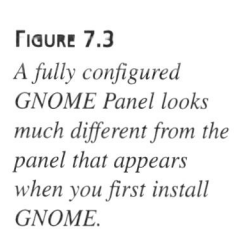

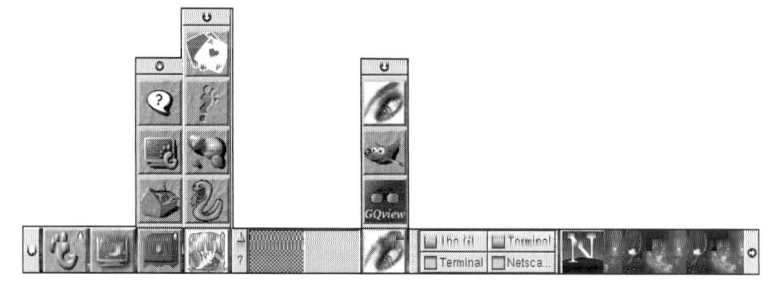

FIGURE 7.3

A fully configured GNOME Panel looks much different from the panel that appears when you first install GNOME.

Global Panel Properties

The Global Panel Properties dialog box contains dozens of options that enable you to customize your GNOME Panel down to the last detail. In the interest of space, I will discuss just a few of the most important options here. For a complete guide to Global Panel Properties, see *The GNOME User's Guide*.

On the Miscellaneous tab, be sure to check the ToolTips Enabled check box. This option causes a pop-up of the launcher or drawer name to appear when you place the mouse over the item. For this option to work, there must be an entry in the ToolTip field (for a drawer) or Comment field (for a launcher) in the Properties section.

Animations control the speed at which drawers will open and close, the panel will open and close, and so on. You can experiment with the animation speeds, or just leave the default values.

The Launcher Icon, Drawer Icon, Menu Icon, and Logout Icon tabs let you configure the depth of these buttons on the panel, how they look when depressed, and so on. Be sure to check the Tiles Enabled check box in the Launcher Icon tab if you want to be able to set background images on empty spaces on the GNOME Panel, as shown in Figure 7.3.

This Panel Properties

The This Panel Properties dialog box lets you configure individual panels. The Orientation boxes—Top, Bottom, Left, and Right—determine the orientation of your panel to the screen. In essence, you can have a panel on all four sides of your screen, oriented to the left, right, top, or bottom. Corner panels conserve space by being only as large as necessary for the items on them. Edge panels take up the entire side of the screen, with background color filling in the empty space on the panel.

The Autohide check box lets a panel be hidden from view until you move your mouse over it. This option is useful for small screens, or if you tend to have many windows open at once.

Use the Background tab to choose a background image for empty sections of your panel. The Standard option gives you the color chosen by the theme you are running. Pixmap lets you choose an image for the background, such as the background design on the panel in Figure 7.3. With the Color option, you can select the exact color you want from a gradient palette.

Adding a Panel

You can have as many panels as your screen will hold. To create a new panel, select Create New Panel from the Panel menu and specify an edge or corner panel. To remove a panel, click on it and select Remove This Panel.

Using the Main Menu

In Microsoft Windows, whenever a new application is added, the installation script usually places a menu icon on the desktop and an entry in the Main Menu "automagically."

In GNOME, you are in full control of what goes on your desktop and in your Main Menu. This requires a bit of thought on your part to decide what belongs on your desktop, in your Main Menu, and on your panel.

The Main Menu, in our configuration, serves as a master list of all applications available to run on your desktop. You learned a bit about the Main Menu in Hour 5. Here you will learn the logic behind the organization of the Main Menu, and how to customize the Main Menu.

You will notice, however, that GNOME starts out with applications already placed in the Main Menu. When you update gnome-core, the Main menu is also updated to reflect new or updated applications. This is the only time that the GNOME Main Menu will be automatically updated. So, when you add a new application, such as StarOffice, if you want to have an entry in the Main Menu, you must manually create it.

In the following section we will study the format of the Main Menu, and then we will add some items to the Main Menu using the Menu Editor.

Parts of the Main Menu

The Main Menu is divided into five sections:

- System menus
- User menus
- Other menus (menus for window managers and other desktop environments, such as KDE)
- Panel menu
- Miscellaneous items

We will go over each section briefly.

System Menus

The System menus have an entry for each application that is bundled into the gnome-core. Some entries include GNOME applications, Internet applications, graphics applications, and utilities. We will not discuss every System menu entry in this hour, but, after you have completed all the hours, you will be familiar with all the applications in the System menus.

These menus can be edited, but you must be logged in as root to do so.

User Menus

When you first install GNOME, the User menus are empty. As you add applications to your system, add an entry for each new application in the User menus. Any application or directory can be added to the User menus. You can also create your own submenus in which to place your applications.

Other Menus

If you have window managers that have menus or even other desktop environments such as KDE, you can access those menus via the GNOME Main Menu. The Red Hat and Debian distributions also place menus here.

Panel Menu

The complete Panel menu can be accessed via the Main Menu. This duplicate menu is very useful if you lose your panel and have to create a new one.

Miscellaneous Items

Below the Panel menus are miscellaneous items such as screen lock, an About the Panel button, an About GNOME button, and the logout button.

Editing the Main Menu

When you want to make a change to the Main Menu, such as adding or deleting an application, you use the Menu Editor. Open the Menu Editor by clicking Main Menu, Settings, Menu Editor. You can also change the Properties of an individual entry in the Main Menu by right-clicking the entry and selecting Properties.

Adding or Deleting Entries in the Main Menu

To add or delete an item, open the Menu Editor by clicking Main Menu, Settings, Menu Editor. The left side of the Menu Editor displays your Main Menu as it currently appears. On the right side of the Menu Editor, you can change the attributes of an individual entry in the Main Menu. The Menu Editor offers the same attribute options as the properties of each menu item.

To add a new entry to the Main Menu, click New Item or New Submenu. You can also move an item around in your Main Menu by clicking on the item and dragging-and-dropping it to the desired position.

Figure 7.4 shows the Menu Editor with the Basic tab displayed.

To learn more about how to use the Menu Editor, see *The GNOME User's Guide* *[Red Hat, 1999]*.

FIGURE 7.4
Use the Menu Editor to add or delete items in the Main Menu, or to change the properties of an individual entry.

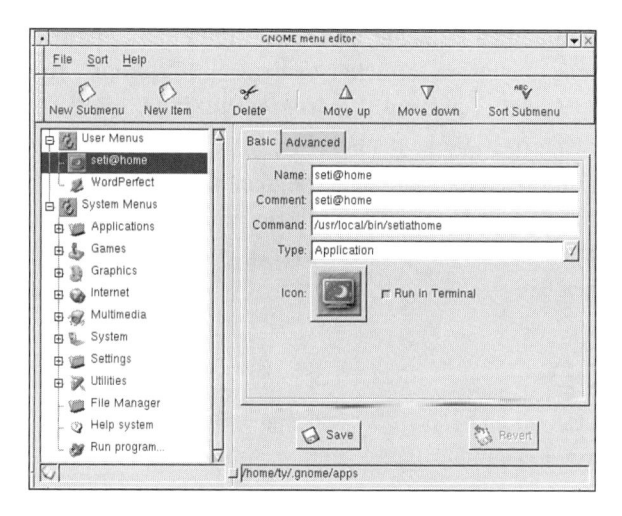

Summary

In this hour we explored the GNOME Panel and the Main Menu. You learned how to add application launchers to the panel and how to organize them into drawers. You also learned how to customize each drawer with an icon that matches the contents of the drawer. You discovered what a panel applet is and explored those currently available. Finally, you looked at the different parts of the Main Menu and learned how to add and remove items in the Main Menu by using the Menu Editor. Now you are ready to customize your desktop to suit your personal work habits. (Just remember that no GNOME Panel is complete without a Games drawer).

Q&A

Q I selected Save before logging out of my last session, but now, when I try to log in, my panel is missing, no windows appear, and my icons are blacked out. What should I do?

A Sometimes something in your session breaks, which can cause unpredictable results the next time you log in to GNOME. To fix a broken session, log out of GNOME (use Ctrl+Alt+Backspace if necessary). From the command line, navigate to ~/.gnome and list the directory contents. Delete the files that include "session," such as `session` and `session-manual`. When you log back in to GNOME you might lose some of your configurations, but the session should start. Check the GNOME FAQ at www.gnome.org for updated information on session management.

Q When moving a launcher or another item on the panel, if I drag the launcher too close to another launcher or drawer, it "jumps," to another place on the panel. How do I prevent this from occurring?

A The GNOME Panel is divided into square regions called *tiles*. If an item on the panel isn't fixed to a particular tile, then the items will moved relative to each other instead of to the panel. To keep the location of items on your panel absolute, go to Global Panel Properties and check Fix Tiles. This will enable you to move each tile independently.

Workshop

The quiz questions and exercises are designed to increase your understanding and to encourage you to continue experimenting. Answers appear in Appendix B, "Answers."

Quiz

1. What is the difference between a drawer and a submenu?
2. Name three ways to add an application launcher to the GNOME Panel. Hint: The hour doesn't explicitly mention three ways. Experiment!
3. How can you tell the contents of a drawer without opening it?
4. Which GNOME Panel applets help you monitor your computer's memory use?

Exercises

1. Add four edge panels to your desktop, one on each side. Change the panels to corner panels. What changes?
2. Most Linux distributions come with a large variety of backgrounds to decorate your edge panel. Open This Panel Properties and browse for a background.
3. Create a drawer and label it "Games." Browse the Main Menu and add three of your favorite games to the drawer.
4. Find an executable file on your system that is not in the GNOME Main Menu. Add it to the User submenu. Start the executable by clicking on its Main Menu entry. Does it start?

HOUR 8

Managing Files in GNOME

GNOME File Manager, or gmc, is the backbone to the GNOME desktop environment. gmc stands for GNOME Midnight Commander; Midnight Commander is a popular UNIX file manager which forms the basis of GNOME Midnight Commander. As a result of excessive memory use and some performance problems, a new GNOME File Manager is being developed for release 2.0 of GNOME.

In this hour, you will

- Open and explore the File Manager window.
- Safely close a File Manager window without killing the gmc process.
- View and understand the contents of the File Manager menus.
- Use right-click windows to accomplish common tasks.
- Use the File Manager toolbar to navigate through the directory tree and learn about the four File Manager views.
- Set File Manager preferences.

The Basics of GNOME File Manager

GNOME File Manager is a graphical interface for manipulating files and performing basic system administration tasks. Although it is often easier to use than the traditional command line, GNOME File Manager is not always intuitive. To help you understand File Manager as a whole, this section explores the parts of the GNOME File Manager window. In the next section, we discuss how to perform simple file manipulation tasks. In Hour 9, "Common File Manager Tasks," we will continue our exploration of File Manager with more advanced tasks.

Opening File Manager

The gmc process is started automatically when you first log in to GNOME, but it runs in the background. To do anything with gmc, you must open a File Manager window. By default, GNOME sets up an icon on the desktop called Home Directory, which opens a File Manager window directly to your home directory, usually in the /home/*username* directory. You can also open a File Manager window from the Main Menu by clicking the File Manager entry.

Closing a File Manager Window

Before we begin our exploration of the File Manager window, it is important that you understand the difference between closing a File Manager window and actually exiting gmc.

A File Manager window should be closed either by clicking File, Close Window or by clicking the Close option on the window bar. This closes the particular File Manager window, but the process gmc continues to run. You can kill the actual gmc process by clicking Commands, Exit on the File Manager menu, or by selecting the Kill/Annihilate option on the window bar. Never exit gmc unless you have a very good reason. Without gmc, the GNOME desktop disappears. Figure 8.1 shows the warning that appears when you click Commands, Exit.

FIGURE 8.1
The warning message can prevent you from crashing GNOME by mistake.

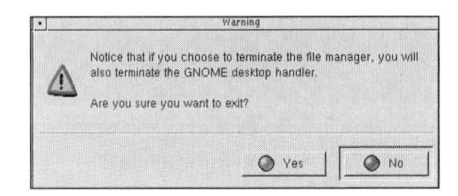

> gmc is central to the GNOME desktop environment. You cannot run GNOME without it. When you log in to GNOME, gmc starts automatically, and you should not close gmc unless you know what you are doing.

File Manager Window

When you first open a File Manager window, it looks somewhat like Windows Explorer, in that it is divided into two subwindows. On the left is a directory tree of folders and subfolders, beginning with the root directory, /, and branching out to the lowest subdirectory. A plus sign (+) next to a folder indicates that there are subdirectories hidden below. Single-click the plus sign and the subdirectories appear beneath the parent directory. When all subdirectories are exposed, a minus sign (–) appears to the left of the directory. (If there are no subdirectories within a directory, no sign appears to the left of the folder icon.)

When you click a directory or subdirectory, the directory's contents appear in the window on the right side of the File Manager window. The directory that is displayed is called the *active* directory. There are several ways to display the contents of the active directory, which we will explore later in this section.

At the bottom of the File Manager window, the status bar displays information about the active directory. You can configure File Manager to display the size of a file or directory on the left side of the status bar. On the right, the status bar displays the filter that is currently active (more on filters in Hour 9). By default, you will see Show All Files at the bottom right of the status bar, which means that all the files you have configured File Manager to display will appear in the window.

Near the top of File Manager window, the Location field displays the full pathname of the active directory like the Location field in an Internet browser. The File Manager window also contains a toolbar with an array of buttons and a row of menus. Figure 8.2 shows a typical File Manager window.

FIGURE 8.2
File Manager is the central GNOME system administration tool.

File Manager Menus

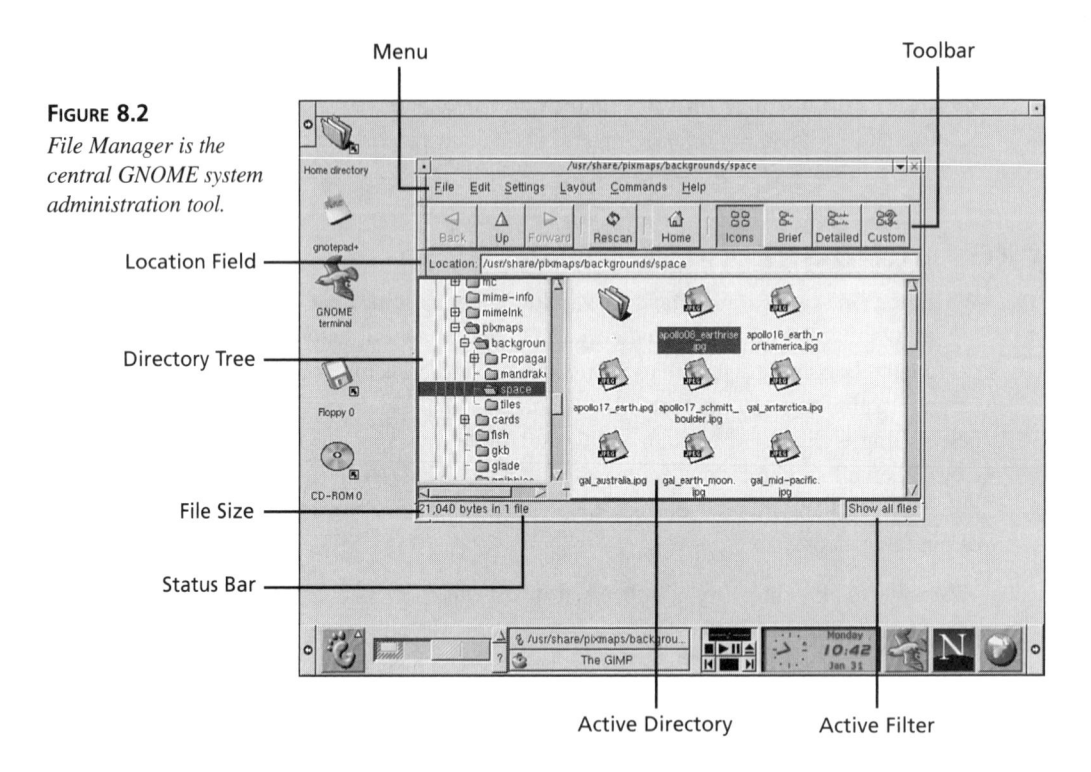

File Manager menus can be a bit confusing because several types of functionality are combined in each menu category. This section gives a brief introduction to each menu item so you won't get lost as you are learning to perform tasks in File Manager.

The File Menu

The File menu contains commands for manipulating files, and some other miscellaneous commands. Note that this section merely introduces the commands. We will use the commands to perform tasks later in the hour and in Hour 9.

- **Create New Window** creates a new File Manager window. It is useful to have more than one File Manager window open when you want to use drag-and-drop to move files around.

  The submenu New contains commands for creating the following items:
  - **Terminal** opens a new GNOME terminal.
  - **Directory** opens a dialog box for creating a new directory. If you enter just a directory name, the directory will be created within the currently active directory. Specify a full pathname to create the directory anywhere in the file system.

- **The Gimp** opens the GIMP graphics application.
- **New File** opens the default editor for you to create a new file.

> You can specify the editor you want to use as the default in GNOME Control Center. We will learn more about configuring GNOME in Hour 11, "Customizing Your GNOME Environment."

- Use **Open** to open a file you have selected in the active window.
- **Copy**, **Delete**, and **Move** open dialog boxes where you can copy, delete, and move files or directories. Each dialog box contains a Browse button so you don't have to remember pathnames.
- **Show Directory Sizes** shows the total size in bytes of the files within the active directory. Note that there is no check box for Show Directory Sizes. Showing the size of a directory is a one-time action for the active directory, not a feature for you to activate and deactivate. After you click Show Directory Sizes, File Manager computes the combined size of every file in the active directory and displays it on the left side of the status bar.
- **Close Window** closes the File Manager window. Note that this does not close gmc.

> Remember, closing a File Manager window and exiting gmc are two different actions! If you exit gmc by clicking the Kill/Annihilate window button or Commands, Exit in the File Manager menu, you actually kill the gmc process. If you click the Close window button or choose the Close Window menu option, you merely close the File Manager window.

The Edit Menu

The Edit menu contains the following commands for selecting and searching for files, as well as refreshing the active directory window:

- **Select All** selects all the files in the active directory.
- **Select Files** opens a dialog box for you to enter a filter to select files with certain attributes.
- **Search** opens the Search feature on the status bar. Search is a simple search tool for finding files and directories within the active directory.

- **Rescan Directory** updates any changes that have been made to the file system. The File Manager does not update the active directory dynamically as changes are made, so you must rescan for changes to appear. Note that there is also a Rescan Directory button on the Toolbar that has the same function.

The Settings Menu and the Layout Menu

The Settings menu contains only one item, Preferences. Use Preferences to configure File Manager.

The Layout menu controls how files appear in File Manager and how they are arranged in the active directory window. The Layout menu includes

- **Sort By**, which opens a dialog box with several choices of how to sort the active directory
- **Filter View**, which opens a dialog box in which you can create a filter to view only certain files in the active directory

Layout also includes menu choices for four possible views of the active directory. These view choices are also included as buttons on the toolbar:

- **Icon View** lists each subdirectory and file with an icon that corresponds to the file type.
- **Detailed View** lists the item, the file size, and the last time the file was modified.
- **Brief View** shows only the name of the item and a folder icon, if the item is a directory.
- **Custom View** enables you to decide exactly what file information to display.

The Commands Menu and the Help Menu

Commands is a miscellaneous menu, which includes only two entries that involve commands:

- **Run Command** is a simple dialog box for running a single command.
- **Run Command in Panel** is a dialog box for running commands within File Manager.

The Commands menu holds two other options:

- **Find Files** is another search tool that searches the entire file system for files, rather than just the active directory.
- **Edit MIME Types** deals with file extensions and launching default applications for certain kinds of files. We will study MIME types in Hour 9.

The Help menu simply opens an About window that gives the version of gmc you are running, the gmc Web site, and an email address where you can submit bug reports.

The Toolbar

The Toolbar buttons help you navigate through your system and control the File Manager display.

As you navigate through your file system, File Manager remembers which directories you have activated. Click Back to go back to the previously active directory. Click Forward to return to the next directory you opened.

> File Manager's Back and Forward buttons work just like the Back and Forward buttons in an Internet browser.

You can also use the Up and Home buttons to navigate through your directory tree. Click Up to go one directory up in the directory tree. Clicking Up opens the parent directory of the active directory. You can click Up to navigate all the way to the root directory.

Click Home to make your Home directory the active directory. If you are logged in as root, this button makes the /root directory the active directory.

Rescan rescans the active directory for changes, just like the Rescan directory in the Edit menu.

The four View buttons—Icon, Brief, Detailed, and Custom—change the view in the same way as the menu items of the same name do in the Layout directory.

Right-Click Menus

File Manager has several menus that are activated by right-clicking in particular places in the File Manager windows, and for certain kinds of files.

Right-Click the Window

Right-click an empty area in the active directory window to open a menu with three entries:

- **Rescan Directory** rescans the active directory for changes.
- **New Directory** creates a new directory in the active directory or, if you give a full pathname, wherever you specify.
- **New File** opens the default text editor to a new file.

Figure 8.3 shows the window's right-click menu.

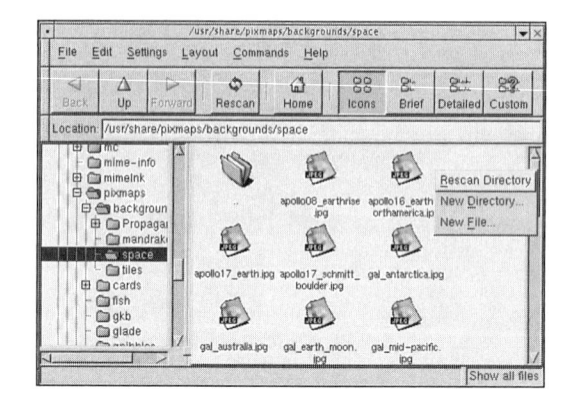

FIGURE 8.3
The active directory window's right-click menu duplicates some of the more commonly used File Manager menu options.

Right-Click a File

Depending on the kind of file, you can access different options when you right-click a file in File Manager. Some options that appear for every file are

- **Open** opens the file in the application specified in MIME Types. If you have no application specified in MIME Types, Open displays a list of applications for you to choose from.
- **Open With** displays a list of applications. Choose the application you want to use to open the file.
- **View** opens the gmc file viewer. You can view the contents of the file, but you can't edit the file.
- **Edit** opens the file in an editor.
- **Copy**, **Delete**, **Move**, and **Symlink** open dialog boxes to copy, delete, move, and create symbolic links for the file. You can use the Move option to actually move the file from one directory to another, as in MS Windows, or you can use Move to rename a file. Symbolic links are similar to shortcuts in MS Windows. You will learn about symbolic links in Hour 9.
- **Properties** opens the file's Properties dialog box.

Figure 8.4 shows a file's right-click menu.

Right-Click Special Files

Certain files have extra right-click menu options as well as the options discussed in the previous section. Some of the extra options include

- HTML files have an option to view the file in Netscape.
- rpm files can be installed, upgraded, and uninstalled directly from File Manager, using right-click menus.

Managing Files in GNOME 97

- Symbolic links have an additional right-click menu option, Edit Symlink. Edit Symlink opens a dialog box with a field to change the file that the symbolic link points to.

FIGURE 8.4
Sometimes the menu that appears when you right-click a file has additional options.

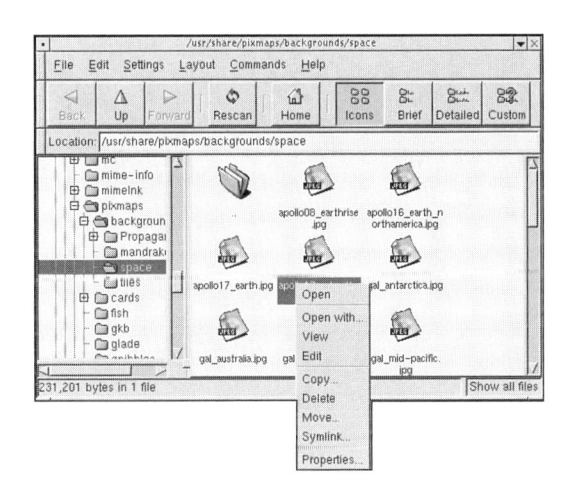

Right-Click Several Selected Files

If you select several files at once and right-click one of the files, a dialog box appears with options to copy, delete, or move the selected files (see Figure 8.5).

FIGURE 8.5
The options that are available in the selected files' right-click menu are also available in the File menu.

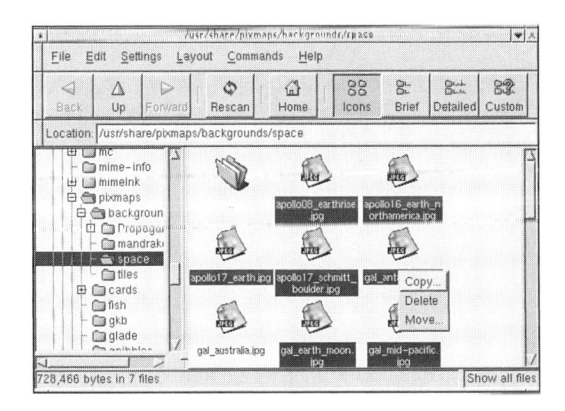

Setting Preferences in File Manager

Use the Preferences dialog box to customize the view of your directory structure in File Manager. The Preferences dialog box is divided into six tabs: File Display, Confirmation, VFS, Caching, Desktop, and Custom View. We will explore some of the tabs in this hour, and the more advanced preference options in Hour 9. Open the Preferences dialog box by clicking Settings, Preferences in the File Manager menus. Figure 8.6 shows the Preferences dialog box opened to the File Display tab.

FIGURE 8.6
File Display lets you control which files appear in the File Manager window.

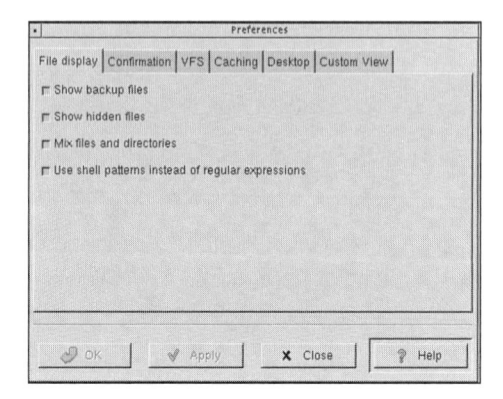

The File Display Tab

The File Display tab has options for you to choose the kinds of files you want to see and how to organize them. By default, special, system-created files such as backup files and hidden files are not displayed in File Manager. Select Show Backup Files and Show Hidden Files to display these files.

A *backup file* is a file that is a duplicate of a file on your system. Backups can be manually created or scheduled automatically. gmc recognizes a backup file as a file that begins with a tilde (~). Hidden files are also called *dot files*, because they have a period in front of the filename. *Hidden files* are usually user-specific files that are created either by the user or by applications and other processes. Hidden files can be directories, such as $HOME/.enlightenment or $HOME/.gnome, or files, such as $HOME/.Xauthority.

By default, directories are displayed at the top of the directory window and files are displayed beneath the directories. Even when you sort a directory, this convention is maintained, unless you select Mix Files and Directories. When you select this option, your files and directories will be sorted together by whatever criteria you determine. Figure 8.7 shows the same directory with the Mix Files and Directories option selected (right) and not selected (left).

The Confirmation Tab

The Confirmation tab has controls for displaying a confirmation dialog box before performing actions such as deleting, overwriting, or executing files. It is always a good idea to confirm deleting and overwriting, even if you are an experienced user.

FIGURE 8.7
The File Manager window on the left shows the default convention, with directories sorted before (above) files. On the right, the Mix Files and Directories option has been selected.

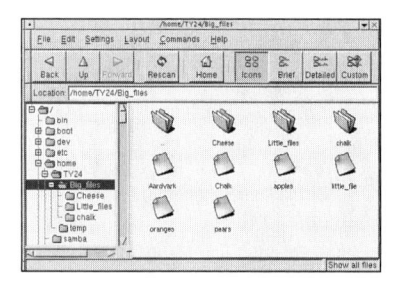

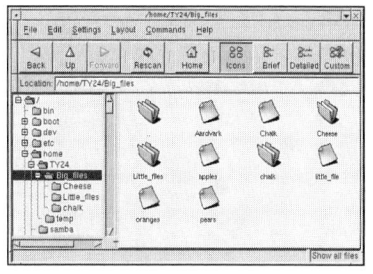

Show Progress While Operations Are Being Performed causes a progress bar to appear when File Manager is performing certain actions on files, such as copying, moving, or deleting. If you have a fast computer you might not even see the status bar as it appears and rapidly disappears, but this option is useful if you are copying a very large file or directory. Figure 8.8 illustrates the Confirmation tab of Preferences.

FIGURE 8.8
Use confirmation options as a safeguard against error.

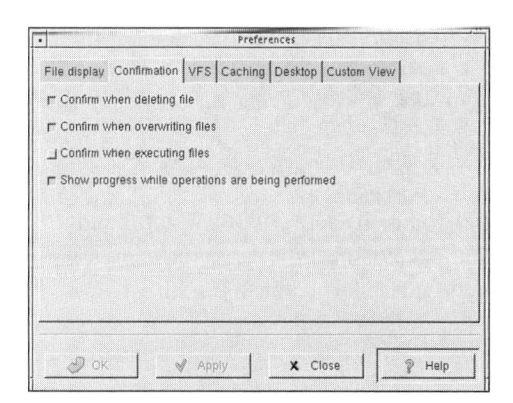

The Desktop Tab

A clever style feature of the GNOME desktop is the use of shaped icons and text. *Shaped* means that the icons and text are transparent. In other words, when you look at a shaped icon or piece of text, the background shows through the spaces between the letters and image, creating a neater appearance.

If you prefer to have unshaped icons and text, deselect the Use Shaped Icons and Use Shaped Text options. Your desktop icons and their accompanying titles will appear framed by a box. Figure 8.9 compares a desktop with shaped icons (left) to one without (right).

FIGURE 8.9
The icons and text on the left are shaped. Those on the right are unshaped.

The Desktop tab also deals with the placement of icons on the desktop. Click in the Icon Position window to indicate how you would like your icons to be oriented. The sample icons in the field move to show how the icons on your desktop will be arranged.

If you select Automatic Icon placement, File Manager will snap icons to position automatically as you create them, and you will not be able to move them manually at all. Snap Icons to Grid gives you a bit more control. You can move the icons where you want them, but when you place an icon near the spot you want, it will snap to position on the desktop so it is lined up to invisible gridlines. Figure 8.10 shows the Desktop tab of the Preferences dialog box.

FIGURE 8.10
The Desktop tab helps you configure the look of your desktop icons.

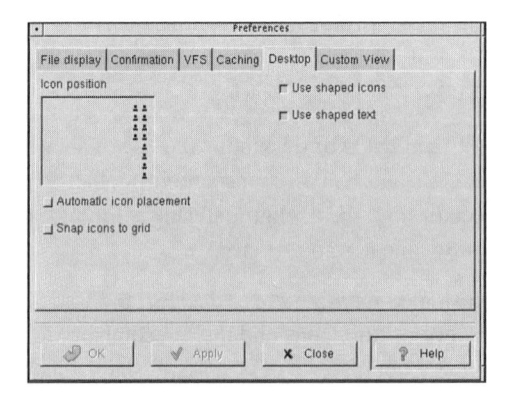

Summary

In this hour, you were introduced to the GNOME File Manager. You explored the File Manager window and learned how to safely close a File Manager window. You studied the menus, toolbar, and right-click menu options, and learned how to configure File Manager using Preferences.

Q&A

Q If I use an X terminal or regular shell session to make changes to my file system, will the changes show up in File Manager?

A Any changes you make to your file system will show up in GNOME just as they would in another shell. Remember that File Manager is just an interface, and that GNOME is just an environment.

Q Can I use the KDE or Enlightenment file manager in GNOME?

A You can use any file manager or any other application within GNOME. You must have gmc running, however, even if you don't use the file management part of gmc.

Q My icons don't appear when I start GNOME, and nothing else seems to work right either. What to do?

A If your session was saved incorrectly the last time you logged in to GNOME, or if GNOME was set up incorrectly, gmc might not start automatically. If this happens, click File Manager from the Main Menu, wait for it to start, then log out of GNOME, saving your session.

Workshop

The quiz questions and exercises are designed to increase your understanding and to encourage you to continue experimenting. Answers appear in Appendix B, "Answers."

Quiz

1. What is the relationship between gmc and File Manager?
2. Name two ways to open File Manager.
3. How would you collapse the directory tree in File Manager so that only the root (/) directory shows?
4. What information does the status bar contain?

Exercises

1. Open a File Manager window. Go to your home directory, and click the /etc directory in the directory tree, then click /usr/bin, and then click /var/tmp. Use the Back and Forward buttons to go back to /etc, then to /var/tmp, then to your home directory again. Note which direction you need to go to reach each file.

2. Open a File Manager window. Click the plus (+) signs next to a directory in your directory tree until the entire directory is open. What happens to the plus signs when you click them?

HOUR 9

Common File Manager Tasks

When you work on a user level with files and directories in Windows or MacOS, you are well shielded from what is happening in the filename. Options are few, unless you are logged in as an administrator. In Linux/UNIX, on the other hand, ordinary users have a wide range of options for working with files and directories. GNOME File Manager makes it easier to understand and more intuitive to use all the tools available for the UNIX filename.

In Hour 8, "Managing Files in GNOME," you were introduced to GNOME File Manager. You learned about the organization of the File Manager window, including the menus, toolbar, and directory windows, and how to customize File Manager using Preferences. In this hour, you will learn how you can use File Manager to accomplish common file administration tasks.

In this hour, you will

- Create a Custom view for your active directory window.
- Use File Manager to accomplish tasks, including selecting, copying, moving, deleting, and renaming files.
- Use drag-and-drop to accomplish tasks in File Manager.
- Search for and sort files and use filters.
- Create symbolic links and learn how File Manager works with hard links and symbolic links.
- Understand the Virtual File System in File Manager.

Customizing Your View

If you would like to see more information about your files than what is shown in the Basic, Icon, or Detailed views, use Custom View to show the information of your choice. You can have up to 14 kinds of file information in the Custom view, in any order you want. To open the Custom View dialog box, click Settings, Preferences, Custom View. Figure 9.1 shows the Custom View dialog box.

FIGURE 9.1
Use the Custom View dialog box to view details about your files and directories in File Manager.

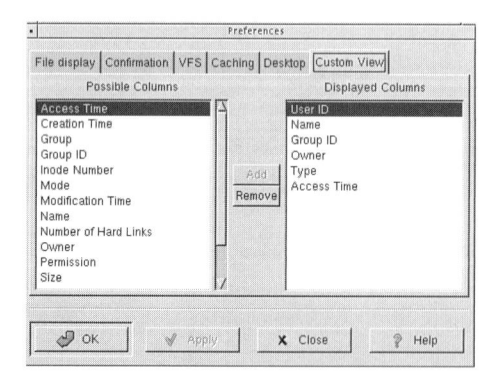

To add a category to your view, select the category title in the Possible Columns field, and click Add. The category title moves to the Displayed Columns list. To remove a category from Displayed Columns, select it and click Remove. A brief description of each category title follows:

- **Access Time** is the time and date the file was last accessed, or opened, either by a user or another program or process.
- **Creation Time** is the date and time the file was created on your computer.

- **Group** is the group that file belongs to. Groups are useful for assigning different access rights to different groups of users. For example, you could give one group of users read and write access to a file, and another group only read access.
- **Group ID**, displayed as GID, is the number that refers to the user's default group. Every file has both a user and group owner. The GID for each group on the system is found in the /etc/group file.
- The **Inode Number** is also called the *Index number*. An *inode* is a datastructure that stores the information about the file, such as owner, group, permissions, modify date, and so on. The *inode number* is the particular inode on the hard disk where information about a file is located.
- **Mode** lists the permissions for the file in octal notation. The mode is a numeric way of displaying the read, write, and execute permissions for the user, group, and others.

> This chapter gives only a cursory discussion of modes and permissions. For a detailed explanation, see the *Linux Installation and Getting Started* guide at http://www.linuxdoc.org/LDP/gs/node1/html.

- **Modification Time** is the date and time the file was last changed by either a user or a process.
- **Name** is the name of the file.
- **Number of Hard Links** lists the number of hard links to the file.
- **Owner** gives the username of the user who owns the file.
- **Permission** lists the file's permissions using symbolic notation.
- **Size** is the size of the file in bytes. Note that the size given for a directory is the actual size of the directory itself, or the number of bytes of space that the directory takes up on the disk. The size of the files and subdirectories within the directory is not given.
- **Size (short)** is slightly different from Size. Size (short) gives the size of files in bytes. For directories, Size (short) indicates whether the file is a parent directory (also called the ".." directory) or a sub-directory. All directories on the system are sub-directories except the root (/) directory.
- **User ID**, or **UID**, is the ID number that represents the user who owns the file.

The Type column contains an icon indicating the type of file. If the file is a directory, Type contains a folder icon. The black arrow symbolic link icon indicates symbolic links, and applications contain an asterisk. Stalled symbolic links, which are symbolic link files whose target file has been deleted, are shown as exclamation points.

Selecting Files

Selecting files in File Manager is similar to selecting files in Windows. To select a single file, left-click the file. The selected file becomes highlighted.

In Icon view, you can graphically select several files at once. While holding down the left mouse button, move the mouse around the files that you want to select, as shown in Figure 9.2. A rectangle is drawn on the screen around the selected files. When you release the mouse button, the selected files are highlighted.

FIGURE 9.2
The rectangle encompasses the files that will be selected as you drag your mouse across the icons.

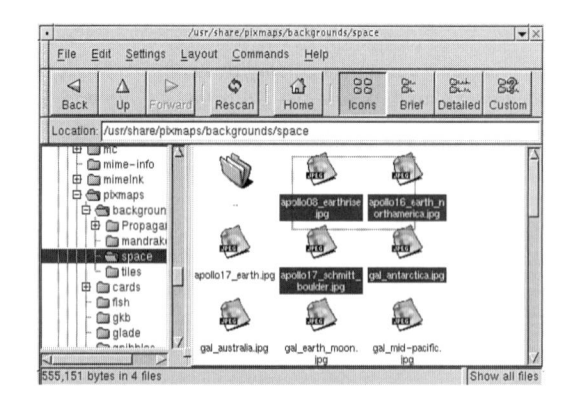

If you are not in Icon view, you can select a group of files in a range, or you can add individual files to the selected group. To select a range of files, click the first file in the range, hold down Shift, and click the last file in the range. All the files in the range are selected.

To add files to a selected group individually, click the first file that you want to select. While pressing and holding the Ctrl key, click the next file to select it, and continue until you have selected all the files you want. When you release the Ctrl button, the files remain highlighted.

Copying, Deleting, Moving, and Renaming Files

From the command line, files are copied, deleted, and moved by using the text commands cp, rm, and mv. Each command has a long list of options and switches that change the behavior of the command. You have to either commit all the options to memory, or constantly check a man page as you enter the commands.

GNOME File Manager has two interfaces to text-based shell commands. You can select Copy, Move, Delete, or Properties from the File or right-click menu to bring up a dialog box to help you perform the task. Alternatively, you can use drag-and-drop. In this section, you will learn about the menu commands. In the section that follows, we will examine some of the ways you can use drag-and-drop in GNOME. Parts of this section and the "Using Drag-and-Drop" section might seem repetitive, but it is important that you be aware of both methods.

Copy

Click File, Copy, or right-click a file and select Copy, to bring up the Copy dialog box. Enter the full pathname of the location to which you want to copy the file. You can use the Browse button if you don't want to type in the pathname manually. Figure 9.3 shows the Copy dialog box.

FIGURE 9.3
The Copy and Move dialog boxes are similar.

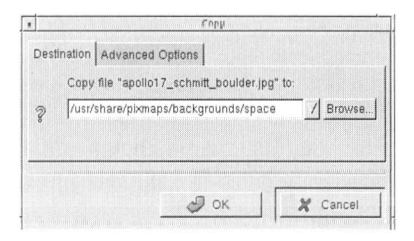

Copy has some advanced options for you to select when copying a file or directory, as shown in Figure 9.4.

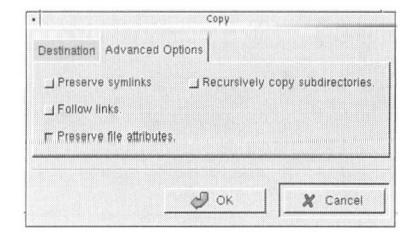

FIGURE 9.4
The Advanced Options tab gives you control over how the files will be copied.

The Advanced Options tab contains the following choices:

- **Preserve Symlinks**   With Preserve Symlinks, if you copy a file that is a symlink, the copy will point to the original file. If you copy a symlink without Preserve Symlinks, the symlink will keep its old value. For example, given the symlink `frog->bull` and `frog` is copied into the subdirectory pond without Preserve Symlinks, we have `frog->bull`, which doesn't exist in the subdirectory pond. If it is copied with Preserve Symlinks, we have `pond/frog->../bull`.
- **Follow Links**   If the directory you are copying contains hard links or symbolic links, the links will be copied as new files containing the contents of the original linked file.
- **Preserve File Attributes**   Select Preserve File Attributes to copy the original files' permissions, creation, access, and modification dates. If you are root, the file's original owner and group will also be preserved.
- **Recursively Copy Subdirectories**   Selecting this option instructs File Manager to copy all subdirectories within a directory as subdirectories, as well as the files within them. In other words, an exact replica of the original directory structure is re-created in the new directory.

Move

To move a file, select Move from the File or right-click menu. The Move dialog box contains the same fields as the Copy dialog box, except that the only advanced option available for Move is Preserve Symlinks.

Delete

To delete a file, select Delete from the File or right-click menu. If you want warning signs about deleting a file or recursively deleting a directory that is not empty, be sure to select the Confirm boxes in the Confirmations tab of Preferences. Figure 9.5 shows a delete warning message.

FIGURE 9.5

If you choose not to be presented with a warning message, you cannot be sure if you deleted the correct file until you rescan the directory.

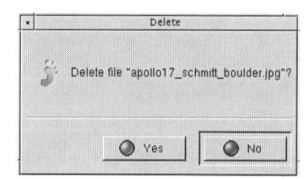

Renaming Files

In UNIX, renaming a file is essentially the same as moving it. You use the mv command to move the file to the same location with a different name. In GNOME, Rename and Move are treated as separate commands, but they are actually both just different interfaces to the mv command.

There are two ways to rename a file in GNOME. The first method requires you to be in Icon view. In Icon view, slowly double-click the filename, first to select it, and then again to open a text box around the filename. Be careful not to click the file quickly enough to actually open it. In the text box, overwrite the old filename and press Enter. Figure 9.6 shows how the text box looks.

FIGURE 9.6
If the text box doesn't appear around the filename, you didn't click the title correctly.

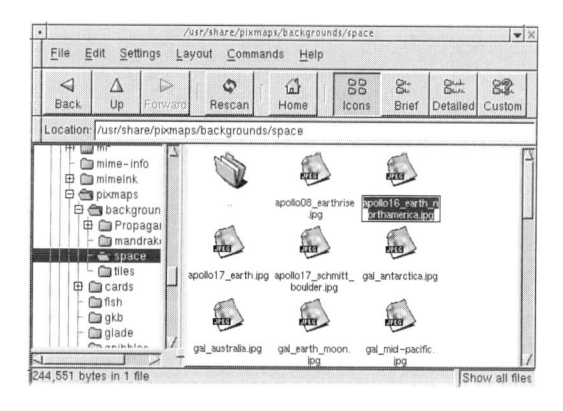

> You must press Enter after renaming the file, or the change will not take place.

Alternatively, you can open the file Properties by right-clicking the file and selecting Properties. Simply overwrite the filename in the dialog box and click OK.

Using Drag-and-Drop

You can use drag-and-drop to move, copy, and link files in your filename or even in remote filenames, if you have mcserv installed.

To move or copy files from one directory to another, open two File Manager windows, one at the location where the file(s) currently resides, and one at target location. Click the file you want to move, copy, or create a symbolic link for, and then drag it to the target directory.

By default, files are moved via drag-and-drop. If you want to copy the file instead of move it, hold down Ctrl as you left-click the file. Drag the file to the desired location. The file is copied when you drop it.

Alternatively, you can hold down the middle mouse button instead of the left mouse button when you click the file to drag it. When you drop the file on the target location, a menu appears with the options: Move Here, Copy Here, Link Here, Cancel Drag (see Figure 9.7). Select the item you want, and the correct action will be performed.

FIGURE 9.7

It is usually easier to simply middle-click when dragging and dropping, rather than to use Shift.

Ways to Use Drag-and-Drop

There are many more ways to use drag-and-drop than simply for copying files, including

- Copy, move, or symlink files or directories.
- Drag the executable file for an application from File Manager to the panel. A launcher for that application is automatically created on the panel.
- Drag a file or directory from File Manager to the desktop. An icon is created on the desktop. When you double-click the icon, one of three actions will occur:
  - If the file is an application, the icon launches the application.
  - If the file is a directory, the icon opens File Manager with the directory in the active window.
  - If the file is not an application, the default application for that file opens the file.
- Drag the executable file for an application from the File Manager onto the panel to create a panel launcher for the application.
- Drag a graphics file such as a jpg file onto the launcher to automatically configure the panel background to be the image stored in the file.
- If you have another partition mounted, use drag-and-drop to copy files from one partition to another.
- If you have the filename of a remote computer mounted, use drag-and-drop to upload files to or download files from the remote computer.
- Use drag-and-drop copy files to a zip drive or floppy.

Viewing Directory and File Sizes

When you click a file in File Manager, the size of the file is displayed in bytes in the status bar. By default, File Manager displays only the size of individual files, not directories. Figure 9.8 shows File Manager with the size of a file displayed in the status bar.

FIGURE 9.8
By default, directory sizes do not appear in the status bar.

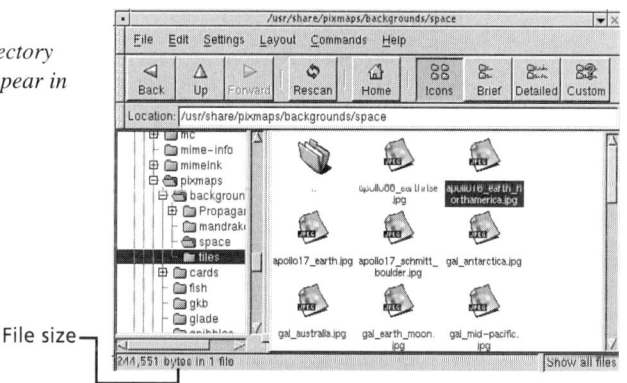

File size

If you want to see the combined size of all the files in a directory, select the directory so that it appears in the active Directory view, and click File, Show Directory Sizes. The size of the combined files in the directory appears. If you want to check the size of another directory, click the next directory and click Show Directory Sizes again. The directory size appears in the lower-left corner of the status bar on the File Manager window, where the file size usually appears.

> Take care when viewing the size of directories at the top of the directory structure. Depending upon the speed of your system and the number of files in the selected directory, it can take quite a few minutes to calculate the directory size.

Finding Files

File Manager has two search tools to help you find files within your filename. The tool Search helps you find a particular file within the active directory. The tool Find File can locate a file anywhere in the filename, by either the filename or a string of characters, such as a word or phrase, within the file. Find File is similar in function to the shell commands `find` and `grep`.

Search

To open Search, from the Edit menu, click Search. The word `Search:` appears in the bottom-left corner of the status bar, as shown in Figure 9.9. Click the status bar and type the first character in the name of the file that you are searching for. The first item in the active directory that begins with that character is selected.

FIGURE 9.9
If no items in the active directory match your search, the character you type will not appear next to Search: in the status bar.

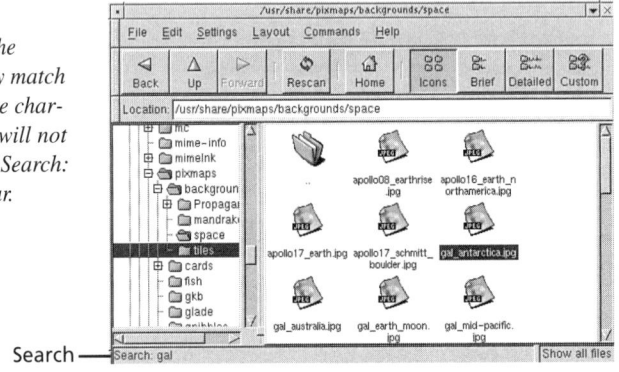

> Search is case sensitive, so be sure that you type the correct case of the letters in the filename.

Search highlights the first file or directory that contains the character you typed. The search can be as specific as you like. You can enter just the first letter or two of the file you are looking for or the entire name.

If no character appears in the status bar when you type it into Search, that means that there is no file or directory in the active directory that begins with that letter.

End the search by leaving the directory, selecting the file you were searching for, or using the arrow buttons or mouse to navigate away from the highlighted file. To start a new search, click Edit, Search again.

Find File

File Manager has a more powerful tool, Find File, that enables you to search for files over your entire filename, not just in the current active directory.

Using Find File is very simple. Open Commands, Find File and enter the directory where you want to start your search. You can also enter a word or phrase if you are not sure of the actual filename. If your search takes too much time, use Suspend to end the search and narrow the search parameters. Find File is illustrated in Figure 9.10.

FIGURE 9.10
In the top figure, search is for files that begin with the string `"gal"` *in the* `/usr/share/pixmaps/backgrounds` *directory. The result of the search is displayed below—six files in that directory begin with* `"gal"`.

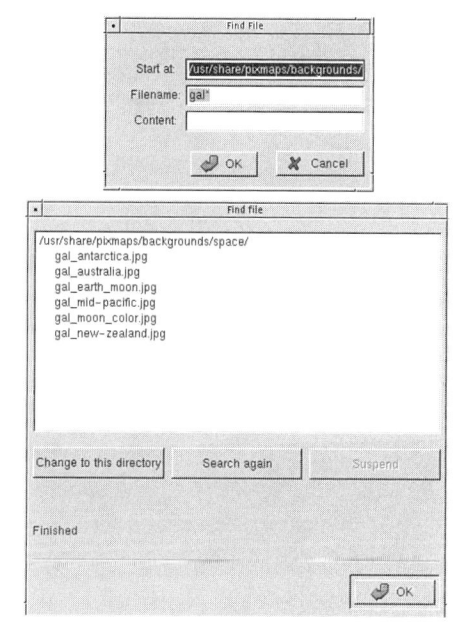

The GNOME Search Tool is a separate utility you can use to search for files. You will learn about GNOME Search Tool in Hour 13, "GNOME Processes."

Sorting Files

There are two ways to sort files within File Manager. In Brief, Detailed, or Custom view, simply click the column title in the active directory window. The files will be sorted according to the column category. To reverse the sort order, click the column title again, and the files will be reversed.

Files can also be sorted using the Sort By tool, located in the Layout menu. The Sort By dialog box contains six sorting options: Sort by Name, File Type, Size, Time Last Accessed, Time Last Modified, or Time Last Changed, as shown in Figure 9.11.

Sort By has an option to ignore case sensitivity, which actually means exactly the opposite of what it seems. If you select Ignore Case Sensitivity, the files are sorted by ASCII convention. Symbols appear first, then numbers, then capital letters, and finally small letters. If you deselect Ignore Case Sensitivity, filenames will simply be sorted alphabetically. Symbols and numbers still appear first, but files that begin with upper- and lowercase letters are sorted alphabetically

FIGURE 9.11

The Sort By tool enables you to perform simple sorts in the active directory.

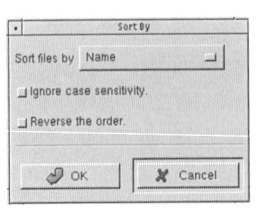

Remember that, by default, directories will still appear before files. If you want directories to be sorted with files, open the Preferences dialog box, File Display, and check Mix Files and Directories. The next time you sort, the directories will be sorted with the files in the manner you specify.

The option Reverse the Order reverses the default sort order. By default, dates are sorted from earliest date to most recent. Sort by Name sorts from non-alphanumeric characters to the lowercase z. Select Reverse to have Sorts by Date display files with the most recent dates first. Select Reverse to make alphanumeric sorts begin with files that start with z.

Symbolic Links Versus Hard Links

Forming a symbolic link is similar to copying a file, except that the new filename actually represents the original file. Changes in one file will show up in the symlinked file as well. If you delete the destination file, or target file, of the symbolic link, the link is no longer valid. The filename will still be there, but there will be nothing in it. This is called a *stalled symbolic link*.

Symbolic links are designated in File Manager by a small black arrow next to the filename or icon, as shown in Figure 9.12. The original file that the symbolic link points to is found in the file properties. The File Type will be Symbolic Link. The Target Name displays the full pathname of the original file that the symbolic link points to.

FIGURE 9.12

The symbolic link symbol denotes symbolic links in Icon and Detailed view.

A hard link is superficially similar to a symbolic link, but there are fundamental differences. A symbolic link is nothing more than a pointer to the original file. Creating a hard link is somewhat like copying the file, in that the files are linked, but appear as separate, distinct files. There is no way to tell which file is the original file and which is the link. If you delete one of the files that are hard linked, the other file remains.

Common File Manager Tasks 115

> Only symbolic links are represented graphically in File Manager. There is no graphical representation of hard links.

Viewing File Properties

The properties of a file—including information about the pathname, extension, creation, access and modification date, permissions, and ownership—can be viewed using File Properties. To open the File Properties, right-click the filename, as shown in Figure 9.13.

File properties can be viewed by anyone who has access to the file, but can only be changed by the owner of the file or the superuser.

FIGURE 9.13
The File Properties/Statistics tab shows basic information about the file. Note that the date of creation is later than the date of modification or access.

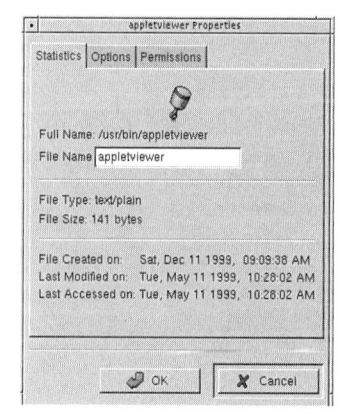

Statistics

The Statistics tab provides basic information about the file. Short descriptions of the file statistics fields follow.

- **Full Name** lists the full pathname of the file.
- The **File Name** appears in a text box so you can rename the file.
- **File Type** is determined by the file's extension. If the file has an extension that is associated with a MIME type, File Manager can determine the type of file.
- **File Size** indicates the size of the file in kilobytes and bytes.
- **File Created On** is the date when the file was created on your computer. This is not necessarily the date that the file was actually created, but the date when the file became part of your filename.
- **Last Modified On** lists the date when the file was last changed.
- **Last Accessed On** indicates the date when a user or a process last opened the file.

Permissions

The Permissions tab is a graphical interface for the ls -l, chown, and chmod commands, for setting permissions and changing the owner of a file.

The three permissions, Read, Write, and Execute, and the three classes of user, User, Group, and Other, are arranged into a grid. The permission for each user class has a button. If the button is selected, that class of user is assigned that particular permission. If the button is deselected, that user class loses that permission. As you press the buttons, the octal notation for the permission is displayed in the Current Mode field. The current mode changes dynamically as you select and deselect the permission buttons. The Permissions tab is shown in Figure 9.14.

FIGURE 9.14
The Permissions tab is a graphical interface to the ls -l, chmod, *and* chown *commands.*

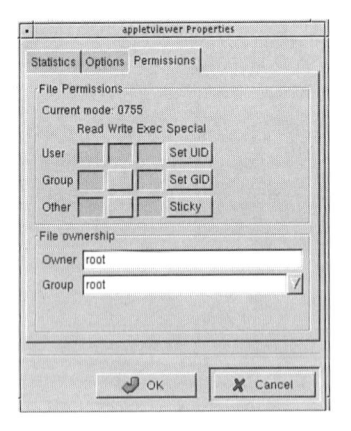

If you understand symbolic notation, octal notation is simple. As with symbolic notation, the read, write, and execute permissions are listed for the user, group, and other users. The mode is a four-place number, where the first number stands for special permissions; the second number represents permissions for the user; the third, permissions for the group; and the fourth, permissions for other users. Each kind of permission is assigned a number value:

- Set UID has a value of 4.
- Set GID has a value of 2.
- Set the sticky bit has a value of 1.
- Read permission has a value of 4.
- Write permission has a value of 2.
- Execute permission has a value of 1.

The permission values are added for each kind of user. For example, mode 0777 is the same as rwxrwxrwx. 0755 is the same as rwxr_xr_x, and 0511 is the same as r_xr__r__.

File Ownership

The bottom of the Permissions tab contains the File Ownership section, with two fields, Owner and Group. By default, the Owner of the file is the User who created the file, or the owner assigned by the superuser with the chown command. The User who owns the file and root are permitted to change the group who owns the file. This field is the interface to the chown command.

The Group field designates the group that the file belongs to. Group ownership is useful if you want only certain users to be able to have, for example, write privileges to a file, while other users have read-only or, in the case of a directory, read and execute-only access.

> Read, write, and execute access mean different things when you are talking about a directory, versus a file. For a directory, read access means that you can list the contents of the directory. If you have write access, you can add or remove files in the directory. Execute access means that you can list specific information about the files in the directory, using ls -l.

Options

Applications have an additional Properties tab, Options. Options enables you to open, view, and edit the file in other than the default manner that is set in the Mime Types capplet of GNOME Control Center. Also, if the file should be opened in an X terminal, select Needs Terminal to Run. The Options tab is shown in Figure 9.15.

FIGURE 9.15
The File Options tab appears if the file is executable.

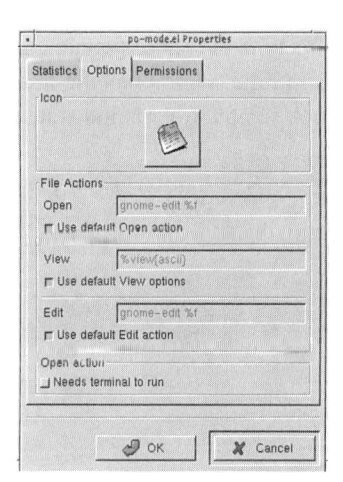

Using Filters

A filter does exactly what the name suggests—it filters out from view the files that you don't want, so that you can more easily see the files that you do want. Filters are useful when you want to work with only certain kinds of files, for example, files with certain extensions, or when you are looking for files in a large directory. By default, File Manager comes with one filter, Show All Files.

Create your own filters by selecting Layout, Filter View. Enter the filter you want to use in the Set Filter dialog box. You can use common shell metacharacters, also called *wildcards*, such as those listed in Table 9.1.

TABLE 9.1 Wildcards to Use in Filters

Wildcard	Description
*	Matches any number of characters
?	Matches any one character
[x-x]	Matches a range of characters
[xxx] or {xxx}	Matches a list of characters

For example, `[AaBbCc]*.txt` matches any files with the extension `.txt` and that begin with the letter A, B, C, a, b, or c. `Alpha*.sgml` matches every file or subdirectory that begins with the string "Alpha". `[^a]*` displays every file and subdirectory except those that begin with "a".

> See the ed man page for more information on forming expressions.

After you set a filter, it remains in effect for the entire filename until you change it or restore it to the default. To restore from Filter view, open the filter dialog box at Layout, Filter View and click Show All Files. A sample filter is illustrated in Figure 9.16.

FIGURE 9.16
Use shell metacharacters to apply filters to your active directory.

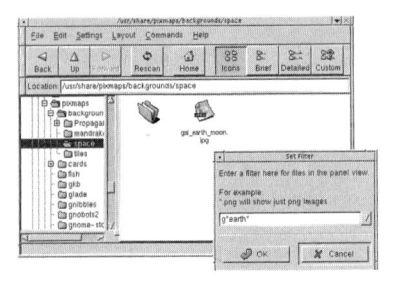

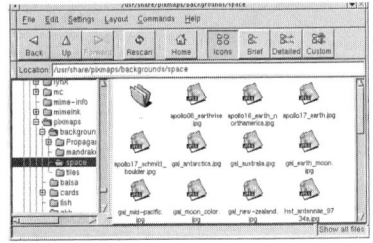

The Virtual File System

A virtual filename makes it possible to access remote filenames as if they were local. The Virtual File System, or VFS, is responsible for File Manager's capability to open tarred and compressed files and to enable you to manipulate files within the tarball without untarring and decompressing. File Manager uses several kinds of virtual filenames to access different systems, but all the filenames appear in the File Manager window to be one interface.

Some of the more common file systems are

- The local file system, which is used to access the files on your computer.
- `ftpfs`, which enables you to manipulate files on a remote computer connected via `ftp`.
- `tarfs`, which is used to open work with files that are tarred and compressed into a tarball. You can open, edit, copy, and delete files within the tarball without untarring and decompressing.
- `mcfs`, which you can use if you are running the mcserv program. `mcfs`, the Midnight Commander network file system, lets you work with files on a remote computer as if the files were on your local computer. The remote computer must also be running mcserv. mcserv can be downloaded from the GNOME ftp site at `ftp://ftp.gnome.org/pub/GNOME/stable`.

Viewing Compressed and Archived Files

When File Manager looks inside and displays the files included in a tarred (archived) and zipped (compressed) file, it is using the Virtual File System to set up virtual directories in your directory tree.

Open a tarball or other archived or compressed file in the same way you would a regular file, either by clicking Open on the File menu, double clicking the file, or right-clicking and selecting Open. The tarred files inside the tarball will appear in the active directory window as distinct, separate files. You can open this files and make changes to them without untarring and decompressing the tarball. If you want to untar the tarball, click Extract from the right-click menu.

Summary

In this hour, you learned how to customize the GNOME File Manager, and to use GNOME File Manager to perform common system administration tasks. You used several different methods for selecting files and used filters to display files. You copied, deleted, moved, and renamed files using File Manager. You learned some common uses for drag-and-drop. You learned two methods, `Search` and `Find File`, for searching your directory tree for files. You learned about symbolic and hard links, and how symbolic links are annotated in File Manager. You viewed the properties of a file. You learned how to change the permissions for files. You also learned how File Manager uses a virtual file system to display remote, archived, and compressed files.

Q&A

Q How can I fix a stalled symbolic file?

A If you can determine what the original target file was, right-click the stalled symlink, select Edit Symlink, and enter the target filename. If you cannot recover the original target file, delete the symbolic link.

Q I find File Manager to be cumbersome and slow. Do I have to use it to use GNOME?

A Although you don't have to use the File Manager window interface to manipulate files, gmc, which is the underlying file manager, is central to the operability of GNOME. And yes, it is cumbersome and slow. A completely new file manager called Nautilus is being developed to replace gmc. Nautilus will have much greater functionality, particularly over networked systems, and will be easier to use than gmc. Nautilus will be released with GNOME 2.0.

Workshop

The quiz questions and exercises are designed to increase your understanding and to encourage you to continue experimenting. Answers appear in Appendix B, "Answers."

Quiz

1. What is the Creation Time, Access Time, and Modification Time for a file?
2. In the Type column of Custom View, what does an exclamation point signify?
3. What is the default action for dragging and dropping a file from File Manager to the desktop?
4. If you want to move a file that is a symbolic link, how do you keep the file linked to its target file when it is moved?
5. How do you view the size of a directory in File Manager?
6. Name two ways to sort a directory by filename in File Manager.

Exercises

1. From File Manager, open the directory where your background files are located, for example, `/usr/share/backgrounds/pixmap`. Drag one of the `.jpg` files from File Manager to the panel. What happens?

2. Create a test directory called `Test`, and the files `alpha`, `bravo`, `charlie`, and `delta`. Turn off the confirmation warnings in File Manager, and delete the file `delta`. What happens?

3. Create a symbolic link called `gorilla` to the file `delta`.

4. Rename `gorilla` as `cheetah`.

5. Open the `Test` directory that you made in exercise 2. Open a Search in the status bar and type `z`. What happens? Now type `a c` in the status bar, and then `a b`. What happens?

6. Open an X terminal and `cd` to your `Test` directory. Enter the command:
   ln bravo mike

   Open File Manager to your `Test` directory. Does a symlink symbol appear next to `mike`?

7. Open the File Properties of `alpha` to the Permissions tab. Change the permissions so that the Current Mode says 0000. Click OK to close Properties, then try to open the file. What happens? Change the permissions to 0755.

HOUR 10

Exploring Enlightenment

Enlightenment is most complex, powerful, and flexible X window manager available today, as well as the default window manager for GNOME. Written for use with Linux, Enlightenment works with every flavor of UNIX. It can be used either in conjunction with GNOME or by itself. In fact, the ultimate goal of the Enlightenment Project is to make Enlightenment a fully functioning desktop shell. There are so many ways to use and configure Enlightenment, it almost deserves its own book. But in this hour, we will merely introduce you to the major features, while keeping our discussion GNOME-centric.

In this hour, you will

- Keep track of open applications with the Enlightenment Iconbox and Pager.
- Customize your environment with configuration tools in the Enlightenment menus.
- Use keybindings to manipulate your windows.
- Communicate with Enlightenment using the Enlightenment External Shell.
- Solve some common Enlightenment problems and where to get help.

Enlightenment Tools

When you start Enlightenment for the first time, you will see two small boxes on the desktop—the Enlightenment Pager and the Iconbox. These tools perform tasks similarly to the GNOME Pager and Desk Guide. Within the GNOME environment they might seem redundant; however, many people prefer them to their GNOME counterparts. Exercise 1 gives you the opportunity to compare tools and decide for yourself.

Iconbox

The Iconbox swallows windows that have been iconified and displays either an icon that represents the application or a miniature version of the window that contains the application. To reopen an iconified window, click the icon in the Iconbox and the window will be raised.

Figure 10.1 shows an Iconbox that contains four icons. The mouse is placed over the GIMP icon, displaying the name of the application in a pop-up.

FIGURE 10.1
The Iconbox keeps track of your iconified applications. Use the Settings menu to configure your Iconbox.

Notice that a ToolTip with the name of the application pops up when you place the mouse over the icon.

The Enlightenment Pager

The Enlightenment Pager is similar to the GNOME Pager in that it keeps track of your active windows. Instead of a list of applications, however, the Enlightenment Pager displays miniature versions of the windows. When you place your mouse over a miniature window, the name of the application pops up. When you click a miniature window in the pager, that window gets the focus.

To configure the Pager settings, right-click the desktop and select Pager Settings from the Settings menu. Figure 10.2 shows the GNOME Pager with the mouse placed over a virtual terminal window. The Pager Settings menu is also displayed.

FIGURE 10.2
When you hold your mouse over an item in the Pager, the window expands. Use the Settings menu to configure your Pager.

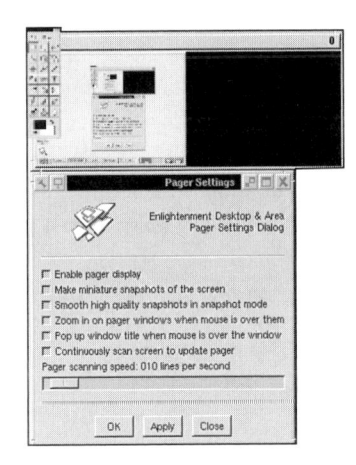

Enlightenment Menus

There are many menus in Enlightenment, with hundreds of configuration options. We will review only a few of the most important menu items in this hour, to give you a feel for the kinds of things Enlightenment can do. Experiment with the menu options as we discuss them so that you really understand their functionality. Next, play with some of the items that are not discussed. Don't be afraid that you'll break your system; at the end of this hour, you will learn how to recover from problems.

Main Enlightenment Menu

The Enlightenment menu is the main menu for all Enlightenment functions. Middle-click the desktop to open the Enlightenment menu, shown in Figure 10.3. We will look at each of the items in the Enlightenment menu in turn.

FIGURE 10.3
Middle-click the desktop to open the Enlightenment menu. All the Enlightenment functions can be accessed from here.

User Menus

You can access the User menus either from the main Enlightenment window, or by left-clicking the desktop. The User menus vary according to your system. In Figure 10.4, the KDE and GNOME menus are included, as well as the user's GNOME menu and a list of commonly used applications. If you are familiar with scripting, you can configure the User menus to hold whatever you want, as we will learn later this hour.

FIGURE 10.4
The User menus vary depending on your system.

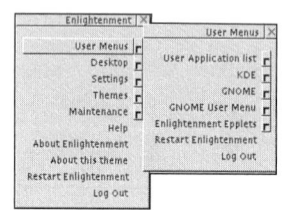

Settings Menu

You can open the Settings menu via the Enlightenment menu, or directly by right-clicking the desktop. Settings control how your windows move and behave, how your mouse behaves, and how to make a window active (also called *setting the focus* of the desktop).

> In Enlightenment version 0.15.x and earlier, there was a tool called E-conf, which enabled you to customize window settings. E-conf was replaced with the Settings menu in the 0.16 release.

Focus Settings

Focus settings help you determine how a window will get the "focus," or become the active window. Table 10.1 lists some common configurations.

TABLE 10.1 Common Focus Settings

Setting	Description
Focus follows pointer	The window the mouse is placed over has the focus.
Focus follows mouse clicks	You must click in a window to give it focus.
All new windows first get the focus	When you start a new application, it automatically gets the focus.
Send mouse pointer to window on focus switch	When you choose an application from the desktop menu, Iconbox, or Pager, the mouse is automatically moved into that window.

Move and Resize Settings

This dialog box lets you control the way your windows look and feel when you move them or resize them with your mouse. Experiment with the different options by checking a new option and then clicking Apply. Click OK when you find a configuration that you like.

ToolTip Settings

If you place your mouse over the desktop or over the border of an open window, the Enlightenment ToolTips appear. These windows are particularly useful when you are first learning Enlightenment, because there are so many ways of doing a task. The ToolTip Settings menu gives you the option of displaying or hiding the window border ToolTips and the Root Window Tips. You can also control how long the mouse must hover until the ToolTips window appears. Figure 10.5 shows the ToolTips windows.

FIGURE 10.5
The ToolTips windows are helpful when you are learning Enlightenment.

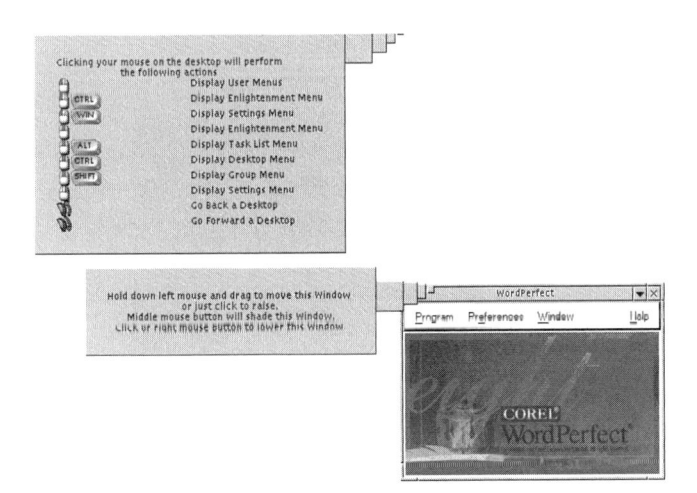

Special FX Settings

Configure the Enlightenment "special effects" with the Special FX Settings. You can control how your desktops look when you are switching between them, or how your windows look as they open or close. You can make your windows look like they are actually rolling up when shading. Experiment with these options and see what happens to your windows. Figure 10.6 shows the Special FX dialog box.

Desktop Background Settings

The Desktop Background Settings menu displays a snapshot of the backgrounds available on your system. The background `pixmap` file must be located in `/usr/share/pixmap/backgrounds` to show up in the Backgrounds menu. You can use either the Enlightenment

Desktop Background Settings dialog box or the GNOME Control Center Background capplet to select a background. If you use Enlightenment, be sure to check Disable Background Selection in the BackgroundGNOME. If you use the GNOME Control Center to choose a background, select No Background in the Enlightenment Desktop Background Settings. Figure 10.7 shows the Desktop Background dialog box.

FIGURE 10.6
Enlightenment Special FX Settings have some unusual configurations to make your desktop more interesting.

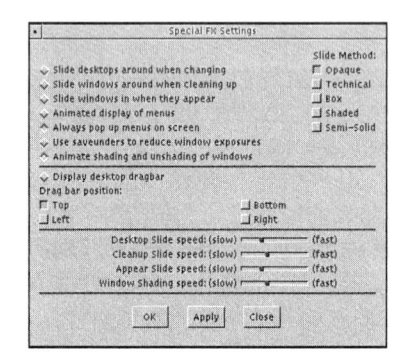

FIGURE 10.7
Enlightenment comes with many beautiful background settings. You can also download backgrounds from the Web, or create your own backgrounds.

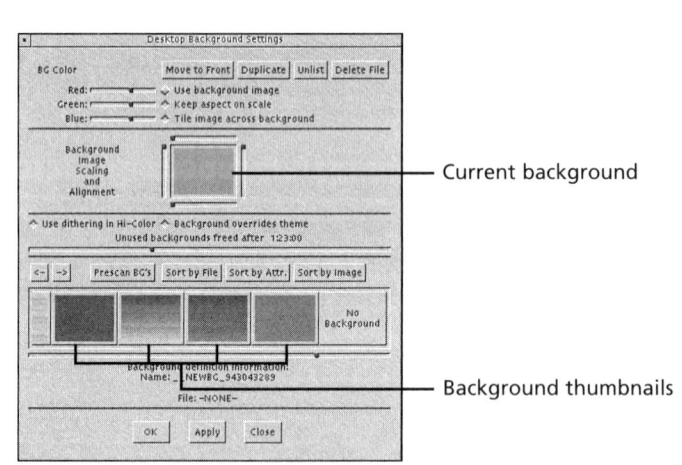

Maintenance Menu

When you make a change in the configuration of Enlightenment, the old configuration files are cached in the directory ~/.enlightenment/cached. The Maintenance menu has options for querying and purging cached files, something you should do periodically when caches get too big, especially if you tend to switch backgrounds and themes often. Figure 10.8 shows a query message for background selector cache usage before and after a purge.

FIGURE 10.8
The size of the cached files can grow quickly. Be sure to purge them often.

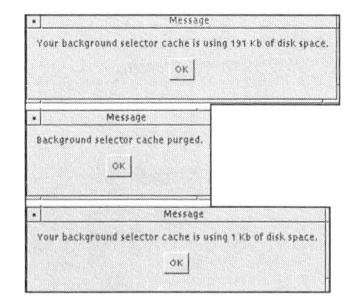

Help

The Help button launches the DOX, or Enlightenment Document Viewer. The Document Viewer contains *The Enlightenment User's Guide*, a list of FAQs, and a link to the Enlightenment Web site, as well as information about the Enlightenment developers.

Window Border Menu

When you right click the window border, the window border menu appears. As you can see in Figure 10.9, the window border menu includes the window options that were discussed in Hour 7, "Using the Panel and the Main Menu," as well as a few others that might not be familiar. We will learn about them in this section.

FIGURE 10.9
The window border menu lets you control the configuration of your windows.

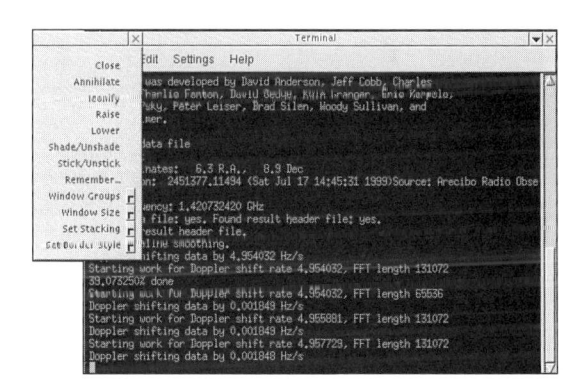

Remember

The Remember dialog box instructs Enlightenment as to which particular window attributes you want it to remember, including window location, size, shaded state, stacking layer (if you have two or more windows stacked on top of each other), border style, whether you have multiple desktops, and the sticky state of the window. You can change any of these attributes at any time; click Remember whenever you make a change you want to keep. Figure 10.10 shows the Application Attributes dialog box, which appears when you click Remember in the window border menu.

FIGURE 10.10
Remember opens the Application Attributes dialog box. Use Remember to keep the configuration of your window the next time you open the same application.

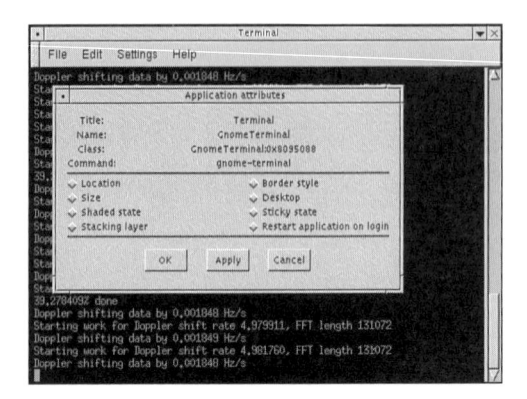

Window Groups

You can organize a set of windows as a window group in order to maintain the same configuration across the group. For example, say that you have 10 GNOME terminals on your desktop. You want to shade them all, and you also want to disable the Kill option. If you place these terminals in a window group, you can set the options for the group and the change will be reflected across every window in the group. As Figure 10.11 shows, you can change the options for border style; iconifying; killing; moving, raising, or lowering the window; stickiness; or shading. The group properties are set in the Group Settings menu, and you can set up your window groups by right-clicking the window border of a member of the group.

Set Border Style

You can configure the kind of border that you want around each individual window on the desktop. Some of the more commonly used border options are

- **Borderless** If you choose this option, your window will have no border and no window menu. To get the border and menu back, hold down Alt and right-click in the body of the window.
- **Border Only** This option will set a thin, colored border around the window, but no menu and no window buttons.
- **Default** Default sets the entire window border around the window, including the window title, buttons, theme, and menu. The Default option is best when you are new to Enlightenment.

FIGURE 10.11
When you organize windows into groups, you can set configurations for the entire group, instead of for individual windows.

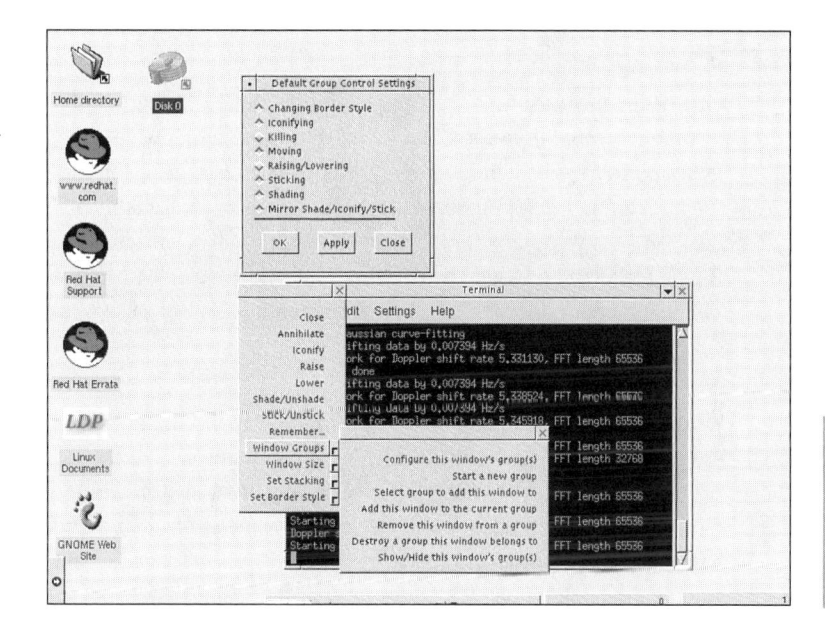

Customizing the Menus

You can change the contents of your Enlightenment User menus by editing the menu configuration files, which are located in $HOME/.enlightenment. The following menus can be edited:

epplets.menu   This file lists the Enlightenment epplets that are installed.

file.menu   This file lists the User menus that appear when you right-click the desktop.

gnome.menu   The GNOME menu appears under Enlightenment, User menus. The gnome.menu file lists the contents of the GNOME menu.

gnome_user.menu   This file displays the contents of the GNOME User Menus, defined on the GNOME Main Menu.

user_apps.menu   This file lists the contents of the User Application list on the Enlightenment main menu. This menu will be the one you are most likely to edit.

You might want to return to section after we have learned more about scripts in Hour 13, "GNOME Processes," but if you look at the examples already in the menu files and follow their example, you will be able to make entries of your own. Have fun! Experiment! If you really break your menus, just delete the .enlightenment file and start over (see the section "Some Common Enlightenment Problems and Solutions," later in this hour).

Desktops

One of the most useful aspects of Enlightenment is its capability to manage multiple and virtual desktops. If you tend to have 10 or more windows open simultaneously, if you want to group your windows according to one task, or if you have applications running in the background that you check on occasion, this feature is ideal. The idea of a virtual desktop goes two steps farther than the traditional X virtual desktop, in which your desktop display can be larger than your actual screen size. With multiple and virtual desktops, you can increase the size of your work area by a factor of two, four, or even twenty.

Virtual Desktops

Virtual desktops, also called *desktop areas*, expand the horizontal size of your workspace. *The Enlightenment User's Guide* compares virtual desktops to multiple sheets of paper placed next to each other on a desk. Just as you would move your pen from paper to paper on a desk, you can drag your mouse to move from one virtual desktop to another. Each desktop has its own GNOME Panel, Iconbox, and Enlightenment Pager. You can make applications sticky so that they appear in each virtual desktop, and you can open different applications in each virtual desktop. For example, you can have your word processing application open in one virtual desktop, games open in another, and a Web site and email open in yet another.

To add or remove a virtual desktop, right-click it and select Virtual Desktop Settings from the Settings menu. You can have virtual desktops oriented vertically, horizontally, or both directions. Select Enable Edge Flip so that you can move to another virtual desktop by dragging the mouse. Use Resistance at Edge of Screen to control the amount of time your mouse must stay at the border of the virtual desktop before moving to the next desktop. Figure 10.12 shows the Virtual Desktop Settings dialog box.

FIGURE 10.12
Use virtual desktops to increase your horizontal workspace.

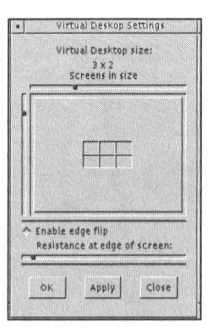

Multiple Desktops

Multiple desktops, like virtual desktops, give you more workspace. Unlike virtual desktops, however, they are "stacked" on top of each other, and act as completely separate desktops. Also, you cannot use your mouse to change from one of these desktops to another. You can define a different theme and background for each desktop.

To add or remove multiple desktops, right-click the desktop and select Multiple Desktop Settings, as shown in Figure 10.13. To add desktops, drag the slider to the right. To remove desktops, drag the slider to the left. You can have up to 32 desktops.

FIGURE 10.13
Each desktop is a complete, separate desktop. Desktops are stacked on top of one another.

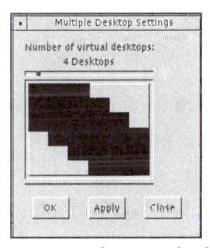

There are several ways to change desktops:

- Click the desktop you want in the GNOME Desk Guide.
- Holding down Ctrl, middle-click the mouse, and then select the desktop you want.
- From the Enlightenment menu, select the Desktop submenu, and then click Goto Next Desktop or Goto Previous Desktop.

There are still more ways to switch desktops in Enlightenment. See *The Enlightenment User's Guide*, which can be opened by middle-clicking the desktop and selecting Help.

Figure 10.14 shows the Desktop submenu of the Enlightenment menu. Use the Desktop menu to move between desktops.

FIGURE 10.14
Features on the Desktop submenu. Try clicking FX—Ripples or FX—Waves, and watch the bottom of your screen. To turn the effect off, click the menu entry again.

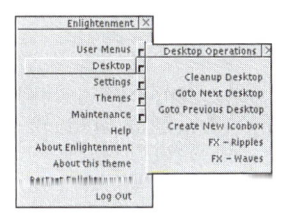

> If you have applications running on a second desktop and you want to remove that desktop, you do not need to close the applications. When you remove the desktop, the windows will automatically move to the original desktop.

Enlightenment Themes

The Enlightenment menu contains a Themes submenu that lists all the Enlightenment themes installed on your machine. Notice that this list is different from the GNOME Control Center theme list. Enlightenment themes work independently of GNOME themes, and you configure them separately.

Enlightenment themes work with the window borders, the Enlightenment Panel, Iconbox, Enlightenment Pager, and ToolTips. GNOME, or gtk, themes affect the GNOME Panel, fonts, icons, and the look and feel of the windows themselves. It is important that you understand this distinction, because the best-looking desktops have GNOME and window manager themes that complement each other. For example, blueHeart is a popular theme that has both Enlightenment and gtk versions.

To change your current Enlightenment theme, middle-click the desktop to open the Enlightenment menu, and select Themes. A menu of themes currently installed on your system will appear. Click the theme you want, and the new theme will replace the old one. We will learn more about themes in Hour 12, "Understanding and Using Themes."

> It is a good idea to purge your cached files after installing a new theme or background.

Keybindings

Keybindings, also called *hotkeys*, are keyboard combinations that accomplish the same task as a mouse or menu item. Keybindings definitions are kept in the `keybindings.cfg` file.

> You can create your own keybindings by editing the `keybindings.cfg` file. See *The Enlightenment User's Guide*.

Table 10.2 lists some of the most useful default Enlightenment keybindings.

TABLE 10.2 Enlightenment Keybindings

Keybinding	Description
Ctrl+Alt+Home	Clean up windows on desktop
Ctrl+Alt+End	Restart Enlightenment
Ctrl+Alt+Left arrow	Go to previous desktop
Ctrl+Alt+Right arrow	Go to next desktop
Ctrl+Alt+X	Close window
Ctrl+Alt+K	Kill window
Ctrl+Alt+R	Shade/unshade window
Ctrl+Alt+I	Iconify window
Ctrl+Alt+S	Stick/unstick window
Ctrl+Alt+F1 to F12	Go to desktop number 1 to 11
Alt+Tab	Switch the focus to next window (cycle through windows)
Shift+Alt+Left arrow	Move to virtual desktop on the left
Shift+Alt+Right arrow	Move to virtual desktop on the right
Shift+Alt+Up arrow	Move to virtual desktop above
Shift+Alt+Down arrow	Move to virtual desktop below

Using the Enlightenment External Shell (eesh)

eesh is a utility for interacting with Enlightenment via IPC (Inter-Process Communication). If you are familiar with Microsoft Windows, it works a bit like Windows DDE (Dynamic Data Exchange). From a terminal, you can send commands to view aspects of Enlightenment or make changes in the configuration. The changes immediately take place in the window manager, and Enlightenment generates a message on the desktop concerning the changes. eesh is most useful to advanced users of Enlightenment, and you should be careful when using it.

Still, novices can use eesh for some things, such as figuring out what is going on when something on the desktop looks wrong or behaves strangely. It is also fun to play with.

Opening eesh

There are three options for opening eesh:

1. eesh -e *[command]*—This option opens eesh, sends the command to Enlightenment, and exits.
2. eesh -wait *[command]*—This option opens eesh and sends the command. eesh waits for input before exiting.
3. eesh—If you enter eesh without an option, eesh will enter interactive mode, which means that the cursor drops down a line and waits for input. At this point, you can enter any eesh command, including help.

If you forget the options, enter eesh -h to see a list.

Getting Help in eesh

To get a list of all the eesh commands, type **help** from within the interactive mode. A list of all the eesh commands will appear. The output of eesh help is shown in Figure 10.15.

FIGURE 10.15

eesh is a handy Enlightenment utility.

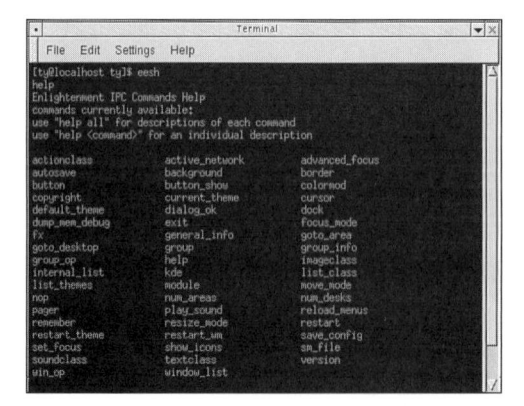

To get more detailed help, you can

- Type **help all** for a brief description of what every command does.
- Type **help *[command]*** for a detailed description of what an individual command does.

Exiting eesh

To exit eesh, enter Ctrl-D or Ctrl-C.

Some useful and harmless eesh commands are included in the Exercises.

Some Common Enlightenment Problems and Solutions

The goal of Enlightenment is to be as stable and easy to use as possible. While it is an outstanding window manager and my personal favorite, it is still in development. Undiscovered bugs and unforeseen problems sometimes occur. This section gives you just a few hints to try before you give up in disgust or post a message to the GNOME or Enlightenment mailing list.

Edit or Delete ~/.enlightenment Directory to Fix a Broken Session

The ~/.enlightenment directory contains files that control your account's Enlightenment sessions. If you lose your Pager or virtual terminals, if your windows appear strange or bare, something in this directory is often responsible. In fact, if anything goes wrong with Enlightenment, try deleting this file first. After you delete ~/.enlightenment, restart Enlightenment. Of course, because this file contains all your configuration information, the system will return to its default state. This usually means that you will have to do your Enlightenment configurations over again.

Enlightenment Is Slow

The flexibility and configurability of Enlightenment, which are two of its greatest advantages, can also cause problems if your system is low on memory. Your system memory, the size of your swap file, and the amount of memory in your video card all affect the speed at which Enlightenment operates. If Enlightenment is slow on startup or when opening a new window, try these steps:

1. Run a "cleaner" theme on both GNOME and Enlightenment. The simpler a theme, the less memory and other system resources it eats up. Try a simple background and a theme such as "Sensible" or "Xclean." You will learn more about obtaining and installing themes in Hour 12.

2. Try a different window manager. Your system simply might not be able to support Enlightenment. Simpler window managers like sawmill are built to be fast, and often work well for users with older hardware or slow X servers.

3. If your X server is on a network, not on the same machine as the X client, you might have a network problem. Problems with X are beyond the scope of this book; visit www.x.org or www.x11.org for more information.

Sound Does Not Work

Sound is not always easy to configure in Linux. Make sure that your sound card is properly configured and that you get sound in other applications. If you are getting sound in other applications, but not in Enlightenment, open the Settings menu (right-click the desktop), select Audio, and verify that sound is enabled.

Segmentation Fault

Enlightenment is seriously broken. Everything freezes, and then you get a segmentation fault message.

You have most likely encountered a bug. Enlightenment is still in development, and bugs still pop up now and then. Hour 22, "Upgrading GNOME and Joining the GNOME Project," and Appendix A, "Troubleshooting," go over debugging in detail.

Getting Help

If you want to learn more about Enlightenment, or have a problem that you can't solve, check the following sources for help:

- *The Enlightenment User's Guide* comes with your Enlightenment package. Click Help on the Enlightenment menu to see it.
- The Enlightenment FAQs are updated every month or so. Check http://www.enlightenment.org or http://e.i-docs.org/.
- I-Docs hosts a Web forum where you can post questions and get answers about Enlightenment, at http://forum.hole.org/list.php3?num=1&collapse=1&.
- If you have a problem that cannot be solved through the previously mentioned channels, try the Enlightenment development mailing list, at http://enlightenment.org/mailman/listinfo/e-develop.

> Check the mailing list archives before posting a question to ensure that a solution to your problem hasn't already been posted. Also, remember that everyone on this project is a volunteer. Flames about how lousy Enlightenment is or demands to help fix a general problem will most likely be ignored.
>
> For some hints on posting mailing list queries, see Hour 22.

Summary

In this hour, you learned how to use the Enlightenment Iconbox and Pager. You navigated the Enlightenment menus and learned how to configure your desktop using the Settings menu. You learned more about Enlightenment windows and virtual and multiple desktops, and were introduced to themes. You also were introduced to `eesh`, the Enlightenment External Shell, and discovered the solutions to some common Enlightenment problems. Finally, you learned where you can get help if you encounter a problem that you can't fix yourself.

Q&A

Q What is the horizontal bar at the top of my desktop and what is its purpose?

A The dragbar is used to navigate around multiple desktops. To move from one desktop to another, drag the dragbar down until you see the other desktop, and then click the mouse in the new desktop.

Q Where do the `.enlightenment` files come from, and won't it hurt my system to delete them?

A The `.enlightenment` files are regenerated by Enlightenment every time there is a change in the configuration of Enlightenment. If you delete the entire directory, Enlightenment will regenerate all the necessary files the next time you start Enlightenment. (This is why Enlightenment takes a long time to start when you log in for the first time.)

Workshop

The quiz questions and exercises are designed to increase your understanding and to encourage you to continue experimenting. Answers appear in Appendix B, "Answers."

Quiz

1. What is the difference in function between the Iconbox and the Enlightenment Pager?
2. Which Enlightenment menu appears when you left-click the desktop? Which menu appears when you right-click it? How else can you access these menus?
3. How do you turn off the ToolTips?
4. What does it mean when a window has the focus?
5. What is the difference between virtual desktops and multiple desktops?

Exercises

1. Compare the GNOME Panel to the Enlightenment Iconbox and GNOME tasklist. Do they have the same functionality? Are there differences? Which set of tools do you
prefer?

2. Open the Focus Settings dialog box and check Focus Follows Pointer, then change the configuration to Focus Follows Pointer Sloppy. What is the difference between the two settings?

3. Query the size of your background cached file, note the size of the file, then change the background of your desktop using Desktop Background Settings. Query your background cache again. What changed?

4. Remove the window border from one of your windows, and then get it back again.

5. Open eesh in interactive mode in a terminal. Enter the following commands: **copyright**, **list-themes**, **window_list**, **restart_wm**. What does each command do?

Hour 11

Customizing Your GNOME Environment

Virtually every aspect of the GNOME desktop can be customized, from the look and feel of the desktop—including font, background, and sounds—to the behavior of GNOME applications. Most customizations are done via the GNOME Control Center. This hour is short and not difficult to understand, but the information is detailed, and there are many instances of practical application.

In this hour, you will

- Use the GNOME Control Center capplets to customize your desktop.
- Select your default text editor and font.
- Customize your keyboard, desktop sounds, and mouse behavior.
- Adjust the look and feel of GNOME applications.
- Conduct advanced session management and reset the session to default values.

Using the GNOME Control Center

The GNOME Control Center, or GCC, is composed of a collection of small configuration applications, or *capplets*, each of which enable you to configure a part of the GNOME desktop. The number and kind of capplets that appear in the GCC varies according to the kinds of GNOME applications you have on your desktop. You might not have all the capplets described in this hour, or you might have some that are not described here, but the information in this hour should be used as a starting point to explore all the capplets that you have. The capplets listed in this hour come with the base October GNOME installation packages.

As shown in Figure 11.1, the GNOME Control Center has two sections. The capplet menu on the left lists all available capplets according to function, and the window on the right is the workspace for the capplet you choose. To open a capplet, click the capplet in the menu, and it will open in the workspace.

FIGURE 11.1

Most customization of the GNOME desktop is done in the GNOME Control Center.

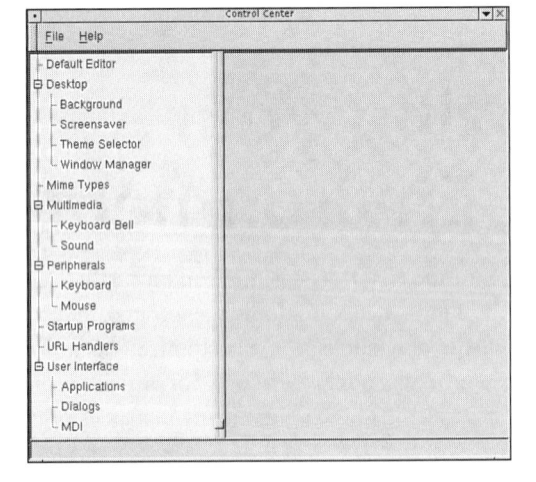

> Some capplets also appear in the Main Menu as individual items. Clicking on these entries will open the GNOME Control Center with the capplet you have chosen.

Not all the capplets in the GCC deal with customization. Capplets such as Theme Selector, MIME Types, URL Handlers, Dialogs, and MDI will be described in the hours that correspond with their function.

Default Editor

Use the Default Editor capplet to select your favorite editor. For every GNOME application that has an Edit feature, the editor you choose here will open. Figure 11.2 depicts the Default Editor capplet.

FIGURE 11.2
The Default Editor capplet is shown with the menu of available editors open.

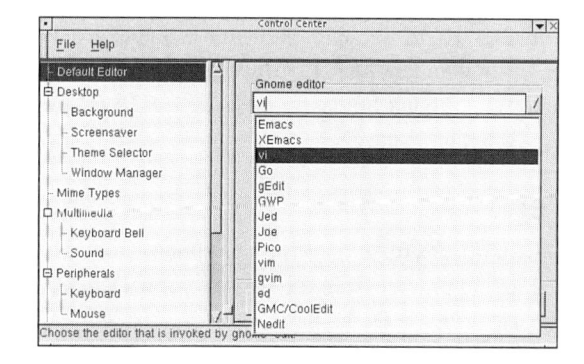

Background

The Desktop Background capplet, shown in Figure 11.3, enables you to choose a background for your desktop. You can select the precise color you want from a color palette, choose two colors for a gradient, or select a pixmap image. The pixmap image can be stored anywhere in the directory tree. Use the Browse button to locate the file you want to use for the image. The image you select can be tiled on the screen, centered, or scaled to fit your screen size.

FIGURE 11.3
Use either the GNOME Desktop Background capplet or the Enlightenment Desktop Background Settings tool to select a background. Do not use both at the same time.

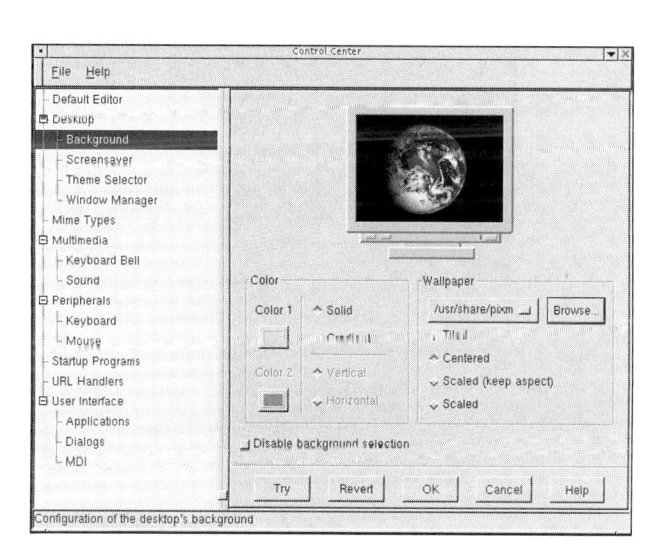

> If you have a virtual screen resolution that is larger than your actual physical screen size, when you select Scaled, the image will scale to the virtual screen size.

As you learned in Hour 10, Enlightenment also has a background configuration tool. If you prefer to use Enlightenment Desktop Background Settings to select a background, then select Disable Background Selection in the GNOME capplet before you select your background using Enlightenment.

Screensaver

GNOME comes with dozens of screensavers to choose from. Highlight the screensaver you are interested in and preview it in the Screen Saver Demo box. Figure 11.4 shows the Xmatrix screensaver in the Demo box.

FIGURE 11.4
GNOME has a much larger variety of screensavers than Windows does.

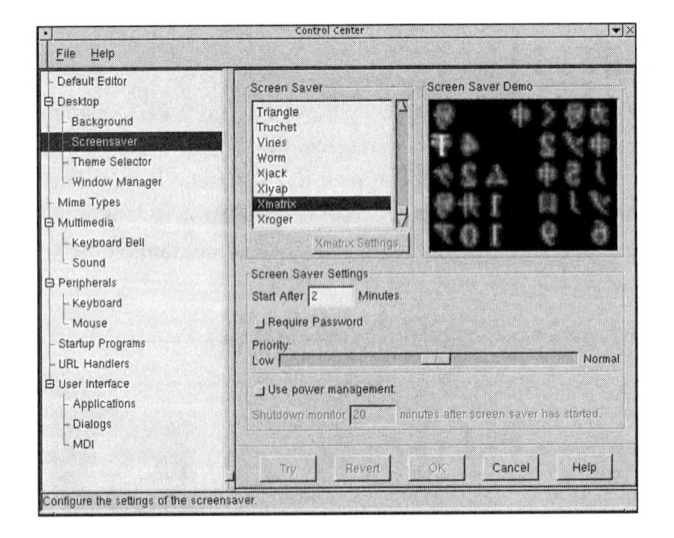

You can control how long the screen will be inactive before the screensaver comes on, and whether a password will be required to unlock the screen. If your monitor supports power management, the entire monitor will shut down after the period of time you dictate, for example, 20 minutes. Some monitors have a fixed time that they wait before shutting down, and some do not support power management. Check your monitor documentation if the power management feature does not seem to work with your monitor.

Changing the Font

If you want to change the GNOME font, use Theme Selector. The primary function of the Theme Selector capplet is to change your desktop theme, but it is also used to change the default GNOME font. We will discuss themes in greater detail in Hour 12, "Understanding and Using Themes," but for now we will look at custom fonts. As you will learn in Hour 12, you can change the look and feel of your desktop with themes. Each theme has a corresponding font, but in many cases you will want to choose a font independent of the theme. To select your own font, check Use Custom Font in the User Font field, as shown in Figure 11.5. The current font appears in a bar. Click the bar and the Pick a Font dialog box appears.

FIGURE 11.5
Select a whimsical font or a clear font in large type with the Custom Font tool.

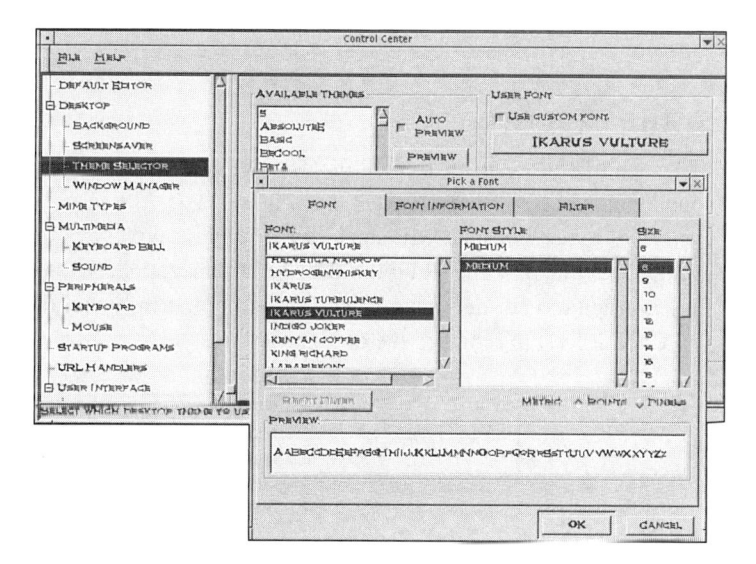

Click a font to preview it in the Preview box. The names of the GNOME font styles are slightly different from the MS Windows font styles: Medium is the same as the Windows regular, oblique is the same as Windows italic, and bold is, of course, bold. You can also select the size of your font, which is particularly useful if you have trouble reading text on the monitor.

Keyboard Bell

Use the Keyboard Bell capplet to customize your keyboard bell to the exact pitch, tone, and duration you want. The Volume slider's values are measured in decibels; the Pitch slider's values, in megahertz; and the Duration slider's values, in milliseconds. Click Test to hear how your bell will sound with each new positioning of the sliders. When you are satisfied, click OK. The Keyboard Bell capplet is shown in Figure 11.6.

FIGURE 11.6
Adjust the keyboard bell to the exact pitch, tone, and duration you want.

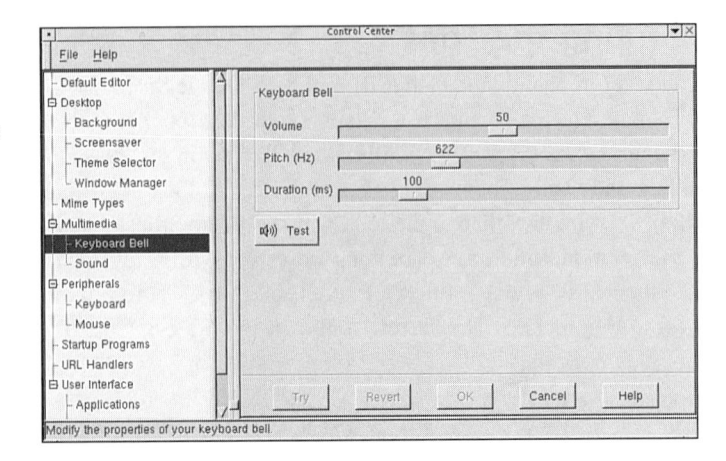

Sound Events

The Sound Events capplet lists all the desktop events and the pathname for the default sound that is played for each event (see Figure 11.7). You can change any of the sound event files to another GNOME sound file or to your own .wav file. To change the sound event, locate the new file using the Browse button, and click the file to select it. Click Play to listen to your new sound, and OK, to permanently include it in the Sound Events list. Click Revert to return to the original settings.

FIGURE 11.7
Use some of the sound events from GNOME games to enliven your desktop events!

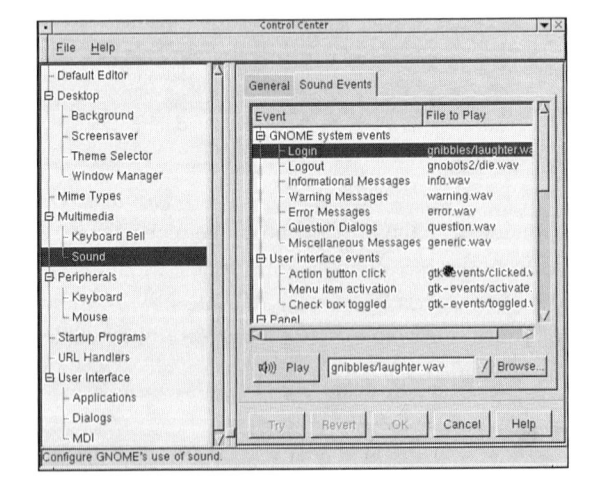

Keyboard

The Keyboard capplet lets you control the key auto-repeat function and the keyboard click, as shown in Figure 11.8. If you turn on the auto-repeat function, you can repeat the action of a key by holding it down. Customize auto-repeat by controlling the amount of time in milliseconds that you must hold the key down for it to repeat, and the number of times the action will repeat when the key is held down. In practice, it can be difficult to discern a difference in the auto-repeat settings, but you can achieve different results if you have very sensitive fingers.

You can also enable the keyboard click, which will cause a soft clicking sound to be played whenever you press a key. Test the settings until you are satisfied. Don't forget to click Try after each adjustment to the settings.

FIGURE 11.8
The Keyboard capplet has just a few customization options.

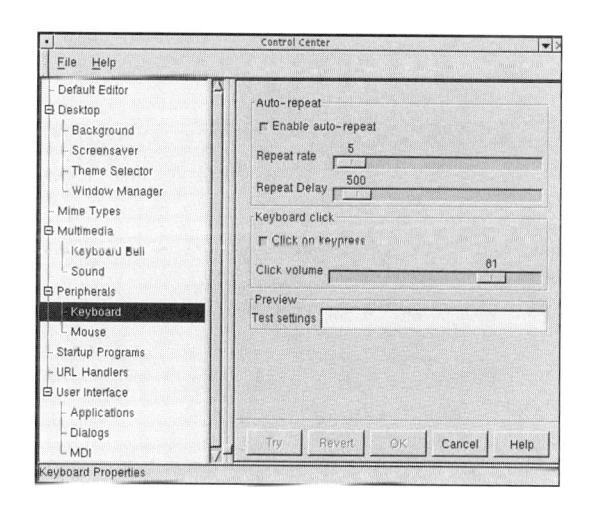

Mouse

The Mouse capplet controls the basic functions of the mouse. You can make the mouse left handed or right-handed using this capplet. You can also control the sensitivity of the mouse by selecting the mouse's acceleration and threshold. The *acceleration* of the mouse is the speed at which the mouse pointer moves across the screen when you move the physical mouse with your hand. The *threshold* controls the speed that you must move the physical mouse before the pointer begins to move. It can help to think of the threshold as the amount of pressure you must apply to the physical mouse before it will move the pointer on the screen, or how many milliseconds you must move the physical mouse before the pointer moves on the screen. To make the mouse the most sensitive (and most difficult to control), move the sliders toward Fast acceleration and Small threshold. For a mouse that's easiest to control(that is, least sensitive), select a Slow acceleration with a Large threshold. Figure 11.9 shows an acceleration and a threshold that should feel comfortable for most users.

FIGURE 11.9
Whether you are impatient and prefer a sensitive mouse, or have trouble controlling the mouse and prefer it to react more slowly, you can customize the mouse's behavior with the Mouse capplet.

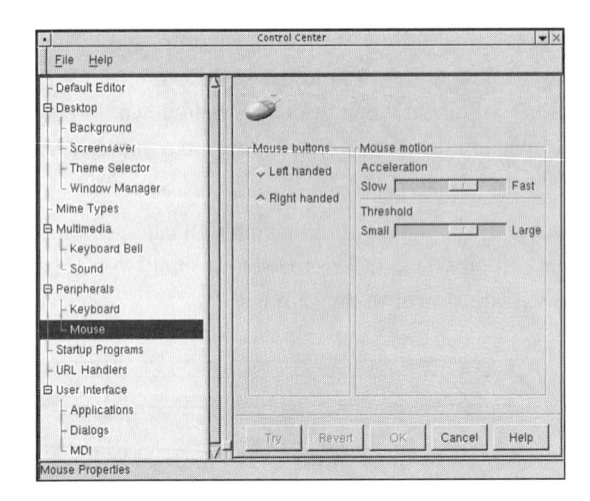

Applications

The Applications capplet, shown in Figure 11.10, contains options for you to customize GNOME and GNOME-compliant applications.

FIGURE 11.10
Customize the behavior of GNOME applications with the Applications capplet.

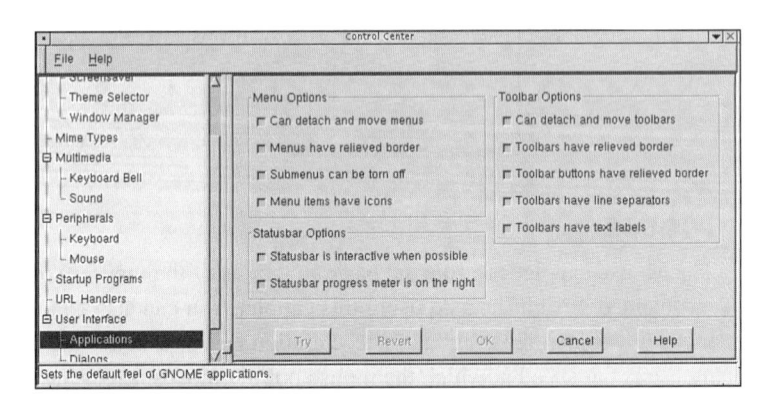

The menus and submenus of a GNOME application can be dragged away from the application itself and stand alone on the desktop as a separate window. Select Can Detach and Move Menus and Submenus Can Be Torn Off to enable this option. Menus Have Relieved Border is a simple appearance option, which will cause a border to appear around menus. Select Menu Items Have Icons if you would like small icons to appear next to each item on GNOME menus. Figure 11.11 illustrates some examples of the options described.

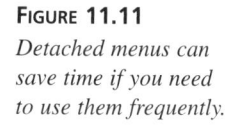

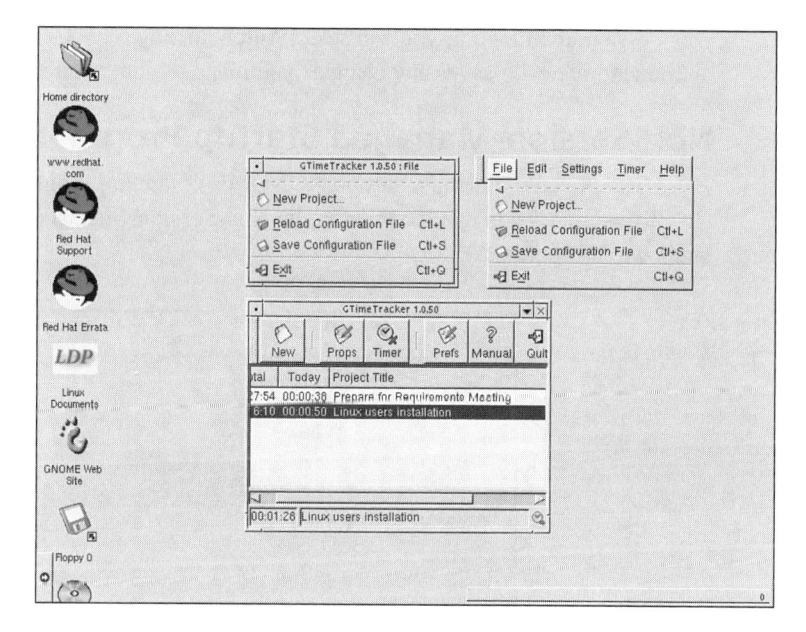

FIGURE 11.11
Detached menus can save time if you need to use them frequently.

The Statusbar Options are self-explanatory; an interactive statusbar will give information about what the application is doing while the statusbar is running. The option Statusbar Progress Meter Is on the Right places the statusbar meter to the right of the statusbar, instead of below it.

The Toolbar Options are similar to the Menu Options. You can detach toolbars from the application and move them around the desktop in the same way as menus. You can also choose to have a text description for each item on the toolbar, instead of just an icon.

Session Management

We touched on session management in Hour 5, "Exploring the Desktop." In this hour, you will use Session Manager to configure your desktop sessions exactly as you want them, and they will be set up that way every time you log in until you change them again.

To open the Session Manager, click Startup Programs in the GNOME Control Center. We will describe each configuration option in detail.

Options

The Prompt on Logout option enables or disables the dialog box that prompts you to save your session when you click Logout. If you do not want to be prompted to save your session upon logout, you can select Automatically Save Changes to Session. This option automatically saves any changes you make to your session when you log out.

Non-Session-Managed Startup Programs

If you want to automatically start non–GNOME-compliant programs when you start your GNOME session, you can list them in the Non-Session-Managed Startup Programs field, as shown in Figure 11.12.

FIGURE 11.12
The non–GNOME-compliant programs seti@home and wvdial will automatically open with every new GNOME session.

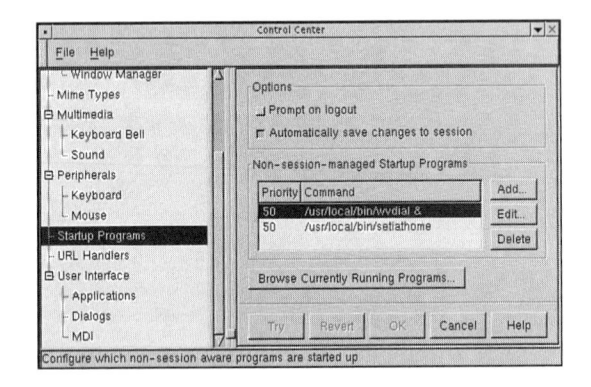

To add an application to the list, click Add and enter the application in the dialog box. The default priority for applications is 50. If you have a program that must be started before other programs, set a lower priority for the first program. Programs that have lower priorities will start before those with higher priorities. For example, if you want your PPP dialer and Netscape Communicator to start automatically, give the PPP dialer a lower priority, so it will start before Communicator.

If you want to start a GNOME-compliant program automatically upon login, simply have it running when you log out, and it will automatically start every time you log in to GNOME.

Browse Currently Running Programs

Before logging out, browse the programs that are currently running so that you can verify that your session is the way you want it. If you want a program not currently running to open upon login, either open it, or simply add it to the list. If the program is on the list, it will automatically start the next time you start GNOME, even if it is not open when you log out. To browse currently running programs, open Startup Programs capplet in the GNOME Control Center and click Browse Currently Running Programs. The Session Properties window displays all the programs currently running. Figure 11.13 shows a typical list of running programs in a GNOME session.

FIGURE 11.13
The programs listed in Session Properties automatically open when you log in to GNOME.

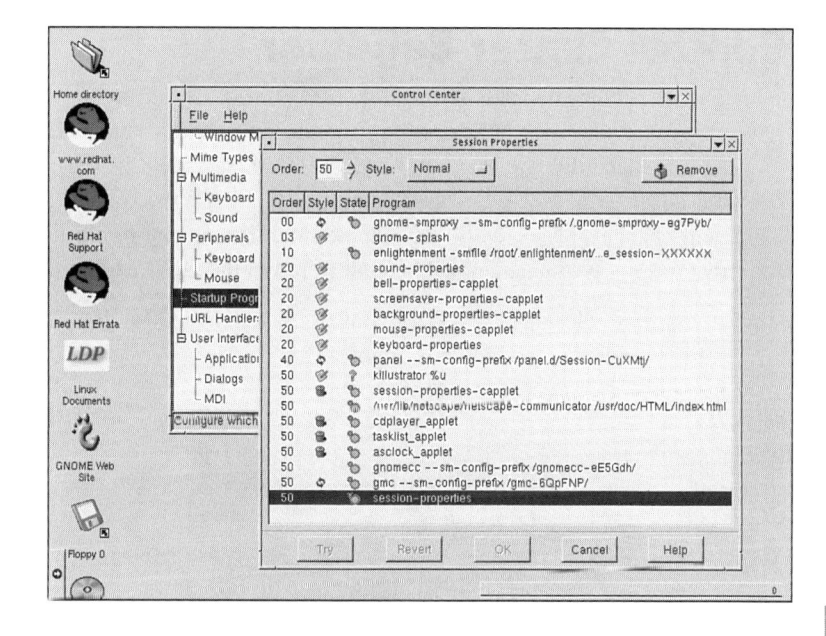

Resetting the GNOME Session

If you want to reset the GNOME session to its default condition, delete the $HOME/.gnome/session file from your home directory and restart GNOME. All configurations you have made to your GNOME session will disappear, and your GNOME desktop will return to the state it was in the first time you logged in. This can be quite a drastic action, because all custom items on your panel, launchers in the Main Menu, all icons you made on the desktop, and all configurations made with GNOME Control Center will disappear. If your session is irrecoverably broken, however, deleting the session file might be the only solution. It is a good idea to log the customizations you have made to your GNOME session, or to make a backup of the $HOME/.gnome/session file before deleting it, so you can recover your customizations later.

Control Center Behavior

There are many capplets in the GNOME Control Center, and if you make several changes at once, it can be easy to forget to save some changes. If you made changes to a capplet and did not click OK or Cancel in the capplet, the capplet name will appear in red in the GCC menu. Before closing GCC, either press Cancel or OK to cancel or save your changes, respectively. The capplet will then appear in black and the next capplet that has unsaved changes will appear in red in the GCC workspace.

If you try to close the GNOME Control Center without saving changes, you will get a warning message, as shown in Figure 11.14.

FIGURE 11.14
If you forget to save changes in a capplet, GCC will remind you.

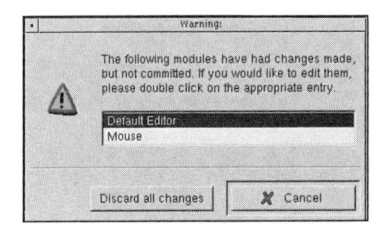

Summary

In this hour, you used the GNOME Control Center to configure and customize your desktop environment. You selected a default editor, a desktop background, a font, and a screensaver. You customized your sound events, keyboard, and mouse behavior, as well as the behavior of the GNOME applications. You used the advanced session management features of the Startup Programs capplet to fully customize your GNOME sessions. You learned how to reset your GNOME session in the event of an irrecoverable session disruption. You also learned how the GNOME Control Center ensures that you save changes to your configuration.

Q&A

Q I used the GNOME Control Center to make changes to the application menus and taskbars, but how do I customize the size and placement of the windows?

A Remember that, although GNOME controls the applications themselves, the window manager controls the size and placement of windows. Review Hour 4, "Working with Window Managers," and Hour 10, "Exploring Enlightenment," for information on customizing your windows.

Q I changed the font in GNOME Control Center. I want to return to the original font, but I don't remember what it was. Do I have to delete my entire session?

A No. If you would like to revert to the previous font, open the Theme Selector capplet and click Revert. If you haven't logged out since you made the change, your original font will reappear.

Q Can I use sound clips from songs or movies for GNOME sound events?

A You can use any sound clip that is in .wav file format as a GNOME sound event, including recordings that you make yourself!

Workshop

The quiz questions and exercises are designed to increase your understanding and to encourage you to continue experimenting. Answers appear in Appendix B, "Answers."

Quiz

1. What is a capplet?
2. What should you do in the GNOME Control Center if you want to use the Enlightenment Background Settings tool to select a background?
3. What kind of file is used for a sound event?
4. How do you add applications that are not GNOME-compliant to your GNOME session?
5. What happens if you try to exit GNOME Control Center without saving your changes?

Exercises

1. Open the GNOME Control Center. Do you have any capplets that are not mentioned in this hour? If so, what does their function appear to be?
2. Open the Default Editor capplet and choose your favorite editor. Try gEdit if you don't have a favorite.
3. Open the Screensaver capplet and select a screensaver that interests you.
4. Exchange the login sound event for a sound from a GNOME game (try gnibbles/laughter.wav).
5. Adjust the mouse controls to the fastest acceleration and the smallest threshold. Is the mouse difficult to control?

6. Configure the Applications capplet so you can drag menus off the application window and onto the desktop.
7. Configure the Applications capplet so that GNOME application menus have no icons. Open a GNOME application, such as gEdit. Do the menu items have icons? Close the GNOME application. Enable menu icons. Reopen the GNOME application. Does the menu contain icons?

HOUR 12

Understanding and Using Themes

One of the fundamental goals of the GNOME Project is to create a desktop environment that can be customized and configured to meet the user's exact desires. To this end, the GNOME developers have set another goal to create a suite of tools that enable an ordinary user to alter his or her desktop without programming, and without understanding anything about the underlying GNOME architecture. One of the most dramatic and visually arresting results of these goals is the use of themes.

> GNOME is not the only desktop project to use themes. KDE/KWM, AfterStep, BlackBox, Enlightenment, IceWM, sawmill and Windowmaker all use themes to change the look and feel of the desktop. This chapter concentrates on GTK and Enlightenment themes, but the same ideas apply to other window managers and desktop environments.

In this hour, you will

- Explore how themes work with the Gimp ToolKit and X to create a graphical user interface on your desktop.
- Learn about the two kinds of gtk themes and the components of a gtk theme.
- Obtain and install gtk themes.
- Obtain and install Enlightenment themes.

The Magic of Themes

If you were to walk into a room of people using GNOME, and you looked at each screen, you would see a dizzying variety of designs. One desktop might have a very bare and sparse look to it (like most of the screen shots in this book). It might have a plain background, ordinary sans-serif fonts, and plain window borders. Another desktop might seem more like the console of a starship than a computer, with glowing green fonts and menus that appear in the center of starbursts. One desktop might remind you of Merlin's spellbook, with black webs and pop-up menus that resemble clouds of smoke. Some people might have desktops that look very much like those of Windows, Macintosh, SGI, or Amiga.

All these looks are created by different themes that work with GNOME and your window manager to make your computer look like anything you can dream of, limited only by the imagination of the theme developers and the amount of memory in your video card.

How Themes Work

In GNOME, you actually choose two themes for your desktop: a gtk theme and a window manager theme. The gtk theme controls the look of your GNOME applications, menus, and Panel. The window manager theme controls the look of the window borders, window manager menus, tools, and pop-ups. Some themes, such as blueHeart, include their own menus. Finally, you choose a background that corresponds with the themes on your desktop.

The gtk theme and the window manager theme work differently, but the general idea is similar. Before we understand how themes work, we must understand a little about how the graphical user interface works.

As we learned in Hour 4, "Working with Window Managers," the X Window system enables you to interact with your computer with a mouse, instead of by merely typing commands on a keyboard. The X libraries interpret a mouse click on a menu item or button into a command that the kernel understands. Before you can use menus and dialog boxes, however, something must give directions to X to create the menu, checkbox, or button, so that it appears on the desktop. In GNOME, the set of libraries that provides this function is called the *Gimp Toolkit*, or GTK. GTK is an API, or application programming interface. An *API* is a programming library that makes it easier to create graphical user interfaces for programs.

Figure 12.1 shows a window from the GNOME Address Book. You see a set of tabs on the top of the window, which you click to go to different dialog boxes. The dialog box shown contains a set of checkboxes on the left and some buttons in the middle. On the right is a box titled Phone List, in which numbers appear after you have entered them in the Number field. The appearance, location, and function of all these items are controlled by GTK.

FIGURE 12.1
GTK controls all the dialog box components that perform some action. The Basic gtk theme is shown here with the X11 Enlightenment theme.

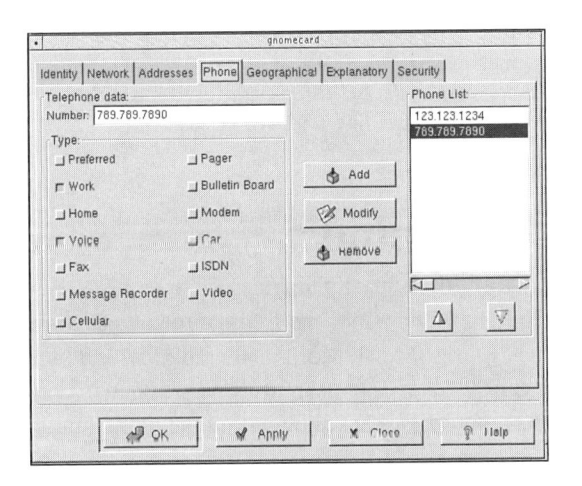

When you apply a theme to your desktop, the theme tells GTK what color to make the box, the buttons, and the fields. It gives instructions on whether the field color will change when you place the mouse over it, what color an active versus an inactive tab will be, and in what font the menu items will appear. Figure 12.2 shows the same dialog box as that in Figure 12.1, but with a different theme. Notice how the look of the dialog box is completely different, but the elements are the same.

FIGURE 12.2

The same window as in Figure 12.1 is shown with the Expensive gtk theme and the Shiny Metal Enlightenment theme. Notice how different it looks!

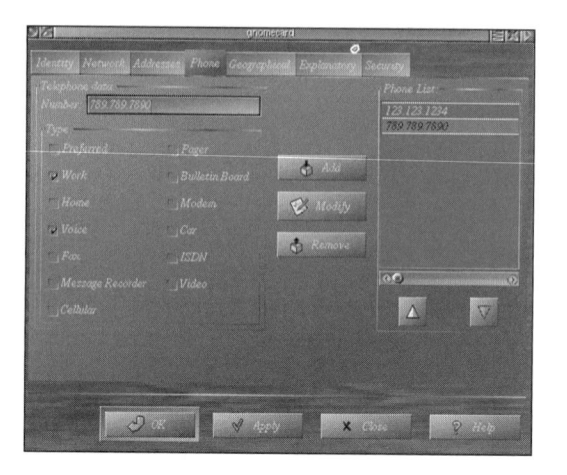

> It is important to understand that only applications written using GTK are affected by gtk themes. Other APIs such as Qt, which is used by KDE, and Motif, which is used by Netscape, will look the same regardless of what gtk theme you use. Keyboard shortcuts are also different when different GUI libraries are used. Do not get confused if a shortcut that works in WordPerfect does not work with gEdit.

Kinds of GTK Themes

There are two kinds of gtk themes: plain (also called gtkrc) themes and pixmap themes. Plain themes only change the colors and fonts of the items in your applications. Some examples are Blue-N-Gray, Metal, MorphiusX, ThinIce, and buffyEro. They tend to be fast, because the GTK widget only deals with color schemes and fonts. Pixmap themes, on the other hand, can look like anything within the limits of the GTK widget itself.

NEW TERM A *pixmap* lets you store a picture as data in a file that can then be used by other files, such as a GTK widget. (This analogy is not totally accurate, but, to help you visualize the concept, you can think of a pixmap as a digital *map* of a *picture*.)

gtkrc themes are much faster than pixmap themes, because with a pixmap theme, each pixmap must be loaded separately into a window on the screen. Pixmap themes eat up system resources and can slow down your whole desktop, but, if you have sufficient memory, they can be well worth it. Figure 12.3 shows the gtk blueHeart theme with the Enlightenment blueHeart theme.

FIGURE 12.3
blueHeart is one of the most popular themes available. To get the full effect, view the screenshot at http://e.themes.org.

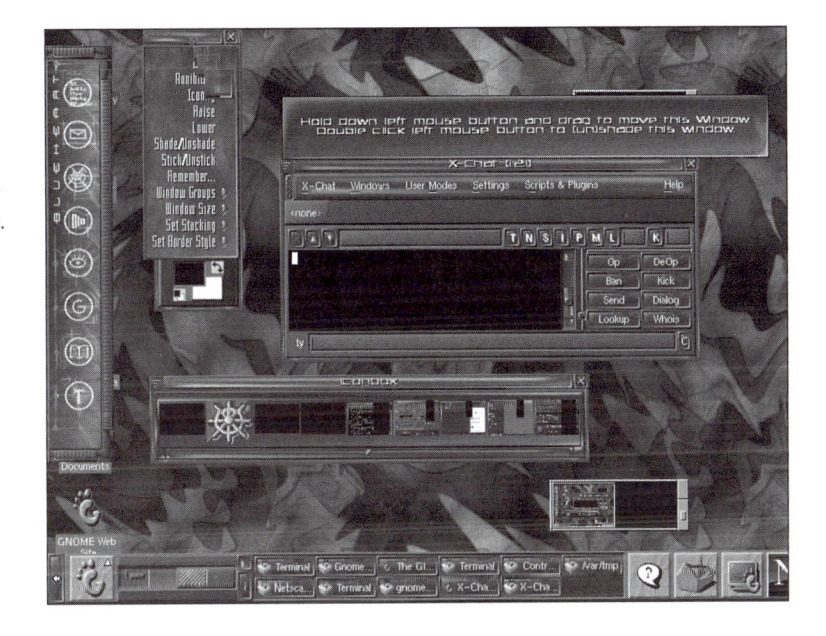

Components of a gtk Theme

There are two parts to a theme: the engine and the gtkrc file, or configuration file. Pixmap themes also have .png files, which are the actual pixmaps. A GTK engine loads the GTK libraries that are needed by the theme so they can be drawn on the screen. The engine "instructs" the theme on how to draw a particular widget. If you look at different themes, you will notice that the components look different. Some have large, flat buttons; some buttons are narrow and look three-dimensional. Some themes use radio buttons, and some use check boxes. Some scrollbars are oblong, and others are rectangular. These differences are because of different engines for the individual themes. You must have the appropriate engine installed on your machine for the theme to work.

NEW TERM A *widget* is an item in a window that performs some task, such as a the function of a button, scrollbar, or menu.

The gtkrc file contains information on the fonts, colors, and engine for GTK to use. Plain themes are made with just the gtkrc file. The pixmap themes also have graphical image, or .png, files.

Libraries Needed for gtk Themes

To run a gtk theme, you must have the following libraries installed:

- glib
- gtk libraries
- gtk-engines

Before you install a particular theme, make sure that you have the correct version of the libraries for that theme; the required library version will be listed in the theme summary on the gtk Themes Web site at `http://gtk.themes.org`. Use GTK Downloads on the Web site to obtain the latest version of glib, gtk+, and gtk-engines.

Obtaining and Installing gtk Themes

The gtk-engines module comes with many popular themes. These themes are automatically installed when you compile gtk-engines. In addition, the gtk Themes Web site, `http://gtk.themes.org`, has more than 100 themes available for download, links to theme sites for window managers, and some excellent tutorials on creating your own themes.

Have a specific location to store all the tarballs that you download. For example, you can download a new theme to `/var/tmp`, and then copy it to `/usr/src/gtk_themes`.

> You should store all your tarballs in a directory such as `/usr/src`. When you want to uninstall or upgrade a module, you must know where the source files are.

Installing a gtk Theme

Installing a theme is easy. Simply open the GNOME Control Center from Main Menu, Settings, GNOME Control Center. Double-click Theme Selector to launch the theme selector capplet. Click Install New Theme, and enter the pathname of the `tar.gz` file in the dialog box that appears. Close GNOME Control Center, and then reopen it and run Theme Selector again. If installed correctly, your new theme will appear in the Available Themes list.

> You can also install a theme manually. `cd` to `/usr/share/themes`, and create a new directory with the theme name. Copy the theme tarball into the new directory, and unpack it using the command
>
> `tar -zxvf [theme_filename].tar.gz`

If your theme does not appear, make sure that your GTK, glib, and gtk-engines libraries are correctly installed, and that you have the most up-to-date versions. If the theme still doesn't work, try installing the theme manually and pay careful attention to any error messages. If you cannot figure out the error on your own, send an email with the complete error message and a description of the problem to the GNOME Mailing List at gnome-list@gnome.org.

Using a New Theme

Using a new theme is even easier than installing it. Open the GNOME Control Center by clicking Main Menu, Settings, GNOME Control Center, and select Theme Selector. Scroll through the Available Themes list until you find one that looks interesting. Check the Auto Preview box and click once on the theme name. The Preview box displays the new theme. If you want to see how the theme looks on your desktop, click Try. Your entire desktop will be transformed to reflect the new theme. If you like the theme, click OK, and the new theme will become your permanent theme. To go back to your old theme, click Revert. Figure 12.4 shows the Theme Selector in the GNOME Control Center.

FIGURE 12.4
Use the Theme Selector to try out a new theme. You can change themes as often as you like.

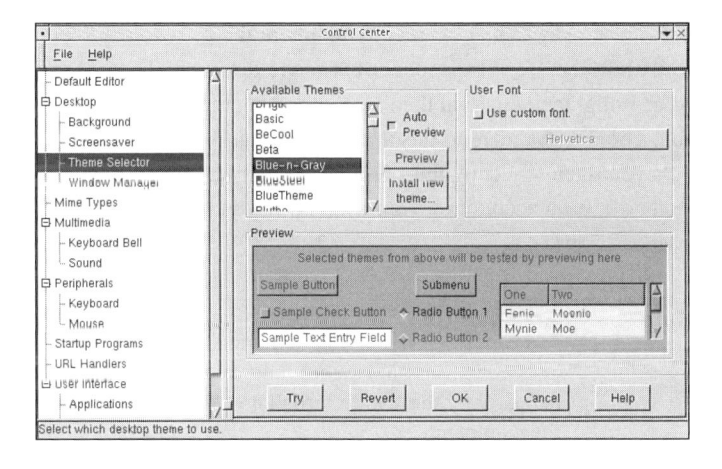

Uninstalling a Theme

Uninstalling a theme is also simple. All the gtk themes are located in the /usr/share/themes directory. To delete a theme, simply delete its subdirectory from /usr/share/themes. The next time you start the Theme Selector, the theme will no longer appear. If you saved the original theme tarball, you can reinstall the theme at any time.

Installing Enlightenment Themes

After you have chosen a gtk theme, you should find a window manager theme that complements it. http://gtk.theme.org has links to theme pages for all the major window managers. Often, the developer of a gtk theme will suggest an Enlightenment theme, and vice versa. Some themes—such as blueHeart, BrushedMetal, and BlueSteel—have theme versions for both GTK and Enlightenment that were specifically designed to go together.

Downloading an Enlightenment Theme

Enlightenment themes are found at http://e.themes.org. Make sure that the theme you are downloading is for your version of Enlightenment. Older themes designed for Enlightenment v15 will not work in newer versions of Enlightenment. Each theme lists the Enlightenment version that it was designed for in its theme summary.

Enlightenment theme download files are ordinary tarballs, but they have the extension .etheme instead of .tar.gz or .tgz. You can install an Enlightenment theme in either of two ways, either for one user account or for all accounts.

Installing an Enlightenment Theme for One User

The simplest way to install an enlightenment theme is to copy the [filename].etheme file directly into the ~/.enlightenment/themes directory. There is no need to untar the file. Restart Enlightenment, and then select the new theme from the Enlightenment, Themes menu. The disadvantage to this approach is that only one account can access the theme, unless you manually copy the [filename].etheme file into the ~/.enlightenment/themes directory of each account on your system. If you have root access, you might want to try the second approach.

> You can also install a theme manually into ~/.enlightenment., cd to ~/.enlightenment/themes, and create a new directory with the theme name. Copy the theme tarball into the new directory, and unpack it using the command
>
> tar -zxvf [theme_filename].etheme

Installing an Enlightenment Theme for All User Accounts

Make a directory for the new theme in /usr/share/enlightenment/themes, for example /usr/share/enlightenment/themes/Absolute_E

Copy the `.etheme` file to that subdirectory, then `cd` to the theme subdirectory. Enter the following command:

```
tar -zxvf [theme_name.etheme]
```

Restart Enlightenment. Middle-click the desktop to open the Enlightenment menu and select Themes. Your new theme will appear in the menu. After you have changed your theme, choose a background for it and purge your cached files, as you learned to do in Hour 10, "Exploring Enlightenment."

Uninstalling an Enlightenment Theme

To delete an Enlightenment theme, simply delete the theme's directory in `~/.enlightenment` or `/usr/share/enlightenment/themes`, and restart Enlightenment.

Summary

In this hour, you learned about how themes work with the GTK application programming interface to control the look and feel of GNOME applications. You learned how to install, change, and uninstall a gtk theme. You also learned about window manager themes and how to install and uninstall the Enlightenment window manager themes.

Q&A

Q After I installed my new theme, I found a great background to go with it. I copied it into `~/.enlightenment/backgrounds`, but it doesn't show up in Enlightenment Background Settings. What should I do?

A After you enter a new background into `~/.enlightenment/backgrounds`, you must regenerate your menus. Middle-click Maintenance, Purge Background Selector Cache to purge your old background list. Then middle-click Maintenance, Regenerate Menus. Your new backgrounds will appear in the Background Settings list.

Q Can I make my own themes?

A Creating your own theme is an excellent way to begin learning about GTK programming. We will learn about GTK programming in Hour 24, "Anatomy of a GNOME Application." Also, there is an outstanding tutorial on creating your own gtk themes at `http://gtk.themes.org`.

Workshop

The quiz questions and exercises are designed to increase your understanding and to encourage you to continue experimenting. Answers appear in Appendix B, "Answers."

Quiz

1. Imagine you are running three applications within GNOME: Gnumeric (a GNOME application), Ktetris (a KDE game), and Netscape Communicator. Which applications will change when you change themes, and which will not? Why doesn't the look of all your applications change when you change your gtk theme?
2. Why is a plain theme usually faster than a pixmap theme?
3. What libraries must you have on your computer before you can use a theme?

Exercises

1. Open the Theme Selector in the GNOME Control Center. Select Basic as your desktop theme. Open a few applications and observe how much time it takes for them to open. Close the applications. Go back to Theme Selector and select Expensive. Open the same applications as you did before. Do they take longer to open?
2. Visit http://gtk.themes.org and download a theme that interests you. Then, link to the theme site of your favorite window manager and download a theme that complements the gtk theme.
3. Uninstall some gtk themes that you don't like, and then open Theme Selector in GNOME Control Center. Do the themes appear in the list?

PART III
System Administration with GNOME

Hour

- 13 GNOME Processes
- 14 Setting Up a Remote Connection in GNOME
- 15 The Internet and GNOME
- 16 Managing Printing with GNOME

HOUR 13

GNOME Processes

In UNIX, system administration has traditionally been conducted from the command line, even on systems that use a window manager. GNOME has some useful graphic system administration tools that make it possible to perform many common system administration tasks within dialog boxes in GNOME.

In this hour, you will

- Use gnoRPM to install, upgrade, and maintain rpm packages
- Perform some common administration tasks with GNOME system administration utilities.
- Maintain the MIME types on your computer.

Installing Packages with gnoRPM

In Hour 2, "Installing GNOME," you learned how to install GNOME packages by using the `rpm` tool on the command line. When you are updating your GNOME components or adding new applications, you can use a handy tool called the GNOME `rpm` Manager, or gnoRPM, for installing `rpm`s via graphical interface. Many chapters in the rest of the book discuss new GNOME software that is not part of the base installation. From this point forward, whenever you install new software, use gnoRPM instead of the command line to install new `rpm` packages.

Exploring gnoRPM

GnoRPM, also called GNOME Package Manager, is a tool for installing, uninstalling, and maintaining the `rpm`s on your computer. Although somewhat buggy and not very intuitive, gnoRPM is the most advanced and useful `rpm` tracking tool available. We will begin our exploration of gnoRPM with a quick tour of the gnoRPM options. We will then use gnoRPM to install, query, and upgrade an `rpm` package and search for `rpm` packages using `rpmfind`. Finally, we will use Preferences to configure gnoRPM. The main gnoRPM window, shown in Figure 13.1, contains a menu bar, a toolbar, a status bar, and two windows.

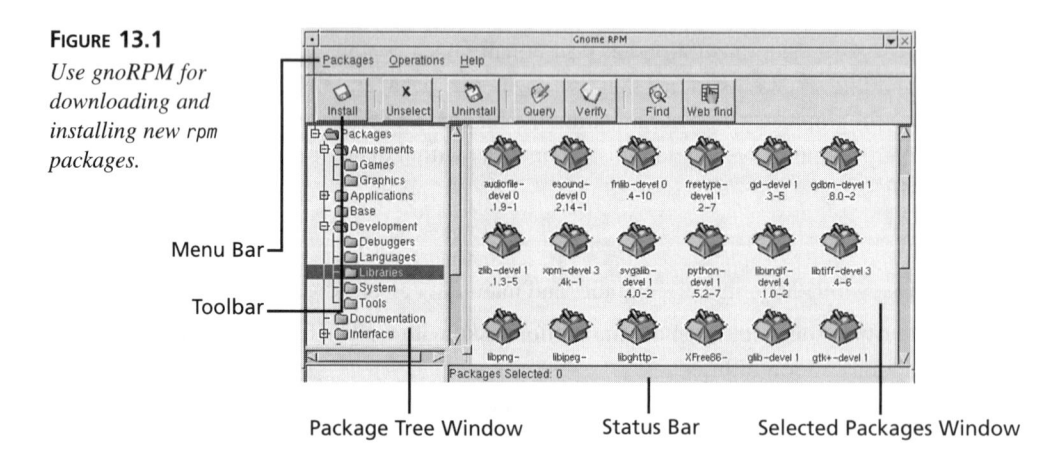

FIGURE 13.1
Use gnoRPM for downloading and installing new rpm packages.

The Package Listing Windows

The left window lists all the `rpm` packages that are in your `rpm` database. The `rpm`s are listed in categories, according to function. The window on the right lists the packages that you select from the tree on the left.

The Toolbar

The toolbar contains buttons for each task you can perform with gnoRPM:

- **Install** raises the `rpm` installation dialog box for installing new `rpms`.
- **Unselect** unselects a package or packages that you have selected in the right window.
- **Uninstall** uninstalls the selected package or packages in the right window
- **Query** opens a message window with details about the package—including a short description of the package, installation date, and files that are installed with the package.
- **Verify** goes through the files in the `rpm` package and makes sure that no file is corrupted.
- **Find** finds `rpm` packages on your computer based on the type of search you choose in a drop-down menu.
- **Web find** invokes the rpmfind database. rpmfind is a database of `rpm` packages and their locations that can be accessed from the Internet.

The Menu Bar

The menu bar contains three menus: Packages, Operations, and Help. Packages and Operations are somewhat inaccurately named, because the operations you can perform on packages are divided between the two menus. All operations in the menus also contain buttons on the toolbar, except for one, Create Desktop Entry.

Create Desktop Entry is an interface for creating a new desktop icon.

Installing and Upgrading `rpms`

If you want to install an `rpm` package that either is on a CD-ROM or has already been downloaded, click Install on the toolbar or in the Operations menu to open the Installation dialog box.

Display the packages to be installed or upgraded according to the filter you choose from the drop-down menu. The display choices are

- All Packages
- All but Installed Packages
- Only Uninstalled Packages
- Only Newer Packages
- Uninstalled or Newer Packages

For example, if you have a new Linux distribution CD-ROM and you want to display only the packages that are newer than those already installed on your computer, then select Only Newer Packages. The gnoRPM Install dialog box is shown in Figure 13.2.

FIGURE 13.2
Use the Install dialog box to install or upgrade packages.

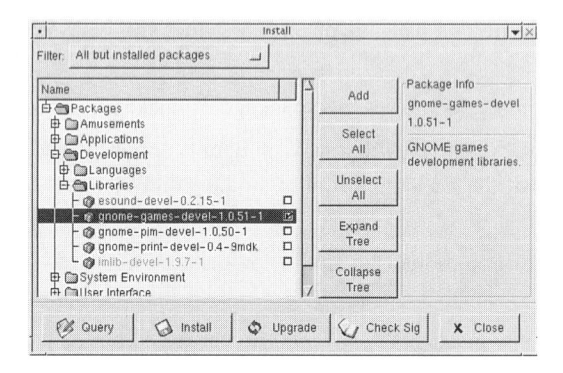

> You can add to or change the directories that are scanned for `rpm` packages in Preferences.

The packages that appear in the package tree are color-coded according to how they compare with packages already installed on your system. By default, packages are coded as follows:

- Packages that are already installed on your computer are colored green.
- A package that is a newer version than what is installed is colored blue.
- A package that is an older version than what is installed is colored grey.
- A package that is not installed is colored black.

The default colors can be changed in Preferences.

To mark a package for installation, check the check box next to the package name. Alternatively, you can double-click a selection, or click Select All to select all the packages in the package tree. If you make a mistake, click Unselect All, or click the check box again to unselect the package.

Aside from installation, you can perform several operations from the Install dialog box:

- **Query** displays information about the package, just like the Query button on the main gnoRPM window.
- **Install** installs the package or packages.

- **Upgrade** performs the same function as Install, but it removes any older packages from the system before installing the new package.
- **Check Sig (Signature)** checks to make sure that the package has not been corrupted, and that it is a valid package.

Finding `rpm` Packages

Click Find to find a particular package that is already installed on your system. Find has several filters that help you search for packages, including

- Contain File
- Are in the Group
- Provide
- Require
- Conflict With
- Match Label

For example, if you are looking for the package that contains a particular file, enter the file you are looking for in the Find field. For example, if you are looking for the file libtext.so.0, enter **libtext.so.0** in the Find field. All rpm packages that include this file will appear. The Find Packages dialog box is illustrated in Figure 13.3.

FIGURE 13.3
Find Packages has several filters to help you find rpm packages on your computer.

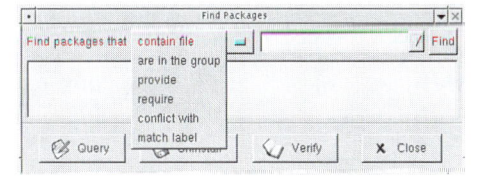

Using Rpmfind

Rpmfind is a database of all the rpm packages in existence. Daniel Veillard created rpmfind and also wrote the code to incorporate it into gnoRPM. rpmfind finds rpm packages on a database on the Internet. You can download and install any package that rpmfind has in the database via gnoRPM. The rpmfind home page is http://rpmfind.net.

Click Web find to open the rpmfind database. The entire database is displayed in the package tree window. The packages in the package tree are colored in the same way as those in the Installation window: black, for not installed; blue, for a newer version; green, for the same version; grey, for an older version.

> Rpmfind displays no information messages when it is downloading. If it seems that rpmfind is doing nothing for a long time, be patient. You might just have a slow connection.

The database includes thousands of packages. A search tool makes it easier to find the package you need. Enter the package you are looking for in the Search field. You can enter the actual package name, a word, or a phrase, and rpmfind will search for and list every package that includes your search parameter in the package tree.

Click a package to display information about it in the right window. The right window displays Query information about the package. You can select simply to download the package, or to actually install it. Rpmfind is shown in Figure 13.4.

FIGURE 13.4
You will learn later this hour how to narrow the packages displayed in rpmfind.

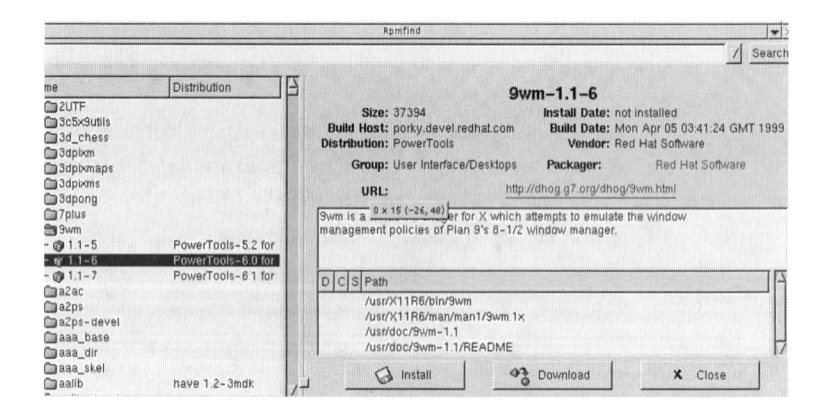

> If you find that gnoRPM tends to crash when you use the Web find tool, you can access the rpmfind database manually using your favorite Web browser. Download the rpm you want, and then use gnoRPM or File Manager to install it.

Querying rpm Packages

Query an rpm package to find out information about it before you install it. To open the query window, select the package or packages you want to query, and then click Query on the toolbar. You can query more than one package at once. To select more than one package at a time, hold down Shift and click the packages you want. A sample query response is shown in Figure 13.5.

FIGURE 13.5

Query a package to determine where the package files are installed.

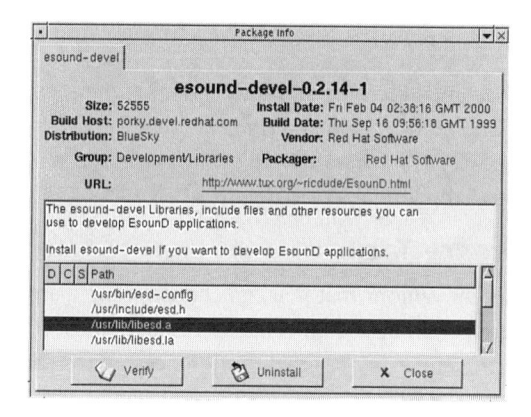

Query information is organized into the following data fields:

- **Size** lists the size of the rpm package in bytes.
- **Build Host** is the host name of the computer where the rpm package was built.
- **Distribution** displays the Linux distribution that the rpm belongs to, if there is one.
- **Group** is the gnoRPM group that the package belongs to. GnoRPM assigns packages to groups according to the function of the package's software.
- **Install Date** is the date the package was installed on your computer.
- **Build Date** is the date the package was created.
- **Vendor** is the individual or organization that created the package.
- **Packager** contains a short description of the package software, and then a list of all the files in the package and their target directories.

> The Packager field is very important, because different packages put files in different places. It is important that you install a package that matches your directory structure. For example, some packages place the executable file in /opt/bin and others in /usr/bin. If you install an rpm that places the files in /opt and your path is /usr, you won't be able to run the application without specifying the full pathname. Other packages that depend on that package won't be able to find it, and it won't be able to find the libraries it needs to run. There are ways to get around this problem, such as adding the new pathname to the PATH environment variable, but it is best if you find the rpm that matches your Linux distribution.

GnoRPM Preferences

GnoRPM includes a detailed Preferences dialog box, in which you can set the many options that are available in the command line version of rpm. There are also many preferences specific to gnoRPM and rpmfind. The following sections describe the Preferences dialog box's option tabs (see Figure 13.6).

Behavior Preference Tab

The Behavior tab lists the options that you can choose when using the rpm command. These options are derived directly from command line options. A pop-up tooltip naming the command line option appears over each Preferences option. Some of the more important options are

- **No Dependency Checks**—When installing or uninstalling a package, gnoRPM will not provide a list of packages that depend on the package you want to install. This option is useful if you are upgrading two packages that depend on each other, for example, gtk and gtk-devel. If you need to, review the information on dependencies in Hour 2. We will address dependencies again in Hour 22, "Upgrading GNOME and Joining the GNOME Project."

- **Upgrade Options**—These options control the difference between the Upgrade and Install commands. If none of the options are checked, Upgrade behaves the same as Install. The Upgrade options are

    - **Allow replacement of packages** instructs gnoRPM to install the package, even if the package has already been installed. This option is useful if you think the original package is broken, or has been corrupted.

    - **Allow replacement of files** enables a package to be installed if the files in it conflict with files already installed from another package. The files from this package will replace the files that belong to the other package that is already installed.

    - **Allow upgrade to older version** enables you to upgrade a newer package with an older package. These options are particularly useful if you upgraded a package and later find that it kills a dependency on a file needed from the older package.

    - **Keep packages made obsolete** instructs gnoRPM to keep a package in the rpm database even if the package has been made obsolete by another package.

- **Database Options**—These options are useful for testing dependencies and for updating your rpm database.

Package Listing Tab

The Package Listing tab controls whether packages appear as icons or lists in the selected package window.

Install Window Tab

The Install Window tab enables you to change the colors for older, newer, and currently installed packages in the Install window.

The RPM Directories field is one of the most important Preferences. This field lists all the directories where gnoRPM searches for `rpm` packages to include in the package tree. Notice that `/mnt/cdrom` is included here by default. If you download your `rpm` packages to a directory that is not listed here, or if your CD-ROM is mounted to a different directory, enter the directory or directories in this field. To enter a directory, place the cursor at the end of an entry and press Enter. Add the new directory pathname and click Apply. The Install Window tab is shown in Figure 13.6 with several directories included in the RPM Directories field.

FIGURE 13.6
Be sure to list all the directories in which rpm packages are located in RPM Directories.

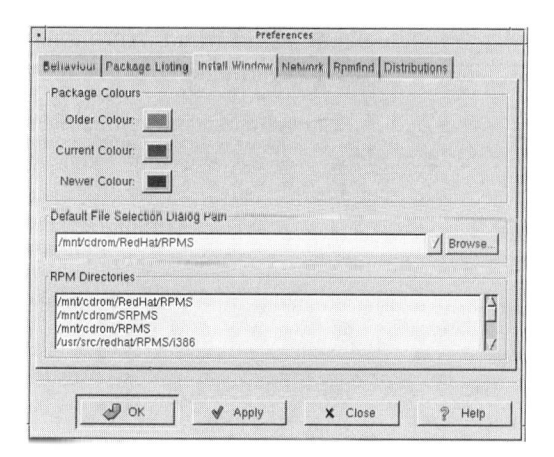

Network Tab

If you use an HTTP or FTP proxy, the Network tab contains fields for entering the proxies and passwords.

Rpmfind Tab

The Rpmfind tab lists the rpmfind server that you connect to in order to download the rpmfind database. There are several mirrors for this database, so if the default server is too slow, try one of the mirrors. A list of mirrors can be found at http://rpmfind.net. In the Download Dir field, enter the full pathname of the directory into which rpmfind should download new rpm packages. Enter your Linux distribution and vendor, and specify whether you want to receive source rpms or the latest binary version.

Finally, enter any packages that you do not want to upgrade in the No Upgrade List field. By default, this list contains packages that have to do with the Linux kernel, because upgrading the kernel is a more complicated process than simply upgrading rpm packages. You can enter any additional package names you want.

Distributions Tab

The Distributions tab is important for filtering and ordering the rpm packages found by rpmfind. Every Linux distribution for which rpmfind has a package is listed in the Distribution Settings field. The Rating drop-down list contains either a -1, a 0, or a positive number rating. Find the distribution, vendor, and processor type that matches your system and select it. In the Rating drop-down, press the arrow until a high rating is reached, for example, 50. Go through the rest of the distributions, and rate them according to how well they match your own system. If you don't ever want to receive rpm packages from a particular distribution, give it a -1 rating. When rpmfind searches for packages, it will not return packages to you from that distribution.

For example, if you have a Red Hat Linux system and an Intel Pentium II processor, rpm packages for Sparc or Alpha machines will not be useful to you, so rate them -1. Also, SuSE rpm packages use a different directory structure than Red Hat, so you don't want SuSE packages either. Give them a -1 rating. The Distributions tab is shown in Figure 13.7.

FIGURE 13.7
The Distributions tab can help you ensure that rpmfind only displays packages that are useful to you.

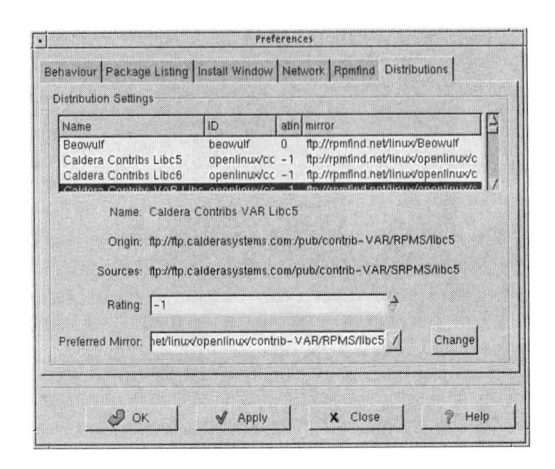

> Be sure to click Change after you change each individual distribution rating; otherwise, the change will not take place.

Some packages will work on your system, but might not be as desirable as your own Linux distribution. For example, Mandrake rpm packages usually work just fine on a Red Hat system, so rate Mandrake i386 packages with a positive number that is less than the Red Hat i386 number, say 15.

GnoRPM and File Manager

When gnoRPM is installed on your system, the options to install, upgrade, check signature, query, and uninstall appear in the right-click menu of rpm packages in File Manager. Each option behaves the same way as in gnoRPM, and any changes you make will appear automatically in the gnoRPM database.

Other GNOME System Administration Utilities

GNOME has dozens of tools and utilities to help you perform system administration on your computer. Some utilities are useful only in a large, networked setting, but most are useful even if you are the only user on your system. Some of the more popular utilities are described here, but there are many more listed on the GNOME Software Map under Utilities. Some of the system administration utilities described in this section are designed to be used by a system administrator logged in as root. If you don't have the necessary permissions, some of these utilities will not run, or will not display any useful data.

Gnome-linuxconf

Gnome-linuxconf is the GNOME version of the graphical administration tool, linuxconf. Better organized than linuxconf, Gnome-linuxconf also contains many more utilities. Generally, you must be root to use GNOME-linuxconf.

Gnome-admin

Gnome-admin will eventually contain a suite of administration tools. Currently, gnome-admin contains two tools, the GNOME Unified Link to Printers, or gulp, and logview.

Gulp

The GNOME Unified Link to Printers is a graphical representation of the command-line tools `lprm` and `lpq`. Gulp provides a comprehensive window of information about every print job on your system going to every printer. Gulp is shown in Figure 13.8.

FIGURE 13.8
Gulp is especially useful on a multiuser environment.

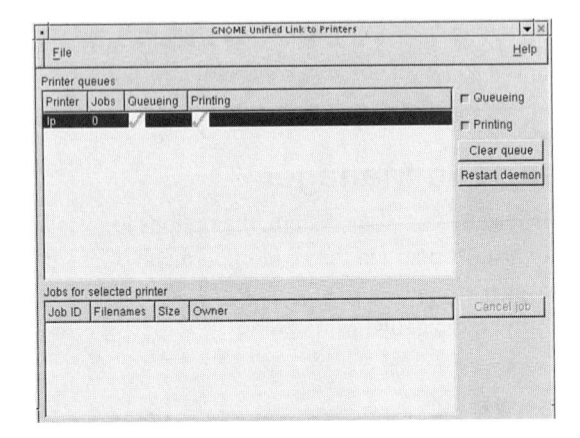

Logview

Logview is a graphic interface for viewing your system logs (see Figure 13.9). Logview includes a calendar that you can click to select a day for viewing, a description/definition of each log, and a menu from which to choose which log to view. If you are new to Linux or UNIX and are not sure how to work with logs, logview is particularly useful. Depending on how your system administrator has set up permissions for logs, usually you must be root to view files in logview.

FIGURE 13.9
Use logview to familiarize yourself with using logs in Linux.

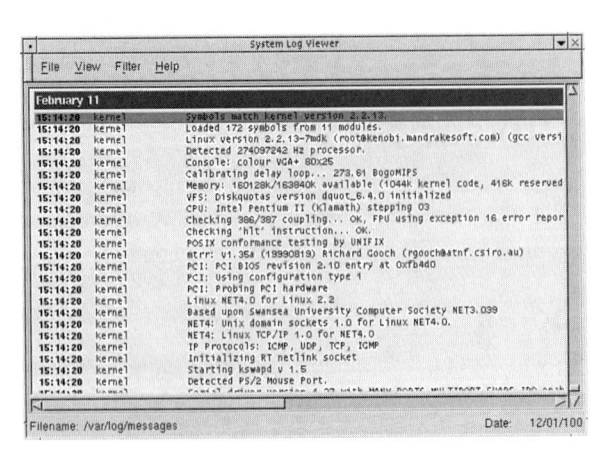

System Information

The System Information utility is particularly useful for when you are having problems and don't want to go to the trouble of typing in all the information about your system. You can save the entire display as a file, or email it.

System Information provides basic information about your system in the main window, including

- Distribution
- Operating System
- Distribution Version
- OS Version and Release
- Processor type
- Computer hostname
- Username
- X Display Name
- Short synopsis of system status

> For a graphical display of your system status, open Stripchart Plotter from Main Menu, Utilities.

Click Detailed Information to open a dialog box that provides detailed information on your

- CPU
- Memory, including use and swap space usage buffers
- Disk information, including partition, mount point, filesystem, usage, and free space

GNOME DiskFree

GNOME DiskFree is a simple utility that shows how much free space is available on each mounted file system. Each file system is displayed as a dial, and the amount of free space is graphed on the dial. A written percentage is also displayed. Figure 13.10 shows a SCSI system with two hard drives, sda and sdb, and four partitions. sda1 is a Windows partition, sdb2 and sdb3 are Linux partitions, and the disk labeled "none" is an empty partition. If you have an IDE based system, your partitions will begin with an "h," for example, hda1, hda2, and so on. For more information on disk partitions, see the installation guide for your Linux distribution.

FIGURE 13.10
DiskFree is a simple utility for tracking disk space.

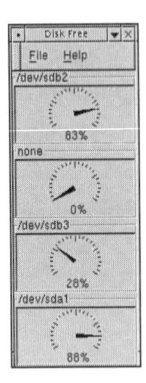

Working with MIME Types

MIME stands for Multipurpose Internet Mail Extensions. MIME was originally a standard for classifying file types for email. In GNOME, the gmc file manager uses MIME types to signify file types for opening and editing applications. After you have a MIME type identified on your computer, a file that contains an extension that matches the MIME type will be recognized by gmc. Gmc can then use that information to open the file using the proper application, and to assign the file a corresponding icon in File Manager.

> The Internet Assigned Numbers Authority (IANA), maintains a list of recognized MIME types. The list is available at
> `ftp://ftp.isi.edu/in-notes/iana/assignments/media-types/`.

MIME types are sometimes assigned by default when you install a new package. More often, you must assign a MIME type to a new kind of file yourself. To view the MIME types on your computer, open GNOME Control Center, MIME Types. The main MIME Types capplet is shown in Figure 13.11.

The extension field lists the extensions that will cause the file to be treated as a particular MIME type. You can give a MIME type more than one extension. For example, for the MIME type `text/html`, File Manager will look for extensions of type `.html`, `.htm`, or `.HTML`.

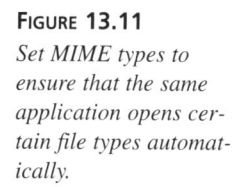

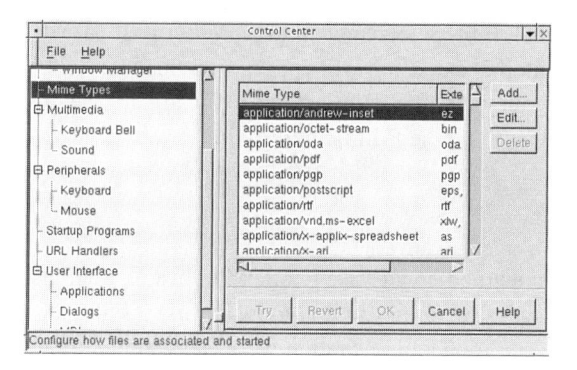

FIGURE 13.11
Set MIME types to ensure that the same application opens certain file types automatically.

Viewing MIME Types

When you open GNOME Control Center, MIME Types, all the MIME types that are defined on your computer appear. To see more specific information about a particular MIME type, click Edit. The icon at the top of the dialog box determines the icon that files of this type will appear under in File Manager. The extensions are listed in the MIME Type list. Any file with one of these extensions will be treated like the file type listed here. The Mime Type Actions section determines the application that will automatically be used to open this kind of file, and the editor that will be used to edit this kind of file.

Editing MIME Types

MIME types can be edited by directly opening the GNOME Control Center, or by selecting Commands, Edit MIME Types in File Manager.

Enter the extensions that you want to associate with a MIME type. For example, for the MIME type text/html, you can add the extensions .HTML, .HTM, .htm, and .html. To change the icon, click the icon in the Set Actions For dialog box and select a new icon from the icon list.

You can also define the kind of application that will automatically start when you select Open, Edit, View in File Manager. If you enter nothing in View, the default internal file viewer will be used.

Adding MIME Types

To add a new MIME type from the GNOME Control Center, open MIME Types and click Add. The Add MIME Type dialog box appears. Enter the new MIME type in the Mime Type field. In the Extension field, enter the extensions that you want gmc to recognize as belonging to your application. After you have created the new Mime Type, click

OK, and then click Edit. Select an icon to represent your MIME type in File Manager. Applications with this extension will appear with this icon in the Icon View of File manager. Enter the command that will start the application in the Open field. The View field will open it in View, and the Edit field, in Edit.

Summary

In this hour, you learned how to use gnoRPM to install, upgrade, uninstall, maintain, and query rpm packages. You used rpmfind to locate and install new rpm packages. You peformed some common administration tasks using gnome-linuxconf, gulp, logview, System Information, and DiskFree. You also used the MIME Types capplet in GNOME Control Center to edit and add the MIME types on your computer.

Q&A

Q Does it matter to gnoRPM where I keep rpm packages on my computer?

A As long as you specify the directory where you keep rpm packages in gnoRPM Preferences, you can put them in any directory you like. You really don't even have to download the packages to install them; you can install them directly from rpmfind without saving the rpms on your local hard drive first.

Q Can I install packages using File Manager?

A Yes. Using File Manager's Virtual File System, you can enter any ftp address in the Location field. Find an ftp site that contains the rpm you want, open it using File Manager, and then right-click the rpm package and select Install. You will learn how to open an FTP site using File Manager in Hour 15, "The Internet and GNOME."

Workshop

The quiz questions and exercises are designed to increase your understanding and to encourage you to continue experimenting. Answers appear in Appendix B, "Answers."

Quiz

1. What is the difference between installing and upgrading an rpm package?
2. How are packages color-coded in rpmfind and the installation window?
3. What is the difference between Install Date and Build Date for rpm packages?
4. What does MIME stand for?

Exercises

1. Open gnoRPM and explore the `rpm` package categories. What are some of the categories?
2. Query the GTK `rpm` package. To which directories does gtk install files? Why do you think there is no executable file added to `/usr/bin` or `/opt/bin`?
3. Find the gnome-core `rpm` package and then verify it.
4. Open the installation window of gnoRPM, and display All but Installed Packages. Do you have any uninstalled `rpm` packages on your computer?
5. Open gnoRPM Preferences and select Distributions. Set all distributions that you cannot use to `-1`. Set the distribution that matches your distribution's vendor and processor type to `50`. Set the other distributions to positive numbers lower than 50, according to your preference. The higher the preference, the higher the number you should assign the distribution.
6. Ensure that you have a remote connection open to the Internet. Open rpmfind and search for gnome-admin. Install the correct distribution of gnome-admin.

HOUR 14

Setting Up a Remote Connection in GNOME

Although GNOME is exciting and fun by itself, eventually you want to connect with the rest of the world via the Internet. The first half of this hour is not concerned with GNOME in particular; it presents the information you need to set up a dial-up, PPP connection either to your ISP or to your office. The second half of the hour deals with GNOME PPP utilities and how to set them up and use them.

If you are already familiar with Linux or a UNIX flavor, most of this chapter will be repetitive. You can skip to "Setting Up a New Account in GNOME PPP Dialer" to read about the GNOME PPP utilities. If you are new to Linux, then this section might reduce some of the mystery and frustration surrounding setting up a remote connection in Linux. This hour will give you the most basic information you need to set up a dial-up connection, and will walk you through the process.

In this hour, you will

- Use the Point to Point Protocol to connect to the Internet.
- Gather information about your ISP account and modem.
- Set up a PPP account in GNOME PPP Dialer.
- Configure GNOME PPP Dialer to your preferences.
- Use the PPP Applet and Modem Lights to make and monitor your PPP connection.

PPP stands for *Point to Point Protocol*. PPP is the protocol that Linux uses to communicate with other computers over a modem, via the TCP/IP protocol. PPP is also used for other serial connections, for example, when you connect one computer directly to another via a serial cable. PPP converts digital packets of data to analog format, which can be sent via a telephone line.

The PPP daemon, or *pppd*, controls ppp in Linux. When you dial in to your ISP, pppd negotiates your PPP client with the ISP's PPP server, and attempts to authenticate your computer as a valid client of the PPP server. Several different authentication procedures can be used to set up a connection: a script-based login, PAP, or CHAP. Contact your ISP to find out which authentication procedure your ISP's PPP server expects.

PPP can also be used if you want to dial up to your company's PPP server. Contact your network administrator for information on how to set up a PPP client account.

Some ISP's use the older SLIP protocol. SLIP stands for Serial Line Internet Protocol. Dialing up to a server that uses SLIP is similar to using PPP. PPP is considered to be an improvement over SLIP, so most ISP's today use PPP.

> This section is geared toward the home user, to help you in the sometimes-complicated process of setting up a PPP connection. If you are using Linux at work, then your administrator should set up the connection for you.

Setting up a PPP connection is quite a bit more complicated in Linux than in MS Windows or MacOS. This section helps you gather all the information you need to set up a connection successfully. First, you should ask some questions about your ISP. Next, you will need some information about your modem.

There is quite a lot of information to gather before setting up a new PPP connection. If you have already set up a PPP connection in Linux using wvdial, minicom, or seyon, you have all the information you need. If you haven't used the Internet in Linux yet, preparations can take some time. You might have to contact your ISP for some of the information you will need.

Gathering Information About Your ISP

Before you set up your account in PPP Dialer, there is information that you must get from your ISP or systems administrator about your account. When you have the following information, you will be ready to create an account in GNOME PPP Dialer:

- **Dial-in telephone number**   The phone number you dial to get a PPP connection.
- **Username**   The username assigned to you, such as `judith@samsonsource.com` or `netfrix/alain`.
- **Password**   Your unique, user password.
- **Protocol**   PPP is the most common, but some ISPs still use the older SLIP protocol.
- **Authentication**   Contact your ISP for the authentication protocol it uses, such as CHAP, PAP, or a login script.
- **Your IP address**   Most ISPs dynamically assign you an IP address each time you log in. If you don't have a fixed IP address, don't worry about this.
- **Dynamic Name Service (DNS) Servers**   Record the addresses of the ISP's primary and secondary DNS servers.
- **Login script**   If you don't use CHAP or PAP authentication, you will need a login script. You can get a login script from your ISP, or you can try to improvise a script.
- **Search domain**   The search domain is often the same as the domain name, such as `umich.edu`, or `netcom.com`. Some ISPs, particularly universities, might have several search domains.

Gathering Information About Your Modem

> If you want to learn more about how modems work in Linux, read the modem HOWTO at `http://www.linuxdoc.org/HOWTO/Modem-HOWTO.html`. The HOWTO explains in layman's terms how modems work, which can be extraordinarily useful if you are having problems getting your modem to work in Linux. The HOWTO is long and might be difficult to understand, but try not to be put off. The extra effort to read it can be well worth it.

Is Your Modem Compatible with Linux?

Most internal and external modems that connect to the computer via a serial port can be used in Linux, with one major exception. If your modem is a Winmodem, that is, if it was designed to work only under MS Windows, then it will not run under Linux. Winmodems contain software that is meant to emulate a chip in hardware modems that converts digital signals to analog signals so that they can be transmitted via telephone. These modems will not work under Linux at all.

Also, if your modem is Plug and Play, you might have trouble configuring it in Linux. Some plug-and-play modems can be manually configured like ordinary modems. Otherwise, there are Linux plug-and-play drivers available. See the LDP Plug-and-Play HOWTO at http://www.linuxdoc.org/HOWTO/Plug-and-Play-HOWTO.html.

To verify that your modem is compatible with Linux, see the Linux Hardware Compatibility HOWTO at http://www.linuxdoc.org/HOWTO/Hardware-HOWTO.html.

Which Serial Port Is the Modem Connected To?

In Windows, serial ports are named COM1, COM2, and so on. In Linux, they are named ttyS0, ttyS1, and so on. Older versions of Linux named serial ports cua0, cua1, and so on. In addition, some versions of UNIX use the cua convention. Table 14.1 compares the three conventions for easy reference.

TABLE 14.1 Linux Nomenclature for Serial Ports

Serial Port	Obsolete Linux Serial Port Name	Serial Port in Windows
ttyS0	cua0	COM1
ttyS1	cua1	COM2
ttyS2	cua2	COM3

Before you can configure your modem, you must know which serial port it is connected to. There are several ways to accomplish this.

Look in the /dev/modem file for the device file it is linked to. Some Linux distributions automatically create this file and a symbolic link to the correct /dev/ttySx device file. Right-click /dev/modem and select Edit Symbolic Link. The correct /dev/ttySx file will be listed. In Figure 14.1, the /dev/modem file is linked to /dev/ttyS2.

Setting Up a Remote Connection in GNOME

FIGURE 14.1
In many distributions, /dev/modem is created automatically during installation. Right-click the /dev/modem file and select Edit Symlink to display this window.

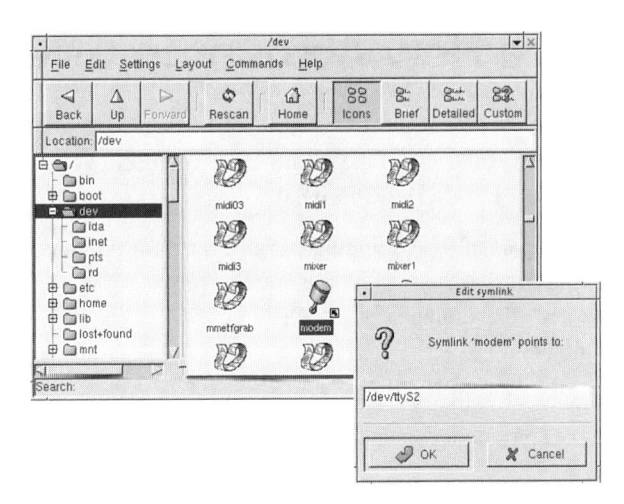

If /dev/modem does not exist or is pointing to the wrong /dev/ttySx file, and if you have a Windows partition on your computer, an easy, cheating way to find the serial port is to look up your system information in Control Panel. Apply the COM port number to Table 14.1 to determine the serial port nomenclature in Linux.

If you have no luck with the methods mentioned previously, you can configure wvdial. Wvdial is a text-based PPP dialer that does all the work for you. After you install and configure it, wvdial checks each serial port until it finds your modem. It then automatically initializes the modem, tests the modem speed, and connects to your ISP. Wvdial is such a wonderful program that many people use it in the desktop environment as well. You can download wvdial from http://freshmeat.net.

After you have determined the correct serial port, create a symbolic link from the serial device file where your modem is located to /dev/modem. This step isn't strictly necessary to get a working PPP connection, but it makes things easier if you ever forget the correct serial port, or if someone else such as a system administrator works on your system. Review Hour 9, "Common File Manager Tasks," if you need help with creating symlinks.

Special Initialization String

Does your modem require a special initialization string? Most modems initialize with the string ATZ, which is the default in PPP Dialer. Check your modem manual if you have a different initialization string.

Setting Up a New Account in GNOME PPP Dialer

Now that you have collected all the information you need, you are ready to set up a connection to your ISP in GNOME PPP Dialer.

GNOME-PPP is part of the gnome-network package. It provides a graphical way to create a PPP connection with your Internet service provider. To use GNOME-PPP, you must first create a new PPP dialup account. Open GNOME-PPP from main menu, Internet and click Account, New.

Shown in Figure 14.2, the PPP Account dialog box has many tabs that will look familiar if you have set up remote connections in Windows. The tabs are described in the following sections.

FIGURE 14.2
The PPP Account dialog box of GNOME PPP Dialer provides a graphical interface for information that once had to be entered manually into scripts.

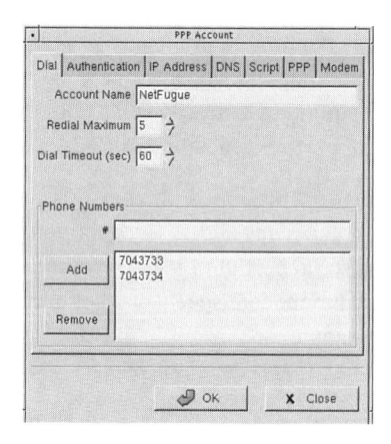

Dial Tab

In the Dial tab, enter the Account Name. This name will appear in the PPP Dialer window.

In Phone Numbers field, enter the phone number or numbers you use to connect. If you add more than one phone number, PPP Dialer will dial each number in turn until it makes a successful connection. Don't forget to include a 1 for a long-distance connection number, or a 9 if you dial 9 to get an outside line. A comma causes a one-second pause in dialing. Two commas will cause a two-second pause.

> If you have call waiting on your phone line, you should disable it before making an Internet connection. Add the code that disables call waiting in front of your ISP dial-up phone number. For example, if the disable call waiting code is *70 and your ISP's phone number is 123-4567, enter *70,,1234567 in the Phone Numbers field to prevent the loss of your connection due to an incoming call.

If your connection time tends to be slow, enter a higher number than the default of 60 seconds in Dial Timeout.

> If you make a successful and connection but your daemon dies soon after you connect, try increasing the Dial Timeout. The timer doesn't stop until all negotiations are complete and a successful PPP connection has been established. If your Dial Timeout expires during an authorization, your ppp daemon can die.

Authentication Tab

Enter your account username and the password in the Authentication tab. If you use CHAP or PAP authentication, the username and password entered here will be used in the authentication process. If you use a login script, the Script tab will use the username and a masked version of the password as part of the script.

IP Address Tab

If your ISP dynamically assigns you an IP address, which is usually the case, check Dynamic for each field in the IP Address tab. If you have a fixed IP address, enter the information in the proper field. If you are dialing in to your company's server, rather than an ISP, you might have to enter specific values for your local IP address, netmask, and remote IP address. Check with your system administrator.

DNS Server Tab

DNS stands for *Domain Name Service*, which is a worldwide database for translating hostnames into IP addresses. Your ISP will usually have a primary and a secondary DNS IP address. In the DNS tab, enter the primary address, then the secondary. If your ISP has several search domains, enter them in the Search Domain field. If you don't know the search domains, enter the ISP domain name or leave the entry blank.

Script Tab

If your ISP gives you a script to connect with, instead of CHAP or PAP identification, enter it in the login script field. Enter the script line by line in the dialog box that appears when you click the Action drop-down menu, and enter Add after each line. You can use the Action drop-down menu to specify what each line of text is.

For example, select Send in the drop-down menu, and then enter your username in the login script field and click Enter. In the complete script field in the lower half of the dialog box, the word Send appears in the Action column and your username in the Text column. This line of the login script is an instruction to Send the string of text in the Text column to the ISP server.

If you forget to add a line, use the Insert button to open a line. Highlight the line below the point where you want to insert a line and click Insert. A blank line is opened above the selected line. A sample script is shown entered into the Script tab in Figure 14.3.

FIGURE 14.3
Your ISP might give you a special script for Linux, if you don't use CHAP or PAP for authentication.

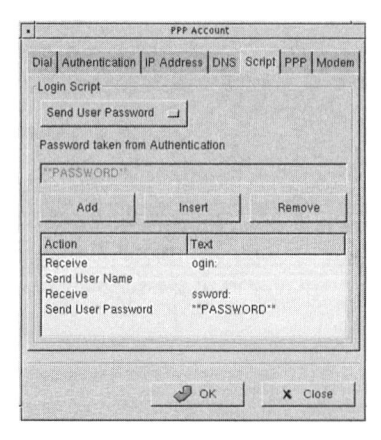

PPP Tab

If your ISP gives you any information for the PPP tab, enter it in the proper fields. Otherwise, leave the default values.

Modem Tab

The Modem tab contains areas for you to configure your modem settings. Check your modem manual for any adjustments you should make to the default values. Usually the defaults will work fine, although if your phone line quality is poor, consider lowering the connection speed. If you choose the highest connection speed, your modem will connect at the fastest speed it can, limited by the quality of your phone connection. If your PPP daemon tends to die at random times, try choosing a lower modem connection speed.

Setting Up a Remote Connection in GNOME

If you have an initialization string other than ATZ or any other edit to make to the modem commands, click Edit Modem Commands and make adjustments. The default modem commands are shown in Figure 14.4.

FIGURE 14.4
Check your modem user's manual for any adjustments you might need to make to the default values.

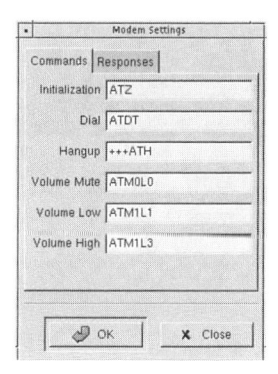

Making a Connection

After you have set up your new account, click OK to close the Account dialog box. Click Connect to start the ppp daemon. A few seconds will lapse while your modem initializes. The modem dials, and then the authorization sequence begins after the server answers. If your PPP daemon dies unexpectedly, check your settings. It sometimes helps to try to make a PPP connection with another utility, such as wvdial. A successful connection is shown in Figure 14.5.

FIGURE 14.5
The small message box on PPP Dialer provides brief messages about the connection status.

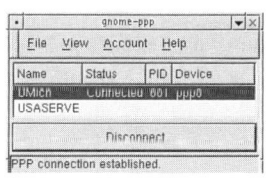

If you have done everything in this chapter, and still can't get a connection, you might have a permissions or ownership problem. Check through these files to make sure that you have read and executed permission for them:

- /etc/chap-secrets
- /etc/pap-secrets
- /etc/resolv.conf

Monitoring Your Connection

If you want to monitor your connection, click View and check Debug Terminal to open a viewer that displays PPP messages. The debug terminal is shown in Figure 14.6.

FIGURE 14.6
The Test window displays more verbose messages about the connection than the main PPP Dialer window.

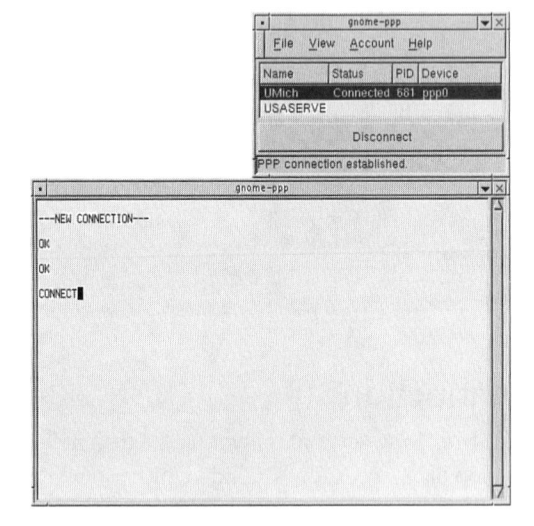

If you are not sure if you are connected, a fast and simple way to verify your connection is to ping an Internet address. For example, in an X terminal, type

`ping www.gnome.org`

If you are connected, ping returns with the IP address of the host you pinged, and the size of the packets of data exchanged. Press Ctrl+C to sever the link. Figure 14.7 shows a ping to www.redhat.com.

FIGURE 14.7
Ping provides the IP address of the host, as well as packet exchange data.

In addition to ping, you can use traceroute for a more detailed test of your connection. Traceroute sends a packet from your computer to the IP address or hostname that you specify, and lists the route that it takes to get there, through each gateway. To use traceroute, enter `traceroute [hostname]`. For example, to trace a route to Red Hat, enter

`traceroute www.redhat.com`

> If you have problems with your connection, read the ISP Hookup HOWTO at `http://linuxdoc.org/HOWTO/ISP-Hookup-HOWTO.html` for guidance.

PPP Applet

The PPP Applet is a simple applet interface to the GNOME PPP Dialer. To start a PPP connection, click the globe icon, choose a PPP account, and click Raise PPP Link. When you are ready to disconnect, click the globe icon and then click Lower PPP Link. The advantage to using the PPP Applet is that it is a simple means to start a ppp connection. A timer lets you know how long you have been connected, and the revolving globe icon lets you know whether the link is connected or severed. A text message also appears to let you know whether you are online or offline. The PPP Applet is shown in Figure 14.8.

FIGURE 14.8
PPP Applet resides in the GNOME panel, so it takes up less space than the main PPP Dialer window.

Modem Lights

Modem Lights is another PPP Dialer applet. The great advantage to Modem lights is that you can choose which dialer you want to use via the Properties tab. While you are connected, the "lights" on the applet light up green. Modem Lights is shown in Figure 14.9.

FIGURE 14.9
The "lights" on Modem Lights turn "on" (get brighter) when you are connected.

Summary

In this hour, you learned how Linux uses the PPP protocol to make remote connections over a phone line using a modem. You created a PPP connection to your ISP using GNOME PPP Dialer. You pinged a Web server to validate your PPP connection, and used the Test window of PPP Dialer to monitor your connection. You also learned about making PPP connections using the PPP Applet and Modem Lights.

Q&A

Q Are there GNOME utilities for networking over a LAN?

A Although they are beyond the scope of this book, GNOME-linuxconf and cpanel provide dialog boxes for networking. Both are available through the GNOME Software Map or the `rpmfind` database.

Q Do I have to use GNOME PPP Dialer to connect to the Internet if I am in GNOME?

A No, you can use any PPP dialer you want. You can create a panel launcher or a main menu entry for your non-GNOME dialer using the techniques you learned in Hour 7, "Using the Panel and the Main Menu."

Q I can't get GNOME PPP Dialer to work. Where can I find another PPP dialer?

A GNOME PPP Dialer is still in development stage, and although stable, doesn't always work for everyone. Wvdial, although text-based, is more user-proof. Download wvdial from your Linux distribution site. Source code is also available at `http://freshmeat.net`. You can also try x-wvdial, which provides a graphical interface for wvdial.

Workshop

The quiz questions and exercises are designed to increase your understanding and to encourage you to continue experimenting. Answers appear in Appendix B, "Answers."

Quiz

1. What does PPP stand for?
2. What is the name of the daemon that starts when you make a PPP connection?
3. What serial port does your modem connect to?
4. What is the `/dev/modem` file?

5. What are two kinds of PPP authentication protocols?
6. If you must dial 9 to get an outside phone line, how would you get the PPP Dialer to pause long enough to connect to an outside line?
7. What does DNS stand for, and what does it do?

Exercises

1. Start a PPP connection using GNOME PPP Dialer. What messages appear in the PPP Dialer window?
2. After establishing a PPP connection, open an X terminal and enter the command ps -a. (If you have many processes running, you might have to enter ps -a|more, and then use the spacebar to scroll through the list of processes. You can also increase the size of the X terminal window.) Look at the list carefully. What processes seem to be involved with the connection?
3. Now disconnect the PPP connection and run ps -a again. Have the processes that you answered in exercise 2 disappeared?

HOUR 15

The Internet and GNOME

Some pundits claim that the Internet is the most fundamentally important addition to human culture since the invention of the printing press. When you think of the countless ways to use the Internet to communicate and share information, it's easy to agree. You can use File Transfer Protocol to share files across the Internet. You can use the World Wide Web to get information about anything you can imagine. Email enables you to send messages instantly. Chat programs let you "talk" with friends and coworkers in real time. Using newsgroups, you can post and read messages on an electronic bulletin board. GNOME has applications to help you with just about anything you want to do on the Internet. This hour, we will talk about just a few of these applications.

In this hour, you will

- Install and configure Balsa, the GNOME email client.
- Use Balsa to send and receive email.
- Configure gFTP, the GNOME FTP client.
- Use gFTP to upload and download files.

A Word About Netscape Communicator

Netscape Communicator is the Internet browser, news, and email client that most people with Linux and UNIX systems use to navigate the World Wide Web. Although there are a few nascent projects to develop a GNOME Web browser, none of the applications are in a very advanced stage of development. Most GNOME users rely on Netscape Communicator or a text-based browser such as Lynx or w3. There are GNOME email, FTP, and news client applications, however, that provide viable and even superior alternatives to Netscape.

We won't go into any detail over Netscape Communicator in this book, because it is not a GNOME or GNU application. Using Netscape is simple if you have used Netscape or Internet Explorer in Windows. Netscape for Linux also comes with a comprehensive user's manual and online support. See http://www.netscape.com for information. The Netscape Navigator window is shown in Figure 15.1.

FIGURE 15.1
Netscape Navigator for UNIX/Linux looks a lot like Netscape for Windows.

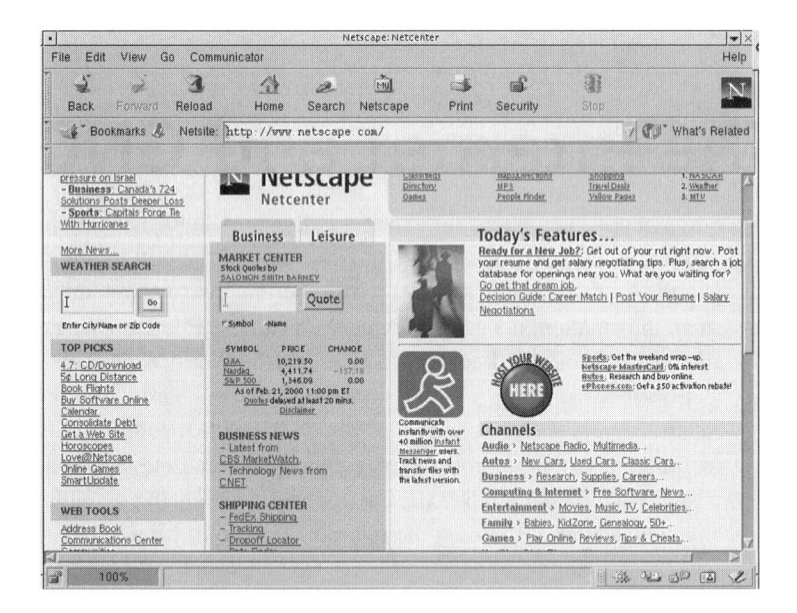

Getting and Sending Email with Balsa

There are several email clients being developed for GNOME. In fact, email has its own category on the GNOME software map. The most advanced email client being developed specifically as part of the GNOME desktop environment is Balsa. To keep up on the development of Balsa, see the home page at http://www.balsa.net. Some of the major features of Balsa include

- Local mailboxes.
- POP3 and IMAP protocols for incoming messages
- SMTP and MTA protocols for outgoing messages.
- Printing messages.
- Multithreaded mail retrieval. (This means that, if you have the bandwidth, you can download several messages simultaneously.)
- MIME support.

> Although Balsa is easy to use and is relatively stable, it does not have many features and has some stability problems. Many people prefer to use Mahogany, as it is more advanced and has features comparable to Microsoft Outlook or Netscape Messenger. Mahogany uses the GIMP Toolkit and some GNOME development tools, but it is not strictly a GNOME application. Learn more about Mahogany at http://www.wxwindows.org/Mahogany/.

> If you use POP3 for incoming messages, it appears as if Balsa is frozen while the messages are downloading. In the 0.6 version of Balsa, you can't use Balsa at all while messages are downloading. Users have reported problems with Balsa crashing if there are many messages to download.

When you start Balsa for the first time, a configuration dialog box walks you through setting up your email account. All you need is your email address and your SMTP address. Balsa suggests folders for your incoming, outgoing, and trash folders, and creates them for you if they don't exist. For example, the default incoming mail folder is /var/spool/mail/*username*. You can change any of these values later in Properties.

If you are familiar with other email programs, Balsa is easy to understand. By default, there is an Inbox and Outbox for send files and Trash. The main Balsa window is shown in Figure 15.2.

FIGURE 15.2
Balsa is a fast and simple email client.

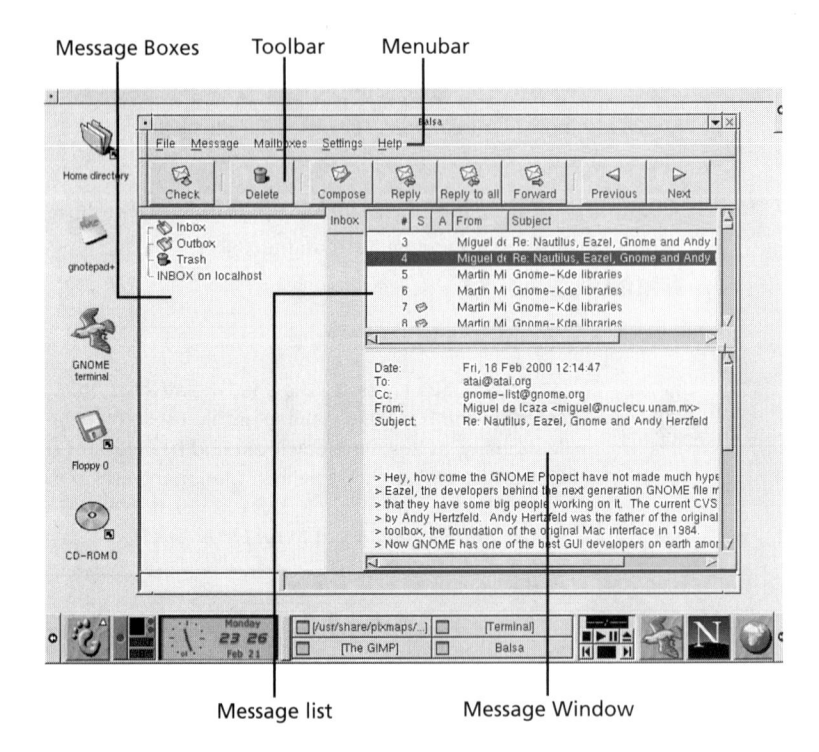

Setting Preferences in Balsa

To configure Balsa the way you like it, use the Preferences in the Settings menu, as shown in Figure 15.3.

FIGURE 15.3
In Balsa Preferences, you can change your identity and other email information that you entered in the Balsa setup dialog box at any time.

Identity Tab

In the Identity Tab of Preferences, set your username, email address, reply-to address (if different from the email address), and the pathname to your signature file.

The reply-to address is useful if you want replies to your messages to go to a different location than where you are. For example, if you are using your Balsa email at work but want to receive a reply at your home email address, change the Reply-to field to your home email address.

Signature files are a great way to personalize your outgoing email messages. You can use them as a business card, to attach your contact information to every email, or you can use them to attach a clever saying of the day or a favorite quote. To create a signature file, create a new text file in your favorite editor and enter the text that you want to appear in the signature. Save the file in your home directory with the filename .signature.

> You can call the signature file anything you want and save it anywhere you want, but *$HOME*/.signature is the default.

If you want to save the signature file in a location other than your home directory, use the Browse button to navigate to your desired location.

Mail Servers Tab

The Mail Servers tab is important, because, although the installation dialog boxes have places for you to enter your SMTP server and outgoing email information, you still have to enter your incoming email information manually here.

To enter an incoming email server, click Add in the Remote Mailbox Servers field. Enter a mailbox name for the messages to be downloaded to, such as Inbox.

Check box is the mailbox that Balsa will download messages to when you click Check. Password is your email password that is assigned by your ISP.

Display and Misc. Tabs

The Misc. tab contains an option for you to customize the prefix that delineates the contents of a message that you are replying to. The default symbol is "<", but you can specify any character, or even a string of characters.

The Display tab has an option to display messages as separate windows or in a preview pane on the main Balsa window. It also contains toolbar display options, with which you can specify to display toolbar items as icons, text, or both icons and text.

Uploading and Downloading Files with gFTP

FTP, which stands for File Transfer Protocol, is used for transferring files and directories between computers via a remote connection, such as PPP. You can use your Web browser or a simple utility such as wget to download single files anonymously from an FTP site. You can also perform simple file manipulations and uploads using GNOME File Manager. If you want to perform tasks that are more complicated, you need an FTP client application such as gFTP. Some of the tasks that gFTP can help you accomplish are

- Log in to FTP sites via user login and password
- Upload files to an FTP site
- Upload or download several files at once or entire directories
- Compare directories on your computer to those of a remote computer
- Manipulate files on a remote computer, including changing permissions, copying, deleting, and moving files
- Edit files on a remote computer

gFTP is an excellent FTP client, with dozens of features, great stability, and speed. Some of gFTP's features include

- ASCII and binary transfer modes
- Multithreaded, so you can transfer several files simultaneously if you have enough bandwidth
- Bookmarks supported, with useful Linux and X11 bookmarks preconfigured
- The capability to resume interrupted file transfers
- Drag-and-drop support
- Support for FTP and http proxy servers
- Automatic connection attempt

Exploring the gFTP Window

If you haven't used an FTP client before, gFTP can look a little daunting at first glance. Although it might not seem so at first, gFTP is as easy to use as a Web browser. After you are familiar with all the buttons and menus, you will want to use gFTP for the simplest to the most complex FTP tasks. Here is a quick exploration of the gFTP window.

The gFTP window is divided into six parts:

- Menu bar
- Toolbar
- Local file system window
- Remote file system window
- Progress window
- Message/log window

Having so many windows helps you to see what's going on during every part of the file transfer, from logging in to breaking the connection. gFTP is shown in Figure 15.4.

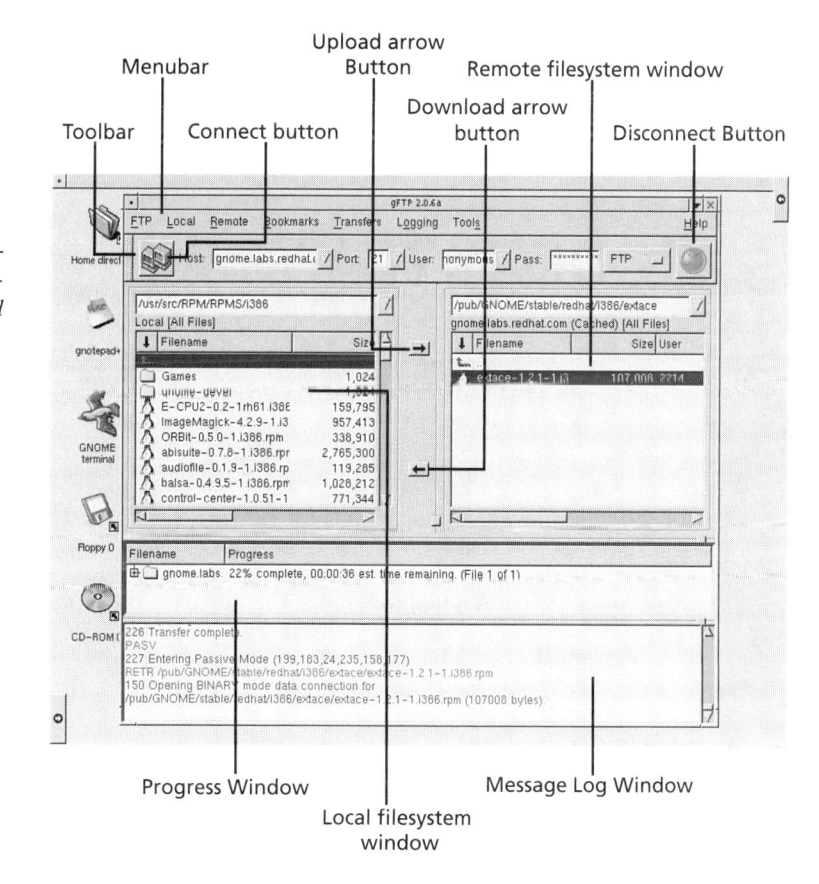

FIGURE 15.4
gFTP can be one of the most useful applications on your desktop if you upload and download files often.

gFTP Menus

The gFTP menus contain all the commands for logging in, downloading, uploading, manipulating files, and comparing directories. A short description of each menu follows. After you have been introduced to the menus and the components of gFTP, each component will be described in detail.

The FTP menu has check boxes to change between ASCII and binary transfer mode and to set options for your remote connection.

The Local menu lets you navigate, select, and manipulate files on your local file system (your hard drive).

The Remote menu lets you navigate, select, and manipulate files on the remote file system.

In the Bookmarks menu, you can create, edit, and list bookmarks for ftp sites.

The Transfers menu contains commands for transferring files via upload and download.

> *Upload* means to transfer files from your computer to a remote computer, via a network connection. Generally, *upload* implies that the files are transferred from a smaller, client system to a larger system, but it is not necessarily so.
>
> *Download* means to transer files from a remote computer to your computer via a network connection. As with an upload, you generally download from a larger server system to a smaller, client system.

The Logging menu contains commands for viewing, saving, and clearing the log and message window.

The Tools menu contains a tool for comparing the remote directory to the local directory.

There is no manual or help for gFTP yet, so the Help menu contains only an About message and a copy of the GNU General Public License (GPL).

Connection Toolbar

The connection toolbar is a detachable toolbar that has fields for you to type in the FTP URL to connect to, your username, and a password. Click the Stop button to break the connection.

Local File System Window

The local file system window displays the directory tree on your hard drive. Files are downloaded to the directory that is currently displayed. You also use the local file system window to select files for upload.

Remote File System Window

The remote file system window displays the directory tree of the remote FTP site to which you are connected. You can download files from and upload files to this directory.

Upload/Download Progress Window

As you download or upload files, the progress window displays the files that are selected for download/upload and the percentage of download/upload that is complete for each file.

Log and Message Window

The log window displays the connection process, any messages from the remote site, messages that your computer sends to the remote site (communication between your computer and the remote computer), and the progress of your file transfers. The log also logs all directory navigation moves you make in the remote and the local file system.

Right-Click Menus

There are several right-click menus in each window, which produce the same items as those in the main menu:

- Local file system window right-click is the same as the Local menu.
- Remote file system window right-click is the same as the Remote menu.
- Progress window right-click is the same as the Transfers menu.
- Log window right-click is the same as the Logging menu.

Using gFTP

Think of using anonymous FTP as if you were a guest on another person's computer. There are certain directories that you are allowed to look in, but most are private. You can read and download files, but you can't manipulate files and directories, you can't move files and directories around, and you can't edit files.

When you establish an FTP connection with a remote site that gives you full permissions, that computer's file system becomes something like an extension of your own. You can copy, move, and delete files and directories. You can create symbolic and hard links. You can open and edit files or upload new files to the remote file system.

Connecting to an FTP Site

The fastest way to connect to an FTP site via anonymous login is to enter the connection information in the Connect toolbar and then click the Connect button. If you don't enter an FTP address in the Host field, a dialog box opens for you to enter an FTP address when you click the Connect button. Enter the URL of the site you want to connect to, as shown in Figure 15.5.

FIGURE 15.5
Enter the hostname of the server you want to connect to. You can enter the IP address instead, if you know it.

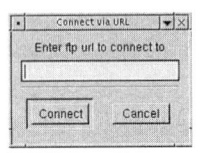

If you want to manually specify the port number, username, and password, enter them in the fields on the connect toolbar. If you leave them blank, gFTP will attempt an anonymous login by default. To break the connection, click the red Disconnect button.

As gFTP connects and negotiates with the remote server, a log of the exchange is displayed in the log window. Messages are color coded to show the origin and purpose of the message:

- Message text from gFTP to you is displayed in red.
- Strings that are sent to the remote server are displayed in green.
- Messages that come back from the remote server are displayed in blue.

Navigating the File Systems

Navigating the local and remote file system windows is much like navigating the windows in File Manager. Double-click a directory to open it and display the files inside. To navigate to a higher directory, double-click the parent, or "..", directory.

> If you log in anonymously to an FTP site and no files or directories appear in the remote directory window, that means that no files or directories are available at that level for anonymous login.

Downloading and Uploading Files

Selecting a file for download is simple. Navigate through the remote directories until you reach the file you want to download. Then, navigate the local file system until you reach the directory where you want to place the downloaded item.

Middle-click the file, files, or directory you want to download and drag the item to the local directory. Alternatively, click the file or directory to select it and click the download arrow button.

> For drag-and-drop to work in gFTP, you must use the middle mouse button.

Uploading files is similar to downloading. Make sure that you have a valid login ID, password, and write permission to the directory you want to upload to before you begin an upload.

> Uploading files anonymously is usually not permitted via anonymous login because you need write permission to the directory. If write permission was given to anonymous logins, a malicious user could easily upload viruses and other nasties to a remote file system.

Comparing Windows

Comparing windows is useful if you already have some of the files in a directory on your local file system, but not others. To determine which files in a remote directory you already have, click Tools, Compare Windows. The files that you already have on your local system will not be selected. Those that do not match the files on your local file system will be selected. Click the download button, and the selected files will be downloaded to your local active directory. Figure 15.6 shows the local directory being compared to the remote directory.

Configuring gFTP Options

The gFTP Options dialog box is similar to Preferences in other GNOME applications. The FTP Proxy and HTTP Proxy tabs have fields for you to enter proxy information, if you use proxies to access FTP and HTTP hosts. The Local Hosts tab has a dialog box for you to enter domain names and hostname information if you are on a network.

The General tab has options for the behavior of gFTP (see Figure 15.7). We will explore the general options in detail.

FIGURE 15.6
After you compare directories, you can synchronize the two directories.

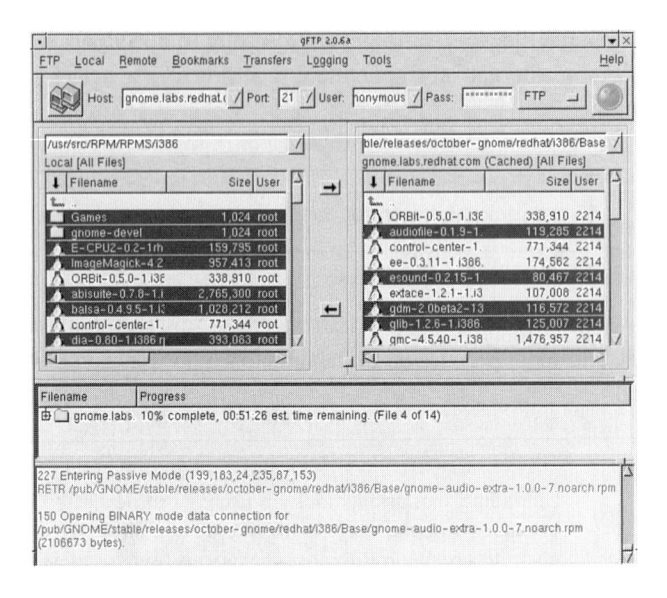

FIGURE 15.7
gFTP has many configuration options.

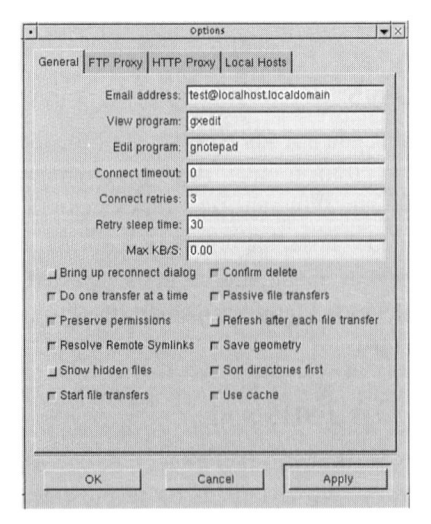

General Options

The most important general options are explained in this section; they are as follows:

- **View program**   If you want to view files with an application other than the gFTP internal viewer, specify the command to run the application in the View Program field. For example, to view files in the GNOME editor gEdit, enter the command gedit in the View Program field. If you leave the field blank, you can view files using the gFTP viewer.

> Not all the files on a remote site can be viewed. If you do not have read permission on a file, you will not be able to view it. Usually, all the files in the /pub directory can be viewed and downloaded via anonymous login.

- **Edit program** If you have write permission to a file on the remote file system, you can edit the file via FTP. Enter the command that starts the file editor of your choice in the Edit Program field. You must specify an editor in the Edit Program field to edit files in gFTP; there is no default editor.

> If you have logged in via anonymous login, or if you do not have write permission on the file, you will not be able to open the file using Edit.

- **Connect timeout** Check this box to have gFTP close the FTP connection if there is no activity within the specified period.
- **Connect retries** Enter the number of times gFTP should try to establish a connection before giving up.
- **Retry sleep time** Enter the number of seconds to wait before trying a busy site again.
- **Bring up reconnect dialog** Check this box if you want to manually reconnect to a site instead of having gFTP automatically try.
- **Do one transfer at a time** gFTP can perform several downloads simultaneously, because it is multithreaded. If you have low bandwidth—for instance, if you are connected via an ordinary telephone line and dial-up modem—check this box to prevent simultaneous download of files.
- **Preserve permissions** Keep the same permissions that the file had on the remote computer for the owning user, owning user's group, and others.
- **Resolve Remote Symlinks** If you want to download a file that is a symbolic link of another file, download the symbolic link as a standalone file with the same contents as the original file, not as a link. You will almost always want to check this option.
- **Show hidden files** Display the hidden files in both local and remote windows.

> Remember that hidden files beginning with a dot, such as .Xauthority, are usually not displayed in a directory listing.

- **Start file transfers** This option instructs gFTP to start the upload or download of a file as soon as you drag and drop it, or select it and click the upload or download arrow.

Using GNOME File Manager for FTP

You can use GNOME File Manager as an FTP client for simple download and file manipulation tasks, thanks to the Virtual File System (VFS). Type the FTP site's URL in the Location box, and File Manager adds it to your directory tree as part of your file system. You can navigate through the directories and download files by dragging and dropping them to a directory on your local file system (hard drive).

You can use File Manager to log in to a remote site and download files via anonymous FTP. If you want to log in to a server using a specific username and password, you need the mcserv package. Download the mcserv package from the GNOME Software Map at http://www.gnome.org/applist/list-martin.phtml.

> Mcserv is a companion utility to gmc that is designed to connect client systems to a network file server. With the new Nautilus file manager that is due to be released with GNOME 2.0, the NFS component will be integrated with the file manager.

Summary

In this hour, you installed and configured Balsa. You used Balsa to send and receive email. You configured gFTP options, and you learned how to use gFTP to upload and download files.

Q&A

Q Can I use Netscape Messenger and Balsa simultaneously?

A You can, although unless you specify that messages should be saved in the same location, you will not be able to read the messages that are saved in the other email client.

Q Can I use a signature file that I create for Balsa in Netscape?

A Yes, by specifying the location of the signature file in both email clients.

Workshop

The quiz questions and exercises are designed to increase your understanding and to encourage you to continue experimenting. Answers appear in Appendix B, "Answers."

Quiz

1. What does "multithreaded" mean for email and ftp?
2. What does a signature file do?
3. What does FTP stand for?
4. Can you upload files via anonymous FTP login?
5. What do the colors in the gFTP message and log window mean?

Exercises

1. Create a signature file for your email messages.
2. Compare the directory where you keep your Linux distribution packages to that of your Linux distribution FTP server. Are you missing any packages? Download packages that you want.
3. Detach the Connection toolbar and place it on the desktop.

HOUR 16

Managing Printing with GNOME

Compared to printing with Windows, printing a document from a Linux or UNIX system can be quite complicated. There are many options to consider. UNIX/Linux is meant to be a multiuser system, so Linux and UNIX act as if print orders are coming from many different users, even if you are the only user on your system. You can print as a user, or print as root, which gives you certain powers. Your printer has a device name, instead of just "Printer." Sometimes different applications use different printing options, and even different drivers. As usual when dealing with UNIX-like systems, all this complexity gives you more power, but it also sometimes makes it difficult to do simple tasks.

In this hour, you will

- Learn about the Linux printing process.
- Use the printing tools lpr, lpd, lpq, and lprm to print files.
- Use the GNOME printer applet to print files.
- Print files from GNOME applications.

Setting Up Your System for Printing

True to their pledge to make UNIX easier to use, the GNOME developers are devising tools to make printing from GNOME applications simpler. Still, there is much that you must configure yourself.

Before you can print any files, you must set your system up for printing. The necessary system information for printing is contained in a file called /etc/printcap. This file defines your printer or printers and stores instructions for sending print jobs to the printers.

> Do not attempt to modify /etc/printcap by hand unless you are experienced with configuring systems for printing and understand the /etc/printcap file.

Because /etc/printcap is rather difficult to modify, most Linux distributions come with print utilities that can create an /etc/printcap file based on your input about your system. For example, Red Hat has a printer configuration utility called printtool (see Figure 16.1), and Caldera comes with a utility called lisa.

FIGURE 16.1
The Red Hat printtool creates the /etc/printcap file based on input from the user.

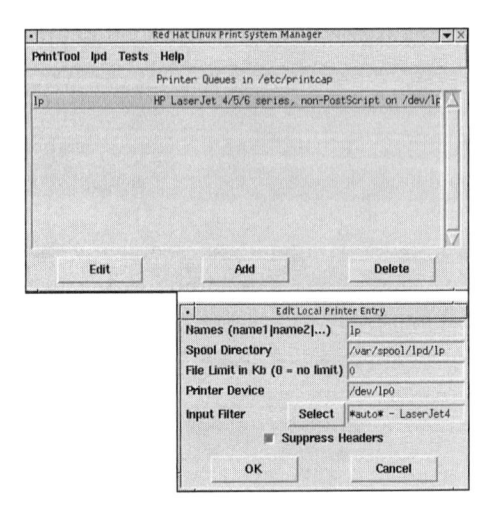

Listing 16.1 illustrates a simple /etc/printcap file for a one-user system with one printer.

LISTING 16.1 Sample /etc/printcap File

```
 1:     # Please don't edit this file directly unless you know what you are doing!
 2:     # Be warned that the control-panel printtool requires a very strict format!
 3:     # Look at the printcap(5) man page for more info.
 4:     #
 5:     # This file can be edited with the printtool in the control-panel.

 6:     ##PRINTTOOL3## LOCAL ljet4 600x600 letter {} LaserJet4 Default 1
 7:     lp:\
 8:        :sd=/var/spool/lpd/lp:\
 9:        :mx#0:\
10:        :sh;\
11:        :lp=/dev/lp0:\
12:        :if=/var/spool/lpd/lp/filter:
```

ANALYSIS Lines 1 to 5 are comments about the /etc/printcap file. Note that line 3 tells you that there is a man page where you can get more information about the printcap file.

Line 6 is a description of the printer, including the default resolution setting of 600 × 600 dpi and letter-sized paper.

Line 7 gives the name of the printer, lp.

Line 8 is the pathname of the print spool directory.

Line 9 defines the maximum file size a print job can have. A definition of 0 means that there is no limit to the file size.

Line 10 gives lpd instructions not to print a header page before each print job.

Line 11 gives the printer name and printer device.

Line 12 provides instructions on using filters for print jobs.

The Printing Process

Selecting a file to print is a simple process. When you click Print, the print dialog box appears with a field to enter the printer name and the print command.

The printer name is the name you gave the printer when you set up printing on your system. You can enter the actual name of the printer, such as **pt002**, or **lp**.

The print command is a bit more complicated. There are several print commands you can use to send a file to the printer. In this hour, we use lpr, which is useful for most print jobs.

Before we get into specific print commands and options, we will review how printing is done in UNIX-like systems. Keep in mind that UNIX—and therefore Linux—is a multiuser system, so all print processes are set up to accept print jobs from many sources simultaneously.

Printing Tools

When you enter the command lpr to print a file, or click Print from an application menu, the print tool lpr looks in the /etc/printcap file for instructions on how to process the file and format it for printing. The formatted print job is then submitted to the print daemon lpd, which accepts the print job and forks a child copy of itself to print the print job. The original lpd waits for the next print job. The file is stored in a temporary directory called the print spool. The print spool stores print jobs from every user on the system and sends them to the printer in the order that the lpd daemon received them. When the file is at the end of the print spool, lpd sends the print job to the printer.

To clarify the process, each tool is described in detail in the following sections.

lpr

lpr is the print utility that accepts each print job and submits it to the printer daemon lpd. Use the lpr command to actually start a print job. The syntax is as follows:

```
$ lpr [ options ] [ filename ... ]
```

Some useful options for lpr are

-P *printer*	Specifies the printer you want to use.
-s	Creates a symbolic link to the printer spool instead of copying the file to the printer spool. Useful for large files.
-#[*number*]	Specifies the number of copies to print. lpr usually prints one copy by default.

lpd

lpd is the printer daemon that manages all print jobs from all users on the system. lpd must be running before a print job is created by lpr, so lpd is usually run at system initialization.

lpq

lpq displays the contents of the print spool, or the print queue, on the screen. lpq displays the rank (active or spooled) of the print jobs, the user who requested the job, the job number, the file name, and the file's size. Listing 16.2 is a sample lpq output.

Managing Printing with GNOME

LISTING 16.2 The `lpq` Tool

```
[root@localhost /root]# lpq
lp is ready and printing
Rank   Owner     Job   Files              Total Size
active root      16    (standard input)   234502 bytes
[root@localhost /root]#
```

lprm

`lprm` removes print jobs from the print spool. You can remove a particular print job by entering `lprm` and the job number, or all the print jobs by entering `lprm -`. Listing 16.3 shows the `lprm` command to remove Print Job # 16.

LISTING 16.3 The `lprm` Tool

```
[root@localhost /root]# lprm 16
dfA016localhost.localdomain dequcucd
cfA016localhost.localdomain dequeued
[root@localhost /root]#
```

> Use `lpq` to get the job number of the print job you want to remove.

GNOME Printing Tools

GNOME has printing tools that make it easier for you to print files from GNOME applications. Some tools, such as the GNOME Printer applet or the `ggv` and `cpanel` utilities, are active tools that help you print or configure your system for printing. Other printing tools, such as `gnome-print`, are included in GNOME applications to help you print.

ggv

`ggv` is a utility that makes it easy to print Post Script files.

cpanel

`cpanel` helps you configure your printers. To set up a printer, right-click and select Properties. In the Printer Properties dialog box, specify the printer name and the command for printing (usually `lpr`).

Gnome-print

Gnome-print is the set of printing libraries that will eventually be included in all GNOME applications that have printing capability. The package is still quite early in its development, so it may seem a little bare in its functionality.

Of all the applications that use gnome-print now, Gnumeric is in the most advanced stage to introduce printing in GNOME, but note that the dialog boxes for printing will be similar for every GNOME application that involves printing.

Like most Windows or MacOS applications, there are three stages to printing a document in GNOME: Print Setup, Print Preview, and Print. Print Setup contains options for you to control exactly how you want your printed page to look. Print Preview displays a screen preview of how the printed page will look. Print involves the printing action itself, including number of copies, printer to print to, and so on.

Print Setup

The first Page tab (the leftmost tab) contains options for you to indicate the size, orientation, and scale of the printout. First, select either letter (upright) or landscape (horizontal) orientation.

Next, if you want a printed page that is larger or smaller than the default, use Scale to adjust the printed size of the document by percentage of original, or by the number of pages the document should take up. The preferred scaling method depends on the kind of document you are printing. Graphics usually do better with a percentage scale, but spreadsheets are easier to read if you can fit them on one or two landscape pages.

If you want to begin printing at a page other than page 1, enter the page number on this tab. For Gnumeric, you can also specify the exact cells to print in the second Page tab.

Every tab in Print Setup has a Print Preview button and a Print button, so you can view changes as you make them, and print as soon as you are satisfied with the layout. The Page tab of Print Setup is shown in Figure 16.2.

In the Margins tab, select the margin size in inches for each edge of the page and for the header and footer. Select paper size from a drop-down menu of standard sizes. A sample sheet changes size and proportion according to the paper size you select. The Margins tab is shown in Figure 16.3.

The Headers and Footers tab contains fields for you to enter a header and footer that will appear on every page. You can use one of the samples provided or enter your own custom header and footer in the Customize Header and Customize Footer fields, as shown in Figure 16.4.

Managing Printing with GNOME 221

FIGURE 16.2
Choose the size and orientation of your printed document in the Page tab.

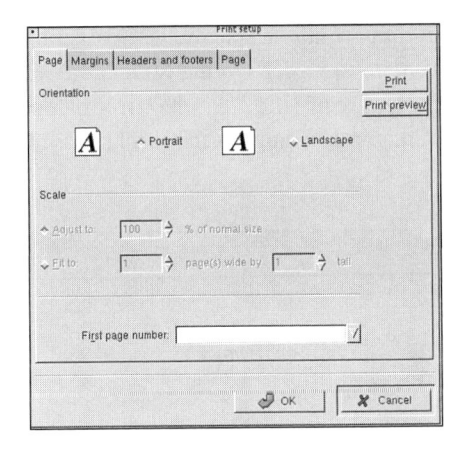

FIGURE 16.3
When calculating margin space around the page, remember that the header and footer are within the margin.

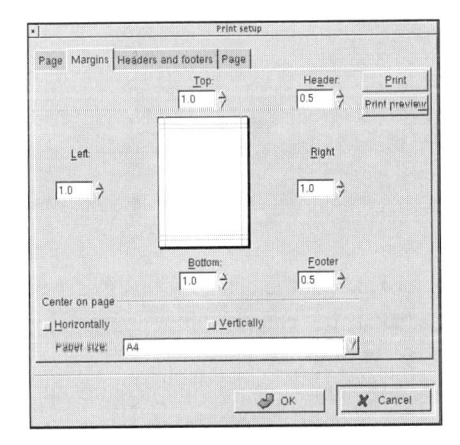

FIGURE 16.4
Add any information that should appear on every page in the Custom Headers and Footers.

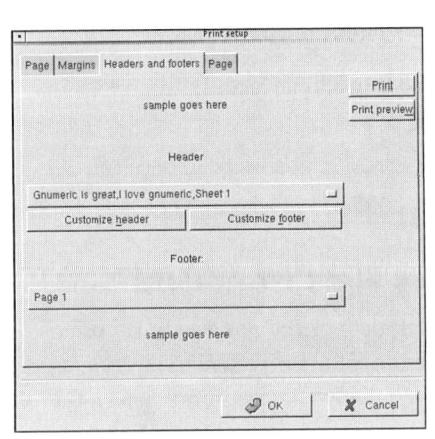

The second Page tab (the rightmost tab) is specific to Gnumeric. Specify the exact area of a worksheet to print by entering the cells in the Print Area field. If you want a row or column heading on every page, specify the column or row name in Titles to Print. You must also select Row and Column Headings in the Print field. The Page tab is shown in Figure 16.5.

FIGURE 16.5
Don't forget to select Row and Column Headings, if you want to use headings on every page.

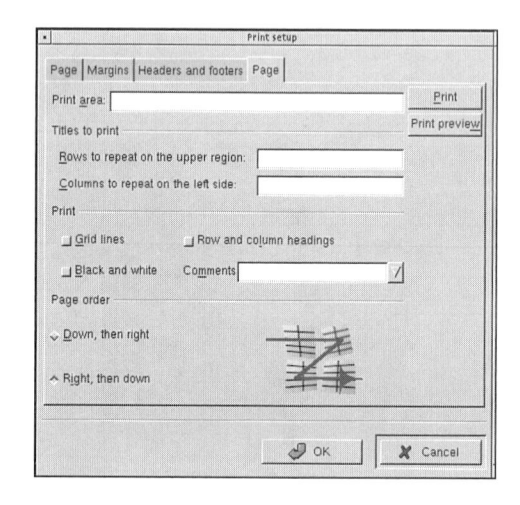

In the Select Printer dialog box, select the category that matches your printer, to ensure that the correct filters are applied. You can print to a printer, in which case you specify the file name, or print to a file to print the document later. The print to file option is useful if you want to print the document using the lp command, so that you can specify special options.

You can also specify which part of the document to print.

- **Active Sheet** prints the sheet that is currently open.
- **All Sheets** prints the enter file
- **Selection** prints the selection you made under Print Setup.

The Select Printer dialog box is shown in Figure 16.6.

Printing Graphics Files from GIMP

Printing graphics files is a little more complicated than printing text files because the files are larger and the formatting is different. Printing a graphics file from the command line can be prohibitively complex. Fortunately, the GIMP has a simple graphical interface, which enables you to print graphics files the way you want them.

FIGURE 16.6
The Select Printer dialog box will eventually support all the printers that Linux supports.

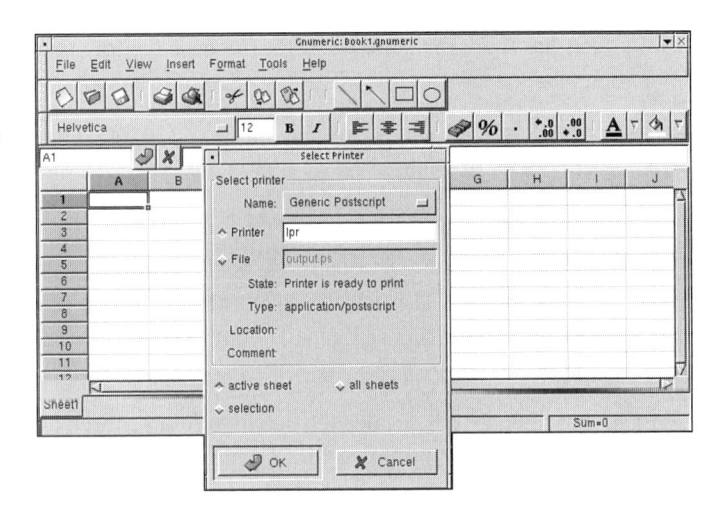

To print a file in GIMP, open the file and right-click it. Select File, Print from the pop-up menu. In the dialog box that appears, shown in Figure 16.7, click Setup. A list of all printers that are supported in GIMP appears. Select your printer.

FIGURE 16.7
The GIMP uses a different set of print libraries than other GNOME applications do.

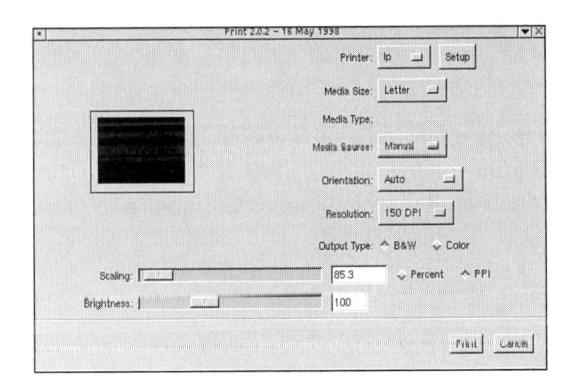

In GIMP, you can either print your job to a file for printing later, or you can send it directly to the print spool. In the Printer field, select either File to print to a file, or the printer name, such as lp.

The Media Size button has three selections for the paper size: letter ($8\frac{1}{2} \times 11$), legal ($8\frac{1}{2} \times 14$), or A4 (11×15).

Some printers have a feature that enables you to choose the kind of paper to print on. If your printer supports it, the Media Type button will appear. Select Plain, Premium, Glossy, or Transparency.

If your printer has more than one paper tray, choose the tray that you want with the Media Source button.

With the Orientation button, select Landscape, Portrait, or Auto. If you choose Auto, GIMP will choose an orientation for you based on how your file would look best.

The Resolution button enables you to choose a high resolution for print jobs when you want high quality, and a low resolution for drafts.

For Output Type, choose either Black and White or Color. If you have a color printer and want a color printout, choose Color. If you have a black-and-white printer, it doesn't matter which you choose.

By default, the scaling slider scales the image to fit an entire page, which means that the image will be stretched or shrunk to fit the page. You can choose a scale of percentage size of the image, or of PPI (pixels per inch), which gives you better control over the quality of the image. As you slide the slider to different values, a preview of the image size and orientation appears in the dialog box.

Brightness controls image contrasts; how it operates depends on your printer. Experiment with this field to see what looks the best.

Summary

In this hour, you learned how printing works in UNIX-like systems. You learned about the various print commands, including `lpd`, `lpr`, `lpq`, and `lprm`. You saw how `/etc/printcap` file is used to store information about your printer and print jobs. You also printed graphics files using GIMP.

Q&A

Q How can I tell if my printer is supported under Linux?

A Check the HOWTO.

Q I ran a very large print job that I wanted to cancel, so I turned off my printer and rebooted Linux. When the computer restarted, my print job continued printing! What should I do?

A Your print jobs remain on the print spool until they are printed or removed from the spool, even if you reboot your computer. Always use `lprm` to cancel a print job.

Workshop

The quiz questions and exercises are designed to increase your understanding and to encourage you to continue experimenting. Answers appear in Appendix B, "Answers."

Quiz

1. How is the `/etc/printcap` file generated?
2. What is the print spool used for?
3. How is `lpd` started? How is `lpr` started?

Exercises

1. Print a file, then use `lpq` to list the print job and `lprm` to remove it from the print spool.
2. Take a screenshot of your computer screen and print it using GIMP.

PART IV
GNOME Applications

Hour

17 Installing and Running GNOME Applications

18 Using GNOME for Your Business

19 Working with Graphics in GNOME

20 Fun with GNOME

HOUR 17

Installing and Running GNOME Applications

GNOME has made a great contribution to the free software movement by making it easier to develop commercial-quality applications. The number of applications is increasing daily, and the range of the software is staggering. The base GNOME packages come with applications, but there are dozens more available. Applications are being developed for everything from spreadsheet and word processing applications to a car diagnostic tool. This hour will help you learn where to find GNOME applications, how applications work in GNOME, and the different ways to run an application.

In Hour 7, "Using the Panel and the Main Menu," you learned how to run applications while exploring the desktop environment.

In this hour, you will

- Learn how applications work within the GNOME desktop environment.
- Open and run GNOME applications using different methods.
- Explore the GNOME Software Map and find interesting applications to download.
- Install new GNOME applications.

Running Applications

As you learned in Hours 7 and 8 ("Managing Files in GNOME"), there are several ways to open applications in GNOME:

- Clicking a launcher in the Main Menu
- Double-clicking an icon on the desktop
- Double-clicking the entry in File Manager
- Clicking a launcher on the panel

You can have as many launchers as you want for the same application in the panel, in the Main Menu, or on the desktop. Figure 17.1 illustrates the different ways to open Iagno, a GNOME game.

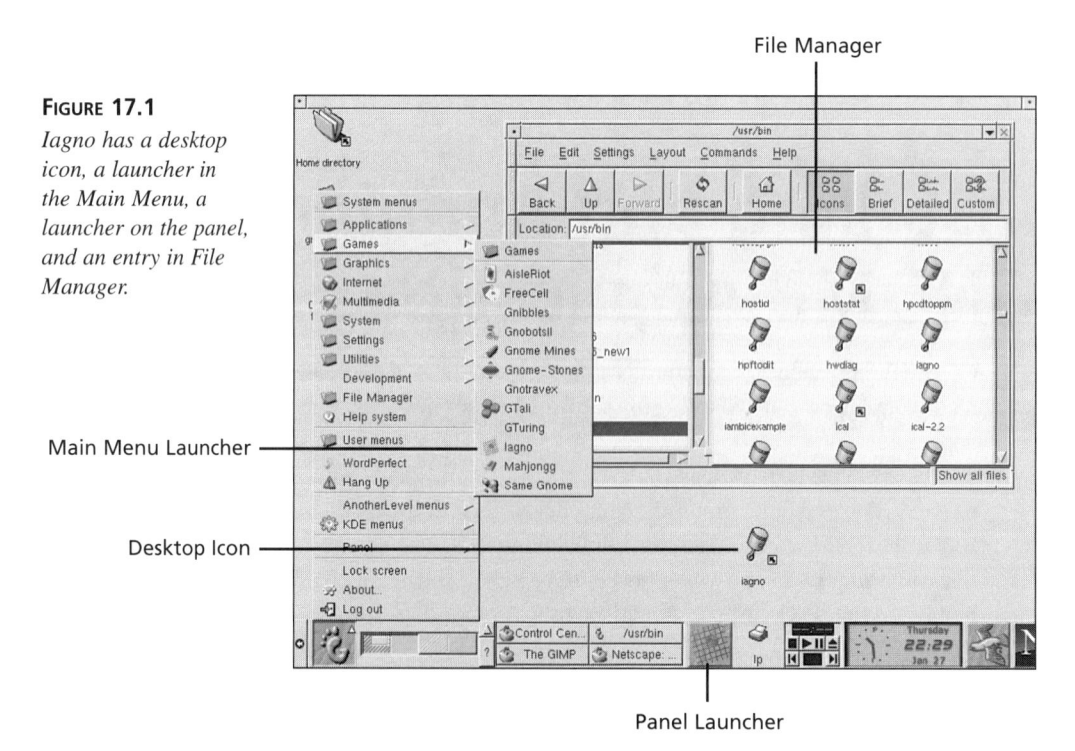

FIGURE 17.1
Iagno has a desktop icon, a launcher in the Main Menu, a launcher on the panel, and an entry in File Manager.

Each time you open an application, you are creating what is called an *instance* of the application. If you open the application twice, then you have two instances of the application on your desktop. Some applications will usually have only one instance per session; others can have several instances. For example, you can have three or more instances of xterm running different processes, or several instances of the GIMP to display different graphics. In Figure 17.2, there are several instances of xterm running.

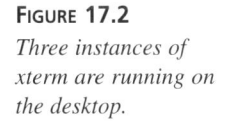

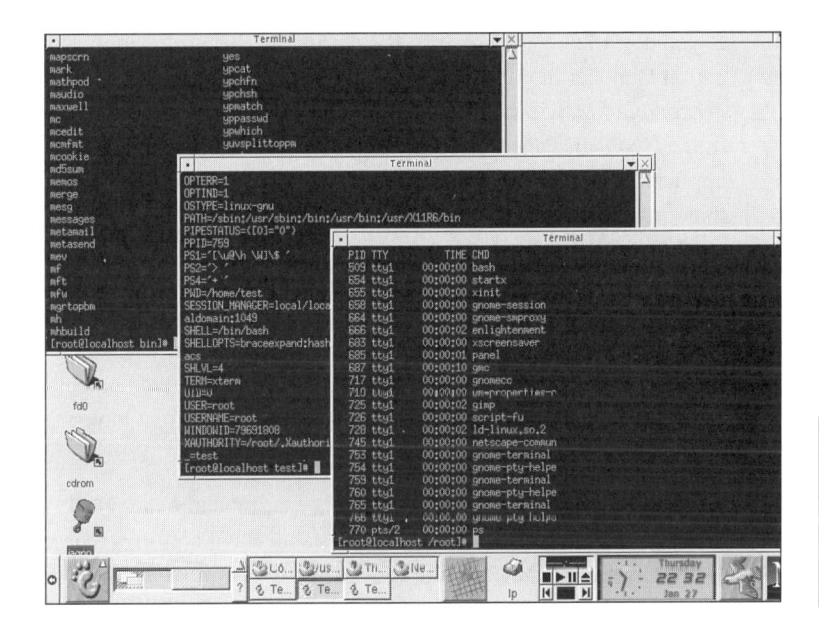

FIGURE 17.2
Three instances of xterm are running on the desktop.

Running Applications from the Command Line

You can also start GNOME applications by running the executable file in a shell session. In other words, you can open an xterm, and enter the command that will start a GNOME application. In Figure 17.3, WordPerfect has been started from the command line.

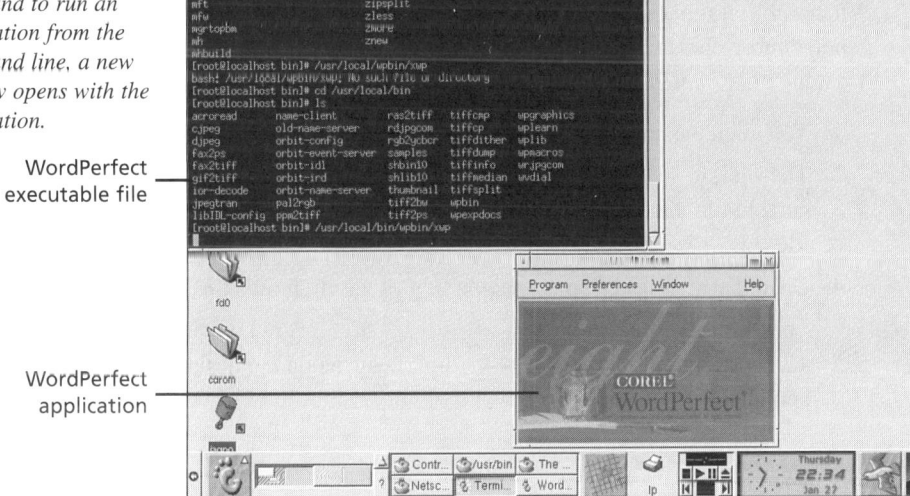

FIGURE 17.3
When you give the command to run an application from the command line, a new window opens with the application.

WordPerfect executable file

WordPerfect application

If you don't know the name of the command to start an application, right-click the application launcher in the Main Menu and select Properties. The command, also called an *executable file*, will be in the Command field. If there is no launcher in the Main Menu, in the GNOME Panel, or on the desktop, read the documentation that comes with the application to find the right command. As a last resort, you can look in the subdirectories that are defined in your path to find the correct command.

The PATH Environment Variable

Your *path* is the full pathname that leads from the root directory to the subdirectory, which contains the executable files, or commands, on your computer. The path is defined for your computer by the environment variable PATH. Some examples of common paths are /usr/bin, /usr/local/bin, or /opt/bin. You might have some or all of these directories defined in your PATH.

To determine what your path is, enter the command echo $PATH at a shell prompt. The output of the echo $PATH command lists all the directories that are in your PATH. The PATH tells the computer where to look for the commands that will run your applications. Listing 17.1 shows a typical path environment variable.

LISTING 17.1 The PATH Environment Variable

```
echo $PATH
/sbin:/usr/sbin:/bin:/usr/bin:/usr/local/bin:/usr/X11R6/bin
```

GNOME Applications—Behind the Scenes

Whenever you run an application—whether you open it by clicking a launcher on the panel, double-clicking the entry in the Main Menu, or double-clicking an icon on the desktop—this same process occurs:

1. You click the launcher or enter the command to run an application.
2. The shell looks at the PATH environment variable to find the location of the executable file that is needed to run the application, and then locates the executable file.
4. Once the shell finds the corresponding program, it tells the kernel to load and run the program.
5. The application runs, and a new window opens on the desktop containing your application.

Now that you have learned how to run applications, you can find and install new GNOME applications that suit your needs. In the next section you will learn how to navigate the GNOME Software Map to find applications that interest you.

Finding New GNOME Applications

There are dozens of GNOME applications available for free download. The core GNOME team develops some applications. Increasingly, developers who are not part of the core team are creating applications based on GNOME tools. At present, the best places to look for new applications are the GNOME Software Map, the GNOME home page, and the GNOME announcement mailing list.

The GNOME Software Map

GNOME applications are proliferating rapidly, because one of the key goals of GNOME is to make it easy to create desktop GUI applications for UNIX. The GNOME Software Map is a central clearinghouse where developers can post information about the applications they are developing for GNOME.

The downside to the Software Map is that it can be hard to find the applications you want. The map is ordered by category of software, and then alphabetically by application name. If you're not sure which category a particular application goes in, finding it can be time-consuming. This can also be an advantage, however, as you can read about other interesting applications along the way.

> Listed under the Internet Tools category, the GNOME Software Map Browser will browse the map for particular applications by keyword, so you don't have to search manually. The browser is still in an early stage of development.

The GNOME Software Map is found at `http://www.gnome.org/applist/list-martin.phtml`. When you open the Software Map page, you will see a list of icons, which give basic information about each item on the Software Map. The icons are shown in Figure 17.4.

Homepage

A Homepage icon indicates that the application has a Web page devoted to it. The Homepage icon usually contains a description of the application, news about the application's development, a link to a server where you can download the application, and sometimes screenshots and additional documentation.

FIGURE 17.4
Use the Software Map icons to find interesting GNOME applications.

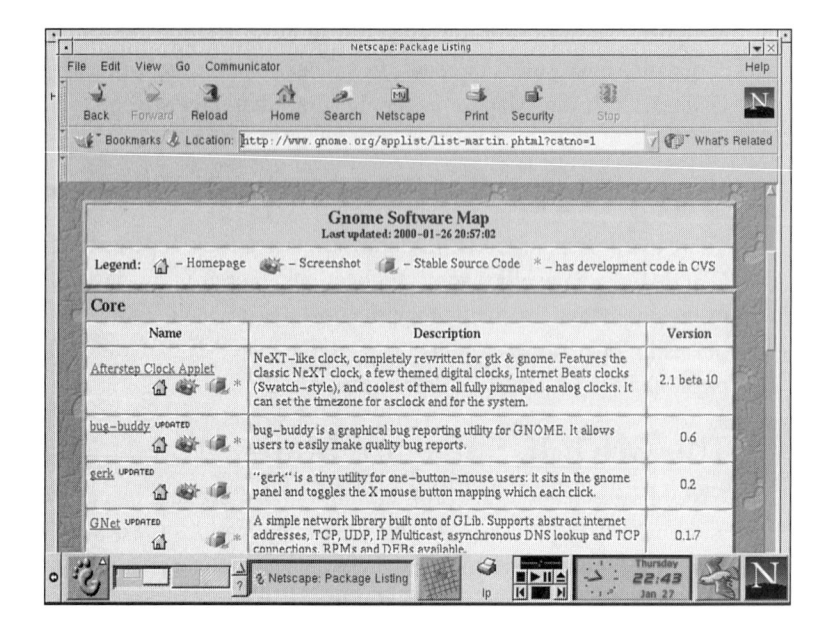

Screenshot

A Screenshot icon means that a screenshot of the application in action is available. Screenshots are usually found on the Website of the application.

Stable Source Code

This icon means that the source code has been released as a stable version. *Stable* means that the source code is bug-free enough for its main functionality to work. Also, under normal conditions the application should not crash. A stable release is not necessarily a 1.0 release; so don't be put off by releases that are numbered in the 0.10s, if the Stable Source Code icon is present.

Development Code in CVS

The red asterisk in the Legend means that the application is checked into GNOME CVS. Not all applications are considered to be part of the GNOME Project, and not everybody who works on GNOME has a CVS account. Some applications are created by individuals who use GNOME tools, but who aren't part of the core GNOME team. If the asterisk appears, that means that the development version of the app has been checked into CVS for everyone to test and debug. You will learn more about CVS in Hour 22, "Upgrading GNOME and Joining the GNOME Project."

Software Categories on the Software Map

To make it easier to find applications, the Software Map is divided into categories. Software within the categories is ordered alphabetically by name. The number in parentheses after the category title indicates the number of applications that are available in that category. This number changes as new applications are added to the Software Map.

Core

The central applications and libraries of the GNOME desktop environment, such as GNOME applets and gnome-core, are included in the Core category. Software that is part of the base GNOME installation but that is developed by another project, such as Imlib and GTK, is not included here.

Development Tools

Tools that are of use to application developers of GNOME are included in this category, as well as tools that are useful for any application development environment. The Development Tools category includes Web editors, compilers, rpm package builders, tools to use with CVS, language bindings, programming environments, and widget sets.

Electrical Design/Programmers

This category currently houses just one application, Oregano, which is used to simulate electrical circuits.

Entertainment

The Entertainment category includes games, multimedia applications, panel amusement apples, network-based gaming tools, and other amusements. Some of the games are described in detail in Hour 20, "Fun with GNOME."

Internet Tools

The Internet Tools category includes tools to use with the Internet, including an HTML editor, an http search tool, an ftp client called DPS-FTP, a Usenet newsreader, a lightweight Web browser called Express, a tool to search for certain files over ftp, Gnomba (a GUI Samba browser), and several PPP dialers based on the GNOME user interface.

Mail Clients

The Mail Clients category contains several mail clients written for GNOME, using IMAP, POP3, and SMTP protocols.

Math and Science Tools

This category contains many interesting tools. Many are of particular interest to people involved in scientific research, but some are useful to the ordinary user. Some of the applications Math and Science Tools contains are

- An automobile diagnostic application (in early stages of development).
- An algebraic calculator.
- A multiple-precision floating-point calculator, as well as many other calculators.
- A fractal generator.
- You'll also find an application that lists the periodic table of the elements, with information about each element, and an astronomy application that describes various astronomical phenomena.

Miscellaneous

The Miscellaneous category is a catch-all for applications that don't fit into any other Software Map category. This category includes applications such as

- A college class schedule program
- A GNOME uncompression utility
- An automatic desktop background changer
- A binary file editor
- A map viewer
- A panel applet that shows the phases of the moon
- A catalog for your zip, CD-ROM, and floppy disks
- A portfolio manager
- An encrypted password manager
- An application installer for making autoinstall CDs
- A Post-It utility
- A Web searching applet

Network Talk Clients

The Network Talk Clients category includes software that is useful for chatting on the Internet. Some of the tools include an instant messaging client similar to AOL Instant Messenger, lots of chat applications, and various utilities to use with IRC (Internet Relay Chat), including the famous XChat and ICQ clients for instant messaging.

Productivity

The Productivity category includes some of the GNOME Office applications, as well as many other applications that are useful at work. Some of the productivity applications include

- Dia, a Visio-like drawing application
- Emma, a money management program
- Electric Eyes and Eye of GNOME, both image viewers
- Gaby, a personal database manager will help you keep track of data like addresses
- Gaspell, a spell checker
- GIMP, the graphics application
- Several GNOME text editors
- Gfax, a fax application
- GNOME-PIM, a personal information management program
- gnome-utils, a package of useful utilities
- Gnumeric, the GNOME spreadsheet program
- Money management and tax prep software

Sound Tools

The Sound Tools category contains lots of applications for sound, including

- gnome-media, the basic multimedia package for GNOME
- Electric Ears, an audio player, editor, and recorder
- Gstring, a guitar tuner
- Midnight, a MIDI player which you can use for karaoke

Rounding out the category are various sound editors, some voice recognition software (early development), and an MP3 organizer and search utility.

System Utilities

The System Utilities category has many utilities to make using and administering your Linux/UNIX system easier. The category includes gdm, which is xdm with a GNOME ui, and cpanel, which helps you configure printers, network cards, modems, partitions, and so on. Gfdisk is a partition program like fdisk. GIP, the Gnome Install Project, makes the installation, upgrade, and deinstallation of software in Linux easier. There are graphical front ends of various UNIX commands; gnome-admin, which contains several system administration tools; gnome-apt, a front end for the Debian package manager; GnoRPM, a front end for the Red Hat package manager; GtkSamba, a front end for configuring Samba; Seahorse, which is a GNOME front end for an encryption/decryption program; and many other tools.

Window/Session/Desktop Managers

This category contains GNOME-compliant window managers—such as IceWM, sawmill, and SCWM—and patches for BlackBox and CTWM to make these non-compliant window managers compliant. There are also some new window managers in early stages of development, and the GNOME Panel package is also included here.

The GNOME Office Homepage

The GNOME Office Project is a sub-project of the GNOME Project. Its goal is to create a suite of office productivity applications that are of commercial quality and that consist entirely of free software. Most of the applications listed in the GNOME Office Homepage are also listed in the Software Map, but there are some that are not included. The GNOME Office Suite includes the word processor AbiWord, the spreadsheet Gnumeric, GNOME-PIM, the GNOME personal information manager, and gnome-db, a database program.

The GNOME Office Project home page is `http://www.gnome.org/gnome-office/`. You will learn more about GNOME Office in Hour 18, "Using GNOME for Your Business." Figure 17.5 shows the home page of the GNOME Office Project.

FIGURE 17.5

The goal of the GNOME Office Project is to produce a suite of productivity software that will be able to compete with commercial office suite software.

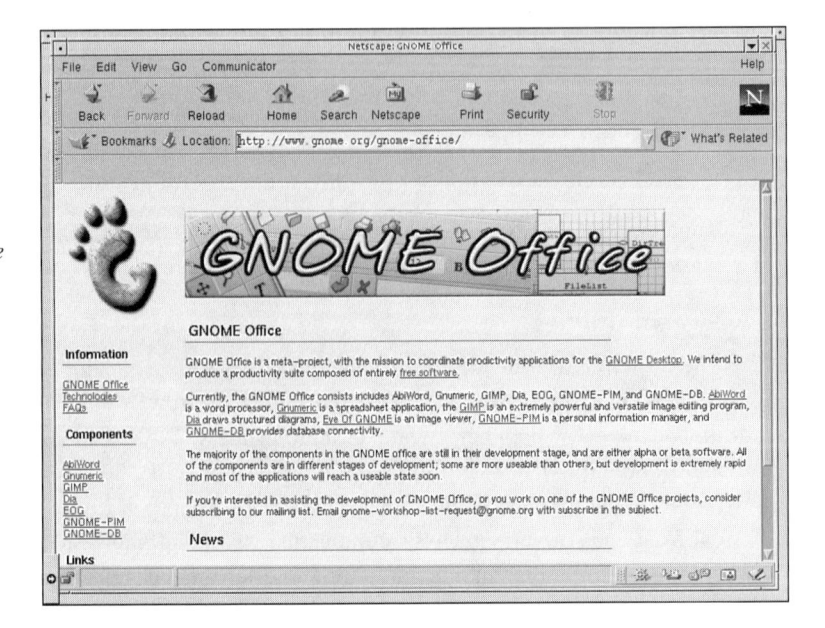

gnome-announce Mailing List

If you want to keep up to date on new releases of GNOME software, subscribing to gnome-announce is a must. GNOME developers use gnome-announce as the fastest way to announce new releases of GNOME software to the community. gnome-announce is also useful for keeping up on GNOME news, interviews, awards, and other items of interest to the GNOME community.

> Announcements are generally made to gnome-announce and gnome-list, the general GNOME mailing list. If you subscribe to gnome-list, it is not necessary to subscribe to gnome-announce.

Downloading and Installing GNOME Applications

Download and install GNOME applications in the same way you downloaded and installed the basic GNOME packages. If you need to, review "Installing GNOME from Downloaded rpms" in Hour 2. Remember, you can download GNOME packages from the ftp sites that contain them using

- Netscape
- wget
- Lynx

After downloading the package, install it using GnoRPM or whatever package installation manager you have chosen.

> Make a habit of using GnoRPM to install rpm packages, so that all the rpms on your system are present in the GnoRPM database.

Tarballs Versus Binary Packages Revisited

The developer of a GNOME application usually releases only the source code in tarball format. Another member of the GNOME project will then make the rpm, usually several weeks later. Sometimes Red Hat Software will make an rpm and post it on the Red Hat ftp server, but only for packages that are part of the base installation. There are two teams on the GNOME Project that are working on making it easier to install GNOME:

the GNOME Install Project and the GNOME packaging team. Both teams are working to make binary packages available faster for more users. Still, the first release of a new application is often a tarball. If you don't want to wait for someone to make an rpm, you have several options, which we discuss in this section.

Request an `rpm` on gnome-list

Sometime the best thing to do is simply send out a general request for an rpm. Often, someone will volunteer to make an rpm and will post it to the GNOME ftp server for download.

Make Your Own `rpm`

Making your own rpm can be surprisingly easy or difficult and frustrating, depending on your own expertise and the condition of the source code. To make an rpm, there must be a file called the *spec file* in the main directory of the unpacked tarball. The spec file provides instructions for how to make the rpm. If the spec file exists, try entering the following command:

`rpm -tb [tarball_name]`

Creating rpms is beyond the scope of this book, but there is some excellent documentation available that covers the subject. The rpm Web site, http://www.rpm.org, provides a good introduction to rpms, as well as an online book that covers rpms in detail. You should also review the rpm man page on your computer.

Install the Application from a Tarball

There are often problems associated with mixing GNOME binary packages and tarballs. When you install an application from source code, there are files called *libraries* that must be present on your system so that the source code can compile into a binary executable file.

If you want to install an application from source code and your base GNOME installation is from rpms or other binary packages, there are some extra steps you must take to get the tarball to compile so you can use it.

First, download and install the development packages from the GNOME Web site or from your Linux distribution CD. The development packages have libraries that are needed for source code to compile.

Attempt to install the GNOME application. Pay careful attention to any errors you get when you run the configure script. Sometimes if you download and install the source code of an application, it won't find the other libraries it needs if the required libraries were created from an rpm. For example, rpms often place executables in /usr/bin and libraries in /usr/lib, whereas most GNOME configure and make files put them in /usr/local/bin and /usr/local/lib.

You might have to add symbolic links to the libraries or define a path to the libraries so the configure script can find them.

The alternative to this problem is to install GNOME from source code and install all applications from source code. Installing from source code is not an easy endeavor and can be time-consuming, but it is the best way to learn about your system.

Summary

In this hour, you ran GNOME applications from the Main Menu, a desktop icon, File Manager, a panel launcher, and from a shell prompt. You learned how File Manager works behind the scenes to run applications. You explored the GNOME Software Map and found interesting applications. Finally, you installed new GNOME applications.

Q&A

Q Most of the applications on the GNOME Software Map appear to be in the early stages of development. Won't there be lots of bugs? Will they crash my system?

A As a project, GNOME is barely two-years-old, so most of the applications are new. If the Stable Source Code icon appears in an application entry, that means the application has been tested sufficiently for the developer to be satisfied with the application's stability. Remember, however, that there are no guarantees.

Q How can I learn to develop my own GNOME applications?

A Hours 23, "GNOME Technologies," and 24, "Anatomy of a GNOME Application," provide basic information on the anatomy of GNOME applications and GNOME programming. You will also learn where to get more information on GNOME application development in these chapters.

Workshop

The quiz questions and exercises are designed to increase your understanding and to encourage you to continue experimenting. Answers appear in Appendix B, "Answers."

Quiz

1. Name five ways to open an application in GNOME.
2. How many launchers can you have for the same application?
3. What is an instance of an application?
4. What is the PATH environment variable used for?

Exercises

1. Open several instances of Gnome Terminal (use a different method each time). Then open a few instances of File Manager and a few instances of GNOME Control Center.

2. From a shell prompt, enter ps-a and see what kind of output you get. Then look in Browse Currently Running Programs in GCC, and see what is there.

3. Open a shell session using your favorite GNOME terminal. At a shell prompt, enter the **set** command. Study the output. What is your path?

HOUR 18

Using GNOME for Your Business

There are a few people in the free software community who think that the concept of free software will eventually turn the entire software industry on its head. If free software breaks out of the technical community and gains a place in the business community, software development, perhaps even the definition of software itself, could change entirely.

This hour is composed of two sections. In the first section, we discuss some possible models for using GNOME in an enterprise, the advantages of GNOME in business, and some of the disadvantages. In the second section, we explore GNOME Office, a group of applications designed to compete with and replace costly commercial productivity software.

In this hour, you will

- Learn about the business future of free software, in general, and GNOME in particular.
- Discover how GNOME can be used in an enterprise setting.
- Examine the advantages and disadvantages of using GNOME for your business.
- Explore GNOME Office and other GNOME productivity applications.
- Compare GNOME Office to commercial office suite applications.

GNOME in an Enterprise

Ever since the advent of the personal desktop computer, personal computers have become a fundamental part of every office. Productivity applications have become more complex as software companies scramble to provide as many features as a customer could possibly want. The end result is huge, disk-space–eating, memory-hogging, bloated software loaded down with features that most users don't need or understand how to use. This licensed, proprietary software costs hundreds of dollars and often doesn't work with any other vendor's software, forcing businesses and individual users to buy "office suites." Few people need all the applications in these suites, but it is easier than trying to get the individual proprietary applications of several vendors to work together.

The problems with modern commercial productivity software can be boiled down to two issues: complexity and cost. As applications become more complex and feature-heavy, it gets harder and harder to make updates and improvements and to add new features. The learning curve for new developers and new users also grows, and the software becomes more expensive.

The GNOME Solution to Complexity

As you will learn in Hour 24, "Anatomy of a GNOME Application," GNOME applications are based on the concept of *component software*. Instead of large, complex applications that contain every imaginable feature, the GNOME Office consists of a string of small, simple, and lightweight applications that easily integrate together to provide whatever feature you need. If a feature you want is not in an application, it is easily developed and added as a component. You then have this component, or mini-application, available for incorporation into any other application you want. In addition, macros are easily attached to any application using any scripting language that has a CORBA binding, including Python and Perl.

Applications just become object servers, or containers that you plug components into to get the functionality you want. It then becomes easy to create designer applications that have all the features you want, with none of the fluff. It is also easier to learn a very complex piece of software if you start out with its simpler functions and add complexity as you get more familiar with the components.

With GNOME Office, for example, companies could design individual word-processing applications based on the needs of each person's job function. People who only needed the basics would get the core application, and others would add components, as they needed them. Accountants would get spreadsheet functionality that they could attach to word processing. A secretary might need only the basics of the spreadsheet to create simple documents, and not need hundreds of other functions. Graphics designers would get the graphics import component included in their word processing software.

The Business Advantage of GNOME

GNOME as a business solution is not quite ready to be unleashed in the office. There are some intriguing aspects to GNOME, however, that deserve notice.

GNOME is free. In the Microsoft era, software is expensive, prohibitively expensive for the small business owner. Even for large corporations, the price tag for licenses for one new application can run into the hundreds of thousands of dollars.

GNOME is customizable. Imagine having a desktop in which your company's logo—not Microsoft's—appears on every open window, where, in fact, your desktop is "themed" to be uniquely different from anyone else's.

It is easy to understand the GNOME applications inside and out. There are no expensive training courses that teach you the undocumented secrets and tricks of the software, or even the basics. If you want to know everything there is to know about a GNOME application, just look at the source code.

You also don't have programming language restrictions with GNOME apps. Because the interface for the components is CORBA, any component can be written in any language. So, if you want to design your own add-on to a GNOME application that was written in C, but your developers prefer to work in C++ or Perl, they can write the plug-in in whatever language they want and it will still work.

Disadvantages of GNOME

The biggest disadvantage of deploying GNOME in business is that it is still new. Documentation is sparse, there is no training, and there are few system administrators with experience installing and implementing it.

GNOME Office applications themselves are still in development. Most have not had a 1.0 release yet, although the applications mentioned in this chapter are all stable.

An outside support organization is probably necessary for anyone seriously considering using GNOME as his main desktop and applications suite. These companies can support your sysadmins in the GNOME installation, design a customized desktop to protect your users from most of the complexity of GNOME, and even design custom applications for you, based on the particular needs of your office.

GNOME Office

The goal of GNOME Office is to create a suite of office productivity applications out of free software. The free software office suite will compete with commercial office suites such as Microsoft Office and Corel Office. The components of GNOME Office are based on the GNOME architecture and development toolkit. The home page for GNOME Office is http://www.gnome.org/gnome-office.

If you are familiar with Microsoft Office, there is virtually no learning curve to using GNOME Office. The interface will look familiar, and the applications work the same. This section provides an introduction to GNOME software that is designed for business use.

AbiWord

AbiWord is the word processing component of GNOME Office. SourceGear, a for-profit corporation that produces open-source software, created AbiWord. Based on the GNOME interface, AbiWord is fast and sleek, takes up only 729Kb of disk space, and is intuitive to use for anyone who has experience using MS Word. It has all the major features of Word, including

- Character formatting
- Dynamic spell check (misspelled words turn red as you type them)
- A rulerbar with interactive tabs
- Type 1 fonts
- Unlimited Undo/Redo
- Multiple columns
- Widow/orphan control
- Find/Replace
- Easy import of graphics

AbiWord is shown in Figure 18.1.

FIGURE 18.1
If you are familiar with Microsoft Word, you can easily use AbiWord.

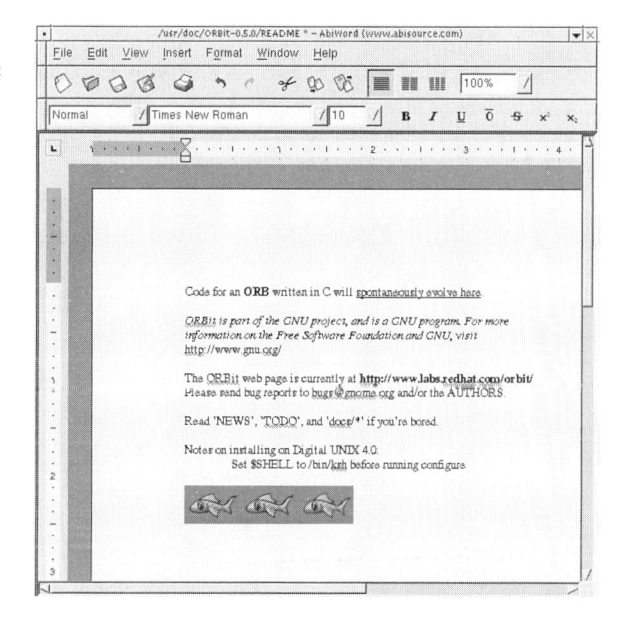

AbiWord has all the major features of MS Word without the bloat. The big advantage of AbiWord is its cross-platform capability. AbiWord runs on UNIX, Win32, BeOS, and MacOS. It can import Word 97 and RTF files and can export documents in RTF, Text, HTML, and LaTeX formats.

AbiWord itself is quite simple, but the base AbiWord application is designed to accept as many components as the user wants. AbiWord also easily incorporates objects created in other GNOME applications that the user will eventually be able to modify within AbiWord itself.

AbiWord does have a way to go before it's ready for a 1.0 release. Many of the menu options produce pop-up messages informing you that the feature is yet to be developed. Typical for free software, the messages also solicit code contributions. At present, the only graphics type that AbiWord can import is the png format, and resizing is not possible yet. Eventually, though, AbiWord will join Corel WordPerfect and StarOffice as definite freeware rivals to the Microsoft Office universe. The Web site for AbiWord is http://www.abisource.com/.

Gnumeric

Gnumeric is the most advanced of the GNOME office applications except for the GIMP, which will be discussed in Hour 19, "Working with Graphics in GNOME." Gnumeric is the brainchild of Miguel Icaza, the founder of the GNOME Project, so it is usually the first GNOME application to incorporate the latest GNOME concepts, libraries, and features.

A venerable rival to MS Excel, Gnumeric incorporates most of Excel's features. Gnumeric uses the XML file format, but it can easily import and export Excel files. The design and user interface is similar to that of MS Excel, so if you are familiar with Excel you will feel right at home with Gnumeric. Gnumeric is pictured in Figure 18.2.

FIGURE 18.2
Gnumeric is one of the most advanced GNOME applications. Notice that the document shown here is an imported Excel file.

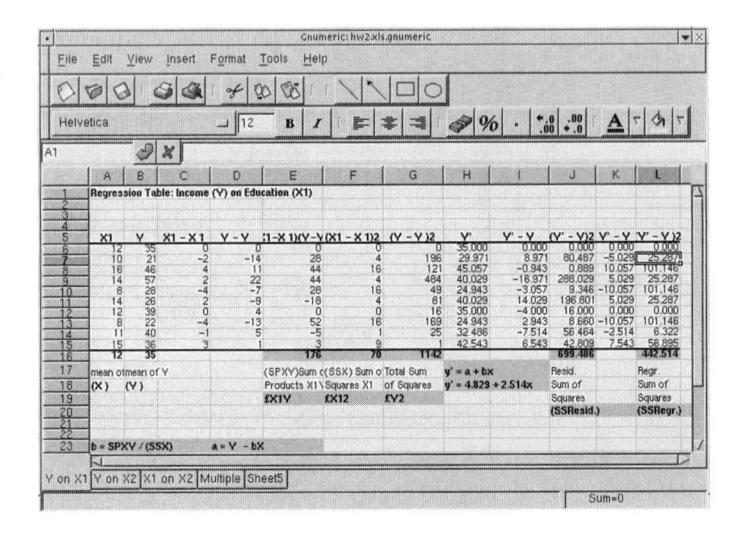

Gnumeric supports many more file formats than Excel. The currently supported file formats for import and export include

- Import
    - XML
    - Excel
    - HTML
    - CSV
    - Lotus 1-2-3
- Export
    - XML
    - Excel
    - HTML
    - LaTeX
    - PDF
    - EPS
    - CSV
    - DVI
    - Troff

Gnumeric comes with a full suite of data analysis tools and a "goal-seek" capability. Also, it can be completely automated to work within other applications, if there are CORBA bindings for the programming language the application is written in.

Gnumeric comes with an online user's manual and a function reference manual. The Web page for Gnumeric is http://www.gnome.org/gnumeric.

GNOME-PIM

GNOME Personal Information Manager includes an address book, calendar, appointment scheduler, and task list. GNOME-PIM is fully compatible with Palm Pilot, and files can be downloaded and synchronized with Palm Pilot via the gnome-pilot tool.

GNOME-PIM is available via tarball and rpm and Debian packages.

> For more information on gnome-pilot, see http://www.gnome.org/gnome-pilot/. The Web page http://eunuchs.org/linux/palm/index.html has useful general information on Palm Pilots and Linux.

GNOME Calendar

Another component to GNOME-PIM, GNOME Calendar is comparable to commercially available calendars, such as Microsoft Schedule or Franklin-Covey Planner. If you are familiar with commercial time management software, GNOME Calendar will look familiar.

The main window of GNOME Calendar contains tabs for daily, weekly, monthly, and yearly views of the calendar. The Daily View has an appointment calendar on the left and a To Do list on the right. You can customize the window in Preferences. GNOME Calendar is shown in Figure 18.3.

FIGURE 18.3

The features of GNOME Calendar are comparable to commercial calendars.

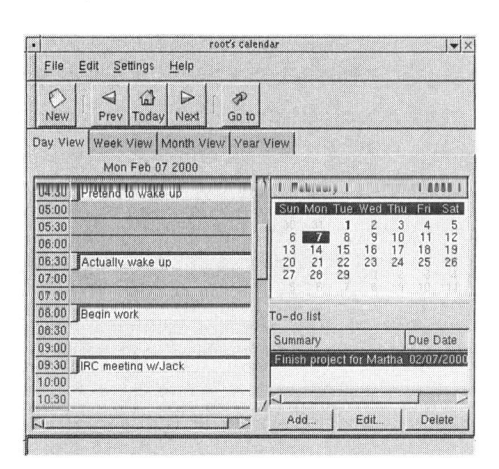

One of the advanced features of GNOME Calendar is its set of alarms. When you create a new appointment, you have several alarms to choose from to ensure that no one will miss the appointment.

The alarms dialog box contains audio, visual, and customized alarms, but it also has an email feature for you to email reminders. For example, you could send automatic email reminders to team members about the upcoming meeting two days before the event. Then you could set up a display reminder for yourself 15 minutes before the event and an audio alarm 5 minutes before, and finally play a .wav file of your mother yelling at you 1 minute before the event.

An appointment can also be classified public, private, or confidential. You can also set up recurring appointments on a daily, weekly, monthly, or yearly schedule. Enter the dates of the recurring appointment or make it continue forever. You can also enter exceptions, which are dates on which the recurring appointment should be skipped.

With GNOME Calendar, you are not limited to an 8:00 a.m. to 6:00 p.m. day. In Preferences, you can decide whether you want a 24-hour calendar or a 12-hour or you can specify the exact times your calendar will begin and end. This feature is extra useful if you're not a 9-to-5 kind of person.

You can customize all the calendar colors, empty days, days that have appointments, a highlighted day, the current day, and a day that contains an overdue To Do item. You can also customize your To Do list to annotate overdue items.

GNOME Calendar comes with a thorough user's manual, and GNOME Calendar—one of the few applications included in *The GNOME User's Guide*.

GNOME Address Book

GNOME Address Book works as both a contact management system and electronic business card database, similar to Act, Goldmine, or Franklin-Covey Planner. When you open Address Book, all your contacts are listed in the window with columns of information that you can customize in Preferences. Press New to make a new entry in the address book. The main window of Address Book is shown in Figure 18.5.

The New Entry dialog box contains fields for you to enter the name, organization, and birthdate of your contact. You can enter as many email addresses as you like, including information on the kind of email address, for example, AOL, Prodigy, IBM, AT&T, MCI, Internet, and so on. There is also a field to include a URL for the contact's Web page.

In the Addresses and Phone tabs, there are spaces to enter multiple addresses and phone numbers for the contact, with checkboxes to indicate the kind of address or phone number. In the geographical tab, you can enter the contact's latitude, longitude, and time zone. GNOME Address Book supports PGP and X.509 public key encryption.

FIGURE 18.4
GNOME Address Book can be synchronized with your Palm Pilot.

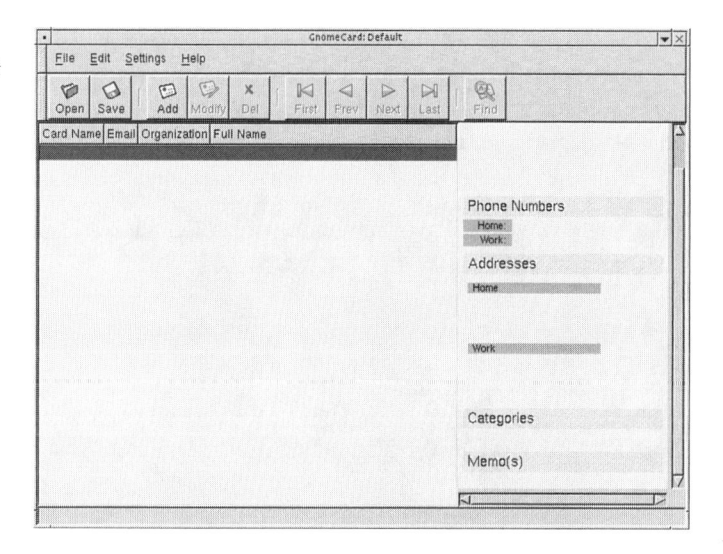

Address Book comes with a sorting feature that enables you to sort your contacts by card name, name of contact, email address, or organization. There is also a Find feature with which you can search for any word or phrase within the entire address book. The Find feature supports shell wildcards such as * or ?.

Dia

Dia is a diagram creation application, similar to the commercial Visio. With the current release of Dia (0.82 at the time of writing), you can make entity relationship diagrams, flowcharts, UML diagrams, electrical circuitry schemas, and network diagrams. Dia comes with 80 shapes, five line thicknesses, and seven arrow designs. You can also create your own objects in the XML file format and add them to the collection. Dia files are saved in XML, so it is easy to port and embed diagrams into different applications. A simple flowchart is shown in Figure 18.5.

Although certainly not as powerful as Visio, Dia is much easier to learn (you can learn how to use it in about five minutes), so it is a superior choice for simple flowcharts and diagrams, whereas Visio can be unwieldy.

Pixmap images can be easily imported and resized quickly, without having to be redrawn by the application.

Dia is organized a little differently from Visio. Instead of a screen with a palette on one side and toolbar at the top, Dia has the palette in a separate window from the diagram grid. To add a shape to the grid, click the object button on the palette, and then click the diagram in the place you want to put the object. To resize the shape, click anywhere on the shape and drag it to the size you want. If you want to delete or move a shape that is already on the diagram field, you must remember to click the Modify Objects button in the diagram editor first. Otherwise, Dia will continue to add the last shape you clicked.

FIGURE 18.5
Dia imports and resizes graphics quickly and easily.

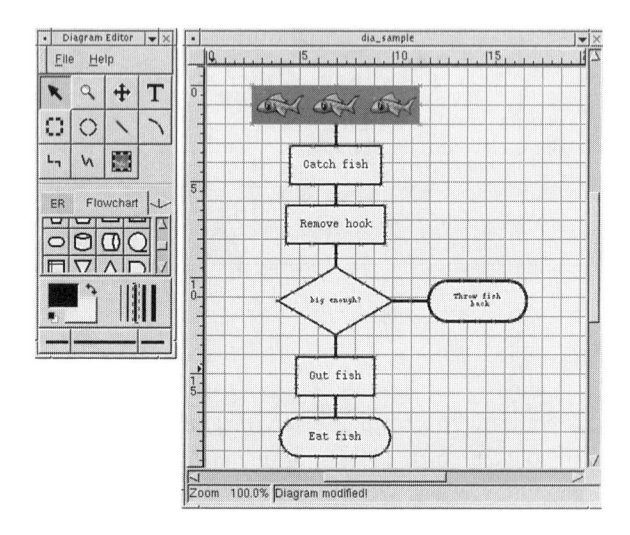

To import an image, double-click Create Image, browse to find the image file you want, and then click Apply. Click on the grid to drop the image where you want it. Resizing images in Dia is very fast compared to resizing in Visio, and the shapes are not as sensitive as those in Visio, so it is easier for a beginner to use Dia.

Dia supports multi-layer diagrams of different colors. Adding text to the diagram is also easier than in Visio. Instead of a text box, Dia uses a text point. The text is centered on the text point as you type it.

The home page for Dia is `http://www.lysator.liu.se/~alla/dia/`.

Other Productivity Applications

In addition to GNOME Office, there are more than 50 productivity applications being developed for office use. Browse the GNOME Software Map at `http://www.gnome.org/applist/list-martin.phtml?catno=10`.

Look in the Productivity category to find software that interests you. As always with GNOME, all the software is available for free download.

Gaby

Gaby is a personal database manager for creating small databases. Built to be extensible, it comes with several plug-ins for different functions, or you can create your own plug-ins in Perl or Python to make the database as simple or complex as you want.

The database can be internationalized, so that the same database can be automatically translated into the language of your choice. The languages currently supported are Danish, Dutch, English, Finnish, French, German, Japanese, Norwegian, Polish, Spanish, and Swedish.

Gaby is packaged with some ready-made database templates, or description files. Some of the templates include

- An index of Freshmeat applications
- A database for Debian packages
- An address book database
- A CD database
- A books database

Gaby comes with a short user's manual and a more detailed programmer's manual. At the time of writing, Gaby is only available in a source code tarball. Gaby is shown in Figure 18.6 with the address book template. The Gaby home page is http://gaby.netpedia.net/.

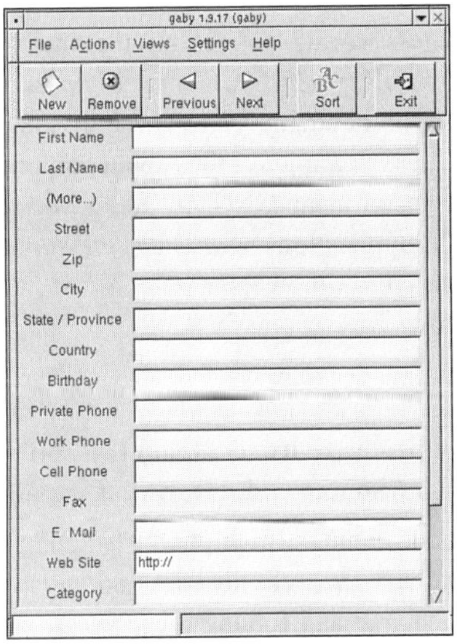

FIGURE 18.6

Gaby is an ideal choice if you want to create a small, simple database.

TimeTracker

TimeTracker is a marvelous little application for timing your tasks. You can track a project by the time you spend on it daily and the total time spent on the project. Click New to start a new project. As soon as you press Enter, the timer begins. In Preferences, specify whether the timer should display hours and minutes, or also show seconds. Whenever you work on your project, click the timer so that the red X shows. When you stop working on the project, click Timer again so that the green arrow shows. TimeTracker is illustrated in Figure 18.7.

FIGURE 18.7

TimeTracker is useful for improving time management skills or for tracking hours for billing purposes.

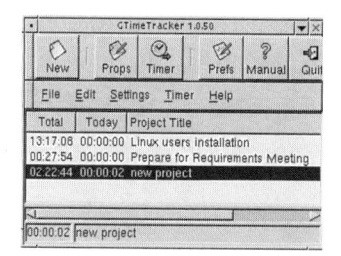

TimeTracker has quite a few advanced options. For example, you can attach the project timer to a logfile for permanent storage. Check the comprehensive user's manual that accompanies the tool for more information.

Summary

Is GNOME ready for the business world? Not yet, but the time when it will be ready is coming fast, perhaps even within the year 2000. Software development—perhaps even the definition of software itself—will change entirely within the next five years. This hour, you learned how GNOME is helping to bring about that change. You learned about the advantages and disadvantages of using GNOME in the workplace. You explored some of the more advanced GNOME applications, including AbiWord, Gnumeric, GNOME Personal Information Manager, Dia, and others.

Q&A

Q I would like to install a productivity tool from the Software Map, but there are no rpms available, only the source code. How do I install the application?

A Installing from source code can be difficult and frustrating—or simple—depending on your setup and if you have the right libraries and tools. Use the information in Hour 22, "Upgrading GNOME and Joining the GNOME Project," to compile and install the source code.

Q I would like to consider using GNOME for my business, but I need help. Where can I get support?

A There are companies forming for the sole purpose of providing GNOME support and application development for business. Two of these companies are International GNOME Support and Helix Code. Check `http://www.gnome.org` for updated links.

Workshop

The quiz questions and exercises are designed to increase your understanding and to encourage you to continue experimenting. Answers appear in Appendix B, "Answers."

Quiz

1. Think about your own work patterns and those of the people in your office. How many features of your current office software do you actually use?
2. How does component software differ from traditional software?
3. What are three advantage of using GNOME in business?
4. What are two disadvantages of using GNOME?
5. What does PIM stand for in GNOME-PIM?
6. True or False: AbiWord can import and export RTF file format.
7. What file format does Dia use?

Exercises

1. Visit the GNOME Productivity Software Map at `http://www.gnome.org/applist/list-martin.phtml?catno=10`. Download and install an application that interests you.
2. Visit the GNOME Office home page at `http://www.gnome.org/gnome-office`. Download an application that interests you.

HOUR 19

Working with Graphics in GNOME

No desktop environment or office suite is complete without the capability to view and manipulate images. GNOME has several graphics applications to view and edit graphics, including Eye of GNOME, Electric Eyes, and the GIMP. Neither Electric Eyes nor Eye of GNOME comes with documentation yet, so this hour provides detailed instructions on how to use them. GIMP comes with a comprehensive user's manual and several tutorials. In fact, GIMP is so powerful that it would take an entire chapter just to describe its capabilities. In this hour, you will receive a basic introduction to GIMP so that you can use it for simple image viewing and editing.

In this hour, you will

- Use Eye of GNOME to view and catalogue images.
- View images and perform simple edits with Electric Eyes.
- Change the default image utility for viewing and editing graphics.
- Receive a brief introduction to GIMP.

Eye of GNOME

Eye of GNOME is a simple, no-frills image viewer. It is fast and takes up a small amount of memory, but still displays high quality images and is also easy to use. Eye of GNOME supports these graphics file formats:

- PNG
- GIF
- JPEG
- BMP
- PNM
- RAS
- TIFF
- ICO
- XPM

Eye of GNOME is new on the GNOME scene, but it is scheduled to replace Electric Eyes as the default image viewer in the GNOME 2.0 release. Electric Eyes is the default image viewer for GNOME 1.0.5.3 (October GNOME) and earlier GNOME versions. Eye of GNOME works as a complete application by itself, but it can also be used as a component in other GNOME applications. Because it uses Bonobo technology, images can be embedded into other GNOME applications as quickly and easily with minimal use of memory. Eye of GNOME is shown in Figure 19.1.

> Bonobo is a CORBA (Common Object Request Broker Architecture) technology for GNOME applications that enables an application to act as a component of another application. You will learn more about Bonobo in Hour 23, "GNOME Technologies."

To install and run Eye of GNOME, you must first ensure that these packages are installed:

- gdk-pixbuf
- gdk-pixbuf-devel
- gnome-libs
- gnome-libs-devel

FIGURE 19.1
Eye of GNOME will replace Electric Eyes as the default image viewer in GNOME 2.0.

Using Eye of GNOME

There really isn't much to using Eye of GNOME. The menu contains only two sub-menus, and the toolbar contains simple file opening, viewing, and sizing options. The File menu contains the usual file manipulation options, as follows:

- **Create New Window** opens a new empty window. Eye of GNOME is useful for cataloguing images because you can open as many windows as you want without slowing the application response time.

- **Open Image** displays the GNOME Open window. The dialog box has Create Directory, Delete File, and Rename File options, so you can use EOG to organize a group of images into a new directory.

- **Close this Window** closes the application if you have only one EOG window open. If you have two or more windows open, Close this Window closes the active window.

- **Exit** closes all windows and exits the application.

The View menu provides options for zooming an image in the viewer:

- **Zoom In** and **Zoom Out** enlarge or shrink the image by increments.
- **Zoom 1:1** returns the image to its original size.
- **Zoom** opens a menu for setting the image enlargement to a particular ratio.
- **Zoom to Fit** enlarges or shrinks the image to fit within the window. If you increase or decrease the dimensions of the window and click Zoom to Fit again, the image will readjust to fit the new window size.

The Toolbar buttons repeat the options in the View menu. In and Out increment a size increase or decrease by the same increment as the menu options Zoom In and Zoom Out.

You can quickly return to the original size by clicking 1:1, or size the image to fit the window by clicking Fit. Figure 19.2 illustrates how large you can zoom an image in using Eye of GNOME. Both windows show the same image.

FIGURE 19.2
Eye of GNOME can quickly zoom in to where a single pixel takes up the entire window.

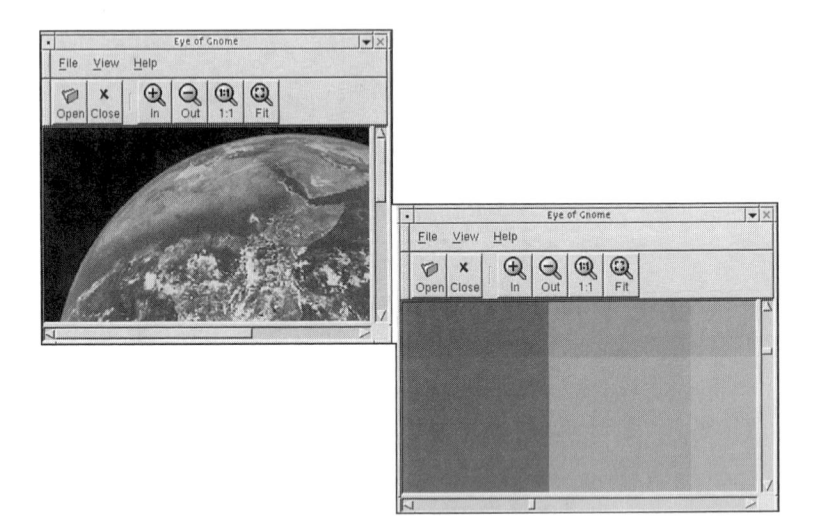

Electric Eyes

Electric Eyes is the default October GNOME image viewer. Although it has more options than Eye of GNOME, it can be tricky to use because the menus are not clearly named. Compared to Eye of GNOME, Electric Eyes is also a bit of a memory hog. On the other hand, Electric Eyes has many more options than the current release of Eye of GNOME.

Electric Eyes supports the following graphics file formats:

- BMP
- GIF
- JPEG
- PPM
- PNG
- RAS
- RGB
- TIFF
- XBM
- XPM

Before installing Electric Eyes, you must have these packages installed:

- imlib
- libjpeg
- libtiff
- libpng

When you first open Electric Eyes, all you see is a window with the Electric Eyes logo. There is no menu or toolbar; all options are accessed with a right-click. The main Electric Eyes window is shown in Figure 19.3.

FIGURE 19.3
Because there is no menu or toolbar, Electric Eyes can be confusing to use on the first try.

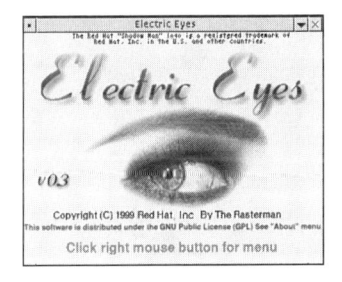

> Electric Eyes can display a toolbar in some Linux distributions. Right-click in the Electric Eyes window, select View, and Toolbar, then select Top, Bottom, Left, Right, or Hide to place the toolbar in the Electric Eyes window. Depending on your version of GTK and Electric Eyes, however, this option does not always work properly.

Viewing Files in Electric Eyes

To open an image in Electric Eyes, right-click the Electric Eyes window and select File, Open. The Open window appears. If you select Use Previews, a preview of the image appears in the Open dialog box, along with information about the image, including file format, 1:1 image dimensions, file size, transparency, and date the file was last modified. The Open window is shown in Figure 19.4.

To view all the files in a directory, click Load All Files in Directory. The first image in the directory appears in the Electric Eyes window. To scroll through the images, right-click in the window and use the directional buttons in the File menu. As you click a button, the new image appears in the window.

- Next Image displays the next image in the directory.
- Last Image displays the last image in the directory.

- Previous image displays the image which is listed in the directory before the current image.
- First image displays the first image in the directory.

FIGURE 19.4
You can see a preview of an image before you open the file in Electric Eyes.

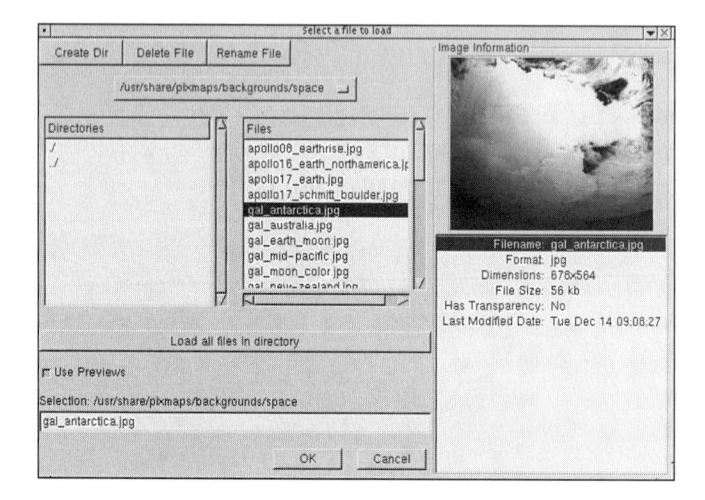

Electric Eyes has a tool called the *list window*, which is useful when you want to open several files at once, or even an entire directory of images. To open the list window, right-click the Electric Eyes window and select View, Show/Hide List Window. Click Open and select the individual files or the directory that you want to display. Select Generate Thumbnails to display a thumbnail image of each file in the list window. Use the forward and back navigation buttons to display each image in the main Electric Eyes window in turn. The list window is shown in Figure 19.5.

> You can use the Space and Backspace keys to scroll through the next and previous pictures, respectively. Press Q to quit Electric Eyes.

> If you are running Enlightenment, the Set as Desktop Background option sets your desktop background to the image in the active Electric Eyes window. Remember to disable the GNOME background control in the GNOME Control Center if you want to use this option.

Figure 19.5
The list window is useful for cataloguing images and for slide shows.

Editing Images in Electric Eyes

Electric Eyes has limited editing capability, but it is not really designed for manipulating images. Ideally, you should use the GIMP for editing images and Electric Eyes or Eye of GNOME for viewing images. To open the editing window, click View, Show/Hide Edit Window. The Edit Controls window is shown in Figure 19.6.

Figure 19.6
Electric Eyes has simple editing capabilities.

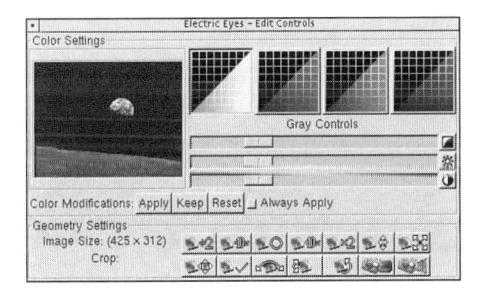

Enlarging and Shrinking the Image

The sizing controls for Electric Eyes are not quite as sophisticated as the resizing controls in Eye of GNOME. The first row of buttons in the Geometry Settings field of the Edit Controls window deals with resizing.

You can reduce or enlarge images by half or in 10% increments. Maximize Image Size Retaining Aspect simultaneously maximizes the window and the image while maintaining the relative horizontal and vertical aspect. Maximize Image maximizes the image to the maximum window size, ignoring the aspect. Be careful when using Maximize Image, as the image can look distorted if the original image was long or wide.

The image size adjustment buttons use the window size to adjust the image size. Set a Custom Size for the Image sets new dimensions of the image. Apply the Current View Size sets the image to the window size. You must save the image to keep the new settings permanently.

Adjusting Colors

You can adjust the saturation, brightness, and contrast of the image for gray, red, blue, and green using the color buttons and sliders. As you manipulate the saturation, brightness, and contrast sliders, the color graph on the button adjusts to show the color percentage graphically. To return to the default value, click the button to the right of the slider.

Rotating the Image

The rotation and flip buttons enable you to rotate the image by 25% increments and to flip the image either horizontally or vertically.

Taking a Screen Shot

The last two geometry buttons control screen shots. You can take a screen shot of the entire screen, or you can select a single window to grab.

If you grab the entire screen, your virtual resolution screen will be grabbed, not your physical screen. For example, if you have a virtual screen size of 1280×1024 but your physical screen size is only 800×600, your screen shot will have dimensions of 1280×1024.

Changing the Default Image Viewer

When you open a graphics file in File Manager or on the desktop, the file opens in Electric Eyes by default. If you want to use Eye of GNOME or the GIMP to open the file, you must change the default image viewer for each graphics file MIME type in GNOME Control Center.

Open the MIME Types capplet in GNOME Control Center. Scroll through the MIME Type list to the image MIME types, as shown in Figure 19.7. An image MIME type entry will have "image" followed by the image type, for example, `image/gif` or `image/ief`.

Select the image type you want to change and click Edit. By default, Electric Eyes is listed under MIME, type Actions to open, view, and edit the file

`ee %f`

Change the command to view and open the file to Eye of GNOME or GIMP as follows:

eog %f

or

gimp %f

Change the command to edit the file to

gimp %f

If you want, you can use GIMP to open, view, and edit your files, but at the time of writing you can't use Eye of GNOME to edit files, only to open or view them. Click OK on GNOME Control Center for the changes to be made. After you have made these changes, when you double-click a graphics file in File Manager, it will open in Eye of GNOME. When you right-click the file and select Open or View, it will open in Eye of GNOME, and when you select Edit, the file will open in GIMP.

FIGURE 19.7
Graphics files have MIME types in the format image/file_type.

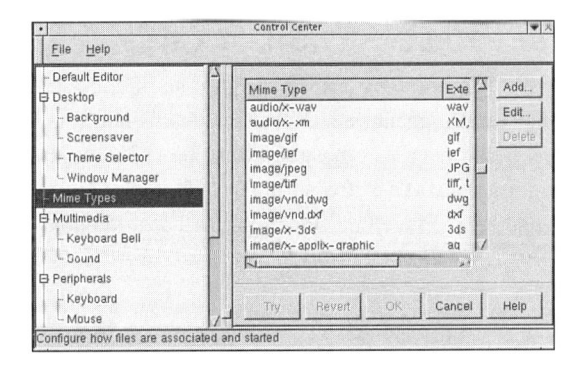

> If you wanted to, you could set up Eye of GNOME as your default image editor, but because Eye of GNOME has no editing capability yet, you wouldn't be able to make any changes to the image files.

Introducing the Graphics Image Manipulation Program (GIMP)

GIMP, affectionately referred to as "The GIMP," was the application that led to the creation of GTK and GNOME. GIMP is the most advanced application available for GNOME, and is arguably the most advanced application created specifically for Linux. GIMP was designed to be a freeware version of Adobe PhotoShop, and many graphics designers find GIMP to be superior to PhotoShop, particularly the GIMP documentation, including GUM, the GIMP User's Manual. More than 900 pages in hard copy, it is also available online at the GIMP Web site, `http://www.gimp.org`. GUM provides a comprehensive guide on just about everything you can do with computer graphics manipulation. The GIMP window is shown in Figure 19.8.

FIGURE 19.8

When you first open GIMP, the GIMP tools window looks deceptively simple.

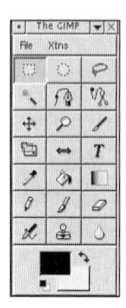

Getting the Latest Version of GIMP

Like most successful free software, GIMP is in a state of constant development. There is usually an unstable, development version that is two or three versions ahead of the stable release, and a new stable release comes out every few months. The best way to keep up-to-date with the progress of GIMP is to visit the GIMP home page at `http://www.gimp.org`. The latest stable and development versions of GIMP are available for download there.

GIMP Basics

GIMP can be used for everyday tasks such as simple image viewing and taking screen shots, or for complex graphics such as creating computer-enhanced film imagery. Some of the features of GIMP include

- Multiple image layers.
- Filters.
- Sub-pixel imaging.
- Anti-aliasing.
- Channel operations and layers.
- Extensibility with scripts.
- A full suite of painting tools.
- Multiple undo/redo.
- Gradient editing and blending.
- Plug-ins for adding new file formats and filters. GIMP comes with 100 pre-defined plug-ins.

GIMP supports virtually every graphic file format under the sun, including

- AA
- BMP
- CEL
- FITS
- FLI
- GBR
- GIF
- GIcon
- HRZ
- HTML
- JPEG
- PAT
- PIX
- PLX
- PNG
- PNM
- PS
- SGI
- SUNRAS
- TGA
- TIFF
- XCF
- XWD
- XPM

> Due to licensing issues, the Debian GIMP does not support the GIF file format.

Further Reading on the GIMP

The best place to learn about the GIMP is the GIMP Web page, http://www.gimp.org. There you can find a beginner's tutorial of the basic paint tools, a full online manual, an overall tutorial of the GIMP, a set of FAQs, and examples of different plug-ins and how to use them. The online manual can be read online or downloaded in pdf or HTML format.

Summary

This hour, you learned how to use Eye of GNOME and Electric Eyes to view images. You performed simple edits on images using Electric Eyes. You changed the default image viewer and editor in GNOME Control Center from Electric Eyes to Eye of GNOME and GIMP, respectively. You also learned about the capabilities and features of GIMP.

Q&A

Q Where can I find other GNOME graphics tools and applications?

A GNOME graphics applications and tools are interspersed between Productivity and Entertainment on the Software Map.

Q Can I use a graphics application besides Eye of GNOME, Electric Eyes, or GIMP in GNOME?

A You can use any graphics application you like that works within the X environment. You can even make your non-GNOME application the default for viewing and manipulating graphics files. Simply substitute the executable command for your graphics application for the Electric Eyes default in MIME types.

Workshop

The quiz questions and exercises are designed to increase your understanding and to encourage you to continue experimenting. Answers appear in Appendix B, "Answers."

Quiz

1. Which graphics program is the default for version 1.0.53 of GNOME (October GNOME)?
2. Can you edit graphics files in Eye of GNOME?
3. What option must you select to see a preview of a file before opening it in Electric Eyes?
4. How do you open the Edit Controls window in Electric Eyes?
5. How do you know that a MIME type is for a graphics file format?
6. Which of the three graphics programs that we explored in this hour supports the most file formats?

Exercises

1. Open a graphics file in Eye of GNOME and Electric Eyes. Zoom the image in as far as you can in both programs. What is the difference?
2. Open a graphics file in Eye of GNOME. Zoom the image out to a ratio of 6:1, then click one button on the toolbar to bring it back to the original ratio.
3. Locate a directory of images on your computer. (The directory where your background pixmap files are located is a good example, for example, /usr/local/share/pixmaps/Backgrounds or /usr/share/pixmaps/Backgrounds.) Load a directory of images into Electric Eyes using the list window.
4. In the list window from exercise 3, scroll through the images using the directional buttons.

5. For fun, try this exercise in GIMP:

   Select File, New.

   Accept the default width and height of 256×256 pixels.

   Set Fill Type = White.

   Click OK. A new image canvas appears.

   Click the black square at the bottom of the GIMP toolbar and select your favorite color from the color palette that appears. Click OK.

   Click the "T" in the GIMP toolbar and click in the workspace.

   In the Text Tool dialog box, select a font like Courier, font size 40 and a Weight of bold.

   Type `"Hello"` in the text field and click OK. Position the text in the box by clicking the text and dragging it to where you want it.

   Right-click in the workspace, and select Script-Fu from the right-click menu, Shadow, Drop-Shadow. Click OK.

   In the GIMP toolbar, select the rectangular select tool and click in the work space to deselect the text.

   Right-click in the workspace, and select filters from the right-click menu, Light Effects, Supernova.

   Click OK in the Supernova dialog box.

HOUR 20

Fun with GNOME

GNOME is a powerful and cost-effective information technology tool. GNOME can help you be more productive in your work, and it can generally enhance the experience of using a UNIX-like operating system. Life is not all about work, however, and neither is GNOME. Because GNOME is free software and the GNOME development project is entirely composed of volunteers, a wide plethora of amusements and games are continuously being developed. GNOME developers are renowned for producing imaginative and complex graphics that grace even the most simple strategy games. Check out Iagno, Gnome Tali, and Gnommind in particular.

In this hour, you will

- Prepare your Linux system to experience sound in GNOME and Enlightenment.
- Play music on the GNOME CD Player and adjust the sound with the Audio Mixer.
- Play some strategy and arcade games that come in the gnome-games package.

- Add some amusements to the GNOME Panel.
- Install and play other games and amusements from the GNOME software map.

Setting Up GNOME for Sound

Like Windows, GNOME and Enlightenment come with sounds that accompany certain desktop events. You can run GNOME without it, but having sound can make the experience more enjoyable. Of course, if you want to play music CDs and certain games, you must have sound configured.

Most Linux distributions do not automatically detect and install the driver for sound cards, although some have scripts or utilities that you can run after installation. For example, Red Hat has a utility called `sndconfig` that will help you select the correct driver for your sound card, install the driver, and recompile the kernel automatically. Configuring your system for sound is beyond the scope of this book, but there are plenty of resources available on the Web to help you. The Linux Sound HOWTO, which can be found online at `http://metalab.unc.edu/linux/HOWTO/Sound-HOWTO.html`, has detailed instructions on how to configure sound in your Linux system.

Configuring Your Desktop for GNOME/Enlightenment Sound

After you have your system configured for sound, you can use the sound features of GNOME and Enlightenment. There are two base packages that must be installed first:

- esound
- gnome-audio

After you have verified that you have the necessary packages, ensure that sound is enabled in your window manager. For Enlightenment, right-click the desktop to open the Settings menu. Select Audio Settings and check Enable Sounds in the dialog box, as shown in Figure 20.1.

FIGURE 20.1
Sounds must be enabled in the window manager before you can hear certain GNOME sounds.

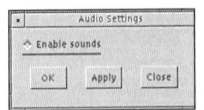

Next, open the Sound portion of the GNOME Control Center by clicking Main Menu, Settings, Multimedia, Sound. Check Enable Sound Server Startup and Sounds for Events, as shown in Figure 20.2. You can also open the Sound dialog box from GNOME Control Center, Sound.

FIGURE 20.2
Enable sound from the GNOME Control Center to hear sounds during a GNOME session.

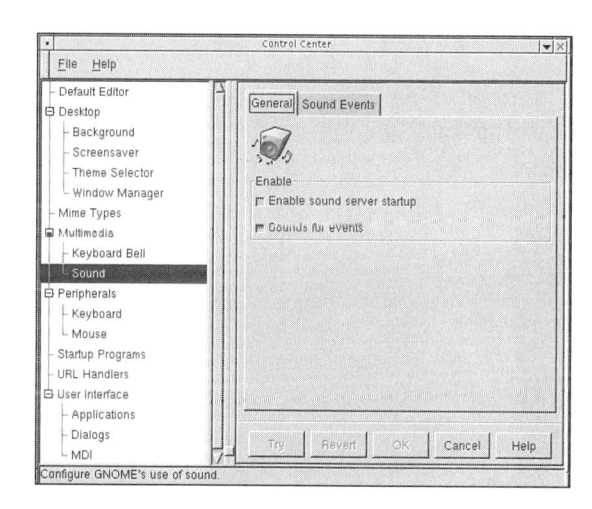

Using the GNOME CD Player

GNOME comes with a CD player application that enables you to play music CDs in your CD ROM drive. Before running the player, verify in the file `/etc/fstab` that your user account has permission to mount the CD-ROM drive. Figure 20.3 shows the parts of the GNOME CD Player.

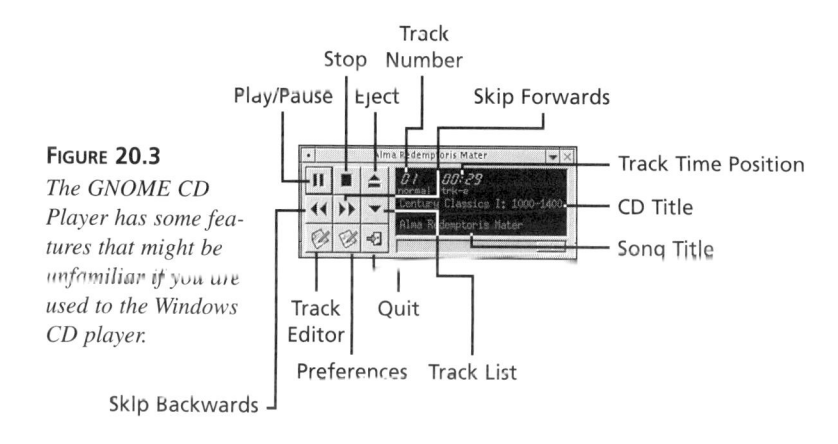

FIGURE 20.3
The GNOME CD Player has some features that might be unfamiliar if you are used to the Windows CD player.

> In this hour, we assume that the mount point for the CD-ROM is /dev/cdrom. If your system has a different mount point, substitute your mount point where appropriate. If you don't know what the mount point for your CD-ROM is, check the /etc/fstab file.

Open the CD Player from Main Menu, Multimedia, CD Player. Click Preferences and check that the correct mount point for your CD-ROM drive is listed under CDROM Device. (You will learn more about Preferences in the next section). Figure 20.4 shows the Preferences tab.

FIGURE 20.4
The CD Player automatically mounts music CDs using the mount point entered in Preferences.

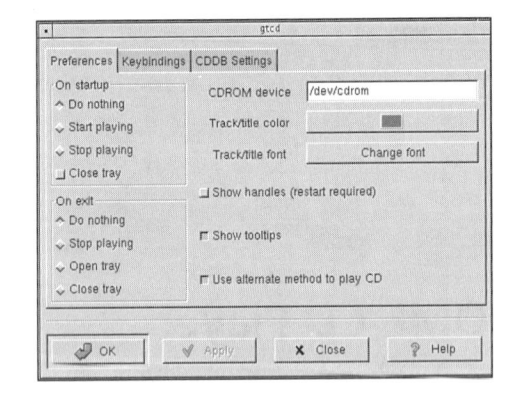

You are now ready to play music CDs. The first six buttons on the player are similar to those on any standard CD player, but we will review them briefly here:

- **Play/Pause**. Click this button to pause the CD track. Push it again to resume play at the same point.
- **Stop**. Click Stop to stop playing the CD. The CD Player will return to the beginning of the first track.
- **Eject**. The Eject button opens the drawer of the CD-ROM drive.
- **Skip Backwards**. Click Skip Backwards to cycle through tracks backward to the first track.
- **Skip Forwards**. Click Skip Forwards to cycle through tracks to the last track on the CD.
- **Track List**. This button supplies a list of all track titles on the CD. Figure 20.5 illustrates a track list for the music CD *Century Classics I: 1000–1400*.

FIGURE 20.5
The Track List button lists all the titles on the CD.

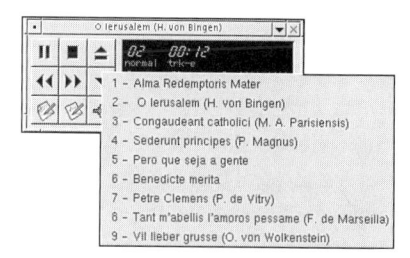

The last three buttons, Track Editor, Preferences, and Quit, add a bit more functionality than most other CD player applications, so we will go over them in greater detail.

Using Track Editor

Use the Track Editor to enter the title of your CD and the titles of each track. You can either enter the titles manually or let the CD Player search a free database called CDDB, for CD Database. CDDB will download the titles of your CD tracks automatically, so you don't have to type them.

Using CDDB to Automatically List CD Tracks

The CD Player connects to the CDDB automatically whenever you play a new CD. CDDB contains the titles and track listings for hundreds of thousands of CDs, and users submit more than 100 new titles to the database every day. See `http://www.cddb.com` for more information on CDDB.

After inserting a CD, wait three to five seconds for the CD Player to connect to CDDB. If your CD is listed in the database, CDDB will automatically download the track titles to your personal CD database. The track titles will automatically appear in the CD Player window every time you play that CD. If CDDB does not download the track titles, than either the CD Player cannot get a connection, or the CD is not listed in CDDB. Click CDDB Status, and then Get CDDB Now. If you get no error message, the CDDB does not have your CD listed. Figure 20.6 shows the Track Editor.

FIGURE 20.6
Use the Track Editor to manually enter track titles for your music CDs.

Entering Track Titles Manually

If CDDB does not contain your CD title, use the Track Editor to manually enter the CD title and track titles (song titles). The CD Player automatically reads the number and length of each track, as well as the total playing time of the CD. When you have finished entering all the tracks, press Submit. Enter the musical category for the CD in the dialog box that appears and press Submit. A special mail message will go to the database with your new entry. You will get no message back unless there was an error in the transmission. Your entry will be added to the CDDB so that anyone else with the same CD will be able to download the titles. Figure 20.7 shows the CD *Century Classics I: 1000–1400* being submitted to CDDB. Click OK to send the submission message.

FIGURE 20.7
When you submit a new CD title to CDDB, you increase the database's usefulness for all other users.

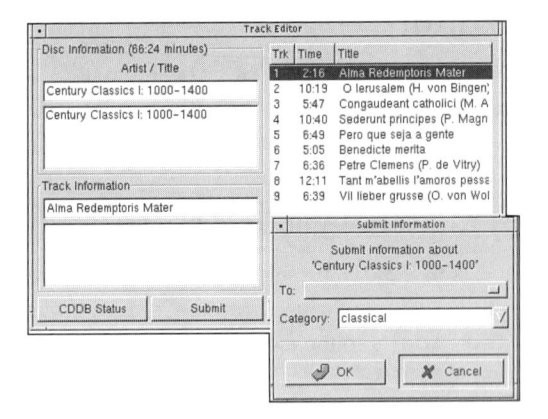

Customizing the CD Player

The Preferences button enables you to customize the look and feel of the CD Player to suit your tastes. There are three tabs in the Preferences dialog box: Preferences, Keybindings, and CDDB Settings. We will discuss each tab in turn.

The Preferences tab enables you to control the behavior of your CD Player. The most important entry is the mount point for the CD-ROM drive. If your player is not working properly, check that the correct mount point is specified in the CDROM Device field.

You can select these events to occur automatically, when the CD Player application starts:

- Have the player stand idle until you click a button to make a selection
- Automatically start or stop playing the CD
- Automatically close the CD tray

When you close the CD Player, you can

- Have the player continue to play the CD even after CD Player closes
- Stop playing the CD
- Automatically open or close the CD tray

The Preferences tab also enables you to select the color and font for the track titles that appear in the Player window. The Show Handles option enables you to drag the CD title window off the Player onto the desktop. Figure 20.8 shows the title window after it has been dragged off the CD Player.

FIGURE 20.8
Drag the title bar onto the desktop if you want to see the title of the music being played without seeing the entire CD Player.

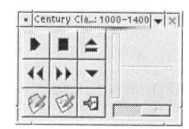

The CD Player has keybindings that you can use to control the player instead of a mouse. Default keybindings are displayed in the Keybindings tab; you can also create your own.

The last tab, CDDB Settings, enables you to specify the server address for CDDB (the default usually works fine). If you are behind a firewall, there is a field to list a proxy address. CDDB Settings also lists your personal, local CD database. Whenever you play a CD and download the track list from CDDB or enter it manually, the list is stored in your local database.

Quit

The Quit button closes the CD Player. If you selected Do Nothing in Preferences in the On Exit field, the CD will continue to play after you close the CD Player. Otherwise the CD will stop playing when you press Quit. You can also specify if you want the CD tray to open or close when you quit the CD Player.

GNOME Games

The GNOME base installation comes with a package called gnome-games that contains several strategy and arcade games. There are dozens of more games in various stages of development available in the Entertainment category of the GNOME software map at http://www.gnome.org/applist/list-martin.phtml?catno=4.

Part of the fun of GNOME games is that most of them are completely configurable. You can change the design and even play with the function of the games in the configuration files. For instance, if you don't like the looks of the hero in Gnobots II, you can redesign him to be anything you like. In this section we will review the games that are included in the gnome-games package, as well as some games that are in advanced stages of development on the software map.

AisleRiot

AisleRiot contains 30 different varieties of solitaire games, including Klondike, Freecell, Beleaguered Castle, Camelot, and Odessa, as well as AisleRiot, which Americans think of as Solitaire. AisleRiot's user manual includes playing instructions for most of the games. If you are a MS Windows Solitaire addict, AisleRiot will keep you happily unproductive for hours. The setup for an AisleRiot game is shown in Figure 20.9.

FIGURE 20.9
Klondike is one of many Solitaire-type games you can play in AisleRiot.

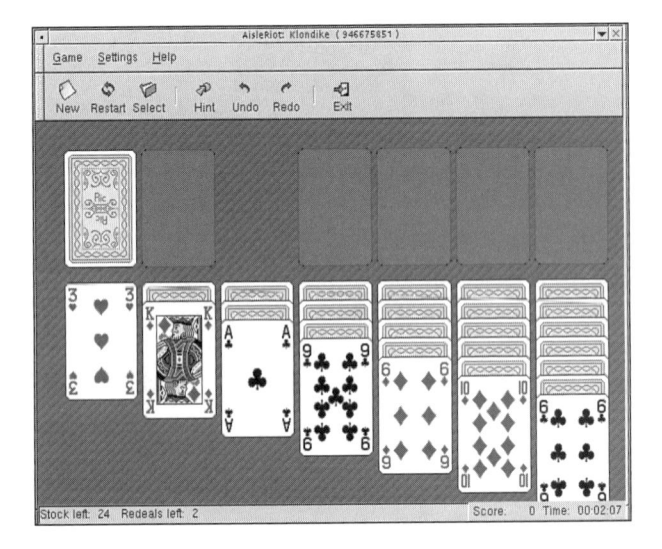

Gnome Mines

Gnome Mines is similar to the game Minesweeper. You are presented with a grid of squares, whose size you can customize. Each turn, click on a square. Some squares contain a number, which tells you that a mine is present so many squares away, but it is up to you to figure out the direction. Other squares contain mines. When you finally hit a mine, the game is over. If you manage to uncover every non-mined space without hitting a mine, you win! Figure 20.10 shows a Gnome Mines game with the smallest default grid of squares.

FIGURE 20.10
Watch the expression of the little man as you uncover mines or hints in Gnome Mines.

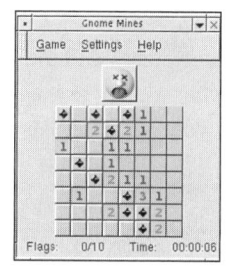

Gnome Tetravex (Gnotravex)

Tetravex is a deceptively simple strategy game. The layout consists of two grids. One grid is empty and the other grid contains from four to 16 squares. Each square is divided into four numbered sections. The idea is to move the squares to the empty grid in a way that the number in each section on every side of every square matches its neighbor. Move the squares around from one board to another to turn the position of the squares around. The fewer moves made, the higher your score. A simple game of Gnome Tetravex is shown in Figure 20.11.

FIGURE 20.11
Gnome Tetravex gets more difficult when there are more squares involved.

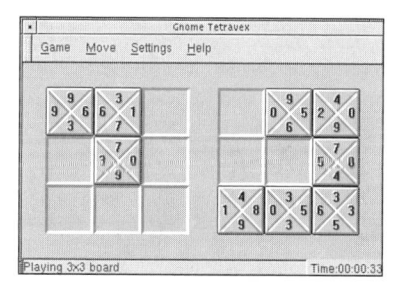

Gnome Tali (GTali)

Gnome Tali is a version of poker played with dice, similar to the board game Yahtzee. In each turn, you are presented with six dice. You can choose to keep the value of the dice, or click on a die to roll it again and try for a better roll. (The die turns into a pumpkin when you click it.) You can have up to six players, either human or computer-generated. A Tali game with one human and three computer players is shown in Figure 20.12.

Iagno

Similar to Reversi, which is based on the board game Othello, Iagno is one of those maddeningly difficult games that appear, at first, to be easy. Play either against a human or the computer, or watch the computer play itself. Play begins with four chips, two black and two white, in the center of a chess/checkers board. Each player places one piece on the board in a way that will flank the opponent's piece or pieces. After you have flanked the opponent's pieces, they become your pieces and the color changes to your color. Iagno has simple, yet stunning, 3D graphics, and you have a choice of designs for the chips. In Figure 20.13, the computer is playing Iagno against itself.

FIGURE 20.12
Don't lose all your money to the computer in Gnome Tali!

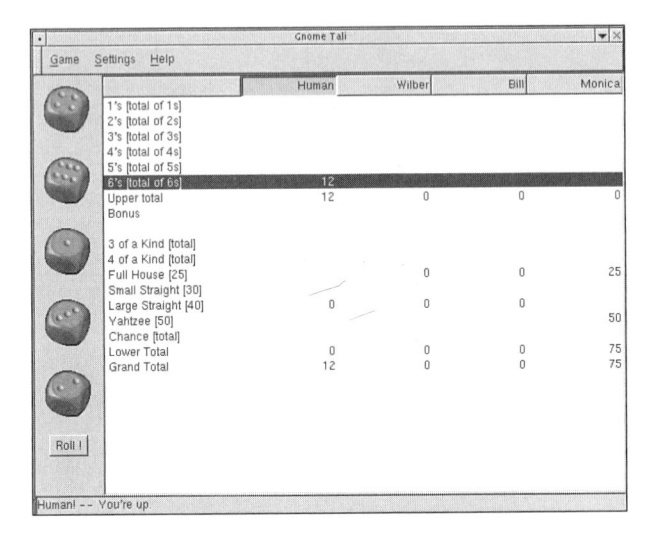

FIGURE 20.13
Let the computer play against itself to learn the strategy of Iagno.

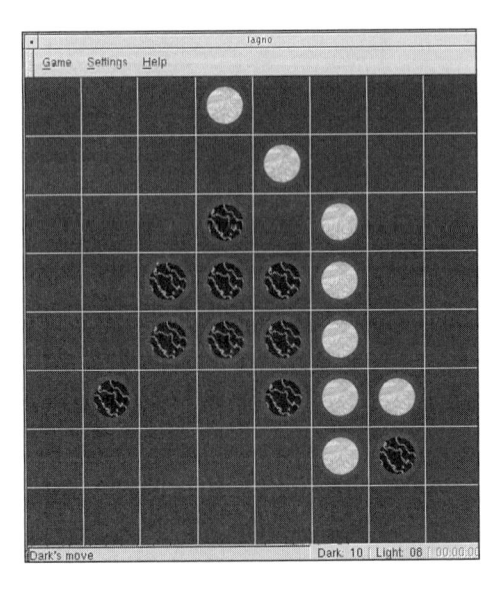

Mah-jongg

Mah-jongg is a strategy game played against the computer in the same ways as the traditional domino game Mah-jongg. I won't go into the rules here, but even if you don't play Mah-jongg, have a look at the game just to appreciate the graphics. Figure 20.14 shows the setup of a game of Mah-jongg.

FIGURE 20.14
The Hint option is useful when you are first learning Mah-jongg.

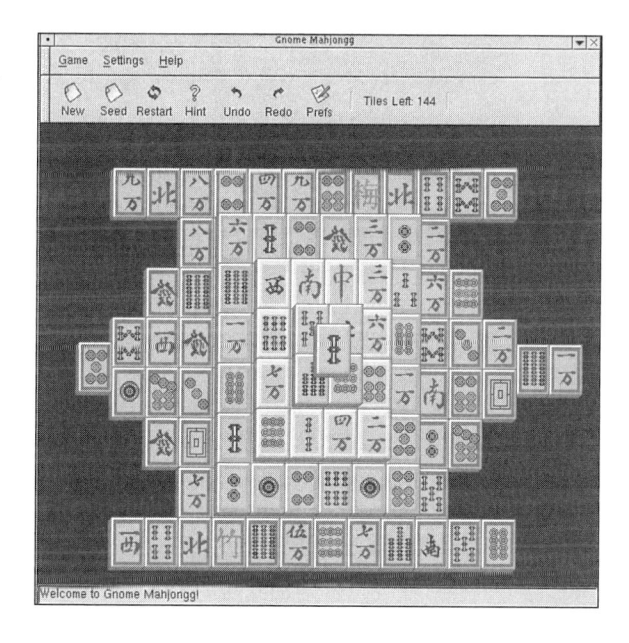

Same Gnome

Same Gnome is a single player strategy game that consists of colored balls placed randomly on the board. When you click on a ball, all the horizontally and vertically adjacent balls disappear. The idea is eliminate all the balls in as few strokes as possible. To help you visualize your strategy, when you place your mouse over a colored ball, all the balls in the color group quiver. When you eliminate a group of balls, the other balls drop down, forming new groups. You cannot eliminate a ball that is not part of a group that does not have any balls of the same color adjacent to it. The game is over when you have eliminated all possible balls. Your score is based on the number of moves it takes you to eliminate all possible balls. If you eliminate all the balls, an extra 1,000 points is added to your score. Figure 20.15 shows a game of Same Gnome in progress.

FIGURE 20.15

Same Gnome appears to be easy until you are down to the last few balls.

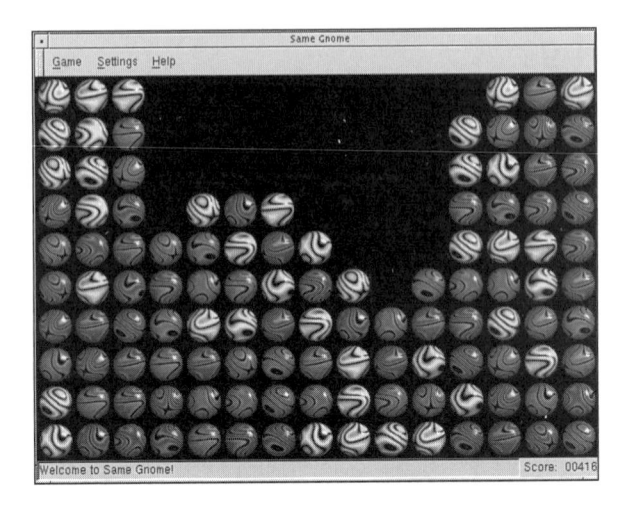

Gnibbles

Also called GNOME Nibbles, this simple video game is a more advanced graphical version of the traditional UNIX Worms game. The game presents you with a worm that you control with a set of keys on the keyboard. The object is to maneuver your worm so that it can eat the diamond crackers without bumping into the wall. There are up to 26 levels of difficulty, and up to four people can play. As your worm eats the diamond crackers, it gets longer. If your worm runs into a wall or turns in on itself while trying to eat the diamonds, it dies, and the game is over. The player whose worm eats the most crackers wins.

GNOME Robots II

GNOME Robots II is another graphical version of an old UNIX game, the text-based Robots. You can also change the robots to eggs, cows, mice, gnomes, or windows. During each move, the robots try to box you in so they can eat you. The object is to move away from them in a way that makes them crash into each other or into the junkheaps left over from collisions. You can also teleport to a far away location. You can wait a turn to see what the robots do, or random teleport, possibly into the waiting arms of a robot.

Gnome-Stones

Gnome-Stones is an arcade-like, one-player game that takes place in a diamond mine strewn with stones and diamonds. The mine also has a labyrinth of brick walls with doors, which you must navigate to find all the diamonds. The object of the game is to collect all the diamonds and then find the mine exit without letting any stones fall on you. Each level of play involves more complicated labyrinths and diamonds that are harder to reach. A game of Gnome-Stones is shown in Figure 20.16.

FIGURE 20.16
In Gnome-Stones, the more diamonds you collect, the greater the likelihood that a stone will fall on you.

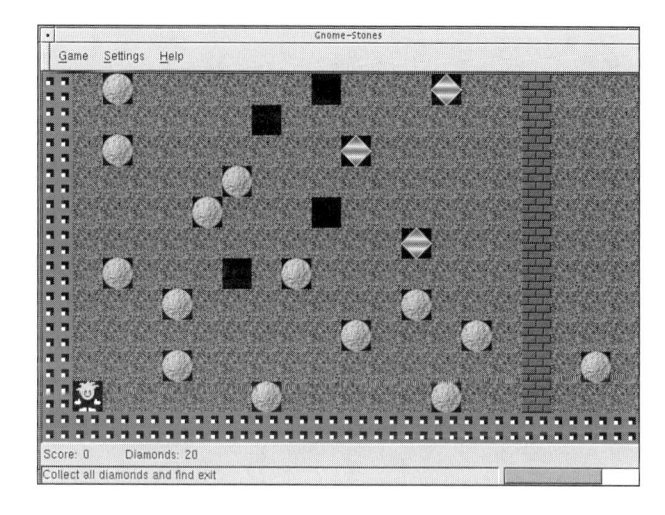

Panel Amusements

Not only does GNOME have full-blown games, it also has small applications, or applets, that you can add to your panel for mild amusement. Install the package `gnome-applets`. At present, there are three panel amusements:

- **Fifteen**. Fifteen is a simple game that consists of 15 numbered squares in a 16-space grid. Randomize the numbers by right-clicking the applet and selecting Randomize. Then arrange the squares sequentially in as few moves as possible.
- **Wanda the Fish**. Wanda the Fish swims in her little bowl on your panel. Click her to hear your daily fortune.
- **Game of Life**. The Game of Life is a non-interactive amusement. Watch microscopic life-forms squirm in the primordial ooze and eat each other.

The panel in Figure 20.17 contains the three panel amusement applets at lower left: Fifteen, Wanda the Fish, and the Game of Life.

FIGURE 20.17
New releases of the panel applets package will contain more panel amusements.

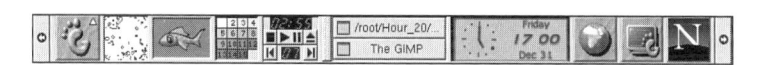

Other GNOME Entertainment

In addition to the games and amusements that come as part of the GNOME base installation, application developers are constantly using GNOME and GTK to create new games. Check the Entertainment section of the GNOME software map for updates.

GnomeHack

GnomeHack is a single-user, graphical role-playing game similar to NetHack, which is loosely based on Dungeons and Dragons. The player controls a D&D-like character who travels through various dungeons, having adventures and encountering danger. NetHack and other games sprung from the original Rogue are wildly popular, and there are many Web pages and newsgroups devoted to the game. See `http://www.xmission.com/~andersen/erik/gnomehack/gnomehack.html` for more information.

GNOME Master Mind

Gnommind is a GNOME version of the game Master Mind. At the beginning of the game, you are presented with four boxes and six colors. The object of the game is to guess the color combination of four balls, which go in the boxes. After you make your guess, the computer sends you another set of boxes to tell you how close you are to the solution. A black ball means that you guessed the correct color in the correct place. A white ball means that you guessed the correct color, but in the wrong place. An empty space means that neither the color nor the place is correct. The fewer moves it takes you to guess the entire sequence correctly, the higher your score. Figure 20.18 shows a game of GNOME Master Mind in progress.

FIGURE 20.18
GNOME Master Mind contains particularly beautiful graphics for a simple strategy game.

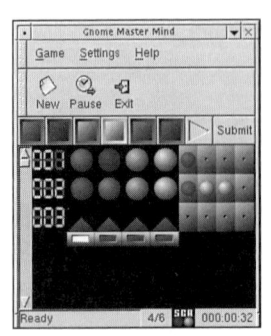

GameStalker

GameStalker is a server browser for Net-based games, that finds game servers based on search criteria that you choose.

Gniall (The GNOME Non-Intelligent AMOS Language Learner)

If you are feeling lonely and friendless, try talking to Gniall. Gniall learns language by remembering the connections between words in the sentences that you input to it. The more you talk to Gniall, the more it talks back! See `http://rat.spunge.org/niall` to learn how Gniall works.

Summary

In this hour, you configured GNOME and Enlightenment for sound. You played music on the GNOME CD Player, and downloaded the CD track titles from CDDB. You also played some GNOME games and learned where to find more GNOME games.

Q&A

Q I installed a driver for my sound card, recompiled the kernel, and enabled sound in GNOME, but I still don't get any sound! What can I do?

A It is not easy to configure your system for sound. It often involves editing configuration files manually, and sometimes you need to also recompile the kernel manually. You also might have an IRQ or I/O conflict with another device. If the Sound HOWTO looks too daunting, try `http://www.opensound.com`. OpenSound is a commercial business that sells sound drivers for Linux, some of which work with sound cards that are not supported by freeware. You can download an evaluation copy of a driver for free.

If you are getting sound in other Linux applications but not GNOME, reinstall the `esound` and `gnome-audio` packages, and make sure that sound is enabled in your window manager.

Q Are there other games I can play in GNOME besides those listed in the GNOME software map?

A You can play any game that works within an X session, including KDE games. Most flavors of UNIX/Linux come with a set of games by default. Check your directory tree for a games subdirectory, such as `/usr/share/games` or `/var/lib/games`.

Q Are there networked games for GNOME?

A There are several games designed for multiple players who play via a server. Although all net games are still in development, some are in very advanced stages. Some examples are Batalla Naval, a battleship game; Gnocatan, which is based on the Settlers of Catan board game; Mystic Arena III; and Quest.

Workshop

The quiz questions and exercises are designed to increase your understanding and to encourage you to continue experimenting. Answers appear in Appendix B, "Answers."

Quiz

1. Where can you set the CD-ROM device mount point in the CD Player?
2. Can you play non-GNOME games in GNOME?

Exercises

1. Go to the Entertainment section of the GNOME software map and download a game that interests you.
2. Play your favorite music CD using the GNOME CD Player. Is your CD listed in CDDB? If not, enter the title tracks manually and submit your CD title to CDDB.
3. Start a KDE or other X-based game in GNOME.

PART V
Advanced GNOME Topics

Hour

21　Uninstalling GNOME and Getting Help

22　Upgrading GNOME and Joining the GNOME Project

23　GNOME Technologies

24　Anatomy of a GNOME Application

Hour 21

Uninstalling GNOME and Getting Help

Uninstalling GNOME is very much like installing GNOME, except that you follow all the steps in reverse. Like installing GNOME, the procedure differs a bit depending on whether you installed from tarball or a binary package.

The biggest weakness of GNOME, which is freely admitted by the developers of the project, is its lack of documentation. Very few GNOME applications have more than the barest help files, and even *The GNOME User's Guide* is not complete. Since the release of October GNOME in October 1999, the members of the GNOME Project have reinvigorated the GNOME Documentation Project, or GDP, and there are many new volunteers. Until more formal documentation is developed, the GNOME mailing lists remain the best place to get help.

In this hour, you will

- Uninstall GNOME from compiled source code and from a binary package (rpm or deb).
- Uninstall Enlightenment in preparation for upgrade and to completely remove Enlightenment from the computer.

- Use the GNOME Help Browser to view help files.
- Explore the options to get help on GNOME, including the mailing lists.

Uninstalling GNOME from Binary Packages

If you installed GNOME from `rpm`, uninstalling each package involves almost the same process as installing the package. In Hour 2, "Installing GNOME," we installed GNOME from the command line; in Hour 13, "GNOME Processes," we in-stalled packages using GnoRPM. In this section, we will uninstall GNOME packages using each method in turn.

As you recall, you installed GNOME one package at time. We will uninstall GNOME using the same method. When you uninstall you must still concern yourself with maintaining dependencies. If you try to uninstall a package that has other packages dependent on it, you will get an error message. To prevent errors, uninstall the packages in the exact reverse order that you installed them. That order is as follows:

```
gnumeric
gnome-users-guide
gnome-games
gnome-utils
gnome-pim
gnome-media
extace
gtop
ee
gnome-print
libglade
control-center
mc
gnome-core
xscreensaver
xloadimage
enlightenment
libghttp
lib-gtop
```

gnome-libs

gnome-audio

Fnlib

Imlib

GTK+

ORBit

libxml

glib

esound

audiofile

Uninstalling GNOME Using GnoRPM

To uninstall a package, open GnoRPM from Main Menu, System, GnoRPM. Find the package you want to uninstall in the GnoRPM rpm list, and then click Uninstall. The package is uninstalled. Repeat this process for each package, in the preceding order. GnoRPM is shown in Figure 21.1.

FIGURE 21.1
GnoRPM, also called GNOME RPM, is the GNOME graphical interface for rpms.

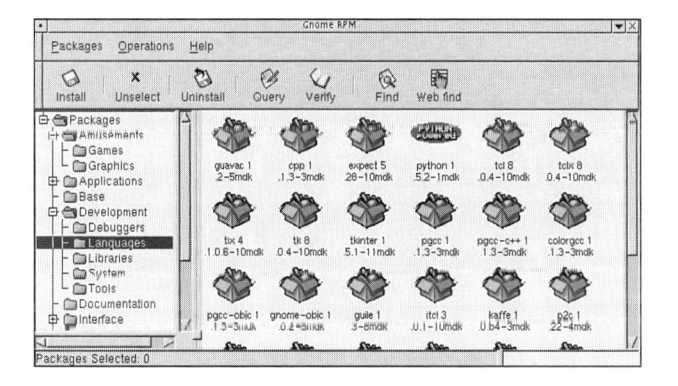

If you use the recommended order for uninstalling packages, you will not have any problems. However, if there are applications or other packages that need the package you want to uninstall, you will get a dependency error. It is similar to the error you get when you want to install a package that requires other packages to be installed first. Figure 21.2 shows an example of a dependency error. If you get a dependency error, determine whether you want to uninstall the other packages as well. If so, uninstall the packages listed in the error message, then uninstall the original package. If you do not want to uninstall the packages listed in the error message, then you should keep the original package on your computer.

FIGURE 21.2
GnoRPM warns you about dependency errors with a dialog box.

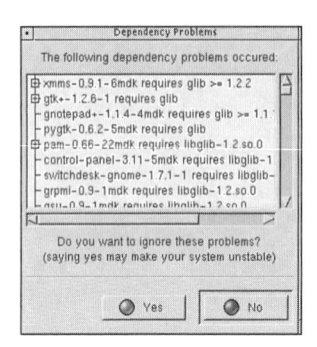

Uninstalling Binary Packages from the Command Line

GnoRPM is useful for people who prefer a graphical interface, but you can also uninstall GNOME binary packages from a shell prompt. To uninstall a package, use the rpm command with the -e switch, for instance:

```
rpm -e [package].rpm
```

There are a few options available if you uninstall from the command line, ones that are not yet available in GnoRPM. Some options that are sometimes useful when uninstalling are as follows:

--allmatches

--allmatches is useful if you have (or think you might have) more than one version of a particular package installed. Using this option will remove all versions of the package you specify, as follows:

```
rpm -e --allmatches
```

If you have more than one package, and you do not use this option, you will get an error message when you try to uninstall.

--nodeps

With the --nodeps option, the package manager will uninstall the package without checking dependencies first. This option is useful if you are uninstalling with the intention of re-installing a package immediately afterwards, to troubleshoot a problem or test an rpm, for instance.

--test

If you don't really want to uninstall but want to see what would happen if you did, use the --test option. Try this option if you want to test for dependencies. Use it with the -v or -vv switch (verbose or very verbose).

Uninstalling GNOME Tarballs

Uninstalling GNOME tarballs is a simple matter if you kept the original uncompiled source code in your directory tree. To uninstall a tarball, cd to the directory that was created when you unzipped and untarred the tarball for installation. For example, if you entered the command **tar -zxvf gnome_core-1.5.3.tgz** in the /usr/src directory, the subdirectory /usr/src/gnome_core-1.5.3 was created. To uninstall gnome_core-1.5.3, enter the following commands:

```
cd /usr/src/gnome_core-1.5.3
make uninstall
```

Uninstall each tarball in the reverse order that you installed it.

> When upgrading, always uninstall the old tarball before installing the new tarball.

Uninstalling Enlightenment

If you installed Enlightenment from a binary package, there is no need to uninstall the old package before you upgrade. Simply download the new version and install it using the Upgrade option. In versions of Enlightenment prior to version 0.16.3, it was recommended that you delete the $HOME/.enlightenment directory. In version 0.16.3 and later, it is no longer necessary to delete these files before upgrading.

> If you are uninstalling Enlightenment permanently, follow the order given in the previous section to uninstall the Enlightenment module and all supporting modules, such as Imlib and Fnlib.

The following steps must be executed from a shell prompt. Log out of GNOME to close the X session before you begin.

Enter the following command to remove the Enlightenment binaries:

```
rm -rf $PATH/enlightenment
```

The path to the Enlightenment files depends on where you originally installed them. Some people install Enlightenment in /usr/local/enlightenment, /usr/enlightenment, or /opt/enlightenment.

If you have customized files such as backgrounds or themes that you do not want to lose, make a backup of the relevant $HOME/.enlightenment directories.

Enter the following command to remove the .enlightenment files from your home directory:

```
rm -rf $HOME/.enlightenment
```

Install the new version of Enlightenment and run it to create a new set of $HOME/.enlightenment files.

Copy the customized files that you backed up previously into the new $HOME/.enlightenment directories.

The GNOME Help Browser

The GNOME Help Browser was designed to enable you to access all help files and other documentation for your system from one place. The help browser can display HTML or text files either from a remote location such as the World Wide Web or from a directory on your computer.

Open the GNOME Help Browser from Main Menu, Help System. *The GNOME User's Guide* is included here, as well as any other GNOME documentation that is installed on your system. Figure 21.3 shows the main window of a GNOME Help Browser that is integrated with Red Hat help.

FIGURE 21.3
The GNOME Help Browser is still in an early stage of development.

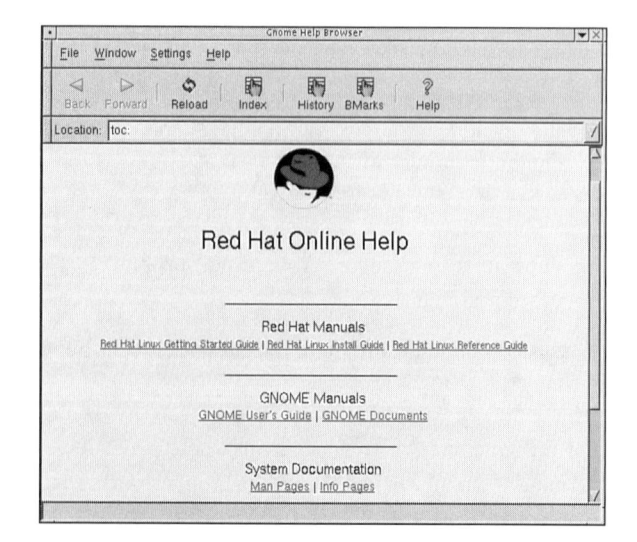

If the document you want to open is on the Web, enter the Web URL in the Location field. If the document is a file on your local machine, enter the file's pathname in the following format:

`file:`*pathname*

For example, to open the Linux Kernel Accessibility page from the Linux FAQ, enter `file:/usr/doc/FAQ/html/Accessability.html`. Note that the misspelling of "accessibility" is intentional.

You can also access man and info pages, if they are installed on your computer. To open a man page or info page, enter the following, respectively:

`man:`*topic*
`info:`*topic*

To look at all man and info pages that are available, enter the Table of Contents, or `toc`, command:

`toc:man`
`toc:info`

The man Table of Contents is displayed in the Help Browser in Figure 21.4.

FIGURE 21.4
The Help Browser can display all the man pages on your computer.

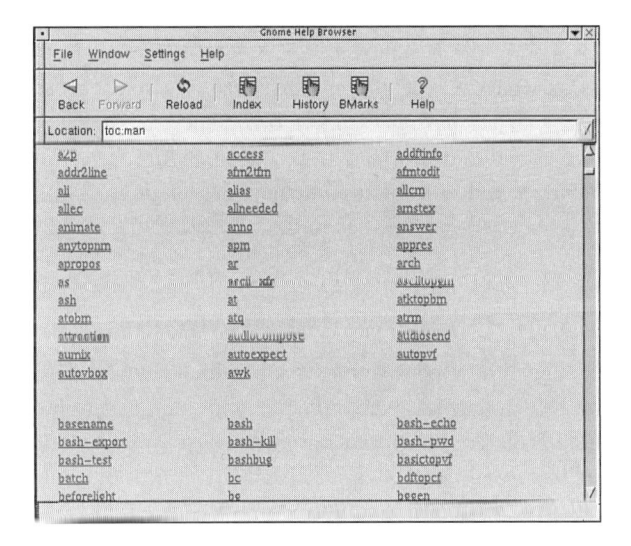

If you are not sure of the exact name of the topic you are looking for, you can use the `whatis` option. The Help Browser will display a list of all documentation on your system that concerns that topic. For example, if you wanted information on the cat command, you would enter `whatis:cat` in the Location field.

For GNOME, the best place to begin looking for help (besides this book) is *The GNOME User's Guide*, the GNOME FAQ, and the GNOME help files. Both are listed on the main page of the GNOME Help Browser.

The GNOME User's Guide

The GNOME User's Guide is the basic manual for getting up and running with GNOME. Written by David Mason and David Wheeler, *The GNOME User's Guide* is sponsored by Red Hat. It is continually updated as new versions of GNOME are released and as the need for documentation for a particular subject is addressed. Although it does not include everything you need to know in order to use GNOME, it is an excellent starting point and reference.

The GNOME FAQ

The GNOME FAQ answers potential questions about material that *The GNOME User's Guide* does not address, such as the history of the Project, installation and configuration of GNOME, and the basic theory behind GNOME. Many of the FAQ questions will eventually be addressed with tutorials and more comprehensive manuals.

Other GNOME Help Documents

Unfortunately, one of the weaknesses of an all-volunteer project is that the contributors tend to focus on what interests them, rather than on what is most needed. In the case of GNOME, that tendency has resulted in a broad spectrum of clever and useful applications that have very little documentation accompanying them. The GNOME Help Browser lists all the help files that come with applications. As you can see from Figure 21.5, the list is short. As we will see in the next section, the situation is improving rapidly.

The GNOME Documentation Project

GNOME has lagged in good documentation, which is why the mailing list is so popular. This problem is being aggressively pursued, with the formation of the GNOME Documentation Project. The Project currently has a Web site that lists items that must be written. Soon there will be a list of all GNOME applications, with the name of the developer of the application and the progress on the documentation. You will be able to see whether there is documentation in progress for the app you are interested in, and will be able to comment on the document as it is posted. The home page of the GNOME Documentation Project is `http://www.gnome.org/gdp`.

FIGURE 21.5
The GNOME Documentation Project is working to write help files for every GNOME application.

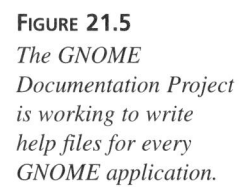

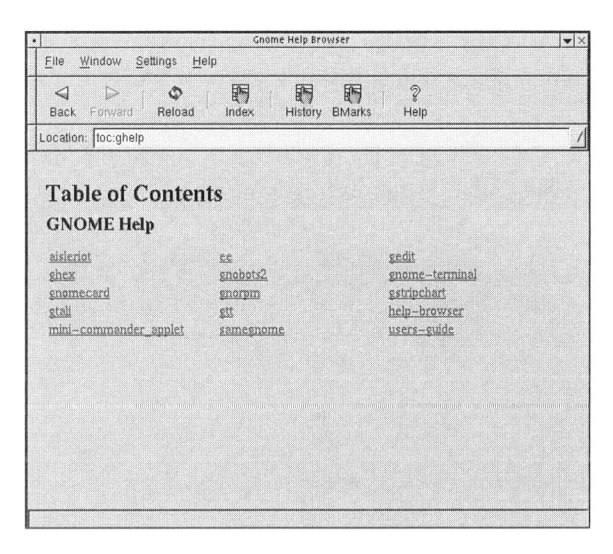

As the user, you can contribute by commenting on documents, requesting documentation on a particular subject, or writing for the GNOME Documentation Project. We will learn more about contributing to the GNOME Project in Hour 22, "Upgrading GNOME and Joining the GNOME Project."

The Mailing Lists

The basic format for communication among members of the GNOME project is via mailing list. Most of the lists are for the developers, documentation writers, and people working on a particular segment of the GNOME Project, but there are two mailing lists of interest to end users: gnome-list and gnome-announce. The complete archives of GNOME mailing lists can be viewed online at http://www.gnome.org.

Anyone interested in GNOME can subscribe to a list and anyone can post—in fact, the list is not really moderated. People can write suggestions for features, ask user questions, point out major bug problems, discuss articles about GNOME, ask questions about future developments, request documentation, or announce that they are working on something and ask for help.

Free software projects are free-wheeling and democratic by nature, but you should follow basic rules of etiquette if you want people to answer your questions and help you. Some items that should not be posted to the list include

- Personal flames directed to or about any individual.
- Negative and non-constructive comments about another person's post. Of course, politely pointing out an error that someone made in a post is always welcome and encouraged, particularly if it is my post!

- General, negative comments, such as "GNOME sucks, KDE rules!" No one will fault you for posting an exuberant "GNOME is GREAT! I LOVE IT! Thanks, guys!"
- Linux/UNIX questions that are not directly applicable to GNOME. Questions about X or window managers might or might not be answered. You might be pointed to the correct mailing list for posting your question if it is not GNOME-related.
- Impassioned missives by newbies about how the project is "all wrong, and we really should be doing it another way instead."
- Impassioned missives by experienced hackers who just joined the project two days ago about how the project is "all wrong, and we really should be doing it another way instead."
- Vague, general questions without much information, such as "um, I don't know what's wrong, but GNOME doesn't work. Can someone help me?" If you really don't know much more, try asking anyway. Often, someone will post specific questions that will help you gather more information, or even email you personally to help.
- Questions with very specific answers easily found in *The GNOME User's Guide* or in the FAQ, such as "How do I log out?"

How to Post a Message

To post a message to the general GNOME mailing list, send a plain text email to gnome-list@gnome.org. Make your question as specific as possible by describing your problem and any error messages you get. Give some basic information about your system, such as flavor of Linux/UNIX and version of GNOME and window manager. If you are a newbie, say so. Also, don't just give the error messages and leave it at that; describe what you were doing when you got the error messages and what you were trying to accomplish.

When you post a question on the list, all the members of the list receive your question as an email. Whoever feels like they have enough knowledge and time posts an answer to the list. Another user or even the developer who wrote the application might answer your question, or you might not get an answer at all. (This doesn't happen very often.)

You might get a personal response or might not; it depends on the person who takes your query. There is no trouble log or person in charge assigning queries. If no one posts an answer to your question, don't despair. It could just be that no one "caught on" to your question, or everyone was tired and busy that night. It could also be that your question was too vague, or even that no one could answer it. Try rephrasing the question and ask again.

Finally, if you get flamed, don't worry. Most GNOMErs are helpful and supportive, but every mailing list has its flamers, and everyone has a bad day that sometimes results in flames.

Summary

In this hour, you learned how to uninstall GNOME and Enlightenment from binary packages and from tarballs. You explored the GNOME Help Browser and learned about the kinds of documentation that can be viewed on the Help Browser. You explored the different kinds of GNOME help and learned how to post a question to a GNOME mailing list.

Q&A

Q I want to upgrade GNOME. Do I have to uninstall the old version first?

A If you installed GNOME from tarballs, uninstall the modules that you want to replace before installing the new modules. If you installed from a binary package, you do not have to uninstall before you upgrade if you specify the Upgrade option when installing the new version (with rpms, the Upgrade option is rpm -U).

Q Do I have to use the GNOME Help Browser to view help files?

A No. The advantage of the Help Browser is that you can bookmark all your help files for easy access. Depending on the help file format, you can use a text editor, GhostView, or Netscape to view files.

Q I clicked the Help button on a GNOME application, but there was no help file. How do I access the help file?

A If there is no help file shown in the GNOME Help Browser and no help file appears when you click Help, then the documentation probably has not been written yet. Check the GNOME Documentation Project Web site for updates at http://www.gnome.org/gdp.

Workshop

The quiz questions and exercises are designed to increase your understanding and to encourage you to continue experimenting. Answers appear in Appendix B, "Answers."

Quiz

1. Must you uninstall a GNOME rpm before upgrading to a newer version?
2. What is the command for uninstalling a tarball?
3. What does the -nodeps option for the rpm command do?
4. What should you enter in the GNOME Help Browser to get a table of contents for all the info entries on your computer?
5. Where are three places to look for help on GNOME?

Exercises

1. If you have an rpm installed on your system, enter the command **rpm -evv --test**. What happens?
2. Open GnoRPM and try to uninstall the glib package. What happens?
3. Open a documentation file in the GNOME Help Browser and bookmark it.
4. Read some messages from the gnome-list archives on a topic that interests you.

HOUR 22

Upgrading GNOME and Joining the GNOME Project

Now that you are more familiar with GNOME, you can begin to use the more advanced components available. As mentioned in Hour 2, "Installing GNOME," GNOME is in such a rapid state of development, that the release included on your Linux distribution CD ROM was probably already out of date when you bought it. rpms are great, but, more often than not, they too do not contain the latest version of a piece of GNOME software. To really keep up to date, you must know how to compile and install source code. Sometimes the newest version of an application fixes bugs and other problems, or adds great new features that you won't want to wait for. Furthermore, if you want to keep absolutely cutting-edge, or if you want to see what the GNOME Project is all about and maybe contribute, you must know how to use CVS. CVS is the code version control system that is used on the GNOME project to track changes in code that GNOME developers submit to a central server as they develop the code.

In this hour, you will

- Install GNOME from source code.
- Install GNOME from CVS.
- Learn how to contribute to the GNOME Project.

> This hour is not meant for beginners, so a lot of material that is not directly related to GNOME is not explained. If you are new to Linux and you don't understand everything in this hour, read through it, note what you don't understand, get more comfortable with your Linux system, and then come back to this hour.

Installing GNOME from Source Code

When you are first learning GNOME and Linux, binary packages such as rpms are useful because they are easy to install and uninstall. To master GNOME and Linux, however, it is necessary to know how to compile and install source code.

GNOME source code is virtually always found in the form of a tarball. A *tarball* is a file that is composed of many smaller files that have been archived, or *tarred*, into one big file. The tar file is then compressed, or *zipped*, with the gzip utility. By historical convention, files that have been tarred and zipped have the .tgz or .tar.gz extension, although this is not strictly necessary.

> For example, the Enlightenment theme packages are tarballs, but they have the extension .etheme. You can untar and ungzip them just like any other tarball.

> Most Linux/UNIX commands are actually abbreviations. For example, tar is short for Tape Archive.

When you install an application from tarballs, you must compile the source code that the developer wrote in C or another programming language into *binary code*, also called *machine code*. Compiling creates executable files that the computer can understand. Compiling source code can seem a bit intimidating at first (unless you are a programmer), but there are distinct advantages in doing so that outweigh the extra level of complexity involved.

The Source Code Advantage

GNOME tarballs comprise the only release of GNOME that is monitored and sanctioned by the GNOME Project. Various groups make binary `rpm` and `deb` packages, but the packages are not always reliable and are not guaranteed to work. The disadvantage of binary packages is that you are at the mercy of the creator of the `rpm`. If the `rpm` does not match your directory tree, or if there is an error in the `rpm`, you will not be able to install the package, or you might not be able to use the application after the package is installed.

When you install from source code, you can control exactly what is installed where. Rather than hoping that the creator of the `rpm` used the same directory tree as you did, you can tell the configure script exactly where to place files.

There is often more documentation in a tarball. All the documentation in a tarball was put there by the developer of the software. When you use an `rpm`, you are dependent on what the creator of the `rpm` thinks is useful. Sometimes `rpm`s lack the man and info files for the utility in a package, and, of course, you will not be able to read the source code or the comments in the source code (often useful in solving problems, even if you can't understand the code).

You can get the most up-to-date version of the software as soon as it is released. When a new application or an upgrade to an existing module is released, there is usually a waiting period of a several weeks to even a few months before the binary packages appear. When you install from source code, you can get the new software as soon as the developer releases it. In addition, if you install from source code, you can get the cutting-edge, development version of software as it is submitted to the code library. The GNOME code library is CVS, and anyone can download the development versions of GNOME packages as they are created.

You can view the source code and learn how the program really works. You can also change features that you don't like, or add features, and recompile the source code. This is an outstanding way to learn about programming, and to begin contributing right away, even if you are new to programming.

You customize the software. When you compile from source code, you can often specify certain options to customize your program to fit your system and your needs. With a binary `rpm`, you have to accept the options that the creator of the `rpm` chose.

Installing software from source code is more secure. It is much easier to insert malicious code into a binary than into source code. If you accept an `rpm` or other binary package from an unknown source, be careful. If the `rpm` doesn't exist from a trusted site such as Red Hat or Freshmeat, it is better to install from source code.

The disadvantage to installing from source code is that, because you are compiling the code and creating the binaries yourself, there is a greater chance that something will go wrong. Of course, you could also look upon that as an advantage, because you will learn more about the inner workings of GNOME! When everything goes perfectly without a hitch, you usually don't learn as much as when you must overcome problems.

How to Install GNOME Software from Source Code

When you know the process of installing from source code, it is actually quite simple. This section is long, but don't be put off. The more you understand about the underlying mechanics of compiling and installing, the easier it will be to recognize and fix problems, and the more likely it is that you will be successful with minimal effort. The first step is to make sure that you have the software you need to compile and install source code on your system.

Obtain the Compilation Tools

The following sections list and describe the compilation utilities that you need. If you installed Linux from a distribution CD, you might already have this software installed. Use the `whereis` or `locate` command to make sure.

> When running the `locate` command, remember to issue the command `updatedb` first, if you haven't done so recently.

Autoconf

Autoconf creates a shell script called `configure` that automatically adapts the source code of a software package to your UNIX system. You don't need autoconf to run the `configure` script; you do need it if you want to re-create the configure script. The `configure` script tests for the presence of each item that the software package might need. As it tests for each feature, the script prints a one-line message on the screen to let you know what it is testing. If the `configure` script tests for an item that is needed and doesn't find it, it exits and displays an error message. It also displays a line number indicating where the configure script was when it exited. You can use this information to look at the script for information that might help you fix the error.

If `configure` runs successfully with no errors, it will create the following files:

- A Makefile and a C header file, which you need to compile and run the software package
- A log file called `config.log` with the results of each test
- `config.cache`, a shell script which saves the results of the tests that `configure` runs
- `config.status`, a shell script that recreates the Makefile and the header file

Make

Make uses the Makefile that was created by the `configure` script to determine which parts of a large program need to be compiled. Make then executes the compilation commands that are in the Makefile, keeping track of which files are newer than other files so that only the files that have changes are re-created. The Makefile contains information on the relationships between the individual files that must be compiled, and the commands needed to compile them.

> Make is not easy to explain or understand in a brief paragraph. For more information on make, see *Managing Projects with make*, by Steve Talbot and Andrew Oram, O'Reilly, 1991.

Gcc

Gcc is the GNU C compiler, which is used to compile the source code from C source code to object files, and then to binary executable code that runs an application. Gcc is a large and advanced C and C++ compiler that you will become very familiar with if you ever program in Linux. To install source code, you only use it indirectly, but if you are interested in learning more about Linux C programming, be sure to study gcc.

> Some good places to start learning about gcc are the gcc info and man pages. If you are interested in learning more about C in general, including gcc, try the C bible, *The C Programming Language: ANSI C Version*, by Brian W. Kernighan and Dennis M. Ritchie, Prentice Hall, 1989. For a gentler introduction, an excellent tutorial book is *Sams Teach Yourself C in 21 Days*, by Peter Aitken and Brad Jones, Sams Publishing, 1999.

Tarball Installation Process

After you have verified that you have the right compilation tools, you are ready to download the tarballs. Before you begin the installation, download all the tarballs into one subdirectory. You can download and untar the tarballs into a shared directory, such as /usr/src or /usr/local/src, or into your home directory. The only step that must be performed by the superuser is to make install.

> If you download the tarballs into your home directory, it is still a good idea to maintain a library directory of all your tarballs in a place such as /usr/src. You must have the original source code in order to uninstall the binaries, once they are compiled.

> Always keep the original tarball and untarred source code directory tree (the directory that appears after you untar the tarball). You will need these files intact to uninstall the software.

Delete Old Versions of the Software

If you have an older rpm version, or a binary of an older version of the software that you installed from source code, uninstall the older version before you install the new version. If you are installing libraries for GNOME or X, it is a good idea to exit from X and do the installation from a shell.

Untar the Tarballs

Now you are ready to unzip and untar the tarballs. You can do this with one command:

tar zxvf [tarball]

This command does several things at once:

- It unzips the tarball.
- It untars the tarball.
- It creates an installation directory.
- It installs all the files from the tar file into the installation directory, if the archived filenames begin with a directory name.

The tar command is extremely useful and versatile. The options used here are

- **z** unzips the gzipped files before extracting them.
- **x** extracts the individual files from the one big archive file.
- **v** means verbose. Lists the files while they are being extracted.
- **f** extracts the files into a new directory with the same name as the archive (tarball).

Figure 22.1 shows the contents of the gNiall tarball.

FIGURE 22.1

gNiall is a simple application. Tarballs for more complex applications and libraries will contain more files.

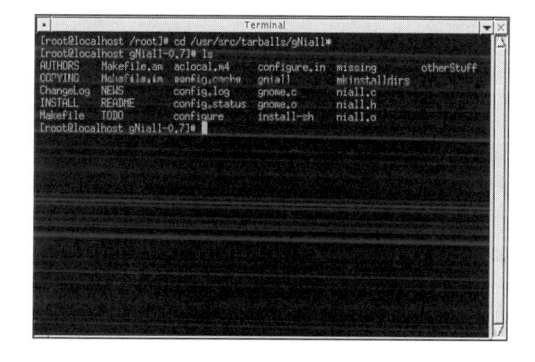

> The process for installing GNOME packages is usually quite standard, but sometimes there are differences that might not be evident unless you read the documentation. Although it is often tempting to skip this step, especially if you have many tarballs to install, always read the README and the INSTALL files before you begin the installation process.

Configure the Makefile

To configure the Makefile, `cd` to the new directory made by the tarball. It usually has the same name as the tarball, but without the `.tgz` extension. If you have read the README and INSTALL files, you will know which of the steps outlined here you should take, and where you should deviate from these general instructions.

Because every system is different, `configure` looks through your system and tries to match the requirements of the software package with the contents and configuration of your system. `configure` makes sure that you have the various libraries and dependencies on your system, and tries to guess the values for system-dependent variables. If no errors are found, `configure` creates a Makefile that matches the configuration of your particular system.

Compile and Install

After you configure your Makefile successfully, you are ready to compile the source code with make. make compiles the source code and produces the binary files and libraries that you need to run the application. To run make, type **make** at the shell prompt.

make can take a long time to run, depending on the size and complexity of the files involved.

After you have made the binary files, you must place them in the correct paths so that you can run the application. To install the binaries, type **make install**.

> You must be root to install the binaries, or the binaries will be installed in your user home directory instead of the shared directories. This might not be a problem if you are on a multiuser system and you are the only person who will use the software. Check with your system administrator.

Clean Up

There are a few more steps to take before you are finished. To remove the object files from your system, enter **make clean**.

If you are running a Linux or another ELF-based system, type **ldconfig** to make sure that the new libraries your package created are found. ldconfig regenerates the file /etc/ld.so.cache. ld.so.cache contains the pathnames for the shared libraries on your system, so that they can be found quickly when needed by programs.

> If something went wrong during one of these steps, particularly if make exited with an error, read the README and INSTALL files to verify that you have not missed a step. Also, check that there are no missing libraries that are needed, and that the location of the libraries is in your path.
>
> Start over at the beginning after you have corrected the error. To return the installation directory to the way it was before you ran configure, type **make distclean**.

Uninstalling a Tarball

Uninstalling a tarball is easy, if you have kept the original untarred installation directory in /usr/src. To uninstall a package, cd to the directory in /usr/src that contains the Makefile for the software package. Enter the command

```
make uninstall
```

The `make` command will go through your file system and remove all the files and links that were originally created by the installation.

Using CVS to Get Development Versions

CVS is the code repository that the GNOME developers use to keep track of GNOME code development. CVS enables many developers to work on the same code at once; it tracks and incorporates changes that every developer makes. There is a lot to learn about CVS, but in this hour, we will concern ourselves only with using CVS to get the most up-to-date GNOME software. To contribute code for the base GNOME packages, you need a CVS account, but anyone can log in to a CVS mirror with an anonymous account and check out code to install it.

> By definition, CVS code is unstable and has not been released for public consumption. You might check out an item that the developer is in the middle of working on, and it might not compile. It might core dump instantly when you try to run it. Be forewarned—don't complain, and use CVS code on your GNOME test system, if you have one. Also, **do not** submit bug reports for CVS code.

- The CVS FTP server is anoncvs.gnome.org. You can log in to this server anonymously.

You need some GNU tools installed on your system in order to use CVS. Your Linux distribution CD-ROM should contain these tools. If it does not, get them from http://www.gnu.org. You will need

- gcc
- GNU autoconf
- automake
- gettext
- libtool
- m4
- indent

Before you begin, you need to set up an environment variable so that you can log in to the CVS server. Enter the following at a bash shell prompt in an Xterm:

```
$ export CVSROOT=':pserver:anonymous@anoncvs.gnome.org:/cvs/gnome'
```

Next, cd into the directory where you want to download the package, and enter the command

`$ cvs login`

At the password prompt, press Enter (there is no password).

Now you are ready to check out CVS modules. For each module that you want, enter

`cvs -z3 checkout [modulename]`

> When you download CVS code, you should put it in a directory separate from your stable GNOME code. For example, if you download your stable GNOME tarballs to /usr/src/gnome, try putting the CVS modules in /usr/src/gnome_cvs or a similar directory.

> You should also create a separate directory to put your GNOME executables in, so that, if things crash, you can easily remove the entire directory without having to worry about inadvertently deleting stable, non-GNOME items. You can put your GNOME exectubles in /usr/local/gnome or /opt/gnome, depending on your system architecture. Remember to add the new pathname to your PATH environment variable.

Next you cd to the directory where you installed the CVS software package. Enter the following command:

`./autogen.sh --prefix=[install_prefix]`

install_prefix is the directory where you want to install the package. For example, if you wanted to install the package to /usr/local/gnome, you would enter

`./autogen.sh --prefix=/usr/local/gnome`

Next, you must enter the new installation prefix to your path. Enter the command

`echo $PATH`

Copy the output to the Clipboard by holding down the left mouse button and dragging it over the string.

Next, at a bash shell prompt, type **PATH=** and paste the original environment path. Add your new CVS GNOME pathname after the current pathnames.

Do the same for libraries. Usually, libraries are installed to /usr/lib or /usr/local/lib. If you are installing GNOME from CVS, you should isolate your libraries as well as your executable files. Enter the new library, such as /usr/local/lib/gnome, in the LD_LIBRARY_PATH.

Continue the installation with `make` and `make install` as described in the last section for installing tarballs.

After you have installed GTK, add the following option, which tells the `autogen` script where GTK is installed.

```
./autogen.sh --prefix=[installprefix] --with-gtk-prefix=[installprefix]
```

This is necessary because there is no configure script to look for things automatically. For more information, see Soren Harward's instructions on installing GNOME from CVS at http://www.cinternet.net/~soren/gnome/cvs.shtml.

Becoming a GNOMEr

If you like what you see of GNOME so far, you might consider contributing to the GNOME Project. It doesn't' matter whether you can program or not; there's lots to be done. Remember, GNOME is a non-profit, community software project, and it can only grow and improve as long as the community is willing to support it. As a user of GNOME, you are now part of that community.

Reporting Bugs

An easy, fast, and extremely helpful way to contribute to making GNOME better is to submit a bug report when you encounter a bug. Appendix A, "Troubleshooting," contains detailed instructions for using Bug Buddy, an ingenious little utility that has graphical dialog boxes you can use to submit bug reports on crashed programs and core dumps. It takes less than five minutes to submit a bug report using Bug Buddy. The more bugs people find and submit, the better the GNOME desktop will be for everyone.

Writing Documentation for GNOME

The biggest weakness of GNOME has been the lack of good user documentation, particularly for applications. If there is an application that you know well enough to write about, or if you are a writer by trade, the GNOME Documentation Project is a great way to contribute. The GDP has its own Web site at http://www.gnome.org/gdp.

At the site you will find links to current documentation, documentation guidelines, and a progress chart, which outlines all the documentation that is needed, its progress, and who, if anyone, is assigned to document it. Browse around, find an application that isn't being worked on, and start writing! Be sure to check out the documentation guidelines first. You should also contact the GDP and the developer of the application to let them know that you're working on the documentation.

Programming for GNOME

If you are an experienced hacker looking for a fascinating project, a novice programmer looking for programs to practice on, or if you want to get more experience in CORBA and other GNOME technologies, becoming a GNOME hacker is ideal.

> If you are new to programming, a good way to begin learning is by looking at the source code of a completed program. Study how it works, change components, and recompile it to see what happens. You can also try to find bugs or ways to improve the program.

Other Ways to Contribute

There are lots of other ways to contribute to the GNOME Project. If you have publicity or marketing experience, if you are familiar with user interface design, or if you operate a business willing to sponsor an employee to work on the GNOME Project, there is a lot to be done.

Summary

In this hour, you installed GNOME packages from source code. You also learned about CVS, and how to download and install development code from CVS.

Q&A

Q Do I have to install GNOME from source code in order to get the full benefit of GNOME?

A No. As long as you are willing to wait for `rpms` or create them yourself, you can install and use GNOME solely from `rpms`.

Workshop

The quiz questions are designed to increase your understanding and to encourage you to continue experimenting. Answers appear in Appendix B, "Answers."

Quiz

1. What format(s) of software releases are monitored and sanctioned by the GNOME Project?
2. What does the z option in tar zxvf mean (GNU tar)?
3. Why is it more secure to install software from source code than from binary package?
4. What files does the configure script create?
5. How do you return the installation directory to its original state after you have run `make` and `configure`?
6. True/False. If you find a bug in CVS software, you should submit a bug report.
7. Who is permitted to log in to CVS anonymously?

Hour 23

GNOME Technologies

In this hour and in Hour 24, we delve into the tools and technologies that are used to create GNOME applications. Most of the documentation available on these subjects is written for developers, from the standpoint of how to use GNOME programming tools to develop applications. In this hour, you will learn about GNOME technologies from the standpoint of how it benefits you as a user.

In this hour, you will

- Learn how GNOME benefits application developers and users.
- Study how GNOME uses CORBA technology.
- Learn how GNOME uses standard Bonobo interfaces to string together software components into custom applications.

GNOME Technologies

GNOME provides tools for creating applications that have a consistent look and feel, and that can be integrated to work together. In the near future, the user will be able to customize the interface to the GNOME desktop and GNOME applications on-the-fly, without programming a single line of code!

Although X and user interfaces have been around for several years, before desktop environments such as GNOME and KDE arrived, there was not a standard interface. Every X application had different standards for windows, dialog, printing, nomenclature, and fonts. GNOME takes the advances made by other desktop environments a few steps further. Not only is GNOME a clever and attractive desktop environment, it is also a set of integrated applications. Most important, it is a collection of application development tools to help developers quickly and easily add to the spectrum of GNOME applications. GNOME provides programmers a consistent and rich API that gives all programs a consistent and customizable look.

At the center of all this integration and componentization is the Common Object Request Broker Architecture, or CORBA.

CORBA

CORBA makes it possible for applications to communicate across any spectrum. It doesn't matter where the applications are physically; they can be on the same local machine, or they can be on a network. It doesn't matter what programming language the applications were written in. It doesn't even matter what operating system the applications are on, as long as there is a CORBA interface written for them that enables them to communicate.

With CORBA, you can

- Use a separate, independent application as a function, or engine, inside another application to perform a task. For example, the CD player applet in the GNOME panel calls whatever CD player application is installed via CORBA.
- Control one application remotely from within another application.
- Create compound documents. A compound document is one file that contains several file formats, because it has been created using several different applications, connected through CORBA interfaces. For example, you can have a document that contains a spreadsheet, word text, and graphics.
- Embed documents inside one another, and edit any part of the document. For example, if you embed a flowchart inside a word processing document, you can edit the flowchart inside the word processing document. When you click the flowchart, the flowchart application is remotely opened within the word processor application, so you can edit the flowchart. When you are finished editing the flowchart, the word processing application closes the flowchart application.

- String together distinct applications as components in order to make one big application, custom-designed the way you need it.

The Object Management Group, or OMG, controls CORBA. For more information on OMG or CORBA, visit the OMG Web site at http://www.omg.org.

ORB

The Object Request Broker (ORB) makes it possible for two applications to communicate—sort of like a middleman, thus it is called *middleware*. An ORB defines and regulates the client/server relationship between two objects. The objects can be hardware and software, two applications, an application and a script, an application and a function, and so on.

ORBit is the CORBA implementation that is used for GNOME. Small and lightweight at only 30KB in size, ORBit was written from scratch specifically for GNOME. Figure 23.1 illustrates the relationship between two objects and the ORB.

FIGURE 23.1
The Object Request Broker enables two objects to communicate and interact with each other.

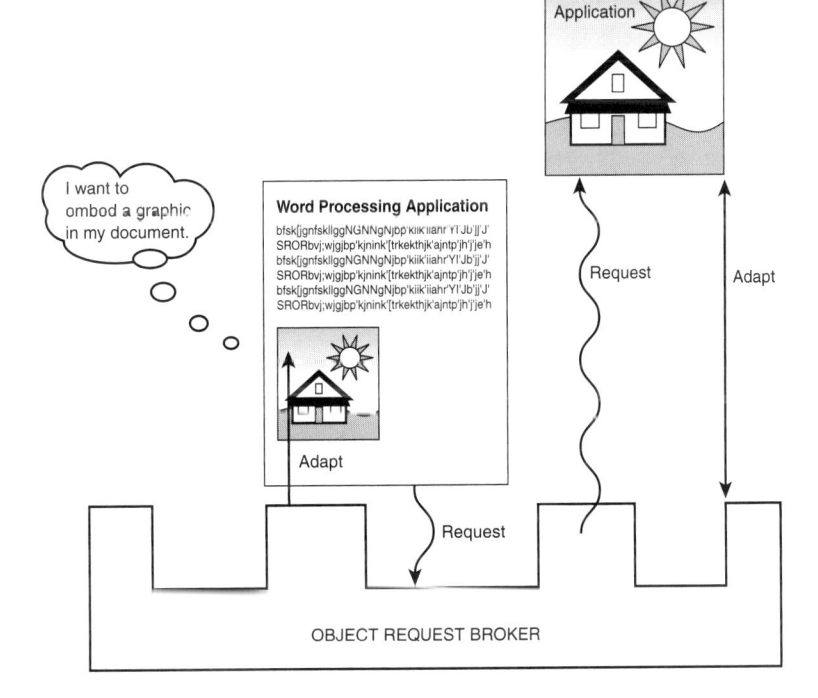

Bonobo

The means by which reusable software components are strung together in GNOME is the Bonobo interface. Bonobo is a CORBA interface, written in the CORBA Interface Definition Language. Bonobo provides standard interfaces for components, so they will fit together in any combination. The result is that any component that has been designed within the Bonobo architecture will fit with any other component.

A rough analogy for this architecture is a LEGO® set. The pieces are of different shapes, sizes, and colors, but they all fit together because they have little holes and handles that fit inside each other. The holes and handles are CORBA. To make all the LEGO pieces that are fitted together into a cohesive whole, you need the holes and handles to be all the same size, designed to fit into one another in any combination. That's Bonobo. In short, you have a ready-made bag of tricks for creating some very interesting software.

The point of Bonobo is to keep an application as simple and small as possible. Greater functionality and complexity is achieved by stringing the small components together using CORBA, not by creating a gigantic hierarchical application. Applications are designed as shells that hold strings of components, rather than a hierarchical program with functions.

Bonobo enables application developers to use components without knowing anything about the internals of the application. Instead of wasting time reinventing the wheel, trying to understand and integrate different functions, or trying to port a component from another language and another application, the developer can simply use the component without knowing anything except what it requires and what it does. The component doesn't even have to be written in the same computer language as the application the developer is creating. All this is achieved by CORBA.

Language Bindings

As discussed in the last section, one of the *raisons d'etre* for CORBA is the ability to concurrently use programs that were written in different languages. For this to be possible, you need some kind of wrapper around each program that will enable the programs to communicate. The wrapper for programs in different languages is called a *language binding*. Most of GNOME and GTK is written in C. Language bindings make it possible to use code that is written in another programming language within the GNOME universe.

Language bindings also make it easy for a user to create scripts to automate tasks within GNOME. With language bindings, the user can write the script in her favorite scripting language, instead of relying on C. GNOME and GTK have many language bindings because they were designed with scripting in mind.

Language bindings for GTK exist for these languages:

Ada95	Objective Caml
C++	Objective Label
Dylan	Pascal
Eiffel	Perl
Guile	Pike
Haskell	Python
JavaScript	Scheme
Objective C	TOM

Language bindings for Java are under development.

Summary

In this hour, you learned how GNOME uses Bonobo interfaces within a CORBA architecture to enable application developers to create new applications using existing code. Objects that are connected with CORBA interfaces do not have to be related in any way to be used together. Using Bonobo, applications can be strung together to create larger, custom applications.

Q&A

Q Where can I learn more about Bonobo and CORBA?

A There is a detailed description of the Bonobo IDL at http://www.gnome.org/gnome-office/bonobo.shtml. There is an extensive amount of documentation available on CORBA at the OMG Web site. For a beginner-level tutorial on CORBA, try OMG's CORBA for Beginners page at http://www.omg.org/corba/beginners.html.

Q Where can I get language bindings?

A Links for all the language bindings supported by GTK are available at the GTK Web site at http://www.gtk.org.

Workshop

The quiz questions are designed to increase your understanding and to encourage you to continue experimenting. Answers appear in Appendix B, "Answers."

Quiz

1. What does CORBA stand for?
2. What is a compound document?
3. What Object Request Broker does GNOME use?
4. What is a language binding?

HOUR 24

Anatomy of a GNOME Application

In Hour 23, "GNOME Technologies," you learned about CORBA and Bonobo, the central technologies of GNOME applications. In this hour, you will look inside a GNOME application to see how it is put together. We will study the components of a GNOME application from a very broad user's perspective, not a more narrow developer's perspective. This chapter is written with the assumption that you have no experience with programming. We gloss over some details that would be difficult to discuss without the developer's vocabulary. We also make some generalizations that are not necessarily useful to a developer, but should help you understand the material as a user. If you would like a more detailed view of GNOME application development, a list of resources is provided at the end of the chapter. Although it certainly won't make you a GNOME programmer, this hour should give you a better appreciation of how object-oriented, graphical interface programs work, and what is actually happening when you open a GNOME application in a window and click a button or drag and drop.

In this hour, you will

- Learn what makes a GNOME application.
- Explore the basics of how graphical interface programs work.
- Discover the libraries that are essential to the GNOME application, including the GNOME libraries, GTK+, GDK, Glib, and Xlib.
- See how Glade makes it easier to develop and change the interface for a GNOME application.

What Is a GNOME Application?

So far, you have learned about GNOME as a desktop environment that provides a graphical interface to UNIX and UNIX-like operating systems. You have also seen GNOME as a collection of applications within the desktop environment that helps you perform tasks. GNOME is certainly both those things, but that's not the whole picture. GNOME is also a set of powerful application development tools that make UNIX and Linux application development easier and provide a standard that makes every GNOME application look immediately familiar to you, the user.

So, what makes a GNOME application a GNOME application? The several ways of answering that question are different ways of stating the same thing:

- A GNOME application is written using the GTK+ and GNOME libraries and application programming interfaces.
- A GNOME application is written to the GNOME standard of architecture.
- A GNOME application is written within the standards of the GNOME desktop environment.
- A GNOME application is an application that has the look and feel of standard GNOME applications, can act as a CORBA object to interface with other GNOME applications, and that can be used as a component within other GNOME applications.

By using the GNOME libraries and adhering to GNOME standard architecture, applications written by different people in totally different settings, who know nothing about each other's code, can not only look and feel the same, but ultimately, if they incorporate Bonobo technology, will be able to work together or as components of each other.

How Do Graphical Interface Programs Work?

Virtually every computer program accepts input from somewhere, does something with that input, and then produces output. In this sense, programs that use a graphical

Anatomy of a GNOME Application

interface behave the same way as text-based programs. The difference is that with a traditional UNIX text-based program, your main interface with the kernel is via the command line. You type in commands, and the kernel calls up the resources and processes needed to carry out the command.

With a program written with a graphical interface, the same process occurs, but through a graphical interface. Instead of typing in commands, you enter commands by clicking in a certain location on a window with the mouse. So how does your mouse click translate into a command?

Some Programming Terms Defined

Before going into any more detail, we must define some programming terms that are immediately pertinent to this chapter.

Every GNOME application uses several groups of *libraries*, which are composed of various *functions*. Some of the most important libraries for GNOME are GTK+ and libgnomeui, which are libraries of *widgets*.

A *function* is a miniature program that performs a certain task within a larger program. If a routine is used many times in a program, the programmer will call a function instead of just writing the code directly into the program. Functions also make the program easier to write and to understand, because it breaks the program into smaller, manageable pieces. Functions also save time, because they can be used and reused, instead of being written directly into the program.

A *library* is a collection of commonly used functions. GNOME has several libraries of functions that programmers can use repeatedly to perform certain tasks in a program.

A *widget* is a special kind of function in a graphic interface library that creates a small graphical piece on the display. For example, buttons, menu entries, scrollbars, and check boxes are all widgets. Some widgets, such as buttons, menu bars, and scroll windows are *containers*, which hold other widgets. Other widgets produce signals, which tell the program to do something. Some examples of signal widgets are menu entries, button labels, and scrollbar entries. Groups of widgets are collected in libraries called *toolkits*.

Parts of a GNOME Application

A GNOME program is made up of several libraries, some of which are specific to GNOME and others that were created for other projects and are used by GNOME. By exploring the libraries, you can begin to understand the many layers of a GNOME application, and how it all fits together. At the bottom, you have the X libraries, which enable the application to work with the X server. The GDK and GTK libraries handle the graphical interface of the application on the desktop, and handle how certain actions trigger an action in the program, such as a mouse click on a button. The top layer, the GNOME libraries, enables the application to fit comfortably in the GNOME desktop environment, and to work with other GNOME applications. Finally, you have the actual application. All the libraries described here are written in the C programming language. The libraries used in GNOME are illustrated in Figure 24.1.

FIGURE 24.1
The GNOME libraries are referred to in the source code, and compiled with the application to make an executable file.

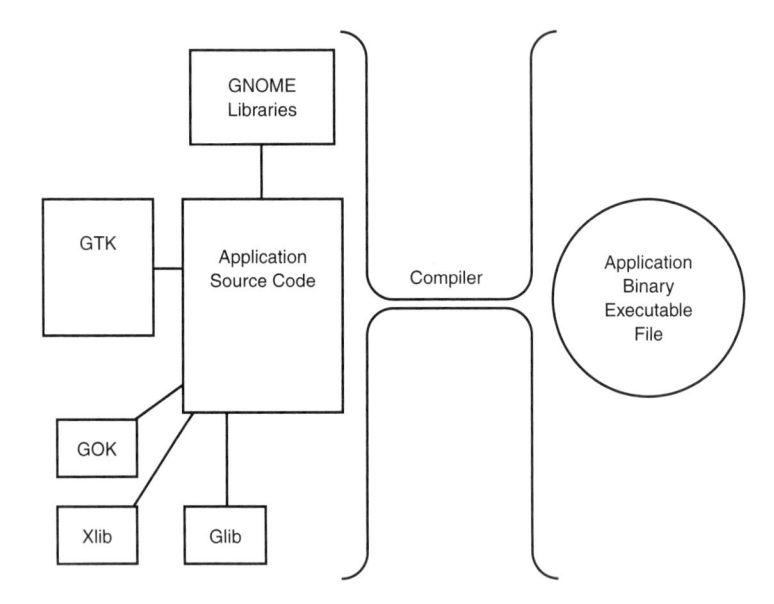

GNOME Libraries

As discussed in the introduction, GNOME is much more than a desktop environment or a set of applications. GNOME is also a set of libraries that help programmers create applications in a streamlined, standard way so that GNOME programs can interact with each other. Microsoft Windows has been doing this for some time, with ActiveX. GNOME brings the ease of programming and the ready-made tools that ActiveX provides Windows programmers to UNIX application programming.

The GNOME libraries enable application developers to build GNOME-compliant applications quickly and easily, within the GNOME standard interface. This means that, although there can be hundreds of programmers working independently, creating their own free software, the applications will have a consistent look and feel and will interact with each other.

From a user perspective, the GNOME libraries add to the GNOME experience, because everything looks and behaves the same way. Rather being than a patchwork quilt of utilities and applications for which you might have to learn 10 different printing dialog boxes, every dialog looks the same for every application. Standards also make GNOME more competitive among the commercial interfaces as well. In addition, the applications use less memory. Instead of each function being loaded into memory when you open an application, the shared library is loaded, and each application that needs it is referred to the library. Application development happens more rapidly, better applications are produced, and the whole project advances. Users get better applications and new releases faster, because developers can concentrate on the application itself, not the user interface.

The GNOME libraries, divided according to functionality, are

- Libgnome
- Libgnomeui
- Libgnorba

Libgnome

Libgnome provides functions for launching applications, identifying application MIME types, storing metadata, and loading and saving configuration files. In Hour 6,"GNOME Under the Hood," you learned about desktop files. The configuration loading function from libgnome uses the desktop files to set up your desktop. Another function from libgnome finds the standard GNOME file locations. Developers using a toolkit other than GTK can use some functions in libgnome to make their programs work with GNOME. Libgnome also contains interfaces to interact with other, non-GNOME libraries, such as esound.

Some examples of utilities and functions that can be found in libgnome follow:

- **gnome-config** is a script that helps compile GNOME applications.
- **gnome-exec** launches applications.
- **gnome-mime** identifies MIME types.

Libgnomeui

Libgnomeui is a toolkit that contains user interface widgets for GNOME applications. The library imposes standards on GNOME programmers, so that the interface of GNOME applications is consistent. It contains standard pixmap icons for open, closing, saving, and other operations, and also has routines that help the developer create dialog boxes, the GNOME application framework, (GnomeApp), the GNOME canvas (GnomeCanvas), and other widgets. Libgnomeui is based on GTK, and the widgets it contains are meant to act as an extension of the GTK+ toolkit.

Some examples of the widgets in libgnomeui follow:

- **GnomeDock** is the widget which enables you to undock your toolbars.
- **GnomeApp** widget creates a standard GNOME window.
- **gnome-about** is a widget that creates the GNOME About box.
- **gnome-canvas-image** creates the GNOME canvas.
- **gnome-spell** is a simple spell-checker widget.
- **gnome-preferences** is a widget for setting GNOME preferences.

The third GNOME library is libgnorba, which provides CORBA interfaces for GNOME applications. We will not discuss libgnorba in this hour, but if you would like to learn more about libgnorba, see `http://developer.gnome.org/arch/component/gnorba.html`.

GTK

Next in the level of a GNOME application comes GTK, which stands for GIMP Toolkit. GTK provides the widgets and other tools for graphical interface applications. Developed for the GIMP graphics application, GTK+ has been extended to all kinds of uses, including GNOME.

The window of an application is made up of hundreds or even thousands of small graphic items called *widgets*. Each widget in an application forms a part of the window on the screen, or acts as a container for another widget. Within some container widgets are *signals* that tell the program to carry out some action. To make the button do something when the signal is emitted, another function called the signal handler catches the signal and calls the right function to perform the action that is called for by the signal. When you interact with a widget that contains a signal, the signal is "turned on," a message is sent to the X server, and the action is carried out.

For example, a scroll window widget will hold a list widget. On screen, you see the scroll window with the list inside it. The scrollbar is yet another widget. A button widget will hold a label widget that names the button. Other widgets will be used to put the container widgets in order, such as the horizontal and vertical box widgets that line up the button widgets.

Some examples of GTK+ widgets are

- Window
- Frame
- Button

- Label that goes into a button
- Scrollbar window
- Scrollbar
- Menu entry
- Horizontal container box
- Vertical container box

GDK, Glib, and Xlib

The next component of a GNOME application is *GDK*, which stands for the GIMP Drawing Kit. Like GTK, GDK was originally developed for the GIMP. GDK acts as a wrapper between GTK and the X libraries, or *Xlib*. The developer uses GDK to set a property for a window or to draw a special object on the window.

GDK increases the *portability* of GTK. Because GTK doesn't interact directly with the X libraries, it is simple to adapt GTK to windowing systems other than X. In fact, GTK has been ported to MS Windows using a modification of GDK.

Glib is a C utility library, which provides routines that are useful in GNOME applications. Glib isn't maintained by the GNOME project, but it is used as the foundation of GNOME applications. The developer uses Glib to create structures that are common throughout the program, and there is a collection of ready-made code for commonly used routines. Glib also contains utilities that help to port GNOME applications to other systems. Glib must be included in a program in order to use GTK.

Xlib is the collection of libraries that the X server uses to create the graphical interface on which GNOME resides.

Glade

Are you ready to start programming? Even if you don't ever want to program in GNOME, you should be familiar with an application development tool called Glade.

Glade is a graphical interface (GUI) design tool that builds the source code and the interfaces for the developer using a menu-driven system. The Glade library, Libglade, loads a Glade project and builds the interface for you. If an application is built using Glade, you can change any part of the GNOME desktop interface yourself, *on-the-fly*, without knowing any programming at all. *On-the-fly* is a programming term for the ability to change an aspect of a program and immediately see the results of the change, without recompiling the source code.

Glade is illustrated in Figure 24.2.

FIGURE 24.2
Glade makes building applications much faster and easier.

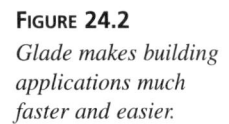

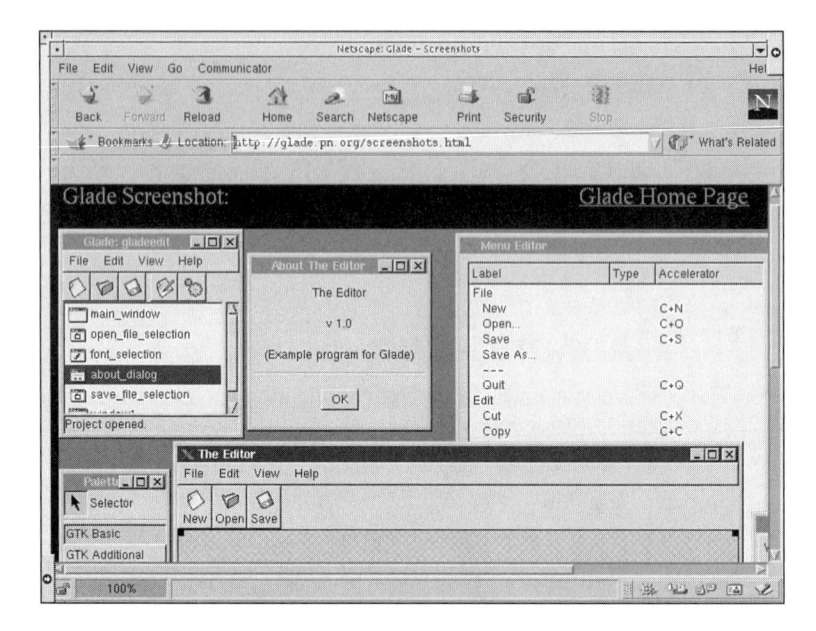

Learning More

This hour is aimed at the user, so that you can better understand the techniques behind the GNOME applications you use. If you would like to learn more about GNOME programming, there are some excellent resources available:

- George Lebl wrote a series of three articles on how to develop GNOME applications, published by IBM DeveloperWorks, at http://www-4.ibm.com/software/developer/library/gnome-programming/index.html#structure.
- A GTK+ tutorial written by Tony Gale is another great resource; it can be found at http://www.gtk.org/tutorial.
- There is also a wealth of information for developers at the GNOME development Web site, http://developer.org.

Summary

In this hour, you learned about the inner workings of a GNOME application. You learned what makes a GNOME program a GNOME program. You delved into the libraries that are used in a GNOME application, and you were introduced to Glade.

Q&A

Q I looked for the GNOME libraries and can't find them in my directory tree. Where are they located?

A You must either have installed GNOME from source code, or have the GNOME devel `rpm` packages installed in order to have the libraries on your system. Most systems have the library header files in `/usr/include` or `/usr/local/include`; these files are useful for learning about the libraries. You can use the `whereis` command to find libraries—for example, to see where the libgnomeui library is installed, enter the following command at a shell prompt:

`whereis libgnomeui`

You could use the command `locate` instead of `whereis`. `locate` does not require the file to be in your PATH.

Workshop

The quiz questions and exercises are designed to increase your understanding and to encourage you to continue experimenting. Answers appear in Appendix B, "Answers."

Quiz

1. What is a function?
2. What is a library?
3. What do you call a widget that holds another widget?
4. Which libraries in a GNOME application handle the actual graphical interface?
5. In what programming language are the GNOME libraries written?
6. In which library is the function `gnome-about`?
7. What do GTK and GDK stand for?
8. True/False: Glade builds the source code for a developer after she chooses an interface for inclusion in an application.

Exercises

1. Open your favorite text editor and enter this small program:

```
/* example-start gnome_love gnome_love.c */

#include <gtk/gtk.h>

void hello( GtkWidget *widget,
            gpointer   data )
{
```

```
    g_print ("I love GNOME\n");
}

gint delete_event( GtkWidget *widget,
                   GdkEvent  *event,
                   gpointer   data )
{
    g_print ("delete event occurred\n");

    /* Change TRUE to FALSE and the main window will be destroyed with
     * a "delete_event". */

    return(TRUE);
}

/* Another callback */
void destroy( GtkWidget *widget,
              gpointer   data )
{
    gtk_main_quit();
}

int main( int   argc,
          char *argv[] )
{
    /* GtkWidget is the storage type for widgets */
    GtkWidget *window;
    GtkWidget *button;

    /* This is called in all GTK applications. Arguments are parsed
     * from the command line and are returned to the application. */
    gtk_init(&argc, &argv);

    /* create a new window */
    window = gtk_window_new (GTK_WINDOW_TOPLEVEL);

    gtk_signal_connect (GTK_OBJECT (window), "delete_event",
                        GTK_SIGNAL_FUNC (delete_event), NULL);

    /* Here we connect the "destroy" event to a signal handler.
     * This event occurs when we call gtk_widget_destroy() on the window,
     * or if we return FALSE in the "delete_event" callback. */
    gtk_signal_connect (GTK_OBJECT (window), "destroy",
                        GTK_SIGNAL_FUNC (destroy), NULL);

    /* Sets the border width of the window. */
    gtk_container_set_border_width (GTK_CONTAINER (window), 10);

    /* Creates a new button with the label "I love GNOME." */
    button = gtk_button_new_with_label ("I love GNOME");
```

Anatomy of a GNOME Application

```c
    /* When the button receives the "clicked" signal, it will call the
     * function hello() passing it NULL as its argument.  The hello()
     * function is defined above. */
    gtk_signal_connect (GTK_OBJECT (button), "clicked",
                        GTK_SIGNAL_FUNC (hello), NULL);

    /* This will cause the window to be destroyed by calling
     * gtk_widget_destroy(window) when "clicked".  Again, the destroy
     * signal could come from here, or the window manager. */
    gtk_signal_connect_object (GTK_OBJECT (button), "clicked",
                               GTK_SIGNAL_FUNC (gtk_widget_destroy),
                               GTK_OBJECT (window));

    /* This packs the button into the window (a gtk container). */
    gtk_container_add (GTK_CONTAINER (window), button);

    /* The final step is to display this newly created widget. */
    gtk_widget_show (button);

    /* and the window */
    gtk_widget_show (window);

    /* All GTK applications must have a gtk_main(). Control ends here
     * and waits for an event to occur (like a key press or
     * mouse event). */
    gtk_main ();

    return(0);
}
/* example-end */
```

When you are finished, save it as gnome_love.c and enter the following command at a shell prompt to compile it:

```
gcc -Wall -g gnome_love.c -o gnome_love `gtk-config --cflags` \
    `gtk-config --libs`
```

APPENDIX A

Troubleshooting

GNOME is a stable, reliable desktop environment, but it is also very new. There are still quite a few bugs to be found, particularly in software with earlier releases. A wonderful little utility called Bug Buddy enables you to troubleshoot crashed programs and report bugs.

The purpose of Bug Buddy is to make sending a bug report easy for the user, while automatically collecting the information that is useful for the developer. It can also help you determine whether a program crashed because of something wrong with your system, or because of a true bug in the program.

Before Bug Buddy, if you had a core dump, you had to start gdb, and then try to re-create the conditions that caused the crash. You had to know about stack traces, and how to run gdb (not an easy prospect), as well as enough about programming to be able to read the results of the trace. With Bug Buddy, *anybody* can submit useful bug reports to the GNOME bug tracking system.

The more ways users discover to crash GNOME applications and the desktop environment itself, and the more bug reports that are submitted, the more stable GNOME will become in the future. Don't be shy about submitting a bug report because you think it's probably a common problem that has already been reported. One of the ways the core GNOME hackers decide on which bugs to fix is the number of bug reports that a particular bug gets.

As the überguru Eric Raymond said, "Given enough eyeballs, all bugs are shallow."

Requirements for Bug Buddy

You must have the following software installed to use Bug Buddy:

- gnome-libs (1.0.53 or later recommended)
- libglade (0.5 or later required)
- gdb (for acquiring stack traces)

Features of Bug Buddy

For such a small utility, Bug Buddy has some extraordinarily useful features:

- It automatically finds and includes the components on your system; there's no need to hunt around for them yourself.
- It gathers a stack trace automatically, either from a crashed application or from the core file.
- It can be started by double-clicking a core file in File Manager, and from the crash dialog box (the one that tells you the applicaton had a segfault).

How to Use Bug Buddy

When you get an error file such as the one shown in Figure A.1, click Submit Bug Report. Bug Buddy starts.

FIGURE A.1

The gnoRPM segfault message contains a button for you to start Bug Buddy directly.

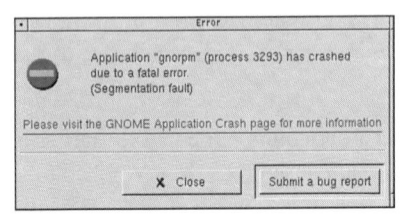

The first time you use Bug Buddy, you must enter your contact information, including your name, email address, and the full path of the `sendmail` command. Bug Buddy searches for this path when it is installed, so the default pathname is probably correct.

The next window contains the system information that Bug Buddy automatically detects, shown in Figure A.2.

FIGURE A.2

Bug Buddy checks your system configuration automatically.

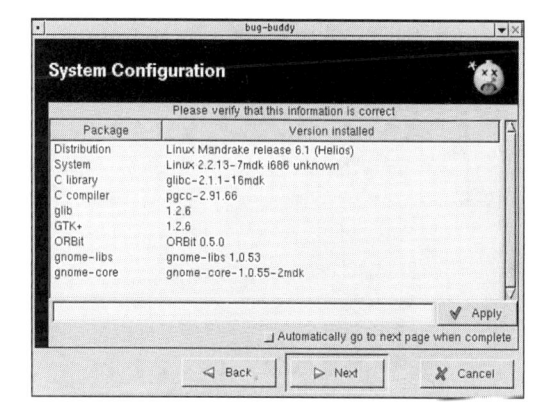

Look over the information to make sure that it is correct. Under the Report Information, shown in Figure A.3, the software that crashed will automatically appear in the window. Enter the version you have manually.

FIGURE A.3

The report information gives basic information about the type of bug report and the application involved. Don't forget to enter the application version number!

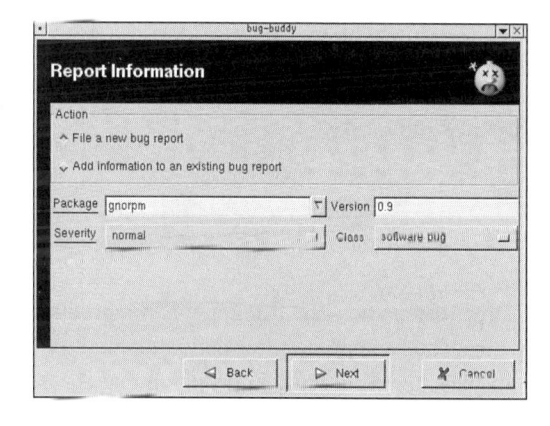

In the Description dialog's Short Subject for the Bug Report field, shown in Figure A.4, enter a bug report title. (This will be the subject of the email you send.) Then in the Full Description of the Bug field, enter all the information you can think of about the bug.

Under More Information, shown in Figure A.5, enter exactly what to do to reproduce the bug. You might have to go through all the steps again, as you describe them to make sure that you don't miss anything.

FIGURE A.4

In the Description dialog box, enter exactly what happened before, during, and after the problem occurred.

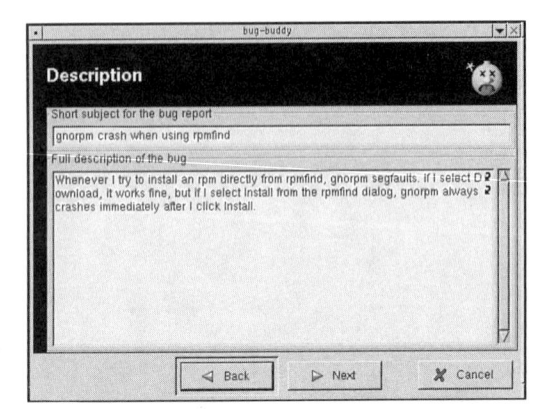

FIGURE A.5

The More Information dialog box.

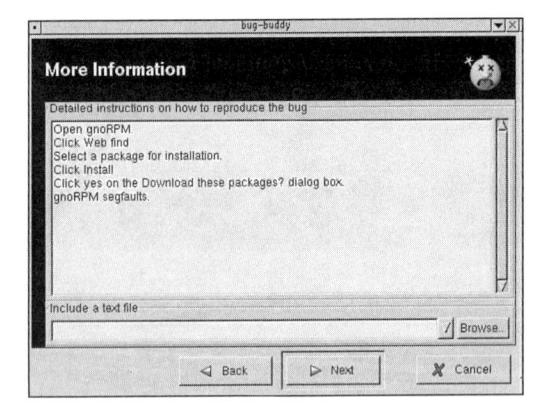

Provide detailed instructions on how the developer can reproduce the bug in the More Information dialog box. The Debugging Information dialog box is important. Here is where Bug Buddy displays the debugging information that is essential to fixing the bug. Check the box that is pertinent to the bug.

- If the application crashed, check Attach to a crashed application.
- If there was a core dump, check Read from a core file.
- If there was some other problem for which there is no record, you can check Skip this step.

Bug Buddy will more than likely have checked the correct box for you, but check to make sure. Bug Buddy should also have entered the correct application and Process ID number automatically, in the case of a crashed app, or the core file pathname in the case of a core dump. This is the most important step in the process, so do not check Skip this step unless you are reporting a documentation bug or making a feature request. The Debugging Information dialog box is shown in Figure A.6.

Troubleshooting

FIGURE A.6

Bug Buddy collects the debugging information automatically after a core dump or crashed application.

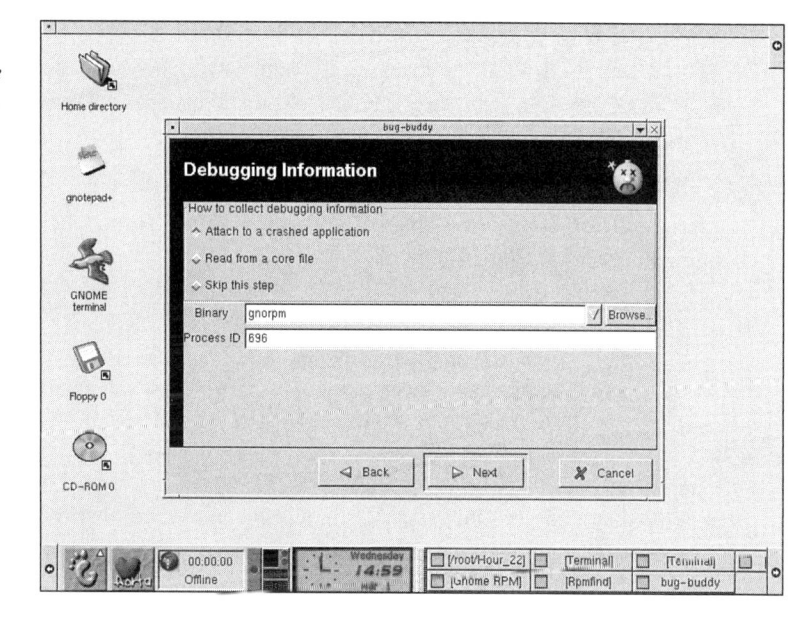

In the next step, Bug Buddy displays the debugging information. An example is shown in Figure A.7.

FIGURE A.7

The debugging information might not mean much to you, but it can mean a lot to the developer of the application.

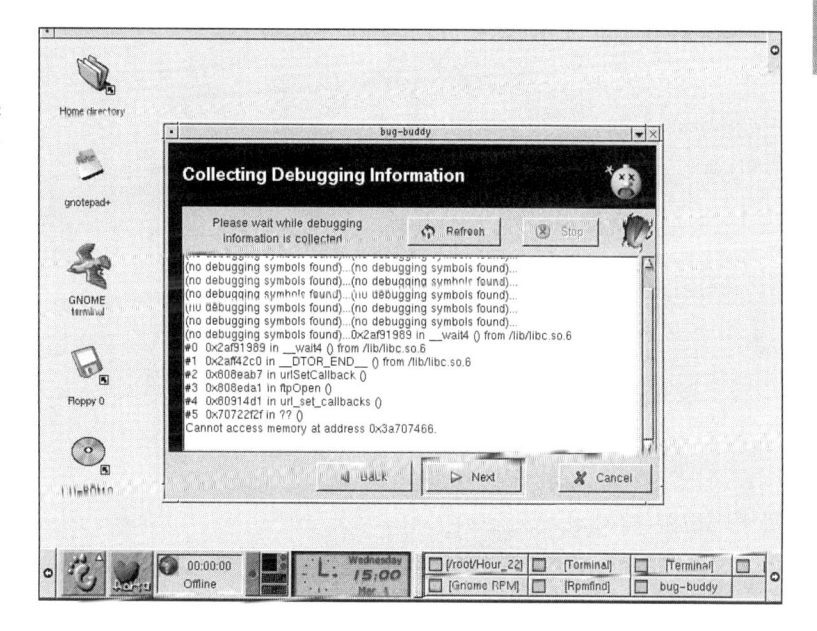

When Bug Buddy is done, click Next. In the Submit Report dialog box, you can select Submit Bug Report to Bug Tracking System, in which your bug report will be entered into the GNOME bug tracking database. You can also send the report in email format to yourself only. After you send it to yourself, you can always forward it to the bug tracking system at submit@bugs.gnome.org. Or, you can save the bug report to a file to send later.

The last dialog box is a synopsis of your email information. Click Finish to submit the bug report.

> Do not close the crashed application until you have filled in all the Bug Buddy dialog boxes. Otherwise, the process will be killed before Bug Buddy can read the results or send a bug report.

After you submit your bug report, you will receive an automatically generated email with your bug ticket number and the name of the person who maintains the package for which you submitted the report. This person will receive the report.

APPENDIX B

Answers

Answers for Hour 1

Quiz

1. What is the difference between free software and open source software?

   The user of free software may run, study, modify, redistribute, improve, and release improvements of software to the public, without any restrictions. The term *open source* is often used in the same context as free software, but actually means only that the software's user can view the source code.

2. What larger project is the GNOME Project a part of?

   The GNOME Project is part of the GNU Project.

3. What is the basic goal of GNOME?

   The basic goal of GNOME is to provide

   A desktop environment for UNIX that is easy to use and free,

   A set of powerful, interoperable applications for use within the destop environment, and

   A framework for application development.

Exercises

1. Explore the GNOME Web Site at `http://www.gnome.org`.

    Answer will vary with the reader.

2. Read the December 14, 1999 article "GNOME: Its Current State and Future" online at *Linux Today*, `http://linuxtoday.com/stories/13678.html`, for a detailed look at the future of GNOME.

    Answer will vary with the reader.

Answers for Hour 2

Quiz

1. Which GNOME installation method is monitored and officially sanctioned by the GNOME Project?

    Installation from source code via tarballs.

2. What does "dependency error" mean?

    A package that you are trying to install requires files from another package in order to run.

3. What should you do if you get a dependency error when installing GNOME?

    You must install the package that will satisfy the dependency first, and then install the original package.

Exercises

1. Enter the command `man rpm` at a prompt and study the output. What does the `-Uvh` in `rpm -Uvh [package_name].rpm` mean?

    `-Uvh` are the options that are passed to the `rpm` command. `U` means update if an old version of the rpm exists, otherwise install. `v` means verbose mode; give error messages if something goes wrong. `h` is the option that causes those neat little dots to appear on the screen as the `rpm` loads.

2. Install GNOME as instructed in this chapter, and then create a file called `.Xclients` using your favorite text editor. (If `.Xclients` already exists, save it under another name, and then return it to its original state after you have finished this exercise.) Enter a single line in the file

    ```
    exec gnome-session
    ```

    Log out of X, and then restart X. Does GNOME appear? If not, don't worry. We'll go over starting problems in the next hour. If it starts, congratulations!

There isn't really an answer for this exercise. If it works, great; if it doesn't, continue to Hour 3.

Answers for Hour 3

Quiz

1. What is the difference between xdm and xinit?

   Xdm is a program that starts the X server at boot-time. Xinit is invoked by the user after logging in.

2. What is the difference between .xinitrc and xinitrc? Between .xsession and Xsession?

   .xinitrc is the X initialization script that resides in the user's home directory, and can differ for each user. xinitrc resides in /etc/X11/xinit and contains the default commands for the system. Same answer for .xsession and Xsession, except that Xsession resides in /etc/X11/xdm/Xsession.

3. Which files does Switchdesk create when it is installed?

   .Xclients and .Xclients-default.

4. What is the magic command when dealing with the X server?

   The magic command is the last command in the X server initialization script, xinitrc or Xsession. When the process started by this command ends, the X server session is also terminated.

Exercises

1. Before installing Switchdesk, determine how the X server is started on your system.

   Answer will vary. To double-check your answer, enter **ps -a** from the command line after you have started an X session. If xinit or xdm is listed, that is what is used on your system.

2. Before installing Switchdesk, create a .xsession, .xinitrc, or .Xclients file and input the correct line to start GNOME. Start X and verify that GNOME starts.

   Answer will vary. If you start an X server using xdm, you should edit .xsession. If you start X using xinit, you should use .xinitrc or .Xclients.

3. After installing Switchdesk, open the .Xclients-defaults file in your favorite editor. What does it look like? Switch from GNOME to KDE using Switchdesk, then open .Xclients-default again within KDE. What has changed?

The file will contain only the line `exec gnome-session`. After switching to KDE, the file will contain only the line `startkde`.

Answers for Hour 4

Quiz

1. Which window managers are fully GNOME compliant?

    Enlightenment and FVWM.

2. Name three aspects of the desktop environment that the window manager controls.

    Window size, window borders, and placement of windows on the desktop.

3. How do you change the default Window Manager?

    Change the environment variable, WINDOW_MANAGER, log out of GNOME, than restart X Window.

4. What is the purpose of a desktop shell?

    The desktop shell lets you run applications and manipulate files in a graphical setting.

Exercises

1. Go to the X11 Web site at `http://www.x11.org`, and find the comparison chart on window managers. Which window manager is GNOME compliant? Which GNOME-compliant window manager has the most features?

    According to the X11.org comparison chart, BlackBox, AfterStep, Enlightenment, WindowMaker, and SCWM are GNOME-compliant. According to the GNOME Project, Enlightenment, sawmill, IceWM, and WindowMaker are fully GNOME-compliant. This exercise is meant to illustrate that there are many places to get information about GNOME and that information is sometimes contradicting. When in doubt, trust the sources that are closest to the GNOME Project itself.

    The GNOME-compliant window manager with the most features is Enlightenment.

2. Run a GNOME session with Enlightenment as the window manager. From the GNOME Control Center, switch window managers to sawmill. What looks different on your desktop? What looks the same?

    The window borders around the open windows change, but the applications themselves and the GNOME Panel look the same. The Enlightenment IconBox and Pager disappear. If you had chosen your background via Enlightenment, it also disappears.

3. From a terminal, change the WINDOW_MANAGER environment variable from the current window manager to IceWM. Restart X. What happens?

   The GNOME session starts with IceWM as the default window manager.

Answers for Hour 5

Quiz

1. What is "session management"?

   Session management is a feature of GNOME that recreates your desktop exactly the way you had it when you last logged out. You will learn more about session management in Hour 7, "Using the Panel and the Main Menu."

2. Name four items that can be iconified on the GNOME desktop.

   Applications

   URLs

   Directories

   Files

3. On the Main Menu, how does the System Menu differ from the User Menu?

   You must be logged in as root to make changes to the System Menu. Any user can add or delete entries to his User Menu, and the User Menu is different for each user.

4. What does "shade" mean when dealing with windows?

   When you shade a window, the window manager "rolls it up" so that you can only see the window border. Unshade the window to display it again. This feature is useful to prevent your desktop from getting too busy.

Exercises

1. Examine the Properties of each icon on your desktop. Can you tell what the icon does? Double-click the icon to check your guess.

   Answer varies according to user.

2. Open the Properties of an icon on your desktop. Select Options, then click the icon. What happens? Select a new icon graphic for your icon.

   The icon window appears, with a list of all available icons. To select a new icon double-click the icon you want in the icon list.

3. Open the Main Menu on your desktop, and compare it to the Main Menu in

Figure 5.4. If you are running a Linux distribution, does a separate distribution menu appear? Does a KDE menu appear? Select an application from one of these menus. How does the application appear when opened in GNOME?

Answer depends on the user.

4. From the Main Menu, open the GNOME Control Center and select Background. Click the Browse button, and navigate to a background filename that interests you. Click it, and then click Try. If you like this background, click OK. Otherwise, click Revert.

Answer depends on the user.

Answers for Hour 6

Quiz

1. What is the difference between a single-user and a multiuser system?

    A single-user system has no login sequence, because only one user uses the system. A multiuser system has a login sequence with the expectation that many users will use the system, even if, in reality, there is only one user.

2. Where are GNOME libraries usually stored?

    /usr/lib or /usr/local/lib.

3. What happens when you type the filename of a GNOME executable file at a shell prompt in an xterm?

    The GNOME application starts.

4. What is the purpose of the /usr/share/gnome directory?

    The /usr/share/gnome directory contains the configuration information for applications that are shared by every user on the system.

Answers for Hour 7

Quiz

1. What is the difference between a drawer and a submenu?

    A drawer contains application launchers which are represented by icons. A submenu contains application launchers which are represented by the name of the application. You can make a drawer out of a GNOME Main Menu submenu by right-clicking the submenu title and selecting "Add this as drawer to panel."

2. Name three ways to add an application launcher to the GNOME Panel. Hint: The hour doesn't explicitly mention three ways. Experiment!

   1. Right-click the GNOME Main Menu entry and select "Add this launcher to panel."
   2. Right-click the panel, and select "Add new launcher." Enter the application pathname and title in the "Create launcher applet" dialog box.
   3. Navigate to the application in the GNOME File Manager, drag the application icon from File Manager on to the Panel. The "Create launcher applet" dialog box appears. Enter the appropriate information and click OK. The new launcher appears in the panel.

3. How can you tell the contents of a drawer without opening it?

   Place the mouse over the drawer. The name of the drawer will pop up.

4. Which GNOME Panel applets help you monitor your computer's memory use?

   CPU/MEM usage and MemLoad.

Exercises

1. Add four edge panels to your desktop, one on each side. Change the panels to corner Panels. What changes?

   Edge panels stretch the entire length of the screen. Corner panels are only as long as the objects on them. When you change from an edge panel to a corner panel, the length of the panel will shrink.

2. Most Linux distributions come with a large variety of backgrounds to decorate your edge panel. Open This Panel Properties and browse for a background.

   Answer varies according to user.

3. Create a drawer and label it "Games." Browse the Main Menu and add three of your favorite games to the drawer.

   Answer varies according to user.

4. Find an executable file on your system that is not in the GNOME Main Menu. Add it to the User Submenu. Start the executable by clicking its Main Menu entry. Does it start?

   Answer varies according to user. If the file does not start, try another executable file.

Answers for Hour 8

Quiz

1. What is the relationship between gmc and File Manager?

   gmc and File Manager are two terms for the same application. When referring to the process that serves as the backbone of GNOME, gmc is the term that is commonly used. When referring to the window interface for viewing and manipulating your files, we usually use the term File Manager.

2. Name two ways to open File Manager.

   File Manager can be opened from the Home Directory desktop icon or from the Main menu.

3. How would you collapse the directory tree in File Manager so that only the root (/) directory shows?

   Click the minus sign (-) next to the root directory to collapse the entire directory tree.

4. What information does the status bar contain?

   On the left of the status bar, the file/directory size is displayed. On the right, the active filter is displayed. If no filter is applied, Show All Files is displayed.

Exercises

1. Open a File Manager window. Go to your home directory, and click the /etc directory in the directory tree, then click /usr/bin, and then click /var/tmp. Use the Back and Forward buttons to go back to /etc, then to /var/tmp, then to your home directory again. Note which direction you need to go to reach each file.

   You would go Back, Back, Forward, Back, and Back.

2. Open a File Manager window. Click the plus (+) signs next to a directory in your directory tree until the entire directory is open. What happens to the plus signs when you click them?

   When the entire directory is open, all (+) icons will be turned to (−) icons.

Answers for Hour 9

Quiz

1. What is the Creation Time, Access Time, and Modification Time for a file?

   The Creation Time is the date and time that the file became part of your computer's filename. The Access Time is the date and time that the file was last opened. The Modification Time is the date and time that the file was last changed.

Answers

2. In the Type column of Custom View, what does an exclamation point signify?

   A stalled symbolic file.

3. What is the default action for dragging and dropping a file from File Manager to the desktop?

   The default is to move the file. Be careful that you don't move a file that you meant to copy!

4. If you want to move a file that is a symbolic link, how do you keep the file linked to its target file when it is moved?

   In the Move dialog box, select Preserve Symlinks.

5. How do you view the size of a directory in File Manager?

   Select the directory whose size you want to check. From the File menu, click Show Directory Sizes. Depending on the size of the directory, it might take a few seconds for File Manager to compute the directory size.

6. Name two ways to sort a directory by filename in File Manager.

   In Brief or Detailed view, click the Name column, or click Layout, Sort and Select Name.

Exercises

1. From File Manager, open the directory where your background files are located, for example, /usr/share/backgrounds/pixmap. Drag one of the .jpg files from File Manager to the panel. What happens?

   The panel background changes to the pixmap image stored in the file you dragged and dropped.

2. Create a test directory called Test, and the files alpha, bravo, charlie, and delta. Turn off the confirmation warnings in File Manager, and delete the file delta. What happens?

   Until you rescan the directory, it appears as if nothing happened.

3. Create a symbolic link called gorilla to the file delta.

   Right-click delta and select Create Symlink. The new file will appear with the symbolic link symbol after you rescan the directory.

4. Rename gorilla as cheetah

   There are two possible answers:

   Slowly double-click gorilla, and then overwrite the filename to cheetah.

   Right-click the file and select Properties. Overwrite the filename as cheetah.

5. Open the Test directory that you made in exercise 2. Open a Search in the status bar and type **z**. What happens? Now type **a c** in the status bar, and then **a b**. What happens?

   Nothing happens. The z does not appear in the status bar and no file is selected, because there are no files in Test that begin with z. When you type **c**, the cheetah file is highlighted. When you type **b**, the bravo file is highlighted.

6. Open an X terminal and cd to your Test directory. Enter the command:
   ```
   ln bravo mike
   ```
   Open File Manager to your Test directory. Does a symlink symbol appear next to mike? Now remove the hard link and create a symbolic link by typing
   ```
   rm -f mike
   ln -s bravo mike
   ```
   Now do you see a symlink symbol?

   At first, no symlink symbol appears next to mike because mike is a hard link. When you recreate mike as a symbolic link, the symlink symbol, a small black arrow, appears next to mike.

7. Open the File Properties of alpha to the Permissions tab. Change the permissions so that the Current Mode says 0000. Click OK to close Properties, and then try to open the file. What happens? Change the permissions to 0755.

   When you try to open the file, a message Permission Denied appears, because nobody has permission to do anything with the file. To change the permissions to 0755, click the Read button for Everybody, the write button for the Owner, and the Execute button for Everybody.

Answers for Hour 10

Quiz

1. What is the difference in function between the Iconbox and the Enlightenment Pager?

   The Iconbox keeps track of iconified windows, and the Pager keeps track of open windows.

2. Which Enlightenment menu appears when you left-click the desktop? Which menu appears when you right-click it? How else can you access these menus?

   The Users menu appears when you left-click the desktop, and the Settings menu appears when you right-click. Both menus are also listed as submenus in the Enlightenment Main Menu, which appears when you middle-click the desktop.

3. How do you turn off the ToolTips?

   From the Settings menu, select ToolTips. Uncheck the Enable ToolTips fields.

4. What does it mean when a window has the focus?

   When a window has the focus, it is the active window, and operations can be carried out with the application inside it. Only one window at a time can have the focus.

5. What is the difference between virtual desktops and multiple desktops?

   Virtual desktops exist side by side (horizontally). You can change virtual desktops by dragging your mouse from one to another. Multiple desktops are stacked on top of one another and can only be changed via dragbar, menu, or the Enlightenment Pager or GNOME Desk Guide.

Exercises

1. Compare the GNOME Panel to the Enlightenment Iconbox and GNOME Tasklist. Do they have the same functionality? Are there differences? Which set of tools do you prefer?

   The Iconbox and E Pager have essentially the same functionality as the GNOME Panel with the GNOME Tasklist and Desk Guide.

2. Open the Focus Settings dialog box and check Focus Follows Pointer, then change the configuration to Focus Follows Pointer Sloppy. What is the difference between the two settings?

   When the focus follows the pointer, the window where the mouse is located has the focus. If you move the mouse off the window to the desktop, that window loses the focus, and no window has the focus until the mouse reaches a new window. When Focus Follows Pointer Sloppy is selected, the window where the mouse used to be retains the focus until the mouse reaches a new window.

3. Query the size of your background cached file, note the size of the file, then change the background of your desktop using Desktop Background Settings. Query your background cache again. What changed?

   When a background is replaced on the desktop, the old background file is copied to the cache. The cache file will increase in size by a few hundred KB. After it is purged, it will be 3KB–10KB in size.

4. Remove the window border from one of your windows, then get it back again.

   Right-click the window border and select Set Border Style. Check No_border. To get the border back, hold down the Alt key and click anywhere in the window. The window border menu appears. Select Set Border Style again, and check Default. The border reappears after you click Apply or OK.

5. Open `eesh` in interactive mode in a terminal. Enter the following commands: **copyright**, **list-themes**, **window_list**, **restart_wm**. What does each command do?

> `copyright` prints the GNU `copyleft`.
>
> `list_themes` lists all currently installed themes.
>
> `window_list` lists all currently active windows.
>
> `restart_wm` restarts Enlightenment.

Answers for Hour 11

Quiz

1. What is a capplet?

   A capplet is a GNOME applet used for configuring aspects of the GNOME desktop environment. Capplets are opened within the GNOME Control Center.

2. What should you do in the GNOME Control Center if you want to use the Enlightenment Background Settings tool to select a background?

   Select Disable Background Selection.

3. What kind of file is used for a sound event?

   `.wav` files are used for GNOME sound events.

4. How do you add applications that are not GNOME-compliant to your GNOME session?

   Add the commands to start the programs to the Non-Session-Managed Startup Programs field in the Startup Programs capplet of the GNOME Control Center.

5. What happens if you try to exit GNOME Control Center without saving your changes?

   When you close a capplet without saving or canceling changes, the capplet turns red in the capplet menu. If you try to close the GNOME Control Center without saving or discarding changes, a warning message will appear.

Exercises

1. Open the GNOME Control Center. Do you have any capplets that are not mentioned in this hour? If so, what does their function appear to be?

   Open the GCC from Main Menu, Settings, GNOME Control Center. Answer varies with reader.

2. Open the Default Editor capplet and choose your favorite editor. Try gEdit if you don't have a favorite.

   Open the GCC, click Default Editor, and click the name of the editor from the drop-down menu on the capplet.

3. Open the Screensaver capplet and select a screensaver that interests you.

   Open the GCC, select Screensaver. Click the screensaver to preview it in the demo window, then click Try to select it temporarily or OK to select it permanently.

4. Exchange the login sound event for a sound from a GNOME game (try `gnibbles/laughter.wav`).

   From GCC, open the Sound Events capplet, click the Login entry to select it. In the drop-down menu next to the Play button, enter `gnibbles/laughter.wav`, and then click Play. If you like the sound, click OK.

5. Adjust the mouse controls to the fastest acceleration and the smallest threshold. Is the mouse difficult to control?

   From GCC, open the Mouse capplet. Slide the Acceleration slider all the way to the right and the Threshold slider all the way to the left. Click Try. Play with the mouse for a while, and then click Revert to revert to your original settings, or adjust the sliders to new settings.

6. Configure the Applications capplet so you can drag menus off the application window and onto the desktop.

   From GCC, open the Applications capplet. Enable Can Detach and Move Menus and Submenus Can Be Torn Off. Open a GNOME application, such as Gnumeric. Drag the menu off the application window using the handle.

7. Configure the Applications capplet so that GNOME application menus have no icons. Open a GNOME application, such as gEdit. Do the menu items have icons? Close the GNOME application. Enable menu icons. Reopen the GNOME application. Does the menu contain icons?

   From GCC, in the Applications capplet, disable the Menu Items Have Icons option and click OK. Open a GNOME application, such as gEdit. The menu will contain no icons. Close the GNOME application. Open the Applications capplet again, enable Menu Items Have Icons, and click OK. Reopen the GNOME application. The menu will contain icons.

Answers for Hour 12

Quiz

1. Imagine you are running three applications within GNOME: Gnumeric (a GNOME application), Ktetris (a KDE game), and Netscape Communicator. Which applications will change when you change themes, and which will not? Why doesn't the look of all your applications change when you change your gtk theme?

   Gnumeric will change to reflect the new theme. Only applications that use gtk are affected by themes. KDE and Netscape use other GUI APIs.

2. Why is a plain theme usually faster than a pixmap theme?

   The plain theme uses only an engine and the gtkrc file. (This is why the plain theme is also called a gtkrc theme.) Each element in a pixmap theme must be loaded as a separate window on the desktop, which takes time and system resources.

3. What libraries must you have on your computer before you can use a theme?

   glib

   gtk

   gtk-engines

Exercises

1. Open the Theme Selector in the GNOME Control Center. Select Basic as your desktop theme. Open a few applications and observe how much time it takes for them to open. Close the applications. Go back to Theme Selector and select Expensive. Open the same applications as you did before. Do they take longer to open?

   This exercise depends completely on the reader's system. There might be no appreciable difference on a machine that has a memory-rich video card and a lot of system memory. Older machines might show a huge difference.

2. Visit http://gtk.themes.org and download a theme that interests you. Then, link to the theme site of your favorite window manager and download a theme that complements the gtk theme.

3. Uninstall some gtk themes that you don't like, and then open Theme Selector in GNOME Control Center. Do they appear in the list?

   They shouldn't.

Answers for Hour 13

Quiz

1. What is the difference between installing and upgrading an `rpm` package?

    When you are installing a new package and there is no older version of the package on your computer, there is no difference. When you want to install a package and there is already an older version on your computer, Upgrade will delete the old version before installing the new version. Install will keep the old files intact.

2. How are packages color-coded in rpmfind and the installation window?

    Package matches what is already installed: green.

    Package is newer than what is installed: blue.

    Package is older than what is installed: grey.

3. What is the difference between Install Date and Build Date for `rpm` packages?

    Install Date is the date an `rpm` package was installed on your computer. Build Date is the date the package itself was created.

4. What does MIME stand for?

    Multipurpose Internet Mail Extension.

Exercises

1. Open gnoRPM and explore the `rpm` package categories. What are some of the categories?

    Answer varies according to the reader.

2. Query the GTK `rpm` package. To which directories does gtk install files? Why do you think there is no executable file added to `/usr/bin` or `/opt/bin`?

    GTK adds an `/etc/gtk` directory, documentation files in `/usr/doc`, and libraries to `/usr/lib` (or `/usr/local/lib`) and shared libraries to `/usr/share` (or `/usr/local/share`). There is no executable file added to the filesystem because GTK isn't an application, but a set of libraries that different applications use. You will learn more about GTK in Hours 23 and 24.

3. Find the gnome-core `rpm` package and then verify it.

    From gnoRPM's main window:

    Click Find.

    Select Find Packages that match label and type gnome-core in the field.

    Click Find.

The Find utility should return the version of gnome-core installed on your system. Click Verify to verify gnome-core.

4. Open the installation window of gnoRPM, and display All but Installed Packages. Do you have any uninstalled `rpm` packages on your computer?

   Answer varies according to reader.

5. Open gnoRPM Preferences and select Distributions. Set all distributions that you cannot use to -1. Set the distribution that matches your distribution's vendor and processor type to 50. Set the other distributions to positive numbers lower than 50, according to your preference. The higher the preference, the higher the number you should assign the distribution.

   This exercise will vary according to your system, but here is an example answer that should help you. The example system has an Intel i686 processor (Pentium II), and is running Red Hat 6.1.

   a. Assign a -1 to all `rpm` types that are built for a different processor than yours. For our example, assign a -1 value to all Alpha, PPC, and Sparc `rpms`.

   b. Assign a -1 for all `rpm` types that are built for Linux distributions that are incompatible with yours. In our example, SuSE, Caldera, and Connectiva are incompatible with Red Hat, so give `rpms` for these distributions a -1.

   c. Assign a -1 for `rpms` that are built with a different C library than yours. In our example, Red Hat 6.1 uses the glibc 2.1 library, so assign a -1 to all `rpms` built for libc5 and libc6.

   d. Assign a high number to your Linux distribution that most closely matches your system. There isn't a category for Red Hat i686, so assign a 50 to `rpms` for Red Hat 6.1, i386.

   e. Assign a high number for `rpms` that are for your Linux distribution and no particular architecture (`noarch`). In our example, assign a 50 to Arch Independent Red Hat contribs.

   f. Assign a lower number for other `rpms` that will work on your system, but were not specifically created for your system. For example, I like freshmeat `rpms`, so I give `rpms` from freshmeat a 40. I don't know much about beowulf, so I give them a 10. GNOME Desktop environment gets a 40. And so on.

   g. Remember to click Change after each value you assign, and to verify that it is changed in the Distributions window.

6. Ensure that you have a remote connection open to the Internet. Open rpmfind and search for gnome-admin. Install the correct distribution of gnome-admin.

   a. Click Web find on the main GnoRPM window.

b. Wait for the database to download. (This could take up to five minutes, depending on the speed of your connection and your bandwidth.)

c. Type `gnome-admin` in the Search field and click Search.

d. Select the version of gnome-admin that you want from the package field.

e. Click Download, and then install it from the main gnoRPM window, or click Install straight from the Web find window.

Answers for Hour 14

Quiz

1. What does PPP stand for?

    Point to Point Protocol.

2. What is the name of the daemon that starts when you make a PPP connection?

    pppd.

3. What serial port does your modem connect to?

    Answer varies according to reader. Possible answers are ttyS0, ttyS1, ttyS2, and so on. On older distributions of Linux, it can be cua0, cua1, cua2, and so on.

4. What is the /dev/modem file?

    /dev/modem is a symbolic link to the device file that represents the serial port that your modem is connected to.

5. What are two kinds of PPP authentication protocols?

    CHAP and PAP.

6. If you must dial 9 to get an outside phone line, how would you get the PPP Dialer to pause long enough to connect to an outside line?

    Enter a comma after the 9 and before the phone number. The dialer will pause for one second. Enter 2 commas to get the dialer to pause two seconds.

7. What does DNS stand for, and what does it do?

    DNS stands for Dynamic Name Service. It is a database that translates hostnames into IP addresses.

Exercises

1. Start a PPP connection using GNOME PPP Dialer. What messages appear in the PPP Dialer window?

    Initializing modem.

    Dialing.

Connected.

PPP connection established.

2. After establishing a PPP connection, open an X terminal and enter the command ps -a. (If you have many processes running, you might have to enter ps -a|more, then use the spacebar to scroll through the list of processes. You can also increase the size of the X terminal window.). Look at the list carefully. What processes seem to be involved with the connection?

pppd and gnome-ppp.

3. Now disconnect the PPP connection and run ps -a again. Have the processes that you answered in exercise 2 disappeared?

pppd disappears, but gnome-ppp remains, unless you close the PPP Dialer window.

Answers for Hour 15

Quiz

1. What does "multithreaded" mean for email and ftp?

   You can send and receive more than one email message or download and upload more than one file at a time.

2. What does a signature file do?

   A signature file can be attached to every email message you send. You can have any text message you want in a signature file.

3. What does FTP stand for?

   File Transfer Protocol.

4. Can you upload files via anonymous FTP login?

   Not unless the remote server gives write permission to users who login anonymously (usually a very stupid move).

5. What do the colors in the gFTP message and log window mean?

   Message and log text from gFTP is red.

   Messages sent from gFTP to the remote server are green.

   Messages from the remote server are blue.

Exercises

1. Create a signature file for your email messages.

   Answer varies according to the reader.

2. Compare the directory where you keep your Linux distribution packages to that of your Linux distribution FTP server. Are you missing any packages? Download packages that you want.

   Answer varies according to the reader.

3. Detach the Connection toolbar and place it on the desktop.

   Click the toolbar handle. Holding down the left mouse button, drag the toolbar off the gFTP window and onto the desktop.

Answers for Hour 16

Quiz

1. How is the /etc/printcap file generated?

   /etc/printcap is usually generated by the printer configuration tool for your Linux
   distribution.

2. What is the print spool used for?

   The print spool stores the temporary files that hold print jobs in the order that they will be printed.

3. How is lpd started? How is lpr started?

   lpd is usually started at system initialization. lpr is started when you enter the command lpr *filename* to print a file.

Exercises

1. Print a file, and then use lpq to list the print job and lprm to remove it from the print spool.

   Print the file by dragging it onto the print applet on the panel. At a shell prompt, type **lpq** to list the print jobs. Note the job number, and then enter **lprm** and the job number of the print job to remove it from the queue, for example

   lprm 16

2. Take a screenshot of your computer screen and print it using GIMP.

   From the GIMP menu, select Scrn Shot. When the screen shot appears onscreen, right-click it, then select File, Print from the menu. Enter the appropriate selections in the Print dialog box, then click Print.

Answers for Hour 17

Quiz

1. Name five ways to open an application in GNOME.

   Open an application with Main Menu, a desktop icon, File Manager, a panel launcher, or a command at the command line.

2. How many launchers can you have for the same application?

   You can have as many launchers as you want.

3. What is an instance of an application?

   When you have the same application open more than once, each manifestation of the application is called an instance of the application.

4. What is the PATH environment variable used for?

   The computer uses the PATH environment variable to find executable files. When an executable file is in your PATH, you can run it without entering the full pathname.

Exercises

1. Open several instances of GNOME Terminal (use a different method each time). Then open a few instances of File Manager and a few instances of GNOME Control Center.

   Use the Main Menu, File Manager, a panel launcher, a desktop icon, or a command at a shell prompt.

2. From a shell prompt, enter ps -a, and see what kind of output you get. Then look in Browse Currently Running Programs in GCC, and see what is there.

   For each instance of GNOME Terminal, File Manager, and GCC, there will be a separate process with a separate PID number.

3. Open a shell session using your favorite GNOME terminal. At a shell prompt, enter the **set** command. Study the output. What is your path?

   Answer will vary according to the user.

Answers for Hour 18

Quiz

1. Think about your own work patterns and those of the people in your office. How many features of your current office software do you actually use?

   Answer varies according to reader.

2. How does component software differ from traditional software?

   Component software is based on small applications, or modules, that are designed to be strung together in whatever combination needed.

3. What are three advantages of using GNOME in business?

   Possible answers: Cost—GNOME is free; GNOME is customizable; GNOME is extensible; GNOME applications can be easily understood.

4. What are two disadvantages of using GNOME?

   Possible answers: There is insufficient documentation; applications are still in development; outside support is probably necessary.

5. What does PIM stand for in GNOME-PIM?

   Personal Information Manager.

6. True or False: AbiWord can import and export RTF file format.

   True.

7. What file format does Dia use?

   XML.

Exercises

1. Visit the GNOME Productivity software map at http://www.gnome.org/applist/list-martin.phtml?catno=10. Download and install an application that interests you.

   Answer varies according to reader.

2. Visit the GNOME Office home page at http://www.gnome.org/gnome-office. Download an application that interests you.

   Answer varies according to reader.

Answers for Hour 19

Quiz

1. Which graphics program is the default for version 1.0.53 of GNOME (October GNOME)?

   Electric Eyes.

2. Can you edit graphics files in Eye of GNOME?

   In version 0.2, you can only view files. Later versions have editing capability.

3. What option must you select to see a preview of a file before opening it in Electric Eyes?

   Check Use Previews in the Open dialog box.

4. How do you open the Edit Controls window in Electric Eyes?

   Right-click the Electric Eyes window and select Show/Hide Edit Window.

5. How do you know that a MIME type is for a graphics file format?

   If you don't recognize the file format by name, the MIME type will begin with the string `"image/"`, followed by the file format.

6. Which of the three graphics programs that we explored in this hour supports the most file formats?

   GIMP.

Exercises

1. Open a graphics file in Eye of GNOME and Electric Eyes. Zoom the image in as far as you can in both programs. What is the difference?

   EE is much slower; EOG can zoom the file in almost immediately.

2. Open a graphics file in Eye of GNOME. Zoom the image out to a ratio of 6:1, and then click one button on the toolbar to bring it back to the original ratio.

   Open View menu, Zoom Factor. Click 6:1. To return the image to its original ratio, click 1:1 on the toolbar.

3. Locate a directory of images on your computer. (The directory where your background pixmap files are located is a good example, for example, `/usr/local/share/pixmaps/Backgrounds`, or `/usr/share/pixmaps/Backgrounds`.) Load a directory of images into Electric Eyes using the list window.

   Click View, Show/Hide List Window. Click the Open icon and select a directory that contains image files.

4. In the list window from the exercise 3, scroll through the images using the directional buttons.

   You can scroll through using the directional buttons or by clicking the image that you want to see.

5. For fun, try this exercise in GIMP:

   Select File, New.

   Accept the default width and height of 256×256 pixels.

   Set Fill Type = White.

   Click OK. A new image canvas appears.

   Click the Black square at the bottom of the GIMP toolbar and select your favorite color from the color palette that appears. Click OK.

Click the "T" in the GIMP toolbar and click in the workspace.

In the Text Tool dialog box, select a font like Courier, font size 40 and a Weight of bold.

Type "Hello" in the text field and click OK. Position the text in the box by clicking the text and dragging it to where you want it.

Right-click in the workspace, and select Script-Fu from the right-click menu, Shadow, Drop-Shadow. Click OK.

In the GIMP toolbar select the rectangular select tool and click in the work space to deselect the text.

Right-click in the workspace, and select filters from the right-click menu, Light Effects, Supernova.

Click OK in the Supernova dialog box.

The result should look like Figure B.1.

FIGURE B.1
Output of exercise 5.

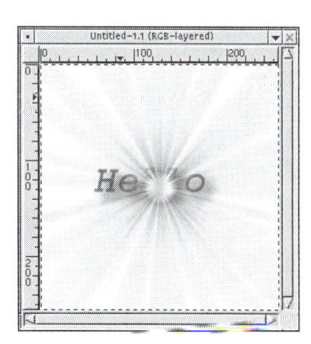

Answers for Hour 20

Quiz

1. Where can you set the CD-ROM device mount point in the CD Player?

    Click the Preferences button, and enter the correct mount point in the Preferences tab.

2. Can you play non-GNOME games in GNOME?

    Yes. Any game that can be played in an X session (including text-based games) can be played in GNOME.

Exercises

1. Go to the Entertainment section of the GNOME software map and download a game that interests you.

   Go to `http://www.gnome.org/applist/list-martin.phtml?catno=4` and download a game. Answer will vary according to the reader.

2. Play your favorite music CD using the GNOME CD Player. Is your CD listed in CDDB? If not, enter the title tracks manually and submit your CD title to CDDB.

   Open Track Editor and edit the track titles. Check Submit to send the list of titles to CDDB. The Submit Information dialog box opens. Select the appropriate music category from the drop-down list and click OK to submit. (Don't worry about the To: field; the CD Player connects to the server that is listed in Preferences.)

3. Start a KDE or other X-based game in GNOME.

   Answer will vary according to the reader. If you can't find the games subdirectory on your system, try using the `locate` command and enter `locate games`.

Answers for Hour 21

Quiz

1. Must you uninstall a GNOME `rpm` before upgrading to a newer version?

   No, only if you installed from tarball.

2. What is the command for uninstalling a tarball?

   From the original tarball source code directory, enter **make uninstall**.

3. What does the `-nodeps` option for the `rpm` command do?

   Uninstalls (or installs) an `rpm` without checking for dependencies. Do not use this option unless you are sure that you will not have dependency errors.

4. What should you enter in the GNOME Help Browser to get a table of contents for all the info entries on your computer?

   `toc:info`.

5. Where are three places to look for help on GNOME?

   The GNOME User's Guide, GNOME FAQ, and gnome-list.

Exercises

1. If you have an `rpm` installed on your system, enter the command **rpm -evv --test**. What happens?

   The messages that would appear if you were really uninstalling the `rpm` will appear on the console, including dependency errors.

2. Open GnoRPM and try to uninstall the `glib` package. What happens?

   A message box appears listing a series of dependency errors. (The exact errors depend on the applications that are installed.)

3. Open a documentation file in the GNOME Help Browser and bookmark it.

   Enter the full pathname of the file in the Location: field. The exact answer will vary with the reader.

4. Read some messages from the gnome-list archives on a topic that interests you.

   Open the mailing list archives from `http://www.gnome.org`. The exact answer will vary with the reader.

Answers for Hour 22

Quiz

1. What format(s) of software releases are monitored and sanctioned by the GNOME Project?

   Source code.

2. What does the z option in tar zxvf mean (GNU tar)?

   The z option unzips the tarball before uncompressing it.

3. Why is it more secure to install software from source code than from binary package?

   It is easier to insert malicious code into a binary package than into source code without it being detected.

4. What files does the configure script create?

   Makefile, C header file, `config.log`, `config.cache`, `config.status`.

5. How do you return the installation directory to its original state after you have run make and configure?

   Type **make distclean**.

6. True/False. If you find a bug in CVS software, you should submit a bug report.

   False. CVS code is, by definition, unstable, and bugs are to be expected.

7. Who is permitted to log in to CVS anonymously?

   Anyone can log into CVS anonymously to download code.

Answers for Hour 23

Quiz

1. What does CORBA stand for?

   Common Object Request Broker Architecture.

2. What is a compound document?

   A compound document is a file that contains items that were created using different applications in different file formats.

3. What Object Request Broker does GNOME use?

   ORBit.

4. What is a language binding?

   A language binding enables applications that are written in different programming languages to work together.

Answers for Hour 24

Quiz

1. What is a function?

   A function is a routine that performs a certain task within a program.

2. What is a library?

   A library is a collection of functions.

3. What do you call a widget that holds another widget?

   A container widget.

4. Which libraries in a GNOME application handle the actual graphical interface?

   gnomeui, GTK, and GDK.

5. In what programming language is the GNOME libraries written?

   The C programming language.

6. In which library is the function gnome-about?

   libgnomeui.

7. What do GTK and GDK stand for?

   GIMP Toolkit and GIMP Drawing Kit.

8. True/False: Glade builds the source code for a developer after she chooses an interface for inclusion in an application.

   True.

Exercises

1. Code.

   Run the program by entering `./gnome_love` at a shell prompt. The window that appears will look like Figure B.2.

FIGURE B.2

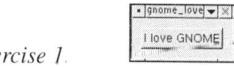

Output of exercise 1.

Read the GTK tutorial at http://www.gtk.org/tutorial if you would like to learn what the details of this program mean. (The program in the GTK tutorial uses the ubiquitous "Hello World" instead of "I love GNOME.")

INDEX

A

abbreviations (commands), 302
AbiSource Web site, 247
AbiWord, 246-247
    AbiSource Web site, 247
    development, 247
    features, 246-247
acceleration (mouse), 147
access
    directories, 117
    remote computers (mcserv), 119, 212
accounts (PPP Dialer)
    Authentication tab (PPP Account dialog box), 191
    Dial tab (PPP Account dialog box), 190-191
    DNS Server tab (PPP Account dialog box), 191
    IP Address tab (PPP Account dialog box), 191
    Modem tab (PPP Account dialog box), 192
    PPP tab (PPP Account dialog box), 192
    Script tab (PPP Account dialog box), 192
    setting, 190-193
active directories (File Manager), 91, 94-95
Add Applet, Clocks command (context menus), 62
Add Applet command (context menus), 82
Add Drawer command (context menus), 81
Add MIME Type dialog box, 181
Add New Launcher command (context menus), 80
Add New Window Manager dialog box, 50
Add This As Drawer to Panel command (context menus), 81
adding
    applets
        clock, 62
        Desk Guide, 62
        GNOME Panel, 61-63, 82-83
        Tasklist, 62
    application launchers (GNOME Panel), 80-81
    applications (Main Menu), 86
    backgrounds (desktops), 163
    Custom View categories (File Manager), 104
    drawers (GNOME Panel), 81
    MIME types, 181
    multiple desktops (Enlightenment), 133
    panels (GNOME Panel), 84
    virtual desktops (Enlightenment), 132
    window managers (Control Center), 50
address books (GNOME Address Book), 250-251

368 administration

administration. *See also* **managing sessions**
  Gnome-admin utility, 177-178
  GNOME DiskFree, 179
  Gnome-linuxconf utility, 177
  outside support organizations, 246
  System Information utility, 179
AfterStep Web site, 49
AisleRiot, 278
APIs (application programming interfaces), 157. *See also* **GTK**
applets. *See also* **applications; capplets**
  clock, adding, 62
  Desk Guide, 62-63
  GNOME Panel
    adding, 61-63, 82-83
    deleting, 82
  gnome-applets package, 283
  Modem Lights (PPP Dialer), 195
  PPP Applet (PPP Dialer), 195
  Tasklist, 62
applications. *See also* **applets; capplets**
  Applications capplet, 148-149
  Big Buddy requirements, 334
  bonobo technology
    CORBA, 258, 318
    documentation, 319
    Eye of GNOME, 258
  browsing (Session Manager), 150
  CD player, 273
    CDDB, 275
    controls, 274-275
    customizing, 276-277
    opening, 274
    quitting, 277
    Track Editor, 275-276

compatibility, 13
component software, 244-245
cost, 245
customizability, 245
developing, 241, 246
documentation, 245
downloading, 239
executable files, 72, 232
free software
  GNU Project, 10
  implications, 13
  open source software comparison, 11
Gniall (GNOME Non-Intelligent AMOS Language Learner), 285
GNOME, 322
  characteristics, 322
  components, 323
  copylefting, 11
  Glade, 327
  GNOME development Web site, 328
  IBM DeveloperWorks Web site, 328
  libgnome library, 325
  libgnomeui library, 325-326
  libgnorba library, 326
  library advantages, 324-325
gnome-announce mailing list, 239
gnome-list mailing list, 239
GNOME Office, 246
  AbiWord, 246-247
  Dia, 251-252
  GNOME Address Book, 250-251
  GNOME Calendar, 249-250
  GNOME Office Project, 238
  GNOME-PIN, 249
  Gnumeric, 220-222, 247-249
GNOME Project Web site, 277

GNOME Software Map, 233
  bugs, 241
  Core, 235
  drawbacks, 233
  Electrical Design/Programmers, 235
  Entertainment, 235
  graphics applications, 267
  icons, 233-234
  Internet Tools, 235
  keyword searches, 233
  Mail Clients, 235
  Math and Science Tools, 236
  Miscellaneous, 236
  Network Talk Clients, 236
  Productivity, 237
  Sound Tools, 237
  System Utilities, 237
  Web site address, 233, 252
  Window/Session/Desktop Managers, 238
GPL, 11
graphical interface, 322, 327
graphics, 267-268
installing, 239
  installation preparation, 16-18
  source code installation, 241, 254
integrating (CORBA), 315-317
language bindings, 318-319
launchers, 230
  adding (GNOME Panel), 80-81
  organizing (GNOME Panel), 81
LGPL, 11
Main Menu, 86
menus, detaching, 148
open source software, 11

opening
  GNOME startup, 150
  Main Menu, 60-61
outside administration support, 246
$PATH/share/gnome directory, 73
productivity
  drawbacks, 244
  Gaby, 253
  TimeTracker, 254
programming language restrictions, 245
rpms, 239-240
running, 230
  background process, 232-233
  command lines, 231-232
  executable files, 232
  instances, 230
  launchers, 230
  paths, 232
simplicity, 245
status bars, 149
tarballs, 239-241
toolbars, detaching, 149
training, 245
Applications capplet, 148-149
attributes (windows), saving (Enlightenment), 129
autoconf utility, 304-305

B

backgrounds
  desktops
    adding, 163
    Desktop Background capplet, 143-144
    Desktop Background Settings, 127
Electric Eyes (Enlightenment), 262

sawmill, 47
usr/share/pixmaps directory, 73
backups, 71-72, 98
Balsa (email client), 200
  configuring, 203-204
    initial setup, 201
    preferences, 202-204
  crashes, 201
  features, 200
  layout, 201
  messages, downloading, 201
  signature files, 203, 213
  Web site, 200
Behavior Preferences tab (gnoRPM), 174
Big Buddy, 333-334
  bug reports, 335-337
  contact information, 334
  Debugging Information dialog box, 336
  features, 334
  software requirements, 334
  starting, 334
  Submit Report dialog box, 338
  system information, 334
binary code, 302
binary packages. *See* **rpms**
BlackBox Web site, 49
bonobo technology
  CORBA, 258, 318
  documentation, 319
  Eye of GNOME, 258
Bookmarks menu (gFTP), 206
booting, starting sessions
  code example, 32
  troubleshooting, 31-32
borders (windows), setting (Enlightenment), 130
Brief View command (Layout menu), File Manager, 94
Bring up reconnect dialog option (gFTP), 211

browsers
  GameStalker, 284
  GNOME Help Browser, 294
    accessing help, 295
    GNOME FAQ, 296
    GNOME User's Guide, 296
    toc command, 295
    viewing help files, 299
    whatis option, 295
  Netscape Communicator, 62, 200
browsing applications (Session Manager), 150
bugs. *See also* **errors**
  Big Buddy, 333-334
    bug reports, 335-337
    contact information, 334
    Debugging Information dialog box, 336
    features, 334
    software requirements, 334
    starting, 334
    Submit Report dialog box, 338
    system information, 334
  Enlightenment, 138
  GNOME Software Map, 241
  reporting, 311
Build Date field (gnoRPM queries), 173
Build Host field (gnoRPM queries), 173
business computing
  GNOME complexity issues, 245
  GNOME cost, 245
  GNOME customizability, 245
  GNOME development issues, 246
  GNOME disadvantages, 245

business computing

GNOME Office, 246
  AbiWord, 246-247
  Dia, 251-252
  GNOME Address
    Book, 250-251
  GNOME Calendar,
    249-250
  GNOME-PIN, 249
  Gnumeric, 247, 249
  GNOME programming
    language issues, 245
  outside administration
    support, 246
  productivity applications
    drawbacks, 244
buttons
  File Manager toolbar, 95
  GNOME Panel
    Control Center, 62
    default, 61-62
    GNOME virtual termi-
      nal launcher, 62
    Help, 62
    Netscape
      Communicator
      launcher, 62
  gnoRPM toolbar, 169
  Help (Enlightenment), 129
  window, 63-64
    Close/Kill, 64
    Iconify, 64, 67
    Maximize/Minimize,
      64
    Shade/Unshade, 64

C

C language
  *C Programming
    Language: ANSI C
    Version, The*, 305
  gcc, 305
  Glib, 327
  *Sams Teach Yourself C in
    21 Days*, 305
C++, 11

**calendars (GNOME
  Calendar), 249-250**
call waiting, 191
capplets. *See also* **applets;
  applications**
  Applications, 148-149
  Control Center, 142
  Default Editor, 143
  Desktop Background,
    143-144
  Keyboard, 146
  Keyboard Bell, 145
  Mouse, 147
  screensavers, 144
  Sound Events, 146, 153
  Startup Programs, 149-151
  Theme Selector, 145, 153
  Window Manager, 49-50
case sensitivity
  Search tool (File
    Manager), 112
  Sort By tool (File
    Manager), 113
**categories (Custom View),
  104-106**
CD Database (CDDB), 275
CD player, 273
  CDDB, 275
  controls, 274-275
  customizing, 276-277
  opening, 274
  quitting, 277
  Track Editor, 275-276
CD-ROMs
  installing GNOME, 19-21
  mount points, 274
**changing themes
  (Enlightenment), 134**
charts (Dia), 251-252
checking
  printer support, 224
  software required for
    installation, 16-18
clients
  email
    Balsa, 200-204, 213
    Mahogany, 201
    Netscape Messenger,
      212

FTP
  File Manager, 212
  gFTP, 204-212
  ORB, 317
**clock (GNOME Panel),
  adding, 62**
**Close Window command
  (File menu), File Manager,
  93**
**Close/Kill buttons (win-
  dows), 64**
**closing windows (File
  Manager), 90, 93.** *See also*
  quitting
**color (graphics), Electric
  Eyes, 264**
COM ports, 188-189
command lines
  executable files, 232
  running applications,
    231-232
  starting sessions, 29-30
commands. *See also* **utilities**
  abbreviations, 302
  Commands menu (File
    Manager), 94
  configure, 307
  context menus
    Add Applet, 82
    Add Applet, Clocks, 62
    Add Drawer, 81
    Add New Launcher, 80
    Add This As Drawer to
      Panel, 81
    Delete, 59
    Move Applet, 81
    Properties, 58-59
    Remove Applet, 82
  cp, 107
  echo $PATH, 232
  Edit menu (File Manager),
    93-94
  File menu
    Eye of GNOME, 259
    File Manager, 92-93
  help (eesh), 136
  Layout menu (File
    Manager), 94

ldconfig, 308
locate, 304, 329
  checking installed
    components, 16-18
  example, 17
  locate esound example,
    19
lpq, 218-219
lpr, 218
lprm, 219, 224
magic, 29
make distclean, 308
mv
  moving files, 107
  renaming files, 109
Panel menu, Create New
  Panel, 84
ping, 194
print, 217
rm, 107
rpm, 292
Settings menu (File
  Manager), Preferences,
  94
tar, 307
toc, 295
traceroute, 195
updateb, 16, 19-20
View menu (Eye of
  GNOME), 259
wget, 23
whereis, 304, 329
**Commands menu
  commands (File
  Manager), 94**
**Common Object Broker
  Architecture.** *See* **CORBA**
**comparing windows (gFTP),
  209**
compatibility
  applications, 13
  Enlightenment, 41
  graphics applications, 268
  hardware compatibility
    HOWTO (Linux
    Documentation Project),
    188
  IceWM, 44

KDE, 26
language bindings,
  318-319
modem Linux
  compatibility issues, 188
Windows compatibility, 26
**compilers (gcc), source code
  compilation, 305**
compiling
  binary code, 302
  source code, 302
    autoconf utility,
      304-305
    gcc, 305
    installing compiled
      code, 308
    make utility, 305, 308
complexity
  applications, 245
  component software,
    244-245
**component software,
  244-245**
compressed files, 119
**compressing files (gzip
  utility), 302**
configure command, 307
configuring
  Balsa
    initial setup, 201
    preferences, 202-204
  configuration files
    backups, 71
    editing, 78
    .gnome directory,
      74-75
    GTK themes, 159
    $PATH/share/gnome
      directory, 73
    XF86Config, 56-57
  desktop files, 76-77
  games, 278
  gFTP options, 209-212
  keyboards, 146
  ldconfig command, 308
  Makefiles, 307
  mouse, 147
  Pager (Enlightenment),
    124

panel properties, 83-84
printers, 219
printing (etc/printcap
  files), 216-217
sessions
  opening applications
    on startup, 150
  Session Manager,
    149-151
sound
  desktops, 272-273
  Linux systems, 272,
    285
  OpenSound, 285
**Connect retries option
  (gFTP), 211**
**Connect timeout option
  (gFTP), 211**
**connection toolbar (gFTP),
  206, 208**
connections
  call waiting, 191
  FTP, establishing (gFTP),
    207-208
  ISP Hookup HOWTO
    (Linux Documentation
    Project), 195
  PPP, 186
    establishing, 193
    ISP information
      needed, 187
    Modem Lights applet,
      195
    monitoring, 194-195
    PPP Applet, 195
    setting PPP Dialer
      accounts, 190-193
    testing, 194-195
    wvdial, 189, 196
  SLIP, 186
containers (widgets), 323
context menus, 207
  accessing Electric Eye
    options, 261
  Add Applet command, 82
  Add Applet, Clocks
    command, 62
  Add Drawer command, 81

Add New Launcher
   command, 80
Add This As Drawer to
   Panel command, 81
Delete command, 59
File Manager, 95-97
gFTP, 207
Move Applet command,
   81
Properties command,
   58-59
Remove Applet command,
   82
**contributing to GNOME
   Project, 311-312**
Control Center
   capplets, 142
      Applications, 148-149
      Default Editor, 143
      Desktop Background,
         143-144
      Keyboard, 146
      Keyboard Bell, 145
      Mouse, 147
      opening, 142
      screensavers, 144
      Sound Events, 146,
         153
      Startup Programs,
         149-151
      Theme Selector, 145,
         153
   GNOME Panel button, 62
   saving changes, 152
   sound, configuring, 273
   Theme Selector, 161
   window managers, adding,
      50
**Copy command (File
   menu), File Manager, 93**
Copy dialog box, 107
copying files
   cp command, 107
   drag-and-drop features
      (File Manager), 109-110
   File Manager, 107-108
copylefting software, 11

**CORBA (Common Object
   Broker Architecture), 315**
   bonobo technology, 318
   documentation, 319
   Eye of GNOME, 258
   features, 316-317
   GNOME Project Web site,
      11
   OMG, 317-319
   ORB, 317
   ORBit, 317
**Core applications (GNOME
   Software Map), 235**
cost, applications, 245
cp command, 107
cpanel utility, 219
crashes
   Balsa, 201
   GNOME Software Map,
      241
   gnoRPM, 172
**Create Desktop Entry
   (gnoRPM), 169**
**Create New Panel command
   (Panel menu), 84**
**Create New Window
   command (File menu),
   File Manager, 92-93**
**Custom View (File
   Manager), 104-106**
**Custom View command
   (Layout menu), File
   Manager, 94**
**Custom View dialog box,
   104**
customizing
   applications, 148-149, 245
   CD player, 276-277
   desktops, 55-56
   Enlightenment, 42
   Main Menu, 84-85
   sawmill, 51
   User menus
      (Enlightenment), 131
   windows, 152
CVS code
   cautions, 309
   downloading, 309-311

   installing, 310-311
   separating from stable
      code, 310
   utilities needed, 309
**CVS icons (GNOME
   Software Map), 234**

D

daemons
   lpd, 218
   pppd, 186, 193
databases
   Gaby, 253
   rpmfind
      downloading rpms,
         171-172
      Rpmfind tab
         (gnoRPM), 176
      Web site, 171, 176
de Icaza, Miguel, 10
debs (sawmill), installing, 48
**debug terminal, monitoring
   PPP connections, 194**
**Debugging Information dia-
   log box (Big Buddy), 336**
decompressing files, 119
Default Editor capplet, 143
defaults, MIME types, 180
Delete command
   context menus, 59
   File menu (File Manager),
      93
Delete dialog box, 108
deleting
   applications (Main Menu),
      86
   Custom View categories
      (File Manager), 104
   files
      File Manager, 108
      rm command, 107
   GNOME Panel, 67
      applets, 82
      panels, 84
   icons (desktops), 59

dialog boxes   373

multiple desktops
  (Enlightenment),
  133-134
object files, 308
print jobs, 219, 224
virtual desktops
  (Enlightenment), 132
dependency errors, 24-25
Desk Guide, 62-63
desktop areas (virtual desktops), 132
Desktop Background capplet, 143-144
Desktop Background dialog box (Enlightenment), 128
desktops. *See also* **KDE; window managers**
  backgrounds
    adding, 163
    Desktop Background
      capplet, 143-144
    Desktop Background
      Settings
      (Enlightenment), 127
    Electric Eyes, 262
  Create Desktop Entry
    (gnoRPM), 169
  customizing, 55-56
  .desktop files, 76-77
  desktop shells, 38, 42
  Enlightenment, 132-134,
    162-163
  focus, 126
  GNOME Panel, 57
    adding applets, 61-63,
      82-83
    adding application
      launchers, 80-81
    adding panels, 84
    clock, 62
    configuring panel
      properties, 83-84
    Control Center button,
      62
    default buttons, 61-62
    deleting, 67
    deleting applets, 82
    deleting panels, 84

Desk Guide, 62
drawers, 61, 81
Global Panel
  Properties, 83-84
GNOME virtual
  terminal launcher, 62
Help button, 62
Netscape
  Communicator
  launcher, 62
organizing application
  launchers, 81
Tasklist, 62
This Panel Properties,
  84
tiles, 88
icons
  creating, 58-60
  defaults, 57-58
  deleting, 59
  editing, 59
  placement, 100
  properties, 58
  shaped, 99
Main Menu, 57
  adding applications, 86
  capabilities, 60
  customizing, 84-85
  deleting applications,
    86
  Menu Editor, 86
  miscellaneous items,
    86
  opening, 60
  opening applications,
    60-61
  Other menus, 86
  Panel menu, 86
  sections, 60, 85
  System menus, 85
  User menus, 85
panel amusements, 283
sound, configuring,
  272-273
switching
  Desk Guide, 63
  Switchdesk utility,
    32-34

text, shaped, 99
themes, 155-156
  Enlightenment, 134,
    162-163
  GTK, 156-163
  GTK Themes Web site,
    160, 163
  window manager, 156
troubleshooting session
  files, 75-78
detaching toolbars, 149
detaching menus, 148
**Detailed View command
  (Layout menu), File
  Manager, 94**
**developing applications,
  241, 246**
**development code (CVS),
  309-311**
Dia
  features, 251-252
  Web site, 252
diagrams (Dia), 251-252
dialog boxes
  Add MIME Type, 181
  Add New Window
    Manager, 50
  Copy, 107
  Custom View, 104
  Debugging Information
    (Big Buddy), 336
  Delete, 108
  Desktop Background
    (Enlightenment), 128
  Find Packages (gnoRPM),
    171
  Global Panel Properties,
    83-84
  Install (gnoRPM), 170
  Move, 108
  PPP Account, 190-192
  Preferences
    File Manager, 97-100
    gnoRPM, 174
  Properties, 58
  Remember
    (Enlightenment), 129
  Select Printer, 222

Submit Report (Big
  Buddy), 338
Switchdesk, 33
Switchdesk Desktop
  Switcher, 32
This Panel Properties, 84
directories
  access, 117
  executable files, 310
  File Manager, 91
    viewing size, 111
    views, 94-95
  .gnome, 74-75
  hidden, 75
  $HOME, 30
  $PATH/share/gnome, 73
  users, 77
  usr/share/pixmaps, 73
Display tab (Balsa preferences), 204
Distribution field (gnoRPM queries), 173
Distributions tab (gnoRPM), 176-177
DNS (Domain Name Service), 191
Do one transfer at a time option (gFTP), 211
Document Viewer (Enlightenment), 129
documentation. *See also* help
  applications, 245
  bonobo technology, 319
  CORBA, 317-319
  GIMP, 266-267
  GNOME Documentation
    Project, 289, 299
      Web site, 296, 311
      writing documentation, 311
  hardware compatibility
    HOWTO (Linux
    Documentation Project), 188
  ISP Hookup HOWTO
    (Linux Documentation
    Project), 195
  limitations, 289, 296

  modem HOWTO (Linux
    Documentation Project), 187
  Plug and Play HOWTO
    (Linux Documentation
    Project), 188
  rpms, 240
  sawmill, 48
  tarballs, 303
dot files. *See* **hidden files**
download/upload progress window (gFTP), 207
downloading
  applications, 239
  CVS code, 309-311
  email (Balsa), 201
  files, 206-208
  GIMP, 266
  installation rpms, 21-23
  mcserv, 119, 212
  rpms, 171-172
  Switchdesk, 32
  tarballs, 306
  themes
    Enlightenment, 162
    GTK, 160
  wvdial, 189, 196
  XFree86, 16
DOX (Enlightenment Document Viewer), 129
drag and drop
  File Manager, 109-110
  gFTP, 209
dragbars (Enlightenment), 139
drawers (GNOME Panel), 61, 81

E

echo $PATH command, 232
E-conf, 126-127
Edit menu commands (File Manager)
  Rescan Directory, 94
  Search, 93

  Select All, 93
  Select Files, 93
Edit MIME Types command (Commands menu), File Manager, 94
Edit program option (gFTP), 211
editing
  etc/printcap files, 216
  files
    configuration, 78
    .desktop, 76-77
  graphics
    Electric Eyes, 263-264
    Eye of GNOME, 265
  icons, desktop, 59
  Main Menu, 86
  MIME types, 181
  XF86Config file, 56-57
editors
  Default Editor capplet, 143
  Menu Editor (Main Menu), 86
  text
    editing XF86Config files, 56
    gEdit, 64
    gnotepad+, 64
eesh (Enlightenment External Shell), 135-136
Electric Eyes
  accessing options, 261
  changing default image viewer, 264-265
  Enlightenment background images, 262
  graphics
    color, 264
    editing, 263-264
    file formats supported, 260
    opening all files, 261
    opening multiple files, 262
    opening single files, 261
    rotating, 264
    screen shots, 264

sizing, 263
viewing, 260-262
list windows, 262
package requirements, 261
toolbars, 261
Electrical Design/Programmers applications (GNOME Software Map), 235
email
Balsa
configuring, 201-204
crashes, 201
downloading messages, 201
features, 200
layout, 201
preferences, 202-204
signature files, 203, 213
Web site, 200
Mahogany, 201
Netscape Messenger, 212-213
emulating three-button mouse, 56-57, 67
emulators, terminal, 65
engines (GTK themes), 159
Enlightenment, 41, 123
benefits, 42
bugs, 138
complexity, 42
customization options, 42
Desktop Background Settings, 127
desktop shell capabilities, 42
desktops, 132
multiple, 133-134
switching between, 133-134
virtual, 132
DOX (Document Viewer), 129
dragbars, 139
drawbacks, 42
E-conf, 126-127
eesh, 135-136

Electric Eyes, background images, 262
Enlightenment menu, 125
file manager, 101
help, 138
Help button, 129
hotkeys, 66, 134-135
Iconbox, 124
installing
installation order, 44
libraries, 44
necessary software, 43
optional software, 43
system requirements, 42
Maintenance menu, 128
Pager, 124
platform compatibility, 41
Settings menu, 126-127
Special FX Settings, 127
themes, 134, 162-163
ToolTips, 124, 127
troubleshooting, 137-139
uninstalling, 293-294
upgrades, 44
User menus, 126, 131
Web site, 21, 41-43, 138
window border menu, 129-130
window groups, 130
Enlightenment External Shell (eesh), 135-136
Entertainment applications (GNOME Software Map), 235
environment variables (PATH), 232
errors *See also* **bugs**
Big Buddy, 333-334
bug reports, 335-337
contact information, 334
Debugging Information dialog box, 336
features, 334
software requirements, 334
starting, 334

Submit Report dialog box, 338
system information, 334
dependency
example, 24
troubleshooting, 24-25
version-dependency, 25
Enlightenment, 138
reporting, 311
source code installation, 308
establishing connections
gFTP, 207-208
PPP, 193
e.themes.org Web site, 159, 162
etc/printcap files
configuring printing, 216-217
editing, 216
example, 216-217
Everything Linux Web site, 249
executable files, 72
directories, 310
paths, 232
running applications, 232
extensions
MIME types, 180-182
tarballs, 302
Eye of GNOME
bonobo technology, 258
changing default image viewer, 264-265
File menu commands, 259
graphics
editing, 265
file formats supported, 258
viewing, 258-260
package requirements, 258
View menu commands, 259

F

FAQs
  Enlightenment, 138
  GNOME FAQ, 296
  GNOME Project Web site, 11
Fifteen (panel amusement), 283
file extensions. *See* **extensions**
File Manager, 89
  Commands menu commands, 94
  context menus, 95-97
  directories, 91
    viewing size, 111
    views, 94-95
  drag-and-drop features, 109-110
  Edit menu commands
    Rescan Directory, 94
    Search, 93
    Select All, 93
    Select Files, 93
  editing MIME types, 181
  File menu commands
    Close Window, 93
    Copy, 93
    Create New Window, 92-93
    Delete, 93
    Move, 93
    Open, 93
    Show Directory Sizes, 93
  File Properties
    file ownership, 117
    opening, 115
    Options tab, 117
    Permissions tab, 116-117
    Statistics tab, 115
  files
    backup, 98
    copying, 107-108
    deleting, 108
    hidden, 98
    moving, 108

renaming, 109
selecting, 106
sorting, 113-114
viewing size, 111
filters, 118
Find Files tool, 112-113
as FTP client, 212
gnoRPM options, 177
graphical interface, 90, 101
help, 95
Layout menu commands, 94
Nautilus comparison, 120, 212
performance issues, 120
Preferences dialog box, 97
  Confirmation tab, 98
  Desktop tab, 99-100
  File Display tab, 98
quitting, 90-91, 93
rpms, installing, 182
Search tool, 112
Settings menu commands, 94
Sort By tool (File Manger), 113-114
starting, 90, 101
symbolic links
  creating, 109-110
  viewing, 114-115
toolbar, 91, 95
troubleshooting, 101
VFS, 119
views, 104-106
windows
  appearance, 91
  closing, 90, 93
  navigating, 91, 95
  opening, 90
  status bar, 91
file managers, 101
File menu commands
  Eye of GNOME, 259
  File Manager, 92-93
File Properties
  file ownership, 117
  opening, 115
  Options tab, 117

Permissions tab, 116-117
Statistics tab, 115
File Transfer Protocol. *See* **FTP**
files
  backup, 71-72, 98
  compressed, 119
  compressing (gzip utility), 302
  configuration
    backups, 71
    editing, 78
    .gnome directory, 74-75
    $PATH/share/gnome directory, 73
  copying (cp command), 107
  decompressing, 119
  deleting (rm command), 107
  .desktop
    editing, 76-77
    user directories, 77
  downloading, 206-208
  etc/printcap
    configuring printing, 216-217
    editing, 216
    example, 216-217
  executable, 72
    directories, 310
    paths, 232
    running applications, 232
  File Manager
    context menu options, 96-97
    copying, 107-108
    deleting, 108
    drag-and-drop features, 109-110
    moving, 108
    renaming, 109
    selecting, 106
    sorting, 113-114
    viewing size, 111
    filtering, 118

formats
   Electric Eyes graphic file support, 260
   Eye of GNOME graphic file support, 258
   GIMP graphic file support, 267
   Gnumeric support, 248
graphic, printing, 222-224
gtkrc, 159
help, viewing, 299
hidden, 212
   creating, 75
   .gnome directory, 74-75
   viewing, 98
Makefiles, configuring, 307
MIME types
   adding, 181
   changing default image viewer, 264-265
   defaults, 180
   editing, 181
   extensions, 180-182
   IANA list, 180
   viewing, 180-181
moving (mv command), 107
object, deleting, 308
ownership, viewing, 117
permissions, viewing, 116-117
.png, 159
PostScript (ggv utility), 219
printing, 217-218
properties
   renaming files, 109
   viewing, 115-117
renaming, 109
searching
   Find Files tool (File Manager), 112-113
   Search tool (File Manager), 112

session, 75-78
signature (email)
   Balsa, 203, 213
   Netscape Messenger, 213
spec, 240
tarballs. *See* tarballs
tarring, 302
uncompressing, 306-307
uploading, 206, 209
viewing
   Custom View (File Manager), 104-106
   remote sites, 211
.wav, 153
XF86Config, editing, 56-57
filesystems
   navigating (gFTP), 208
   space (GNOME DiskFree), 179
   VFS, 119
Filter View command (Layout menu), File Manager, 94
filtering files, 118
filters
   File Manager, 118
   searching rpms, 171
Find Files command (Commands menu), File Manager, 94
Find Files tool (File Manger), 112-113
Find Packages dialog box (gnoRPM), 171
fixing tiles (GNOME Panel), 88
flipping graphics (Electric Eye), 264
focus (desktops), setting, 126
fonts (Theme Selector capplet), 145, 153
footers, setting, 220
footprint symbol (GNOME Project), 8

formats (files)
   Electric Eyes graphic file support, 260
   Eye of GNOME graphic file support, 258
   GIMP graphic file support, 267
   Gnumeric support, 248
free software
   GNU Project, 10
   implications, 13
   open source software comparison, 11
Freshmeat.net Web site, 16, 189, 196
FTP (File Transfer Protocol), 204
   File Manager, 212
   gFTP
      Bookmarks menu, 206
      capabilities, 204
      configuring options, 209-212
      context menus, 207
      connection toolbar, 206-208
      downloading/uploading files, 208-209
      drag and drop, 209
      establishing connections, 207-208
      features, 204
      FTP menu, 206
      Help menu, 206
      Local menu, 206
      Logging menu, 206
      navigating file systems, 208
      Remote menu, 206
      Tools menu, 206
      Transfers menu, 206
      View program option, 210
      windows, 204-209
   sites
      File manager, 182
      MIME types list, 180
FTP menu (gFTP), 206
ftpfs (VFS), 119

functions, 323
  libraries, 72, 323
  widgets, 326
FVWM Web site, 49

G

Gaby, 253
Game of Life (panel amusement), 283
games, 277
  AisleRiot, 278
  configuring, 278
  GameStalker, 284
  Gnibbles, 282
  Gnome Mines, 278
  GNOME Robots II, 282
  Gnome-Stones, 282
  Gnome Tali, 279
  Gnome Tetravex, 279
  GnomeHack, 284
  Gnommind, 284
  Iagno, 279
  KDE, 285
  Linux, 285
  Mah-jongg, 281
  networked, 285
  panel amusements, 283
  Same Gnome, 281
  UNIX, 285
GCC (GNOME Control Center). *See* Control Center
gcc (GNU C compiler), 305
GDK (GIMP Drawing Kit), 327
GDP (GNOME Documentation Project), 289, 296, 299, 311
gEdit, 64
gFTP
  Bookmarks menu, 206
  capabilities, 204
  connection toolbar, 206-208

connections, establishing, 207-208
context menus, 207
downloading/uploading files, 208-209
drag and drop, 209
features, 204
file systems, navigating, 208
FTP menu, 206
Help menu, 206
Local menu, 206
Logging menu, 206
options, configuring, 209-212
Remote menu, 206
Tools menu, 206
Transfers menu, 206
windows, 204-06
  comparing, 209
  download/upload progress window, 207
  local file system window, 207-208
  log window, 207
  remote file system window, 207-208
ggv utility, 219
GIMP (Graphics Image Manipulation Program), 265
  changing default image viewer, 264-265
  documentation, 266-267
  downloading, 266
  features, 266
  GDK, 327
  graphics, file formats supported, 267
  GTK. *See* GTK
  printing graphics, 222-224
  Web site, 266-267
  windows, 266
GIMP Drawing Kit (GDK), 327
GIMP ToolKit. *See* GTK
GIMP User's Manual (GUM), 266

Glade, 327
Glib, 327
Global Panel Properties, 83-84
gmc (GNOME Midnight Commander). *See* File Manager
Gniall (GNOME Non-Intelligent AMOS Language Learner), 285
Gnibbles, 282
GNOME (GNU Network Model Environment), 8
  application compatibility issues, 13
  applications
    characteristics, 322
    components, 323
    copylefting, 11
    Glade, 327
    GNOME development Web site, 328
    IBM DeveloperWorks Web site, 328
    libgnome library, 325
    libgnomeui library, 325-326
    libgnorba library, 326
    library advantages, 324-325
    KDE comparison, 11-12
    languages, 11
    programming, 312
GNOME Address Book, 250-251
Gnome-admin, 177-178
gnome-announce mailing list, 239
gnome-applets package, 283
GNOME Calendar, 249-250
GNOME Control Center. *See* Control Center
GNOME CVS icons (GNOME Software Map), 234
GNOME Developer's Site, 326
GNOME development Web site, 328

GNOME Software Map 379

.gnome directory
  configuration files, 74-75
  hidden files, 74-75
  viewing, 75
GNOME DiskFree, 179
GNOME Documentation Project (GDP), 289, 296, 299, 311
GNOME FAQ, 296
GNOME File Manager. *See* **File Manager**
gnome-games, 277
  AisleRiot, 278
  configuring, 278
  Gnibbles, 282
  Gnome Mines, 278
  GNOME Robots II, 282
  Gnome-Stones, 282
  Gnome Tali, 279
  Gnome Tetravex, 279
  Iagno, 279
  Mah-jongg, 281
  Same Gnome, 281
GNOME Help Browser, 294
  accessing help, 295
  GNOME FAQ, 296
  GNOME User's Guide, 296
  help files, viewing, 299
  toc command, 295
  whatis option, 295
Gnome-linuxconf, 177
gnome-list mailing list, 239-240
GNOME Mailing List, 161
GNOME Master Mind, 284
GNOME Midnight Commander (gmc). *See* **File Manager**
Gnome Mines, 278
GNOME Nibbles, 282
GNOME Non-Intelligent AMOS Language Learner (Gniall), 285
GNOME Office, 246
  AbiWord, 246-247
  Dia, 251-252
  GNOME Address Book, 250-251

GNOME Calendar, 249-250
GNOME Office Project, 238
GNOME-PIN, 249
Gnumeric, 220-222, 247-249
GNOME Package Manager. *See* **gnoRPM**
GNOME Panel, 57
  applets
    adding, 61-63, 82-83
    deleting, 82
  application launchers, 80-81
  clock, 62
  configuring panel properties, 83-84
  Control Center button, 62
  default buttons, 61-62
  deleting, 67
  drawers, 61, 81
  GNOME virtual terminal launcher, 62
  Help button, 62
  Netscape Communicator launcher, 62
  panels, 84
  Tasklist, 62
  tiles, fixing, 88
gnome-pilot tool, 249
GNOME-PIN (Personal Information Manager)
  GNOME Address Book, 250-251
  GNOME Calendar, 249-250
GNOME PPP Dialer. *See* **PPP Dialer**
gnome-print
  Print Preview, 220
  Print Setup, 220-222
GNOME Project
  contributing, 311-312
  de Icaza, Miguel, 10
  footprint symbol, 8
  goals, 9, 12

history, 8-10
reporting bugs, 311
GNOME Project Web site, 49, 87
  applications, 277
  bonobo technology information, 319
  FAQ, 11
  GNOME Office, 246
  GNOME Office Project, 238
  gnome-pilot tool, 249
  GNOME support, 255
  Gnumeric, 249
  installation information, 21
  installation packages, 21-23
  mailing lists, 297
GNOME Robots II, 282
GNOME rpm Manager. *See* **gnoRPM**
GNOME Software Map, 233
  bugs, 241
  Core applications, 235
  drawbacks, 233
  Electrical Design/Programmers applications, 235
  Entertainment applications, 235
  graphics applications, 267
  icons, 233-234
  Internet Tools, 235
  keyword searches, 233
  Mail Clients, 235
  Math and Science Tools, 236
  Miscellaneous applications, 236
  Network Talk Clients, 236
  Productivity applications, 237
  Sound Tools, 237
  System Utilities, 237
  Web site address, 233, 252
  Window/Session/Desktop Managers, 238

Gnome-Stones, 282
Gnome Tali, 279
GNOME Tasklist
    GNOME Panel, adding, 62
    window managers, 40
GNOME Terminal, 65
Gnome Tetravex, 279
GNOME Unified Link to Printers (gulp), 178
GNOME User's Guide, The, 86, 296
GNOME virtual terminal launcher, 62
GNOME virtual terminals. *See* **virtual terminals**
GnomeHack, 284
Gnommind, 284
gnoRPM (GNOME rpm Manager). *See also* **rpms**
    crashes, 172
    Create Desktop Entry, 169
    File Manager, 177
    main window, 168
    menu bar, 169
    package listing windows, 168
    preferences
        Behavior Preferences tab, 174
        Distributions tab, 176-177
        Install Window tab, 175
        Network tab, 175
        Package Listing tab, 175
        Rpmfind tab, 176
    rpmfind database
        downloading rpms, 171-172, 176
        Web site, 171, 176
    rpms
        installing, 168-171, 239
        querying, 172-173
        saving rpm packages, 182

        searching, 171
        uninstalling, 291
        upgrading, 169-171
    toolbar, 169
gnotepad+, 64
Gnotravex, 279
GNU C compiler (gcc), 305
GNU General Public License (GPL), 11
GNU Lesser General Public License (LGPL), 11
GNU Network Model Environment. *See* **GNOME**
GNU Project
    CVS code utilities, 309
    free software, 10
    gnu symbol, 9
    history, 8-10
    Stallman, Richard, 9
    Web site, 9, 309
Gnumeric, 247-249
    features, 248
    file formats supported, 248
    printing, 220-222
GPL (GNU General Public License), 11
grabbing screen shots (Electric Eyes), 264
graphical interfaces, 322. *See also* **graphics**
    File Manager, 90, 101
    Glade, 327
    window managers, 38-39
graphics. *See also* **graphical interfaces**
    applications
        compatibility issues, 268
        GNOME Software Map, 267
    changing default image viewer, 264-265
    Electric Eyes
        accessing options, 261
        color, 264
        editing, 263-264
        Enlightenment background images, 262

        file formats supported, 260
        list windows, 262
        opening all files, 261
        opening multiple files, 262
        opening single files, 261
        package requirements, 261
        rotating, 264
        screen shots, 264
        sizing, 263
        toolbars, 261
        viewing, 260-262
    Eye of GNOME
        bonobo technology, 258
        editing graphics, 265
        file formats supported, 258
        File menu commands, 259
        package requirements, 258
        View menu commands, 259
        viewing, 258-260
    GIMP, 265
        documentation, 266-267
        downloading, 266
        features, 266
        file formats supported, 267
        GDK, 327
        GTK. *See* GTK
        printing graphics, 222-224
        Web site, 266-267
        windows, 266
    importing (Dia), 252
    usr/share/pixmaps directory, 73
Graphics Image Manipulation Program. *See* **GIMP**
Group field (gnoRPM queries), 173

grouping windows (Enlightenment), 130
GTali, 279
GTK (GIMP ToolKit), 12, 157, 326
  help, 328
  language bindings, 318-319
  themes, 156
    components, 159
    creating, 163
    downloading, 160
    GTK Themes Web site, 160, 163
    installing, 160-161
    libraries needed, 160
    limitations, 158
    pixmap, 158
    plain, 158
    selecting, 161
    uninstalling, 161
  Web site, 319, 328
  widgets, 326-327
gtkrc files, 159
gtkrc themes, 158
gulp (GNOME Unified Link to Printers), 178
GUM (GIMP User's Manual), 266
gzip utility, 302

H

hard disks, inode numbers, 105
hard links, 114
hardware
  hardware compatibility HOWTO (Linux Documentation Project), 188
  installation preparation, system requirements, 16
Harpei, John, 47
headers, setting, 220
Helix Code, 255

help. *See also* documentation
  C Programming Language: ANSI C Version, The, 305
  eesh, 136
  Enlightenment, 138
  File Manager, 95
  files, viewing, 299
  GNOME FAQ, 296
  GNOME Help Browser, 294-296
    accessing help, 295
    toc command, 295
    viewing help files, 299
    whatis option, 295
  GNOME mailing list, 161
  GNOME User's Guide, 86, 296
  GTK, 328
  Helix Code, 255
  Help button (Enlightenment), 129
  HOWTOs
    checking printer support, 224
    hardware compatibility HOWTO, 188
    ISP Hookup HOWTO, 195
    modem HOWTO, 187
    Plug and Play HOWTO, 188
    Sound HOWTO, 272
  International GNOME Support, 255
  Linux Installation and Getting Started guide (Linux Documentation Project Web site), 105
  Linux System Administrator's Guide, 31
  mailing lists, 297
    etiquette, 297-298
    posting messages, 298-299
  man pages (X11), 29

Managing Projects with make, 305
rpms, 240
Sams Teach Yourself C in 21 Days, 305
ToolTips (Enlightenment), 124, 127
Help button (GNOME Panel), 62
Help menu (gFTP), 206
hidden directories, creating, 75
hidden files, 212
  creating, 75
  .gnome directory, 74-75
  viewing, 98
history
  GNOME Project, 8-10
  GNU Project, 8-10
$HOME directory, 30
Homepage icons (GNOME Software Map), 233
hostnames (DNS), 191
hotkeys
  Enlightenment, 66, 134-135
  GNOME support, 66
HOWTOs
  checking printer support, 224
  hardware compatibility HOWTO, 188
  ISP Hookup HOWTO, 195
  Linux Sound HOWTO, 272
  modem HOWTO, 187
  Plug and Play HOWTO, 188

I

Iagno, 279
IANA (Internet Assigned Numbers Authority), 180
IBM DeveloperWorks Web site, 328

IceWM
  installing, 45-47
  keyboards, 45
  Macek, Marko, 44
  mouse, 45
  platform compatibility, 44
  rpms download site, 46
Icon View command (Layout menu), File Manager, 94
Iconbox (Enlightenment), 124
Iconify buttons (windows), 64, 67
icons
  desktop
    creating, 58-60
    defaults, 57-58
    deleting, 59
    editing, 59
    placement, 100
    properties, 58
    shaped, 99
  GNOME Software Map, 233-234
Identity tab (Balsa preferences), 203
images. *See* **graphics**
importing images (Dia), 252
index numbers, 105
initialization strings, 189
inode numbers, 105
Install Date field (gnoRPM queries), 173
Install dialog box (gnoRPM), 170
Install Window tab (gnoRPM), 175
installation, 15. *See also* **uninstalling**
  applications, 239
    source code
      installation, 241, 254
    tarball installation, 240-241
    CD-ROM installation, 19-21

  component installation order, 20-21
  CVS code, 310-311
  Electric Eyes package requirements, 261
  Enlightenment
    installation order, 44
    libraries, 44
    necessary software, 43
    optional software, 43
    system requirements, 42
  Eye of GNOME package requirements, 258
  GNOME Project Web site, 21, 23
  IceWM, 45-47
  KDE compatibility issues, 26
  preparation
    hardware requirements, 16
    locate command, 16-18
    software requirements, 16-18
  rpms, 21
    dependency errors, 24-25
    downloading packages, 21-23
    File Manager, 182
    gnoRPM, 168-171, 239
    installing packages, 23-24
    saving rpm packages, 182
    upgrades, 299
  sawmill, 48-49
  source code
    advantages, 303-304, 312
    compiling, 302, 308
    configuring Makefiles, 307
    customizing, 303
    deleting object files, 308
    documentation, 303

    downloading tarballs, 306
    errors, 308
    installing compiled code, 308
    ldconfig command, 308
    security, 303
    uncompressing/untarring tarballs, 306-307
    uninstalling old versions, 306
    uninstalling tarballs, 308
    upgrades, 303
  themes
    Enlightenment, 162-163
    GTK, 160-161
  Windows compatibility issues, 26
instances (applications), 230
integrating applications (CORBA), 315-317
interfaces
  CORBA
    bonobo technology, 258, 318-319
    features, 316-317
    GNOME Project Web site, 11
    integrating applications, 315-316
    OMG, 317-319
    ORB, 317
    ORBit, 317
  graphical, 322
    File Manager, 90, 101
    Glade, 327
    window managers, 38-39
  shells, 70
International GNOME Support, 255
Internet Assigned Numbers Authority (IANA), 180
Internet connections and call waiting, 191
Internet Tools (GNOME Software Map), 235

ISPs (Internet Service Providers)
  information needed for PPP connections, 187
  ISP Hookup HOWTO (Linux Documentation Project), 195

J-L

KDE (K Desktop Environment), 11. *See also* desktops; window managers
  C++, 11
  file manager, 101
  games, 285
  GNOME comparison, 11-12
  GNOME compatibility, 26
  Qt library, 11
keybindings. *See* hotkeys
Keyboard Bell capplet, 145
Keyboard capplet, 146
keyboards
  hotkeys
    Enlightenment, 66, 134-135
    GNOME support, 66
  IceWM, 45
  Keyboard Bell capplet, 145
  Keyboard capplet, 146
keyword searches (GNOME Software Map), 233
killing. *See* quitting

language bindings, 318-319
languages
  application restrictions, 245
  C
    C Programming Language: ANSI C Version, The, 305
    gcc, 305

Glib, 327
    Sams Teach Yourself C in 21 Days, 305
  C++, 11
  compatibility (language bindings), 318-319
  Gaby, 253
  Gniall (GNOME Non-Intelligent AMOS Language Learner), 285
  GNOME, 11
LANs (local area networks), 196
launchers
  adding (GNOME Panel), 80-81
  organizing (GNOME Panel), 81
  running applications, 230
Layout menu commands (File Manager), 94
ldconfig command, 308
LGPL (GNU Lesser General Public License), 11
libgnome library, 325
libgnomeui library, 325-326
libgnorba library, 326
libraries, 324-325
  developer benefits, 324
  Enlightenment installation, 44
  functions, 72, 323
  Glib, 327
  GNOME application components, 323
  gnome-print
    Print Preview, 220
    Print Setup, 220-222
  GTK. *See* GTK
  ldconfig command, 308
  libgnome, 325
  libgnomeui, 325-326
  libgnorba, 326
  Qt, 11
  searching, 329
  tarball installation (applications), 240-241

user benefits, 325
  widgets, 323
  Xlib, 327
links
  hard, 114
  symbolic
    drag-and-drop features (File Manager), 109-110
    stalled, 114, 120
    viewing (File Manager), 114-115
Linux
  games, 285
  shells, 70
  sound
    configuring, 272, 285
    OpenSound, 285
Linux Documentation Project
  hardware compatibility HOWTO, 188
  ISP Hookup HOWTO, 195
  Linux Installation and Getting Started guide, 105
  Linux System Administrator's Guide, 31
  modem HOWTO, 187
  Plug and Play HOWTO, 188
  Sound HOWTO, 272
Linux Installation and Getting Started guide (Linux Documentation Project Web site), 105
Linux System Administrator's Guide, 31
list windows (Electric Eyes), 262
listing PATH environment variable, 232
listings
  dependency errors, 24
  etc/printcap file, 216
  locate command, 17-19

lpq command, 218
lprm command, 219
starting sessions
    boot startups, 32
    xinit scripts, 30
version-dependency error, 25
XF86Config script, 56
local area networks (LANs), 196
local file system window, 207-208
Local menu (gFTP), 206
locate command, 304, 329
    checking installed components, 16-18
    example, 17
    locate esound example, 19
log window (gFTP), 207
Logging menu (gFTP), 206
logins, root, 71
logoffs, 65-66, 87
logs, viewing, 178
logview, 178
lpd daemon, 218
lpq command, 218-219
lpr command, 218
lprm command, 219, 224

M

Macek, Marko, 44
machine code, 302
magic command, 29
Mah-jongg, 281
Mahogany (email client), 201
Mail Clients (GNOME Software Map), 235
Mail Servers tab (Balsa preferences), 203
mailing lists
    Enlightenment, 138
    etiquette, 297-298
    gnome-announce, 239

gnome-list, 239-240
GNOME Mailing List, 161
posting messages, 298-299
Main Menu, 57
    applications
        adding, 86
        deleting, 86
        opening, 60-61
    capabilities, 60
    customizing, 84-85
    Menu Editor, 86
    miscellaneous items, 86
    opening, 60
    Other menus, 86
    Panel menus, 86
    sections, 60, 85
    System menus, 85
    User menus, 85
Maintenance menu (Enlightenment), 128
make distclean command, 308
make utility
    deleting object files, 308
    make distclean command, 308
    Managing Projects with make, 305
    source code compilation, 305, 308
    source code installation, 308
    uninstalling tarballs, 308
Makefiles, configuring, 307
making rpms, 240
man pages, 29
managing sessions, 65-66, 87. *See also* **administration**
Managing Projects with make, 305
margins, setting, 220
Math and Science Tools (GNOME Software Map), 236
Maximize/Minimize buttons (windows), 64
mcfs (VFS), 119

mcserv, downloading, 119, 212
menu bar (gnoRPM), 169
Menu Editor (Main Menu), 86
menus, detaching, 148. *See also* **specific menus**
messages
    email, downloading (Balsa), 201
    mailing lists, 297-299
middleware (ORB), 317
Midnight Commander (UNIX), 89. *See also* **File Manager**
Midnight Commander network file system (mcfs), 119
MIME (Multipurpose Internet Mail Extensions), 180
MIME types
    adding, 181
    defaults, 180
    editing, 181
    extensions, 180-182
    files, 264-265
    IANA list, 180
    viewing, 180-181
Misc. tab (Balsa preferences), 203
Miscellaneous applications (GNOME Software Map), 236
miscellaneous items (Main Menu), 86
Modem Lights applet, 195
modems
    initialization strings, 189
    Linux compatibility, 188
    modem HOWTO (Linux Documentation Project), 187
    serial ports, viewing, 188-189
monitoring PPP connections, 194-195
mount points (CD-ROMs), 274

mouse
    acceleration, 147
    IceWM, 45
    Mouse capplet, 147
    right click, accessing
        Electric Eye options, 261
    three-button mouse
        emulation, 56-57, 67
    threshold, 147
Mouse capplet, 147
**Move Applet command
    (context menus), 81**
**Move command (File
    menu), File Manager, 93**
Move dialog box, 108
moving files
    drag-and-drop features
        (File Manager), 109-110
    File Manager, 108
    mv command, 107
**multiple desktops
    (Enlightenment), 133-134**
**Multipurpose Internet Mail
    Extensions (MIME), 180**
mv command
    moving files, 107
    renaming files, 109

N-O

names
    DNS, 191
    printers, 217
    tarballs (extensions), 302
Nautilus, 120, 212. See also
    File Manager
navigating
    file systems (gFTP), 208
    windows (File Manager),
        91, 95
**Netscape Communicator,
    62, 200**
**Netscape Messenger,
    212-213**
Netscape Web site, 200

Network tab (gnoRPM), 175
**Network Talk Clients
    (GNOME Software Map),
    236**
networks
    LANs, 196
    networked games, 285

object files, deleting, 308
**Object Request Broker
    (ORB), 317**
objects (ORB), 317
**office applications
    (GNOME Office Project),
    238**
**OMG (Object Management
    Group) Web site, 317-319**
**on-the-fly programming,
    327**
**Open command (File
    menu), File Manager, 93**
open source software, 11
opening. See also starting
    capplets, 142
    compressed files, 119
    eesh, 136
    File Properties
        file ownership, 117
        Options tab, 117
        Permissions tab,
            116-117
        Statistics tab, 115
    GNOME Terminal, 65
    graphics (Electric Eyes),
        261-262
    Main Menu, 60
    man pages, 29
    Preferences dialog box
        (File Manager), 98
    Search tool (File
        Manager), 112
    windows (File Manager),
        90
    xterm, 65
OpenSound Web site, 285
**ORB (Object Request
    Broker), 317**
ORBit, 317

organizing application
    launchers (GNOME
    Panel), 81
**OSs (operating systems),
    multiuser, 70-71**
**Other menus (Main Menu),
    86**
ownership (files), viewing,
    117

P

**Package Listing tab
    (gnoRPM), 175**
**Packager field (gnoRPM
    queries), 173**
packages. See also **rpms**
    Electric Eyes package
        requirements, 261
    Eye of GNOME package
        requirements, 258
    gnome-applets, 283
    gnome-games, 277
        AisleRiot, 278
        Gnibbles, 282
        Gnome Mines, 278
        GNOME Robots II,
            282
        Gnome-Stones, 282
        Gnome Tali, 279
        Gnome Tetravex, 279
        Iagno, 279
        Mah-jongg, 281
        Same Gnome, 281
    gnome-print
        Print Preview, 220
        Print Setup, 220-222
page size, setting, 220
Pager (Enlightenment), 124
Palm Pilots, 249
panel amusements, 283
**Panel menu (Main Menu),
    86**
**Panel menu commands,
    Create New Panel, 84**

panel properties
 configuring, 83-84
 Global Panel Properties, 83-84
 This Panel Properties, 84
panels. *See* **GNOME Panel**
paper size, setting, 220
partitioning test partitions, 72
PATH environment variable, 232
$PATH/share/gnome directory, 73
paths, 232
performance (File Manager), 120
permissions
 files, viewing, 116-117
 Options tab (File Properties), 117
 Permissions tab (File Properties), 116-117
PIN (Personal Information Manager), 249-251
ping command, 194
pixmap themes (GTK), 158
pixmaps, 158
plain themes (GTK), 158
playing CDs (CD player), 273
 CDDB, 275
 controls, 274-275
 customizing, 276-277
 opening, 274
 quitting, 277
 Track Editor, 275-276
Plug and Play HOWTO, 188
.png files, 159
Point to Point Protocol. *See* **PPP**
POP3, Balsa conflicts, 201
ports, serial, 188-189
PostScript files (ggv utility), 219
posting mailing list messages, 297-299

PPP (Point to Point Protocol). *See also* **PPP Dialer**
 connections
  establishing, 193
  ISP information needed, 187
  Modem Lights applet, 195
  monitoring, 194-195
  PPP Applet, 195
  setting PPP Dialer accounts, 190-193
  testing, 194-195
  wvdial, 189, 196
 dialers
  selecting, 196
  wvdial, 189, 196
  pppd, 186
PPP Account dialog box
 Authentication tab, 191
 Dial tab, 190-191
 DNS Server tab, 191
 IP Address tab, 191
 Modem tab, 192
 PPP tab, 192
 Script tab, 192
PPP Applet, 195
PPP Dialer
 accounts
  Authentication tab (PPP Account dialog box), 191
  Dial tab (PPP Account dialog box), 190-191
  DNS Server tab (PPP Account dialog box), 191
  IP Address tab (PPP Account dialog box), 191
  Modem tab (PPP Account dialog box), 192
  PPP tab (PPP Account dialog box), 192
  Script tab (PPP Account dialog box), 192
 setting, 190-193

 connections, establishing, 193
 initialization string, 189
 Modem Lights applet, 195
 PPP Applet, 195
 selecting, 196
pppd, 186, 193
preferences
 Balsa, 202-204
 gnoRPM, 174-176
Preferences command (Settings menu), File Manager, 94
Preferences dialog box
 File Manager, 97
  Confirmation tab, 98
  Desktop tab, 99-100
  File Display tab, 98
  opening, 98
 gnoRPM, 174
Preserve permissions option (gFTP), 211
print jobs, deleting, 219, 224
Print Preview (gnome-print), 220
Print Setup (gnome-print), 220-222
printers. *See also* **printing**
 configuring (cpanel utility), 219
 gulp, 178
 names, 217
 selecting, 222
 support, 224
printing, 215. *See also* **printers**
 configuring (etc/printcap files), 216-217
 files, 217-218
 footers, 220
 ggv utility, 219
 gnome-print
  Print Preview, 220
  Print Setup, 220-222
 Gnumeric, 220-222
 graphics (GIMP), 222-224
 headers, 220
 lpd daemon, 218

lpq command, 218-219
lpr command, 218
lprm command, 219, 224
margins, 220
page size, 220
paper size, 220
print commands, 217
print jobs, deleting, 219, 224
print spools, 218
scaling, 220, 224
processes
  gmc. *See* File Manager
  window managers, 39-40
productivity applications
  drawbacks, 244
  Gaby, 253
  Productivity applications (GNOME Software Map), 237
  TimeTracker, 254
programming
  Glade, 327
  GNOME, 312
  GNOME development Web site, 328
  IBM DeveloperWorks Web site, 328
  on-the-fly, 327
programming languages. *See* **languages**
properties
  desktop icons, 58
  files, renaming, 109
  panel
    configuring, 83-84
    Global Panel Properties, 83-84
    This Panel Properties, 84
Properties command (context menus), 58-59
Properties dialog box (desktop icons), 58
protocols
  POP3, Balsa conflicts, 201
  PPP. *See* PPP
  SLIP, 186

Q-R

Qt widget library, 11
querying rpms (gnoRPM), 172-173
queues, print, 218
quitting
  eesh, 136
  File Manager, 90-93

Red Hat Web site
  installation packages, 21
  Switchdesk download, 32
  XFree86 downloads, 16
Remember dialog box (Enlightenment), 129
remote computer access (mcserv), 119, 212
remote file system window (gFTP), 207-208
Remote menu (gFTP), 206
Remove Applet command (context menus), 82
renaming files, 109
repairing
  sessions, 87
  stalled symbolic links, 120
reporting bugs, 311, 335-338
requesting rpms, 240
Rescan Directory command (Edit menu), File Manager, 94
resetting sessions, 151
Resolve Remote Symlinks option (gFTP), 211
Retry sleep time option (gFTP), 211
right click. *See* **context menus**
rm command, 107
root logins, 71
rotating graphics (Electric Eyes), 264
rpm command, 292

rpmfind database
  downloading rpms, 171-172
  Rpmfind tab (gnoRPM), 176
  Web site, 171, 176
Rpmfind tab (gnoRPM), 176
rpms. *See also* **gnoRPM; packages**
  applications, 239-240
  documentation, 240
  help, 240
  IceWM, 45-46
  installing
    dependency errors, 24-25
    downloading packages, 21-23
    File Manager, 182
    gnoRPM, 168-171, 239
    installing packages, 23-24
    saving rpm packages, 182
  making, 240
  querying, 172-173
  requesting, 240
  rpm Web site, 240
  rpmfind database
    downloading rpms, 171-172
    Rpmfind tab (gnoRPM), 176
    Web site, 171, 176
  sawmill, 48
  searching, 171
  spec files, 240
  uninstalling, 290
    component uninstallation order, 290-291
    gnoRPM, 291
    rpm command, 292
  upgrading, 169-171, 299
Run Command command (Commands menu), File Manager, 94
Run Command in Panel command (Commands menu), File Manager, 94
running. *See* **starting**

S

Same Gnome, 281
Sams Teach Yourself C in 21 Days, **305**
saving
    Control Center changes, 152
    sessions
        options, 149
        repairing sessions, 87
        session management, 65-66
    window attributes (Enlightenment), 129
sawmill
    backgrounds, 47
    benefits, 48
    customizing, 51
    documentation, 48
    Harper, John, 47
    installing
        rpms/debs, 48
        tarballs, 48-49
    Web site, 47-48, 51
scaling (printing), 220, 224
screen shots, grabbing (Electric Eyes), 264
screensavers (capplets), 144
Screenshot icons (GNOME Software Map), 234
scripts
    startup
        starting sessions, 28-29
        Switchdesk, 33-34
        troubleshooting, 34-35
    XF86Config, three-button mouse emulation, 56
    xinit, 29-30
Search command (Edit menu), File Manager, 93
Search tool (File Manger), 112
searching
    files
        Find Files tool (File Manager), 112-113
        Search tool (File Manager), 112

gnome-announce mailing list, 239
gnome-list mailing list, 239
GNOME Office Project, 238
GNOME Software Map, 233
    bugs, 241
    Core applications, 235
    drawbacks, 233
    Electrical Design/Programmers applications, 235
    Entertainment applications, 235
    icons, 233-234
    Internet Tools, 235
    keyword searches, 233
    Mail Clients, 235
    Math and Science Tools, 236
    Miscellaneous applications, 236
    Network Talk Clients, 236
    Productivity applications, 237
    Sound Tools, 237
    System Utilities, 237
    Web site address, 233, 252
    Window/Session/Desktop Managers, 238
libraries, 329
locate command, 304, 329
rpms
    gnoRPM, 171
    rpmfind, 171-172
whereis command, 304, 329
security (source code installation), 303
Select All command (Edit menu), File Manager, 93
Select Files command (Edit menu), File Manager, 93

Select Printer dialog box, 222
selecting
    files (File Manager), 106
    fonts (Theme Selector capplet), 145, 153
    PPP dialers, 196
    printers, 222
    themes (GTK), 161
Serial Line Internet Protocol (SLIP), 186
serial ports, 188-189
servers
    game
        GameStalker, 284
        networked games, 285
    ORB, 317
    X, 16
session files, 75-78
session management, 65-66, 87
Session Manager, 151
    applications, 150
    sessions
        configuring, 149-151
        resetting, 151
        saving options, 149
sessions
    configuring
        opening applications on startup, 150
        Session Manager, 149-151
    resetting, 151
    saving options, 149
    starting, 27
        booting, 31-32
        command lines, 29-30
        packaged Linux distributions, 28
        startup scripts, 28-29
        Switchdesk, 28, 33-34
        troubleshooting, 34-35
setting
    Custom View (File Manager), 104-106
    focus (desktops), 126
    footers, 220
    headers, 220

icons placement, 100
margins, 220
page size, 220
paper size, 220
PPP Dialer accounts,
 190-193
  Authentication tab
   (PPP Account dialog
   box), 191
  Dial tab (PPP Account
   dialog box), 190-191
  DNS Server tab (PPP
   Account dialog box),
   191
  IP Address tab (PPP
   Account dialog box),
   191
  Modem tab (PPP
   Account dialog box),
   192
  PPP tab (PPP Account
   dialog box), 192
  Script tab (PPP
   Account dialog box),
   192
 preferences
  File Manager, 97-100
  gnoRPM, 174-177
 shaped icons/text, 99
 test partitions/systems, 72
 window border options
  (Enlightenment), 130
Settings menu
 Enlightenment, 126-127
 File Manager, 94
**Shade/Unshade buttons
 (windows), 64**
shaped icons/text, 99
shells, 70
 desktop shells, 38, 42
 eesh, 135-136
shortcuts
 Enlightenment, 66,
  134-135
 GNOME support, 66
**Show Directory Sizes
 command (File menu),
 File Manager, 93**

**Show hidden files option
 (gFTP), 211**
signals (widgets), 326
signature files (email)
 Balsa, 203, 213
 Netscape Messenger, 213
sites
 AbiSource, 247
 AfterStep, 49
 Balsa (email client), 200
 BlackBox, 49
 CDDB, 275
 Dia, 252
 e.themes.org, 159, 162
 Enlightenment, 21, 41-43,
  138
 Everything Linux, 249
 Freshmeat.net, 16, 189,
  196
 FTP
  File Manager, 182
  MIME types list, 180
 FVWM, 49
 Gaby, 253
 gEdit, 64
 GIMP, 266-267
 Gniall (GNOME Non-
  Intelligent AMOS
  Language Learner), 285
 GNOME Developer's Site,
  326
 GNOME development
  Web site, 328
 GNOME Documentation
  Project, 289, 296, 299,
  311
 GNOME Project, 49, 87
  applications, 277
  bonobo technology
   information, 319
  FAQ, 11
  GNOME Office, 246
  GNOME Office
   Project, 238
  gnome-pilot tool, 249
  GNOME support, 255
  Gnumeric, 249
  installation
   information, 21

 installation packages,
  21-23
 mailing lists, 297
 GNOME Software Map,
  233, 252
 GnomeHack, 284
 GNU Project, 9, 309
 GTK, 319, 328
 GTK Themes, 160, 163
 IBM DeveloperWorks, 328
 IceWM rpms download
  site, 46
 Linux Documentation
  Project
   hardware compatibility
    HOWTO, 188
   ISP Hookup HOWTO,
    195
   Linux Installation and
    Getting Started guide,
    105
   Linux System
    Administrator's
    Guide, 31
   modem HOWTO, 187
   Plug and Play
    HOWTO, 188
   Sound HOWTO, 272
 Mahogany (email client),
  201
 mcserv download ftp site,
  119, 212
 Netscape, 200
 OMG (Object
  Management Group),
  317, 319
 OpenSound, 285
 Red Hat
  installation packages,
   21
  Switchdesk download,
   32
  XFree86 downloads,
   16
 rpm Web site, 240
 rpmfind database, 171,
  176
 sawmill, 47-48
 Window Maker, 49

X11 Web site, 42, 49
XFree86, 16
size
   directories, 111
   files, 111
   graphics, 263
   page, setting, 220
   paper, setting, 220
Size field (gnoRPM queries), 173
SLIP (Serial Line Internet Protocol), 186
sndconfig utility, 272
software. *See* **applications**
Sort By command (Layout menu), File Manager, 94
Sort By tool (File Manager), 113-114
sorting files, 113-114
sound
   CD player, 273
      CDDB, 275
      controls, 274-275
      customizing, 276-277
      opening, 274
      quitting, 277
      Track Editor, 275-276
   desktops, 272-273
   Enlightenment, 138
   Keyboard Bell capplet, 145
   Linux system
      configuring, 272, 285
      OpenSound, 285
   Sound Events capplet, 146, 153
   troubleshooting, 285
   .wav files, 153
Sound Tools (GNOME Software Map), 237
source code. *See also* **tarballs**
   applications, installing, 241
   compiling, 302
      autoconf utility, 304-305
      make utility, 305, 308

CVS
   cautions, 309
   downloading, 309-311
   installing, 310-311
   separating from stable code, 310
   utilities needed, 309
documentation, 303
gcc, 305
GNOME installation, 302
   advantages, 303-304, 312
   configuring Makefiles, 307
   customizing, 303
   deleting object files, 308
   downloading tarballs, 306
   errors, 308
   installing compiled code, 308
   ldconfig command, 308
   security, 303
   uncompressing/untarring, 306-307
   uninstalling old versions, 306
   uninstalling tarballs, 308
   installing, 254
   stability, 234
   upgrades, 303
space (file systems), 179
spec files, 240
speed (Enlightenment), 137
spools, print, 218
spreadsheets (Gnumeric), 247-249
stability (source code), 234
Stable Source Code icons (GNOME Software Map), 234
stalled symbolic links, 114, 120
Stallman, Richard (GNU Project), 9
Start file transfers option (gFTP), 212

starting. *See also* **opening**
   applications
      background process, 232-233
      command lines, 231-232
      executable files, 72, 232
      GNOME startup, 150
      instances, 230
      launchers, 230
      Main Menu, 60-61
      paths, 232
   Big Buddy, 334
   File Manager, 90, 101
   PPP connections, 195
   sessions, 27
      booting, 31-32
      command lines, 29-30
      packaged Linux distributions, 28
      startup scripts, 28-29
      Switchdesk, 28, 33-34
      troubleshooting, 34-35
Startup Programs capplet, 149-151
Statistics tab (File Properties), 115
status bars
   applications, 149
   File Manager windows, 91
strings, initialization, 189
Submit Report dialog box (Big Buddy), 338
subscribing to mailing lists, 239
support. *See also* **documentation; help**
   Helix Code, 255
   International GNOME Support, 255
   outside administration support, 246
   printers, checking, 224
Switchdesk
   desktops, switching, 32-34
   downloading, 32
   editing startup scripts, 33-34

troubleshooting 391

starting sessions, 28
Switchdesk Desktop
  Switcher dialog box, 32
Switchdesk dialog box, 33
switching
  desktops
    Desk Guide, 63
    multiple desktops
      (Enlightenment),
      133-134
    Switchdesk utility,
      32-34
  window managers
    (Window Manager
    capplet), 49-50
symbolic links
  drag-and-drop features
    (File Manager), 109-110
  stalled, 114, 120
  viewing (File Manager),
    114-115
system administration. *See*
  administration
System Information utility,
  179
System menus (Main
  Menu), 85
System Utilities (GNOME
  Software Map), 237

T

taking screen shots (Electric
  Eyes), 264
tar command, 307
tarballs. *See also* source
  code
    applications, 239-241
    compressing (gzip utility),
      302
    documentation, 303
    extensions, 302
    GNOME installation
      advantages, 303-304,
      312

compiling source code,
  302
configuring Makefiles,
  307
customizing, 303
downloading, 306
security, 303
uncompressing/untar-
  ring, 306-307
uninstalling old
  versions, 306
IceWM, 46-47
sawmill, 48-49
uninstalling, 308
uninstalling GNOME,
  293, 299
upgrades, 303
tarfs (VFS), 119
tarring files, 302
Tasklist
  GNOME Panel, adding,
    62
  window managers, 40
tasks, tracking
  (TimeTracker), 254
templates (Gaby), 253
terminal emulators, 65
terminals, virtual, 62, 65
testing
  PPP connections, 195-195
  test partitions/systems, 72
text, shaped, 99
text editors
  gEdit, 64
  gnotepad+, 64
  XF86Config file, editing,
    56
Theme Selector (Control
  Center), 161
Theme Selector capplet,
  145, 153
themes, 155-156
  e.themes.org Web site,
    159, 162
  Enlightenment, 134
    downloading, 162
    installing, 162 163
    uninstalling, 163

GTK, 156
  components, 159
  creating, 163
  downloading, 160
  GTK Themes Web site,
    160, 163
  installing, 160-161
  libraries needed, 160
  limitations, 158
  pixmap, 158
  plain, 158
  selecting, 161
  uninstalling, 161
  Theme Selector capplet,
    145, 153
  window manager, 156
This Panel Properties, 84
three-button mouse
  emulation, 56-57, 67
threshold (mouse), 147
tiles (GNOME Panel),
  fixing, 88
TimeTracker, 254
toc command, 295
toolbars
  detaching, 149
  Electric Eyes, 261
  File Manager, 91, 95
  gnoRPM, 169
tools. *See* **utilities**
Tools menu (gFTP), 206
ToolTips (Enlightenment),
  124, 127
traceroute command, 195
Track Editor (CD player),
  275-276
tracking tasks
  (TimeTracker), 254
training applications, 245
Transfers menu (gFTP), 206
Troll Tech, 11
troubleshooting
  Big Buddy, 333
  bug reports, 335-337
  contact information,
    334
  Debugging Information
    dialog box, 336

features, 334
software requirements, 334
starting, 334
Submit Report dialog box, 338
system information, 334
boot startups, 31-32
dependency errors, 24-25
desktops, session files, 75-78
Enlightenment, 137-139
File Manager, 101
sessions, repairing, 87
sound, 285
startup scripts, 34-35
xinit startup scripts, 30

U

uncompressing
files, 306-307
tarballs, 306-307
uninstalling. *See also* **installation**
Enlightenment, 293-294
old installation versions, 306
rpm installation component uninstallation order, 290-291
gnoRPM, 291
rpm command, 292
tarballs, 293, 299, 308
themes
Enlightenment, 163
GTK, 161
UNIX
benefits, 8
drawbacks, 8
games, 285
Midnight Commander, 89
untarring tarballs, 306-307
updateb command, 16, 19-20

upgrades
Enlightenment, 44
rpms, 169-171, 299
tarballs, 303
uninstalling tarballs, 293, 299
upload/download progress window (gFTP), 207
uploading files, 206, 209
User menus
Enlightenment, 126, 131
Main Menu, 85
users
directories (.desktop files), 77
.gnome directory, 74-75
multiuser OSs, 70-71
root logins, 71
usr/share/pixmaps directory, 73
utilities. *See also* **commands**
autoconf, 304-305
Big Buddy, 333-334
bug reports, 335-337
contact information, 334
Debugging Information dialog box, 336
features, 334
software requirements, 334
starting, 334
Submit Report dialog box, 338
system information, 334
Control Center, 62
cpanel, 219
Find Files (File Manager), 112-113
ggv, 219
Gnome-admin, 177-178
GNOME DiskFree, 179
Gnome-linuxconf, 177
gnome-pilot, 249
gnoRPM, 168
Behavior Preferences tab, 174
crashes, 172

Create Desktop Entry, 169
Distributions tab, 176-177
File Manager, 177
Install Window tab, 175
installing rpms, 168-171
main window, 168
menu bar, 169
Network tab, 175
Package Listing tab, 175
package listing windows, 168
querying rpms, 172-173
rpmfind database, 171-172, 176
Rpmfind tab, 176
saving rpm packages, 182
searching rpms, 171
toolbar, 169
uninstalling rpms, 291
upgrading rpms, 169-171
gzip, 302
Iconbox (Enlightenment), 124
make
deleting object files, 308
make distclean command, 308
Managing Projects with make, 305
source code compilation, 305, 308
source code installation, 308
uninstalling tarballs, 308
Pager (Enlightenment), 124
Search (File Manager), 112

sndconfig, 272
Sort By (File Manager), 113-114
Switchdesk
  downloading, 32
  editing startup scripts, 33-34
  starting sessions, 28
  Switchdesk Desktop Switcher dialog box, 32
  Switchdesk dialog box, 33
  switching desktops, 32-34
System Information, 179
working with CVS code, 309

V

variables, PATH, 232
Vendor field (gnoRPM queries), 173
version-dependency errors, 25
VFS (Virtual File System), 119
View menu commands (Eye of GNOME), 259
View program option (gFTP), 210
viewing
  directories, size, 111
  file properties, 115-117
  files
    backup, 98
    Custom View (File Manager), 104-106
    hidden, 98
    ownership, 117
    permissions, 116-117
    remote sites, 211
    size, 111
  .gnome directory, 75

graphics
  changing default image viewer, 264-265
  Electric Eyes, 260-262
  Eye of GNOME, 258-260
help files, 299
hidden files (.gnome directory), 74-75
logs, 178
MIME types, 180-181
modem serial ports, 188-189
paths, 232
print spools, 218
symbolic links (File Manager), 114-115
views (File Manager)
  Custom View, 104-106
  directories, 94-95
virtual desktops (Enlightenment), 132
Virtual File System (VFS), 119
virtual terminals
  GNOME Terminal, 65
  GNOME virtual terminal launcher, 62
  xterm, 65

W

Wanda the Fish (panel amusement), 283
.wav files, 153
Web browsers. *See* browsers
Web Find (gnoRPM), 171-172
Web sites. *See* sites
wget command, 23
whereis command, 304, 329
widgets, 159
  containers, 323
  GTK, 326-327
  libgnomeui library, 326

libraries, 323
signals, 326
wildcards, filters (File Manager), 118
Window Maker Web site, 49
Window Manager capplet, 49-50
window managers, 37-39.
  See also **desktops; KDE**
  AfterStep Web site, 49
  BlackBox Web site, 49
  Control Center, 50
  Enlightenment, 41, 123
    benefits, 42
    bugs, 138
    complexity, 42
    customization options, 42
    Desktop Background Settings, 127
    desktop shell capabilities, 42
    DOX (Document Viewer), 129
    dragbars, 139
    drawbacks, 42
    E-conf, 126-127
    eesh, 135-136
    Electric Eyes background images, 262
    Enlightenment menu, 125
    file manager, 101
    help, 138
    Help button, 129
    hotkeys, 66, 134-135
    Iconbox, 124
    installing, 42-44
    Maintenance menu, 128
    multiple desktops, 133-134
    Pager, 124
    platform compatibility, 41
    Settings menu, 126-127
    Special FX Settings, 127

switching between desktops, 133-134
themes, 134, 162-163
ToolTips, 124, 127
troubleshooting, 137-139
uninstalling, 293-294
upgrades, 44
User menus, 126, 131
virtual desktops, 132
Web site, 41-43, 138
window border menu, 129-130
window groups, 130
FVWM Web site, 49
GNOME-compliant, 40-41, 51
IceWM
   installing, 45-47
   keyboards, 45
   Macek, Marko, 44
   mouse, 45
   platform compatibility, 44
   rpms download site, 46
KDE windows manager comparison, 37
necessity, 50
processes, 39-40
sawmill
   backgrounds, 47
   benefits, 48
   customizing, 51
   documentation, 48
   Harper, John, 47
   installing, 48-49
   Web site, 47-48, 51
   switching (Window Manager capplet), 49-50
Tasklist, 40
themes, 156
Window Maker Web site, 49
windows, customizing, 152
Window/Session/Desktop Managers (GNOME Software Map), 238

windows
   appearance, 63
   attributes, saving (Enlightenment), 129
   borders, setting (Enlightenment), 130
   buttons, 63
      Close/Kill, 64
      Iconify, 64, 67
      Maximize/Minimize, 64
      Shade/Unshade, 64
   customizing, 152
   File Manager
      appearance, 91
      closing, 90, 93
      context menu options, 95
      directories, 91
      navigating, 91, 95
      opening, 90
      status bar, 91
      toolbar, 91, 95
   gFTP, 204-205
      comparing, 209
      download/upload progress window, 207
      local file system window, 207-208
      log window, 207
      remote file system window, 207-208
   GIMP, 266
   gnoRPM, 168
   grouping (Enlightenment), 130
   list (Electric Eyes), 262
   widgets, 159
Windows, GNOME compatibility, 26
word processing (AbiWord), 246-247
wrappers
   GDK, 327
   language bindings, 318-319

writing documentation (GNOME Documentation Project), 311
wvdial (PPP dialer), 189, 196

X-Z

X. *See* X11
X servers (GNOME installation preparation), 16
X Windows system. *See* X11
X11
   man pages, 29
   X11 Web site, 42, 49
   Xlib, 327
X11 Web site, 42, 49
XF86Config file, editing, 56-57
XFree86, 16
xinit
   magic command, 29
   starting sessions, 29-30
Xlib, 327
xterm, 65

Other Related Titles

Sams Teach Yourself GIMP in 24 Hours
0-672-31509-2
Joshua and Ramona Pruitt
$24.99 US/$35.99 CAN

Sams Teach Yourself StarOffice 5 for Linux in 24 Hours
0-672-31412-6
Nicholas Wells and R. Dean Taylor
$19.99 US/$29.95 CAN

Linux Unleashed, Fourth Edition
0-672-31688-9
David Pitts, Bill Ball
$49.99 US/$67.95 CAN

Red Hat Linux Unleashed, Third Edition
0-672-31410-x
David Pitts, Bill Ball
$39.99 US/$57.95 CAN

Sams Teach Yourself SuSE Linux in 24 Hours
0-672-31843-1
Bill Ball
$24.99 US/$37.95 CAN

Sams Teach Yourself Linux-Mandrake in 24 Hours
0-672-31877-6
Coletta and Craig Witherspoon
$24.99 US/$37.95 CAN

Sams Teach Yourself Linux in 10 Minutes
0-672-31524-6
John Ray
$12.99 US/$18.95 CAN

SAMS
www.samspublishing.com

All prices are subject to change.

Windows 95/98/NT/2000 Installation Instructions

1. Insert the CD-ROM into your CD-ROM drive.
2. From the Windows 95 desktop, double-click the My Computer icon.
3. Double-click the icon representing your CD-ROM drive.
4. Open the README.txt file for descriptions of Third Party products.

Linux and UNIX Installation Instructions

These installation instructions assume that you have a passing familiarity with UNIX commands and the basic setup of your machine. As UNIX has many flavors, only generic commands are used. If you have any problems with the commands, please consult the appropriate man page or your system administrator.

1. Insert the CD-ROM into your CD drive.
2. If you have a volume manager, mounting of the CD-ROM will be automatic. If you don't have a volume manager, you can mount the CD-ROM by typing

```
Mount   -tiso9660   /dev/cdrom   /mnt/cdrom
```

NOTE: /mnt/cdrom is just a mount point, but it must exist when you issue the mount command. You can also use any empty directory for a mount point if you don't want to use /mnt/cdrom.

Open the README.text file for descriptions of Third Party products, author code, and how to create a boot disk for installing the distribution.

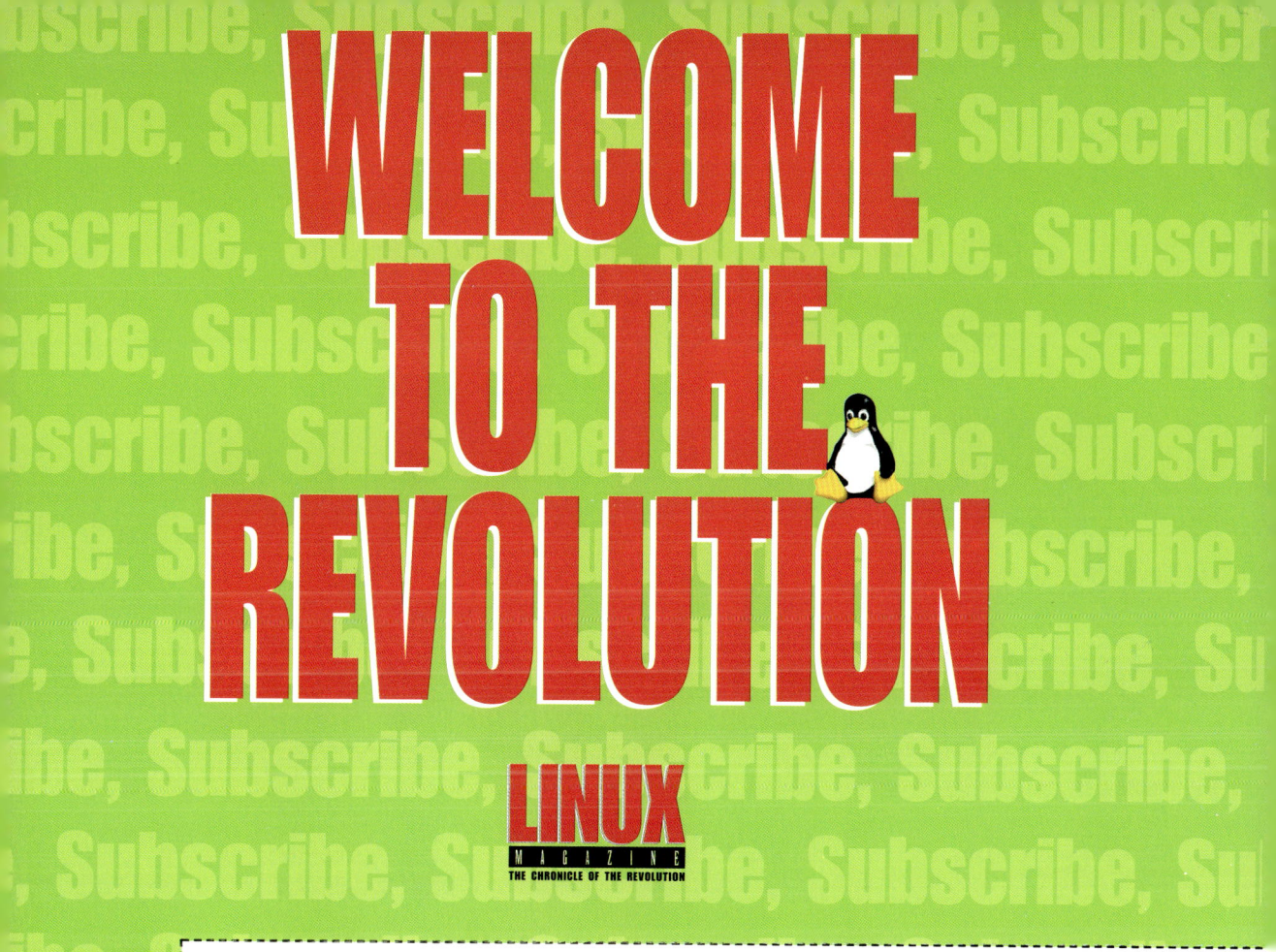

WELCOME TO THE REVOLUTION

LINUX MAGAZINE
THE CHRONICLE OF THE REVOLUTION

I DON'T WANT TO MISS THE REVOLUTION!

WWW.LINUX-MAG.COM

PLEASE SIGN ME UP FOR:

☐ 1 year (12 issues) **$34.95**   ☐ 2 years (24 issues) **$64.95**

Name

Company

Address

City/State/Zip

Country

Phone   Fax

E-mail

☐ Check Enclosed   ☐ Bill Me

International Rates:
Canada/Mexico Rates: ☐ 1 year (12 issues) $59.95   All other countries: ☐ 1 year (12 issues) $69.95
All non-U.S. orders must be pre-paid in U.S. funds drawn on a U.S. bank. Please allow 6-8 weeks for processing.

9MCB6

DON'T MISS AN ISSUE!

Linux Magazine is the monthly information source for the whole Linux community. Whether you are a system administra[tor,] developer, or simply a Linux enthusiast, *Linux Magazine* delivers the information and insight you need month after month.

Our feature stories, in-depth interviews, and reviews will help you navigate and thrive in the ever-changing world of Linux a[nd] Open Source Software. What does Microsoft really think of Linux? What's the best way to build a Linux machine from scratch? H[ow] can you integrate Linux into a Windows-based network? Whatever you are looking for, *Linux Magazine* is where you will find [it.]

With regular columns from such Open Source luminaries as Alan Cox, Paul 'Rusty' Russell, Randal Schwartz, and Larry August[ine,] you know you can't go wrong...

So don't miss an issue — Subscribe today to *Linux Magazine*, "The Chronicle of the Revolution."

Check out our website at www.linux-mag.com

BUSINESS REPLY MAIL
FIRST-CLASS MAIL   PERMIT NO. 1384   BOULDER CO

POSTAGE WILL BE PAID BY ADDRESSEE

NO POSTAGE
NECESSARY
IF MAILED
IN THE
UNITED STATES

INFOSTRADA COMM
PO BOX 55731
BOULDER CO 80323-5731